Library and Information Science

for

UGC-NET/SLET

and Other Competitive Examinations

(Paper II and III) According to the Latest Syllabus

Theory and Objective Type Questions with Answers

Md Gulnawaz Azam
Arun Kumar Sinha

ATLANTIC
PUBLISHERS & DISTRIBUTORS (P) LTD

ATLANTIC
PUBLISHERS & DISTRIBUTORS (P) LTD
7/22, Ansari Road, Darya Ganj, New Delhi
Tel.: +91-11-4077 5252, 2327 3880
E-mail: orders@atlanticbooks.com
Web: www.atlanticbooks.com

Reprint 2026

Published by Atlantic Publishers & Distributors (P) Ltd.

Printed & bound in India by Atlantic Print Services

Preface

Library and Information Science started as a multidisciplinary field based on literature, psychology, sociology, management, computer science, etc. and which is now developing towards an academic discipline in its own right. The theories and practices in Library and Information Science are applied across various disciplines. It is increasingly being recognized as one of the most important subjects for the intellectual development of society as library professionals act as catalysts of generating academically and socially beneficial knowledge and skill to the potential study and research activity. As Library and Information Science provides proper arrangement of knowledge and its dissemination to teachers, students, scholars, and all other knowledge-seekers, its importance has increased. With the application of technology, especially computer and telecommunication technology, library and information services have become faster, more accurate and have facilitated collection, storage, organization, processing, analysis, presentation, communication and dissemination of information in a better and more accessible manner.

In colleges and universities, the status of qualified and trained library professionals has been raised to be at par with teaching faculty. The categories of various nomenclature posts, including teaching and non-teaching, have been categorized.

The University Grants Commission (UGC) (now CBSE) holds National Eligibility Test (NET) on various subjects every year, in June and December. There are three papers: Paper I, which is common to all candidates, is a general paper on teaching and research aptitude, while Paper II and III are on the subject selected by the candidate. NET aims to determine eligibility for college and university level lectureship and for award of Junior Research Fellowship (JRF) for Indian nationals in order to ensure minimum standards for the entrants in the teaching profession and research.

The book presents a unified overview of the major areas in Library and Information Science. The objective is to present the facts with clarity and completeness from the point of view of the candidates preparing for UGC-NET Paper II and Paper III in the subject. The book is written in simple style and lucid manner for easy comprehension by the readers. It follows the current pattern of examination. An attempt has been made to select important topics and questions relating to latest developments in the discipline.

The subject matter has been divided into 11 chapters keeping in view the syllabus provided by the UGC in the subject. The book contains various type of objective-type questions on the subject. Answers have been given at the end of each chapter for self-check. All the 11 chapters comprehensively deal with the topic taken. Chapter 8 and 10 specially lay emphasis on Information and Cummunication Technology (ICT). Chapter 11 contains many questions on the latest developments in Library Automation, Computer Hardware and Software, Computer and Resource Sharing Networking, etc. In addition, there are rich Appendices providing useful information in the form of abbreviations, abstracts, catalogue codes, classification schemes and their inventors, citation manuals, ICT tools, terminologies, computer languages and their developers, indexing systems, subject headings, and list of important books, among others. There are also rich Bibliography and References.

The book will be useful for those preparing for any type of examination in Library and Information Science, like NET/SLET for the post of Asstt. Librarian, Asstt. Professor, Professional Asstt., Information Scientist for colleges, universities and institutions; School Librarians at Kendriya Vidylaya Sangathan (KVS) and Navodaya Vidyalaya Samiti (NVS); and technical posts in Library and Information Science in Defence Research & Development Organization (DRDO) and other such type of examinations.

Md Gulnawaz Azam
Arun Kumar Sinha

Acknowledgments

It is difficult to individually mention all the resources tapped to compile this type of book. We hereby acknowledge all the resources used to prepare the book.

We are thankful to Atlantic Publishers and Distributors (P) Ltd., for the interest evinced in publishing this book. We specially thank Mr. Harjeet Singh who encouraged us to write the book. His team took care in rectifying the errors in the text in a short time. We are thankful to all the members of the editorial team.

Md Gulnawaz Azam
Arun Kumar Sinha

Contents

CHAPTER 1 Information, Communication and their Properties

Introduction

Information and communication are vital aspect in any intellectual society and a library of the society enact to cater the need of the social aspect in respect of various altitudes.

Information is processed data with an organized, meaningful and useful interpretation of data. Library is a kind of Information System (IS). To gain maximum user oriented services from the library systems, we have to exploit all its capabilities. Information System is a set of objects such as tools, machine and the environment controlled by the humans.

In any organization, information is an essential entity and in 21st century world, information is assets and it plays a vital role in modern world in terms of technology, economics, and the agriculture growth. Information Technology (IT) applications help for organizing the data that comes from the various sources.

Data, information, knowledge and wisdom are the entities of information and the communication system which works as a hierarchical pattern. Data is a raw facts whereas information is a meaningful fact. Knowledge is the aggregation of information (after processing of data) which makes decision-making easier and the wisdom comes from knowledge that will be needed to make sensible decisions and judgments.

Thus we will take notice of various important points and questions arise in this area and what will be the right choice among four options like competitive examination.

Important Points

- After processing of data, we can get information.
- Claude Shannon's Information Theory is a mathematical theory related to the data transmission and storing.
- Knowledge is the structured form of information.
- The founder of 'documentation movement' worldwide was Paul Outlet and Henri La Fontaine.
- The term social epistemology was coined by J. Shera and Margaret Egan.
- The term 'Information Scientist' was first used by J.E.L. Farradane.
- The acronym DIKW (Data, Information, Knowledge and Wisdom) was first given by International Society for the Systems Sciences (ISSS) in 1988.

- Among Data, Information, Knowledge and Wisdom, the Knowledge is a highly organized intellectual product of humans mind.
- International Society for the Systems Sciences formerly known as Society for General System Research established in 1954.
- According to Russell Ackoff, the human mind can be classified into five categories namely Data, Information, Knowledge, Understanding, and Wisdom.
- Wisdom deals with the future because it incorporates vision and design.
- Data, Information, Knowledge, and Understanding are related to the past because they deal with what has been or what is known.
- The appropriate collection of information is knowledge.
- When data are processed, interpreted and make them meaningful is called information.
- Knowledge is dynamic, ever expanding and infinite.
- Data collected directly from first-hand experience or research output by the investigator himself is called primary data.
- Data collected by someone else or other parties is called secondary data.
- The advantage of primary data is that, there is no doubt about the quality of the data collected.
- Thesis, dissertation, and textbook are the example of knowledge in abstraction level.
- The advantage of secondary data is that, it is less expensive.
- Surveys, experiments, questionnaires, and direct observation are the sources of primary data.
- It is fact that secondary data cannot be converted to primary data.
- Theoretically, primary and secondary data are categorized based upon who collected the data.
- The sequence of flow of model of the Information Theory is Source → Message → Channel → Receiver.
- Error Coding Codes deals with redundancy added to the signal to correct transmission errors.
- The Information Theory model, Information source → Source Encode → Channel Encoder → Channel → Channel Decoder → Source decoder → Destination is known as Shannon Paradigm.
- Channel includes signaling equipment and pair of coaxial cables, optical fiber and may be copper wires for linking a transmitter to a receiver.
- The main purpose of ASCII (American Standard Code for Information Interchange) is to standardization of character-sets for communication and data processing in a common format developed in 1963.
- ASCII consists of $2^8 = 256$ (from 0 to 255) binary code-words for data representation with same length.

- There are three categories of ASCII characters from 0 to 255.
  - ⇒ ASCII Control Characters (Character code from 0 to 31)

    In this category of ASCII character, there are 32 characters for unprintable control codes that are used to control various computer peripherals such as printers.
  - ⇒ ASCII Printable Characters (Character code from 32 to 127)

    There are 96 characters are represented for printable characters such as letters both capital and small, digits, punctuations marks and almost keyboard characters.
  - ⇒ Extended ASCII Codes (Character code from 128 to 255)

    This is variation of 8 bit ASCII table, the character codes is based on ISO 8859-1 and in this range of characters code is specially for non-keyboard board characters.
- Morse Code (developed by Samuel F.B. Morse in 1844) is a method of sending text messages by keying in a series of electronic pulses in the form of short electrical signals (called "dot") and long electrical signals (called "dashes").
- The Information Theory of Digital Communication System model is, Binary Source → Transmit Filter → Channel → Receive Filter → Sampler → Decision Device.
- Sampling is a process where we convert continuous time signals (i.e. analog signals) into discrete time signals (i.e. digital signal system) commonly called Sampling Theorem.
- In communication system, the baud rate is the number of symbols which can be transmitted in one second.
- The bit rate is the number of bits which can be transmitted in one second and bit rate is usually measured in Kbps (thousands of bits per second), Mbps (millions of bits per second) or Gbps (billions of bits per second).
- Information is the building block of knowledge.
- Processing of information with applying of reasoning, the information becomes knoweldge.
- When knowledge is interpreted intelligently and analyzed with past experience and taking sagacious judgments is known as wisdom.
- Cumulation of vast amount of data and various file formats of digital data are the examples of information barrier.
- The interpretation of the Fifth Law of Library Science may be Information Institution is Growing Organism.
- The data in CD-ROM/DVD-ROM is the example of physical media of modes of information.
- The Explicit Knowledge sometimes referred to as know-what.
- The Tacit Knowledge sometimes referred to as know-how.
- Tacit Knowledge regarded as most valuable source of knowledge.
- Tacit Knowledge can be founded from cultural beliefs, mental models, human skills and capabilities, etc.

- Information from textbooks, notes, encyclopedia, Internet, etc. are the examples of Explicit Knowledge.
- Explicit Knowledge can be expressed in the form of words and numbers and also easily communicated and shared in terms of textual, scientific formula or any codified procedures.
- Tacit Knowledge not easily sharable, visible and expressible and it is highly personal and something insights.
- Personal Knowledge is short-lived and Tacit Knowledge are not possible to be recorded and therefore, Explicit Knowledge is required for social developments.
- Embedded Knowledge can be founded from organizational culture, products manuals, processes procedure, etc.
- In organizational knowledge, the process of knowledge sharing, developing, capturing with effectively is known as Knowledge Management (KM).
- In Library and Information Science, the KM making the right knowledge available to the exact sources of information.
- In Modes of Formation of Knowledge, Fission is the process of division or splitting of knowledge.
- An organized form of knowledge in Modes of Formation of Knowledge is Subject.
- The branch of metaphysics dealing with the nature of being is known as ontology.
- The collective body of knowledge which produced by community is known as Social Knowledge and that knowledge freely and equally available to all the members of society.
- At present, information is a valuable commodity to everyone, in terms of information supplying, demanding and marketing.
- Information is intangible and it can be used without being used up and can be sold without being given up, unlike goods.
- In modern IT era, the digital data storage technologies change the number of ways where data can be altered, summarized, evaluate, and repackaging to produce new or newly tailored information.
- For reference service, the goal of information suppliers is to fit data into the users' frame of reference.
- The public domain information refers to intellectual information that is not protected by intellectual property laws such as copyright, patent laws or trademark and also freely access and use without any limitation.
- The flow of information between sender and recipient is known as communication.
- A communication channel refers to the way where information flows within the organization.
- The written communication is known as documentary communication.

- The communication where expressed through facial expressions, body posture, gestures, etc. are called non-verbal communication.
- The device used to carry out the message is called channel.
- The processing of translating ideas, converting data into a required format for data transmission and storage is known as encoding.
- The conversion of an encoded format back into the original data format is known as decoding.
- In communication process, the encryption is the conversion of electronic data into another encrypted form called ciphertext and decoding and encryption both are not same in term of data processing between communication channels.
- In encryption, the data is intentionally altered for the purpose of content concealing.
- Noise is unwanted any types of data, electronic signals, or electromagnetic energy that degrades the quality of signal and data.
- For any type of communication process, there are three elements are necessary; source, message and destination.
- The communication channel is directly related to the success or failures of communication.
- Theodore Newcomb communication model is also known as ABX model, where someone (A) sending information to the other (B) about something (X) by assuming that A's orientation to B and to X depends on each other.
- Theodore Newcomb's model is like a triangle.
- Lasswell Model (Harold Dwight Lasswell) suggests the message flow in a multicultural society with multiple audiences and the flow of message is through various channels; this communication model is similar to Aristotle's communication model.
- Gerbner's Model (George Gerbner) is an expansion of Lasswell Model which consist from verbal model and diagrammatic model, based on dynamic nature of communications and their factors affecting the reliability of communication.
- In Gerbner's Model, the verbal model where someone observes an event and participant's perception in terms of feedback in a situation, through communication and diagrammatic model where someone observes an event and response the situation in terms of messages sending to transmitter.
- According to the Social Scientist, the communication is completely observable or measurable and almost ubiquitous.
- Between 1940s and 1960s, the seminal theories of communication were developed to be embraced a linear design in which message and information are transmitted from a source to a receiver.
- General System Theory (GST) was founded by Ludwig von Bertalanffy and the basic aim of this theory is to integration of accumulated knowledge with a clear and realistic framework and making a relationship between system members.

- AIETA Model (developed by E.M. Rogers and F.F. Shoemaker) of decision-making can be used to described the role of different sources and channels of information also known as diffusion of innovation process.
- In Information Theory, the diffusion is an information process of knowledge.
- When an innovation is communicated through certain channel over time among the members of a social system is known as diffusion process.
- A piece of information (knowledge) is spread and reaches individual through medium is known as diffusion process.
- The diffusion process involved the three elements: Sender, Receiver and Medium.
- The types of information diffusion are herd behaviour, information cascades, diffusion of innovation, and epidemics.
- The Epidemic Model (also known as Linear Model) consist of a pathogen (i.e. disease being spread); among hosts (human, animals, plants, etc.) and a spreading mechanism
- The feature of Epidemic Model (also known as Linear Model) is the analogy drawn from the spreads of diseases and it consists of a hosts population and their spreading mechanism.
- The Epidemic Model of communication process is more suitable when we are interested in global patterns.
- Information diffusion process is one of the kind of information dissemination over social networking platforms such as Twitter, Facebook, Instagram, LinkedIn, Youtube, Google Plus, Pinterest, Tumblr, Flickr etc.
- The process of optimal conversion without losing the original information content is known as sampling theorem.
- The signals we have listened and use in the real world such as our voices are called analog signals.
- To process analog signals in computers we need to convert it into digital form.
- The analog signals in continuous in both time and amplitude.
- The digital signal is discrete in both time and amplitude.
- The process of converting of analog signal from continuous time to discrete time is known as sampling.
- According to Claude E. Shannon, source coding is helpful for efficient representation of information from a given source before transmission.
- The channel coding is a mechanism for error-free transmission of digital signals over transmission channels.
- The average information content per message of a source is known as information entropy or source entropy.
- The equation of source information rate (R) is = rH, where R is information rate, H is entropy or average information, and r is the rate at which messages are generated.

- The maximum rate at which the channel can transfer information with perfect accuracy is known as channel capacity (C).
- For information communication, the channel must have a minimum capacity that is equal to or greater than the rate at which information is delivered by the source, therefore, $C \geq R$ or $R \leq C$.
- In digital transmission, when output information does not match with the input information due to noise (that means 0 bit may change to 1 or 1 bit may change to 0), the condition is known as errors in transmission.
- The error detection codes added the addition bits along with the source message to help us detect if an error occurring during information transmission.
- There are three types of errors occur in data transmission from source to receiver, Single bit errors, Multiple bit errors, and Burst errors.
- The codes which are used for error detection as well as error correction are called error correction codes and there are two correction techniques, Single bit error correction and Burst error correction.
- The Hamming Code and Redundancy Bit (Block Parity) are two popular error correction codes.
- Hamming Code is developed by R.W. Hamming.
- Parity Checking, Cyclic Redundancy Check (CRC), Longitudinal Redundancy Check (LRC), and Check Sum are the example of error detection codes.
- The 4-bit and 8-bit string is called a nibble and a byte respectively.
- The EBCDIC (Extended Binary Coded Decimal Interchange Code) is used 8-bit length for characters representation specially in IBM computers.
- There are three primary colours for image processing in computer, Red, Green, and Blue commonly known as RGB colours.
- The audible frequency range at which humans can hear is known as audio spectrum.
- The audio spectrum of human ears is range between 20 Hz to 20 kHz.
- Markup languages, for examples Hypertext Markup Language (HTML), Extensible Markup Language (XML), Extensible Hypertext Markup Language (XHTML) are used for metadata forming of bibliographic information in electronic domain.
- Internet is an expression of society and the most important is that Internet can't be controlled, technically or politically expect by disconnecting a communication system from the global network.
- Information Technology (IT) based information system deals with the use of computers to store, retrieve and transmit information.
- Information is not only academic asset of intellectual society but also it is economic resource in modern world.
- Information is shareable but not exchangeable.

- Technologies are not socially neutral and they affected by society.
- Information is a source of economic and political power.
- Internet has changed the way people to one another and their social environment, as well as how humans organize their work with intellectual societies.
- The impact of Information Technology (IT) not only education but also research, media, government activities, even whole societies.
- The key component of Knowledge Economy (KE) can be existed an innovation organization using information technology tools to introduce process, organizational and presentational innovation.
- The principal work of any knowledge economy organization is to allow to store and share information through knowledge management practices and principles.
- Industries involved in the production and distribution of information is known as Information Industry.
- To the library and information professionals, the Information Policy means that documents contents will carry all forms of information, textual, images, audio, video, etc. are store, disseminate and retrieved according to the easily accessible format for all types of users groups and their requirements.
- A National Information Policy (NIP) is a set of decisions or task by government appropriate to laws and regulations, to direct the harmonic government of information transfer activities, in order to satisfy the information needs of the country.
- A National Information Policy (NIP) for library and information systems and services needs provisions of necessary means or instruments such as information resources, institutional mechanism, information products and services for implementation.
- A kind of institution that generates and store knowledge and information, as well as gives services those who need them known as Information Institution.
- When a communication path has been established before the actual information transfer is known as Circuit Switching Network commonly called dedicated line.
- When small unit of data called packets are routed through entire network address within packet address is known as Packet Switching Network and this type of data communication between sender and receiver is known as connectionless.
- Internet is basically a connectionless network because it uses packet switching network.
- The modern Wide Area Network (WAN) protocols, including TCP/IP, X.25, and Frame Relay are based on Packet Switching Network.
- In data communication, the data is transmitted between devices in multiples of fixed length units, typically 8-bits.
- For asynchronous data transfer, there is no common clock signal between the sender and receiver.
- For synchronous data transfer, both the sender and receiver access the data according to the same clock.

- Asynchronous data transfer mode is also known as start-stop mode and this mode is used when data to be transmitted is generated at random intervals.
- Synchronous data transfer mode is characterized by a continuous stream of data in the form of signals.
- A type of private network which extends across a public network or Internet with encrypted connection over a less secure network is known as Virtual Private Network (VPN).
- Tunneling is a protocol which allows for the secure movement of data from one network to another such as Internet, through a private network communication.
- The expression of knowledge as a composite way for all the knowledge, skills, abilities, training, intelligence, experience, judgment, and wisdom possessed individually, and collectively by individuals in a population is known as Human Capital.
- The term human capital is popularized by Gary Becker and Jacob Mincer.
- The process of discovering useful knowledge from a data warehouse is known as Knowledge Discovery (KD).
- A system that supports the process of developing new tacit and explicit knowledge from data warehouse is known as Knowledge Discovery System (KDS).
- In database management system, the Knowledge Discovery in Database (KDD) is the process of searching for hidden knowledge in the data warehouse.
- A data warehouse is a relational database management system component that is designed for query and analysis of data rather than for transaction process of data.
- The analysis of data from data warehouse, on the basis of relationship that have not previously been discovered and summarizing into useful information is known as Data Mining (DM).

QUESTIONS

1. Who coined the term 'Intellectual Technology'?
(A) Daniel Bell
(B) Samuel C. Bradford
(C) Thomas D. Wilson
(D) Paul B. Kantor

2. In modern time, the organizing principle for Information System (IS) and Services is the mixing of
(A) Science, Technology and Social Information (STSI)
(B) Information and Communications Technology (ICT)
(C) Knowledge Based Information Technology (KBIT)
(D) All of the above

3. Which of the following is the product of mind?
(A) Data (B) Knowledge
(C) Wisdom (D) All of the above

4. Who defined that "Data are facts, concepts or instructions in a formalized manner suitable for communication, interpretation or processing by human or automatic means"?

(A) Paul B. Kantor (B) UNESCO
(C) IFLA (D) Thomas D. Wilson

5. The unorganized and unprocessed facts is
(A) Information (B) Knowledge
(C) Wisdom (D) Data

6. ....can be considered as an aggregation of data which makes decision-making easier.
(A) Information (B) Data
(C) Knowledge (D) Wisdom

7. Which of the following is the exact sequence?
(A) Information, Data, Wisdom, and Knowledge
(B) Data, Knowledge, Information, and Wisdom
(C) Data, Wisdom, Information, and Knowledge
(D) Data, Information, Knowledge, and Wisdom

8. ....can be considered as the integration of human perceptive processes that helps them represent meaningful conclusion.
(A) Information (B) Wisdom
(C) Knowledge (D) Data

9. ....is the ability to make right use of knowledge.
(A) Information (B) Data
(C) Wisdom (D) All of the above

10. After processing of data we can get
(A) Knowledge (B) Wisdom
(C) Information (D) Both (A) and (B)

11. In Information Theory, 'DIKW' stands for
(A) Display, Information, Knowledge, and Worldwide
(B) Data, Integration, Knowledge, and Wisdom
(C) Digital, Integration, Knowledge, and Worldwide
(D) Data, Information, Knowledge, and Wisdom

12. In Science, the affirmative or negative types of data i.e. Yes or No, 1 or 0 can be categorized in
(A) Determinable data
(B) Stochastic data
(C) Quantitative data
(D) Semi-Quantitative data

13. In Social Science, which of the following is the example of Interval data?
(A) Total number of books in a school library
(B) Total number of books in the subject of Physics
(C) Total number of female members in a library
(D) Total number of users between age 20 and 30 in a library

14. The term............includes facts, figures, symbols, graphs or charts, that represent an idea
(A) Information (B) Data
(C) Knowledge (D) Wisdom

15. In which year CODATA were established?
(A) 1955 (B) 1958
(C) 1961 (D) 1966

16. CODATA stands for
(A) Committee on Data for Science and Technology
(B) Committee on Database for Science and Technology
(C) Coordination of Digital Data for Science and Technology
(D) Committee on Data Transmission and Technology

17. The headquarters of CODATA is located at
(A) Washington (B) New York
(C) Paris (D) Sydney

18. The book titled *The Mathematical Theory of Communication* was written by
(A) Claude E. Shannon & Warren Weaver
(B) B.C. Vickery & A. Vickery

(C) Lyon Gorman & David McLean
(D) Pascal Preston & Daniel Bell

19. One of the first designs of the Information Theory was the 'Model of Communication' by
(A) Vickery & Vickery
(B) Gorman & McLean
(C) Buckland & Daniel
(D) Shannon & Weaver

20. The correct sequence of Shannon & Weaver Model of Communication is
(A) Source, Transmitter, Channel, Receiver, and Destination
(B) Source, Channel, Transmitter, Receiver, and Destination
(C) Channel, Source, Receiver, Transmitter, and Destination
(D) Source, Channel, Receiver, Transmitter, and Destination

21. In Shannon & Weaver Model of Communication..................is the person (or thing) for whom the message is intended.
(A) Transmitter (B) Receiver
(C) Channel (D) Destination

22. Match the following:

	LIST-I	LIST-II
(1)	33	(i) Information
(2)	Roll no. 33	(ii) Wisdom
(3)	Textbook of Physics	(iii) Data
(4)	Judgment	(iv) Knowledge

Codes:

	(1)	(2)	(3)	(4)
(A)	(iii)	(i)	(iv)	(ii)
(B)	(i)	(ii)	(iii)	(iv)
(C)	(iv)	(ii)	(i)	(iii)
(D)	(ii)	(iv)	(iii)	(i)

23. ....encompasses intentional information seeking as well as unintentional information encounters.
(A) Information need
(B) Information seeking
(C) Information access
(D) Information behaviour

24. ....is known for Anomalous State of Knowledge for Information Retrieval.
(A) Brenda Dervin (B) Robert S. Taylor
(C) T.D. Wilson (D) Nicholas J. Belkin

25. The fundamental equation of Information Science ($K[S] + \Delta I = K[S + \Delta S]$) is defined by
(A) T.D. Wilson
(B) Nicholas J. Belkin
(C) Bertram C. Brookes
(D) Robert S. Taylor

26. In $K[S] + \Delta I = K[S + \Delta S]$ fundamental equation of Information Science, here ΔS is
(A) Effect of modification
(B) Changed to the new modified structure
(C) An input of information
(D) None of the above

27. Who renamed the term 'Post-industrial Society or Information age' to 'Information Society'?
(A) Daniel Bell
(B) Bertram C. Brookes
(C) Nicholas J. Belkin
(D) Robert S. Taylor

28. Information Science is the field of
(A) Data collection and classification
(B) Data storage and retrieval
(C) Data movement and protection
(D) All of the above

29. The Greek word 'gnosis' is the root word of
(A) Information (B) Knowledge
(C) Wisdom (D) Data

30. Knowledge is
(A) Finite (B) Dynamic
(C) Expanding (D) Both (B) and (C)

31. Which of the following is true?
(A) Explicit knowledge is formal and systematic
(B) Explicit knowledge is easily communicated
(C) Tacit knowledge is not easily expressed
(D) All of the above

32. The term 'Tacit knowledge' was first introduced into philosophy by
(A) Michael Polanyi (B) John M. Ziman
(C) D.A. Kemp (D) Bertram C. Brookes

33. ....is the building block of knowledge.
(A) Data (B) Information
(C) Knowledge (D) Wisdom

34. The barrier to information is
(A) Redundant data (B) Errors
(C) Digital divide (D) All of the above

35. In Library & Information Science, data are either
(A) Statistical or non-Statistical
(B) Bibliographic or non-Bibliographic
(C) Numerical or non-Numerical
(D) Science or Social-Science

36. Among five laws of Library & Information Science, which law stresses the value of information in its use?
(A) First Law (B) Second Law
(C) Third Law (D) Fifth Law

37. The Citation index and Citation studies are invented by
(A) Eugene Garfield (B) Frank Gardner
(C) Mary Gaver (D) Richard Garnett

38. According to Modes of Formation of Knowledge, 'Biochemistry' is the example of
(A) Denudation (B) Loose Assemblage
(C) Fission (D) Fusion

39. Match the following:

LIST-I	LIST-II
(1) Tacit and Explicit knowledge	(i) S.R. Ranganathan
(2) Three Worlds of knowledge	(ii) John M. Ziman
(3) Perception of Public Knowledge	(iii) Karl Popper
(4) Modes of Formation of Knowledge	(iv) Michael Polanyi

Codes:

	(1)	(2)	(3)	(4)
(A)	(ii)	(iii)	(iv)	(i)
(B)	(iii)	(ii)	(iv)	(i)
(C)	(iv)	(iii)	(ii)	(i)
(D)	(i)	(iii)	(iv)	(ii)

40. ....is the knowledge of the individual and available to others only, if it communicated.
(A) Public Knowledge
(B) Personal Knowledge
(C) Social Knowledge
(D) Both (A) and (B)

41. Which kind of knowledge provided by the Libraries and the Information Centers?
(A) Personal Knowledge
(B) Public Knowledge
(C) Social Knowledge
(D) Both (B) and (C)

42. Match the following:

LIST-I	LIST-II
(1) Branch of metaphysics dealing with the nature of being	(i) Discipline
(2) A branch of knowledge	(ii) Ontology
(3) An organized form of knowledge	(iii) Private Knowledge
(4) Knowledge of mind of an individual	(iv) Subject

Codes:

	(1)	(2)	(3)	(4)
(A)	(i)	(iii)	(ii)	(iv)
(B)	(iv)	(ii)	(iii)	(i)
(C)	(iii)	(i)	(ii)	(iv)
(D)	(ii)	(i)	(iv)	(iii)

43. Which of following is true about 'Information'?
(A) It is a resource
(B) It is the representation of knowledge
(C) It is the part of communication process
(D) All of the above

44. The word 'Communication' is derived from the Latin word
(A) Comminus (B) Comminuo
(C) Comitatus (D) Communis

45. Channel of Communication is
(A) Oral Communication
(B) Documentary Communication
(C) Both (A) and (B)
(D) Only (B)

46. Signs, Signals, and Symbols are the example of
(A) Non-Vocal Communication
(B) Vocal Communication
(C) Verbal Communication
(D) All of the above

47. The communication between human called
(A) Non-Vocal Communication
(B) Non-Verbal Communication
(C) Verbal Communication
(D) Vocal Communication

48. Hand movement without talking is the example of
(A) Verbal Communication
(B) Non-Verbal Communication
(C) Vocal Communication
(D) None of the above

49. The sharing of information between individual by using speech is called
(A) Non-Verbal Communication
(B) Vocal Communication
(C) Verbal Communication
(D) None of the above

50. Smile, wink or wave without talking are the example of
(A) Vocal Communication
(B) Non-Vocal Communication
(C) Non-Verbal Communication
(D) Verbal Communication

51. A level of communication where sending and receiving of information between two or more persons called
(A) Intrapersonal (B) Interpersonal
(C) Public (D) None of the above

52. Which of the following is the example of 'Intrapersonal Communication'?
(A) Taking to oneself
(B) Daydreaming
(C) Internal Monologue
(D) All of the above

53. The Source and Recipient of information become one person called
(A) Interpersonal Communication
(B) Intrapersonal Communication
(C) Mass Communication
(D) Public Communication

54. Communications that indicates how Verbal Information should be interpreted is a/an
(A) Datacommunication
(B) Metacommunication
(C) Interpersonal communication
(D) Intrapersonal Communication

55. The literally meaning of Greek word 'meta' is
(A) After (B) Previous
(C) Beyond (D) Both (A) and (C)

56. At least three basic elements are required for communication processes, these are
(A) Source, Channel, and Person
(B) Source, Message, and Destination
(C) Source, Transmitter, and Interpreter
(D) Source, Metadata, and Person

57. Which of the following is the final link for any communication chain?
(A) Source (B) Message
(C) Transmitter (D) Destination

58. ....is the process of converting data into a format required for the data transmission.
(A) Decoding (B) Channel
(C) Encoding (D) Communication

59. ....refers to anything introduced into the message that is not included by the sender.
(A) Encodes (B) Decodes
(C) Destination (D) Noise

60. The information about arrival of new books in library through SMS is the example of
(A) Conventional media
(B) Non-Conventional media
(C) Hypertext media
(D) None of the above

61. Which of the following is true about Social Media?
(A) All activities are time stamped
(B) It always depends by people activities
(C) Information updating and deletion frequently
(D) All of the above

62. Which of the following was enumerated the 'Linear Model of Communication from Source to Destination'?
(A) Shannon & Weaver
(B) H.D. Lasswell
(C) G. Gerbner
(D) W. Schramm

63. The question pattern 'Who, Says What, In Which Channel, To Whom, With What Effect' was interpreted by
(A) Harold Dwight Lasswell
(B) Shannon & Weaver
(C) George Gerbner
(D) Wilber Schramm

64. According to Lasswell's Communication process model, 'In Which Channel' means
(A) Communicator (B) Message
(C) Medium (D) Receiver

65. Match the following:

	LIST-I		LIST-II
(1)	Books	(i)	Who
(2)	Knowledge	(ii)	To Whom
(3)	Library users	(iii)	In Which Channel
(4)	Book's editor	(iv)	With What effect

Codes:

	(1)	(2)	(3)	(4)
(A)	(i)	(iv)	(iii)	(ii)
(B)	(iii)	(iv)	(ii)	(i)
(C)	(iv)	(iii)	(i)	(ii)
(D)	(i)	(ii)	(iii)	(iv)

66. In which year George Gerbner defined the term 'General Theory of Communication'?
(A) 1956 (B) 1958
(C) 1960 (D) 1962

67. In George Gerbner's General Theory of Communication, 'M' stands for
(A) Event (B) Signal
(C) Both (A) and (B) (D) Man or Machine

68. In which year Wilber Schramm proposed the concept 'Model of Communication Theory'?
(A) 1944 (B) 1946
(C) 1948 (D) 1954

69. The disadvantage of Lasswell's Model of Communication is

(A) Linear Model
(B) Noise not mentioned
(C) Feedback not mentioned
(D) All of the above

70. In Lasswell's Model of Communication, 'Says What' is refers to
(A) Control Analysis (B) Content Analysis
(C) Media Analysis (D) Audience Analysis

71. Which of the following is true about Information Diffusion?
(A) It is essential for social changed
(B) It is the source of advancement
(C) Barriers for social changed
(D) Both (A) and (B)

72. Which of the following is associated for the development of Geographical Information System and data movement?
(A) Torsten Hagerstrand
(B) David Easley
(C) C. Taylor
(D) H.C. Kelman

73. In 1962, Everett Rogers propounded ....model of communication for solving communication tasks between organizations and their customers.
(A) SAPTA (B) KAFTA
(C) TIETA (D) AIETA

74. In AIETA model, 'I' stands for
(A) Interest (B) Information
(C) Intellectual (D) Intrapersonal

75. In AIETA model, 'T' stands for
(A) Transmission (B) Transfer
(C) Tracks (D) Trial

76. Which one is wrong in AIETA?
(A) A=Awareness
(B) E=Evaluation
(C) A=Adoption
(D) All above are correct

77. The writer of *The Mathematical Theory of Communication* is
(A) C.E. Shannon (B) W. Weaver
(C) W. Dutton (D) Both (A) and (B)

78. Which of the following is propounded the Information Diffusion Theory and Information Behaviour?
(A) Elfreda A. Chatman
(B) Frank Webster
(C) Tim Walker
(D) T. Allen

79. For diffusion of information related to the innovations, which of the following is a necessary condition?
(A) Data storing
(B) Information preserving
(C) Information stopping
(D) Information flow

80. The Diffusion of Innovation (DOI) theory is developed by
(A) M. Turner (B) C. Danielson
(C) G.E. Hall (D) E.M. Rogers

81. In which year E.M. Rogers was developed the Diffusion of Innovation (DOI) theory?
(A) 1956 (B) 1959
(C) 1962 (D) 1965

82. A specific book has been spreads among library users, is the example of
(A) Compact (B) Succinct
(C) Confined (D) Diffusion

83. Which of the following is the form of 'Information'?
(A) A printed research paper
(B) An electronic file send through email
(C) An audio tape
(D) All of the above

84. The literally meaning of 'metadata' is
(A) Data for data (B) Data about data
(C) Data in data (D) Data in data out

85. Who was quoted "Information is the pattern of organization of matter and energy"?
(A) Edwin B. Parker (B) M. Abrahams
(C) Gray Cleveland (D) Peter F. Drucker

86. The Class Number of Forestry in DDC is 634.9 is the example of
(A) Simplified Form of Information
(B) Translated Form of Information
(C) Printed Form of Information
(D) Coded Form of Information

87. Information is
(A) Tangible (B) Intangible
(C) Either (A) or (B) (D) Only (A)

88. A tool that helps for the study of quantitative analysis and impact of the scholarly articles and the scientific communication in the Internet
(A) Cyberphobia (B) Cyberspace
(C) Cybrarian (D) Cybermetrics

89. The study of the way in which Information and Information Technology (IT) influenced the economy is called
(A) Information behaviour
(B) Information and Knowledge
(C) Information flow
(D) Information economic

90. The ultimate level of understanding is
(A) Information (B) Wisdom
(C) Data (D) Knowledge

91. Which of the following is false?
(A) Data is generated through research
(B) Information and Knowledge are static
(C) Information is static, but Knowledge is dynamic
(D) Ultimate level of understanding is Wisdom

92. Which of the following is true?
(A) Data and Information deal with the past
(B) Knowledge deals with the present
(C) Wisdom deals with the future
(D) All of the above

93. The correct sequence of Knowledge Continuum is
(A) Data, Information, Wisdom, and Knowledge
(B) Information, Wisdom, Data, and Knowledge
(C) Knowledge, Wisdom, Data, and Information
(D) Data, Information, Knowledge, and Wisdom

94. In Knowledge Continuum, novelty is
(A) Data (B) Information
(C) Knowledge (D) Wisdom

95. Which of the following is associated with 'Theory of Information Measure'?
(A) Claude E. Shannon
(B) R.V.L. Hartley
(C) Johan Jensen
(D) All of the above

96. The concept of Information Entropy was defined by
(A) Claude E. Shannon
(B) John Jensen
(C) R.V.L. Hartley
(D) Irwin Lebow

97. In Information Equation $I(p) = -\log_b(p)$, here b is
(A) Base (B) Probability
(C) Bypath (D) Byword

98. The unit of information is determined by
(A) Data (B) Base
(C) Probability (D) Frequency

99. Which one is odd?
(A) Base 2 = decit
(B) Base 3 = trits
(C) Base 10 = Hartleys
(D) Base e = nats

100. The average or expected amount of the information from an event is

(A) Information Entropy
(B) Information Source
(C) Information Storage
(D) Information Arrangement

101. 'If someone is told something that they already know' is the example of
(A) High Entropy (B) Low Entropy
(C) Both (A) and (B) (D) Average Entropy

102. For the measurement of data storage capacity, EB stands for
(A) Executablebyte (B) Exabyte
(C) Extendablebyte (D) Expectedbyte

103. According to the International System of Units (SI), 1 EB is equal to
(A) 10^{18} bytes (B) 10^{15} bytes
(C) 10^{12} bytes (D) 10^{21} bytes

104. According to recent studies, prediction of the estimated volume of the whole Internet data will be
(A) 966 EB (B) 400 EB
(C) 977 TB (D) 600 TB

105. In Information Entropy, SIR stands for
(A) Source Information Rate
(B) Specific Information Rate
(C) Standard Information Rate
(D) Storage Information Rate

106. A given communication system, the maximum rate at which the channel can transfer information with perfect accuracy is called
(A) Channel Capacity
(B) Channel Communication
(C) Channel Transmission
(D) High Bits Transmission

107. In Shannon's Channel Capacity Theorem $C=B \log_2(1+S/N)$ bits/s, here C is
(A) Channel Capacity
(B) Communication Path
(C) Comparative Path
(D) Cumulative Path

108. In Shannon's Channel Capacity Theorem $C=B \log_2(1+S/N)$ bits/s, here S/N is
(A) Signal to Noise Ratio
(B) Sender to Receiver Ratio
(C) Source to Receiver Ratio
(D) Sender to Noise Ratio

109. ....is the detection of errors caused by noise or other impairments from the Transmitter to Receiver.
(A) Error correction
(B) Error detection
(C) Error modification
(D) Transmission failure

110. Which of the following is the Errors Detection Scheme?
(A) CRC (B) Parity bits
(C) Checksums (D) All of the above

111. In Error Detection Schemes, CRC stands for
(A) Cyclic Redundancy Code
(B) Capacity Redundancy Code
(C) Communication Redundancy Code
(D) Capability Redundancy Code

112. In Shannon-Hartley Theory, the Information Rate is represented by
(A) Ir (B) Hr
(C) rH (D) R

113. ....is a single bit added to a binary data transmission used to finding errors that may occur during data transmission.
(A) Checksum (B) CRC
(C) Parity bit (D) Multiplexer bit

114. When data are well-formed and meaningful, the result is known as
(A) Semantic content
(B) Artificial content
(C) Natural content
(D) Communication content

115. In Semantic Information Theory, the number of atomic constituents in a message is called its
(A) Data Length
(B) Width
(C) Capacity
(D) Communication Length

116. Which of the following is true?
(A) Larger width, lower information content
(B) Lower width, higher information content
(C) Larger width, higher information content
(D) No relation between width and information content

117. Which logical connective provides higher information content?
(A) OR (B) AND
(C) NOT (D) Both (A) and (B)

118. Which logical connectivity increases the number of occurrences, but decreases the precision of the information content?
(A) AND (B) OR
(C) NOT (D) Both (A) and (B)

119. Which of the following is true?
(A) Digital documents are transferable
(B) The text of digital documents are searchable
(C) Digital documents can be dynamically linked to anywhere
(D) All of the above

120. The basic unit of information for computing and data transmission is
(A) byte (B) bit
(C) character (D) nibble

121. 1 byte is equal to
(A) 4 bits (B) 6 bits
(C) 8 bits (D) 12 bits

122. A bit is represented by binary symbol as
(A) 0 (B) 1
(C) Either by 0 or 1 (D) ASCII

123. A four-bit aggregation of binary number is called
(A) byte (B) bit
(C) word (D) nibble

124. Which of the following is the addition of 1+1+1?
(A) 10 (B) 3
(C) 11 (D) 111

125. The decimal equivalent of binary number 101 is
(A) 7 (B) 8
(C) 5 (D) 9

126. Which of the following is the code that represents texts, images and the devices reorganization for electronic computer?
(A) ASCII (B) EBCDIC
(C) UNICODE (D) All of the above

127. In ASCII, the decimal number 75 is represent by
(A) A (B) K
(C) L (D) P

128. Total number of specified characters in ASCII encode is
(A) 122 (B) 124
(C) 128 (D) 135

129. Who coined the term 'Digital Divide'?
(A) Larry Irving Jr (B) William S.
(C) K.J. McGarry (D) Daniel Bell

130. Which of the following is an identification system for intellectual property of digital objects in digital environment?
(A) Digital Object Identifier (DOI)
(B) Digital Data Processing (DDP)
(C) Digital Data Storage (DDS)
(D) Digital Object Storage (DOS)

131. The term 'pixel' is the short for
(A) Photo element
(B) Photo synthesis element

(C) Picture element
(D) Picture depth element

132. Which of the following is graphics image format?
(A) .bmp (B) .png
(C) .jpg (D) All of the above

133. In graphics image format, TIFF stands for
(A) Tagged Image File Format
(B) Total Image File Format
(C) Transparent Image File Format
(D) Transcribed Image File Format

134. In graphics image format, JPEG stands for
(A) Joint Photographic Experts Group
(B) Joint Pixel Experts Group
(C) Joint Pixel Express Group
(D) Joint Photo Express Group

135. In Image Compression Equation, the ratio between the uncompressed size and compressed size is known as
(A) Compression Ratio (CR)
(B) Pixel Ratio (PR)
(C) Image Ratio (IR)
(D) Image Depth Ratio (IDR)

136. In character recognition method, OCR stands for
(A) Optics Character Recognition
(B) Optical Character Recognition
(C) Object Character Recognition
(D) Optical Character Reader

137. Disadvantage of analog signal is
(A) Affected to external noise
(B) Data qualities depends on voltage and frequency
(C) Temperature sensitive nature
(D) All of the above

138. Advantage of digital signal is
(A) Better noise immunity
(B) Consistency of reproduction
(C) Easy to storing and processing
(D) All of the above

139. Sampling Theorem is also known as
(A) Nyquist Theorem (B) Shannon Theorem
(C) Jensen Theorem (D) Weaver Theorem

140. The reproduction of analog signals to digital signals without losing the information content is called
(A) Samples (B) Quantization
(C) Optimization (D) Filtration

141. ....is the process of converting a continuous analog audio signal to a digital signal with discrete numerical value.
(A) Quantization (B) Sampling
(C) Optimization (D) Filtration

142. Which of the following is true?
(A) Sampling is directly related to Zooming
(B) Quantization is opposite to Sampling
(C) Both (A) and (B)
(D) Only (B)

143. In data conversion method, PCM stands for
(A) Pulse Code Modulation
(B) Picture Code Modulation
(C) Pixel Code Modulation
(D) Parallel Code Modulation

144. Which of the following is odd?
(A) .vob (B) .avi
(C) .mp4 (D) .jpg

145. In document format, PDF stands for
(A) Portable Document Format
(B) Printed Document Format
(C) Pixel Document Format
(D) Picture Document Format

146. Who invented the PDF format of document?
(A) John F. Warnock (B) W.J. Martin
(C) Jenifer Rowley (D) R. James Beniger

147. Which of the following is odd?
(A) HTML (B) XML
(C) PHP (D) C++

148. In document format, RTF stands for
(A) Rich Text Format
(B) Real Text Format
(C) Readable Text Format
(D) Recorded Text Format

149. Which of the following is odd?
(A) .mp3 (B) .wav
(C) .bmp (D) .wma

150. The book titled *The Changing Context of Information: An Introductory Analysis* was written by
(A) K.J. McGarry (B) Daniel Bell
(C) Peter F. Drucker (D) W.J. Martin

151. Which of the following is an agent for changing in societies?
(A) Information Technology (IT)
(B) World Business
(C) World Bank
(D) US Economy

152. Who says "The basic economic resource in the knowledge society is Knowledge and not Information"?
(A) Peter F. Drucker (B) Daniel Bell
(C) K.J. McGarry (D) W.J. Martin

153. A system of consumption and production that is based on Intellectual Capital is called
(A) Data Economy
(B) Information Economy
(C) Knowledge Economy
(D) Wisdom Economy

154. A/an...............is a policy, regulation, use, storage, access and communication and dissemination of information
(A) Government Policy
(B) National Policy
(C) Information Policy
(D) Library Policy

155. Which of the following is the feature of National Information Policy?
(A) To established the free public libraries
(B) A network of public libraries from village to district should be established
(C) Each school/college library should have qualified library personnel
(D) All of the above

156. Which of the following organization actively involved for the development of Information Policy worldwide?
(A) UNESCO (B) IFLA
(C) FID (D) Both (A) and (B)

157. In which year FID was dissolved?
(A) 2000 (B) 2002
(C) 2005 (D) 2006

158. Who governs the Internet?
(A) Specific government
(B) Specific groups of people
(C) Government agencies
(D) There is no governing body

159. In which year NIC (National Informatics Centre) was established?
(A) 1970 (B) 1974
(C) 1976 (D) 1978

160. Which of the following organization has provides financial assistance of NIC?
(A) UNDP (B) UNFPA
(C) NISCAIR (D) RRRLF

161. In India, which of the following organization provides e-Government solutions?
(A) NIC (B) IISc
(C) IIST (D) NIELIT

162. The National Institute of Science Education and Research (NISER) is located at
(A) New Delhi (B) Kolkata
(C) Bhubaneswar (D) Mumbai

163. Which of the following is a communications standard for sending voice, video, and data over telephone wires?

(A) ISDN (B) PSDN
(C) PSTN (D) SLIP

164. On the Internet, a/an............is an access point from one place to the rest of the Internet.

(A) Protocol (B) POP
(C) VPN (D) PSTN

165. A society that organized itself around knowledge in the interest of social control, and the management of innovation and change is called

(A) Digital Society
(B) Information Society
(C) Knowledge Society
(D) Wisdom Society

166. Knowledge that is locked in processes, products, culture, routines, artifacts, or structures

(A) Explicit Knowledge
(B) Tacit Knowledge
(C) Embedded Knowledge
(D) Both (A) and (B)

167. The term 'Knowledge Economy' is coined and popularized by

(A) Peter F. Drucker (B) Frederick F. Taylor
(C) John Ribeiro (D) Alvin Toffler

168. Which of the following is possible situation in 'Digital Dark Age'?

(A) Unable to processing of files due to obsolete file formats
(B) Unable to accessing of database files due to their file format
(C) Incapable to read e-documents due to their file format
(D) All of the above

169. A condition where people can't able to accessing the modern communication tools such as Internet or restrict accessing of IT is known as

(A) Information Barrier
(B) Communications Barrier
(C) Language Barrier
(D) Digital Divide

170. For getting the right knowledge to the right person at the right time, for this the essential component is

(A) Knowledge Transmission (KT)
(B) Data Transmission (DT)
(C) Knowledge Management (KM)
(D) Resource Management (RM)

171. In Data Mining, KDD stands for

(A) Knowledge Discovery in Database
(B) Knowledge Data in Database
(C) Knowing Data in Database
(D) Knowing Discovery in Database

172. Investigation of knowledge, processes and the techniques for retrieving potential knowledge from database is called

(A) KDD (B) KM
(C) KMS (D) GIS

173. A type of Text Mining where extract relevant textual data from a corpus of text and then provides a dynamic and navigable index is called

(A) Search Engine
(B) Discovery Engine
(C) Information Engine
(D) Knowledge Engine

174. WIPO stands for

(A) World Intellectual Property Organization
(B) World Internet Processing Organization
(C) World Information Processing Organization
(D) World Intellectual Protection Organization

175. The formation date of WIPO is
(A) 14 July, 1968 (B) 13 July, 1965
(C) 14 July, 1967 (D) 12 August, 1980

176. The headquarters of WIPO is located at
(A) Berlin (B) Geneva
(C) Amsterdam (D) Chicago

177. The World Intellectual Property Day is observing annually on
(A) 12 August (B) 13 November
(C) 24 December (D) 26 April

178. At present who is the Director-General of WIPO?
(A) George Bodenhausen
(B) Arpad Bogsch
(C) Kamil Idris
(D) Francis Gurry

179. Match the following:

LIST-I	LIST-II
(1) Paris Convention for the Protection of Industrial Property	(i) 1952
(2) Berne Convention for the Protection of Literary and Artistic Works	(ii) 1883
(3) Copyright, Act in India	(iii) 1886
(4) Universal Copyright Convention	(iv) 1957

Codes:

	(1)	(2)	(3)	(4)
(A)	(iv)	(ii)	(i)	(iii)
(B)	(ii)	(iii)	(iv)	(i)
(C)	(iii)	(ii)	(iv)	(i)
(D)	(i)	(iii)	(ii)	(iv)

180. The Universal Copyright Convention (UCC) was developed by
(A) WIPO (B) UNESCO
(C) WTO (D) OAS

181. Which of the following is under copyright work?
(A) Books writing
(B) Musical compositions
(C) Sculpture
(D) All of the above

182. In India, Copyright Office is currently located at
(A) Mumbai (B) Kolkata
(C) New Delhi (D) Ahmedabad

183. The most recent amendment of Copyright Act, India was in the year
(A) 2009 (B) 2011
(C) 2012 (D) 2014

184. In Copyright treaty, WCT stands for
(A) WIPO Copyright Treaty
(B) World Copyright Treaty
(C) Washington Copyright Treaty
(D) World Wide Copyright Treaty

185. Which of the following organization, India as a member country?
(A) WPPT (B) TRIPS
(C) Phonograms (D) Both (B) and (C)

186. According to the WIPO, the patent protection period generally granted up to
(A) 15 years (B) 20 years
(C) 22 years (D) 25 years

187. Intellectual Copyright can be included
(A) Patents (B) Trade marks
(C) Trade secrets (D) All of the above

188. Multistage Model of Human Information Processing was developed by
(A) H.W. Auden (B) Douglas Adams
(C) George Orwell (D) Charles Osgood

189. 'The Third Wave' was written by

(A) Alvin Toffler (B) Irwin Lebow
(C) R.L. Brewster (D) D.W. King

190. In which year Digital Millennium Copyright Act (DMCA) was passed into law?
(A) 1995 (B) 1998
(C) 2000 (D) 2004

191. In..........., Claude E. Shannon published a paper titled "A Mathematical Theory of Communication" in the *Bell Systems Technical Journal.*
(A) 1945 (B) 1948
(C) 1950 (D) 1952

192. Information Theory developed by ....during World War II.
(A) C.E. Shannon (B) R.L. Ackoff
(C) Warren Weaver (D) Both (B) and (C)

193. Claude E. Shannon was a research mathematician at the
(A) Bell Telephone Laboratories
(B) Massachusetts Institute of Technology (MIT)
(C) California Institute of Technology
(D) General Electric (GE)

194. Which of the following is encoding method?
(A) Unipolar (B) Polar
(C) Bipolar (D) All of the above

195. In which year IEEE Information Theory Society was established?
(A) 1954 (B) 1956
(C) 1959 (D) 1961

196. International Nuclear Information System (INIS) is located in
(A) Badajoz, Spain
(B) Vienna, Austria
(C) Geneva, Switzerland
(D) Helsinki, Finland

197. ....is a medium where coded message is transmitted.
(A) Decoder (B) Encoder
(C) Source (D) Channel

198. Pulse Code Modulation (PCM) is based on ....for voice encoding.
(A) Sampling Theorem
(B) Calculating Theorem
(C) Bandwidth Theorem
(D) Signaling Theorem

199. .... is ephemeral and timely whereas .... is a summation of information.
(A) Data, Information
(B) Data, Wisdom
(C) Information, Knowledge
(D) Knowledge, Wisdom

200. The book titled *Putting Knowledge to Work: An American view of Ranganathan's Five Laws of Library Science* was written by
(A) Pauline A. Atherton
(B) Mary Adams
(C) Carla O'Dell
(D) Edna Pasher

201. Who coined the term 'Cybernetics'?
(A) Ted Nelson
(B) Norbert Wiener
(C) William Ford Gibson
(D) Pauline A. Atherton

202. For Analog-to-Analog encoding, which of the following modulation method is used?
(A) Amplitude Modulation (AM)
(B) Frequency Modulation (FM)
(C) Phase Modulation (PM)
(D) All of the above

203. The..........is a measure of the intensity and volume level of a signal.
(A) Amplitude (B) Frequency
(C) Wavelength (D) Period

204. *IEEE Transactions on Information Theory* has been published since

(A) 1950 (B) 1953
(C) 1955 (D) 1961

205. According to the Information Theory, data is..........into signals to send them from one place to another.
(A) Decoded (B) Encoded
(C) Encrypted (D) All of the above

206. The maximum data rate at which data can be transmitted over a given communication link is called
(A) Channel Length (B) Channel Capacity
(C) Channel Load (D) Wavelength

207. Assertion (A): Nowadays each and every person needs information according to their requirements.

Reason (R): In early time, there was no Internet; therefore they can't get latest information.
(A) Both (A) and (R) are true
(B) Neither (A) nor (R) is true
(C) Both (A) and (R) are false
(D) (A) is true, but (R) is false

208. Assertion (A): No research and experiment are possible without analysis of existing data.

Reason (R): For growth of knowledge, data should be interpreted in the form of information.
(A) Both (A) and (R) are true
(B) (A) is true, but (R) is false
(C) (A) is false, but (R) is true
(D) Both (A) and (R) are false

209. Assertion (A): Universe of Knowledge is infinite, dynamic, and continuously expanding.

Reason (R): The growth of knowledge structure and the development have not a pattern.
(A) Both (A) and (R) are true
(B) Both (A) and (R) are false
(C) (A) is true, but (R) is false
(D) (A) is false, but (R) is true

210. Assertion (A): For Scientific development of any society, it is necessary to develop an integrated scientist group.

Reason (R): In modern civilized societies, information sharing thinking is not very strong.
(A) Both (A) and (R) are false
(B) Both (A) and (R) are true
(C) (A) is false, but (R) is true
(D) (A) is true, but (R) is false

211. Assertion (A): Through Social Networking, the diffusion of information is faster than organizational sources.

Reason (R): Nowadays, the civil societies are fully depends on Internet for information retrieving.
(A) Both (A) and (R) are true
(B) Both (A) and (R) are false
(C) (A) is true, but (R) is false
(D) (A) is false, but (R) is true

212. Assertion (A): A basic problem of communication is that of reproducing at one point either exactly or approximately.

Reason (R): Noise is only responsible for this problem.
(A) Both (A) and (R) are false
(B) Both (A) and (R) are true
(C) (A) is true, but (R) is false
(D) (A) is false, but (R) is true

Answers Keys

1. (A)	2. (D)	3. (D)	4. (B)
5. (D)	6. (A)	7. (D)	8. (C)
9. (C)	10. (C)	11. (D)	12. (D)
13. (D)	14. (B)	15. (D)	16. (A)
17. (C)	18. (A)	19. (D)	20. (A)
21. (D)	22. (A)	23. (D)	24. (D)
25. (C)	26. (A)	27. (A)	28. (D)
29. (B)	30. (D)	31. (D)	32. (A)
33. (B)	34. (D)	35. (B)	36. (A)
37. (A)	38. (D)	39. (C)	40. (B)
41. (C)	42. (D)	43. (D)	44. (D)
45. (C)	46. (A)	47. (D)	48. (B)
49. (C)	50. (C)	51. (B)	52. (D)
53. (B)	54. (B)	55. (D)	56. (B)
57. (D)	58. (C)	59. (D)	60. (B)
61. (D)	62. (A)	63. (A)	64. (C)
65. (B)	66. (A)	67. (D)	68. (D)
69. (D)	70. (B)	71. (D)	72. (A)
73. (D)	74. (A)	75. (D)	76. (D)
77. (D)	78. (A)	79. (D)	80. (D)
81. (C)	82. (D)	83. (D)	84. (B)
85. (A)	86. (D)	87. (C)	88. (D)
89. (D)	90. (B)	91. (B)	92. (D)
93. (D)	94. (D)	95. (D)	96. (A)
97. (A)	98. (B)	99. (A)	100. (A)
101. (B)	102. (B)	103. (A)	104. (A)
105. (A)	106. (A)	107. (A)	108. (A)

109. (B)	110. (D)	111. (A)	112. (D)
113. (C)	114. (A)	115. (B)	116. (C)
117. (B)	118. (B)	119. (D)	120. (A)
121. (C)	122. (C)	123. (D)	124. (C)
125. (C)	126. (D)	127. (B)	128. (C)
129. (A)	130. (A)	131. (C)	132. (D)
133. (A)	134. (A)	135. (A)	136. (B)
137. (D)	138. (D)	139. (A)	140. (A)
141. (A)	142. (C)	143. (A)	144. (D)
145. (A)	146. (A)	147. (D)	148. (A)
149. (C)	150. (A)	151. (A)	152. (A)
153. (C)	154. (C)	155. (D)	156. (D)
157. (B)	158. (D)	159. (C)	160. (A)
161. (A)	162. (C)	163. (A)	164. (B)
165. (B)	166. (C)	167. (A)	168. (D)
169. (D)	170. (C)	171. (A)	172. (A)
173. (B)	174. (A)	175. (C)	176. (B)
177. (D)	178. (D)	179. (B)	180. (B)
181. (D)	182. (C)	183. (C)	184. (A)
185. (D)	186. (B)	187. (D)	188. (D)
189. (A)	190. (B)	191. (B)	192. (A)
193. (A)	194. (D)	195. (B)	196. (B)
197. (D)	198. (A)	199. (C)	200. (A)
201. (B)	202. (D)	203. (A)	204. (B)
205. (B)	206. (B)	207. (D)	208. (A)
209. (C)	210. (D)	211. (C)	212. (C)

CHAPTER

2 Library and Society

Introduction

The growth of the relation between library and society was just a matter of importance after the thought of the human being to store and conserve the knowledge for the future generations and present utility.

Library and society are depends on to each other in terms of mutual relations. They are key actors for establishment of educated and the knowledgeable societies. Library especially public libraries make an important role to establishment a learning society. The entire world especially Europe understand the importance of public library too early and unfortunately in India, a well and user oriented library system was established after 1947. However before this, various regional library movements were played a vital role for establishment of public libraries.

In this time, across the country, the library movements are spreads from villages to cities, from schools to universities and from academic institutions to research institutions. Without considering the caste, religions and the sects, library movements in our country are successfully running from Kashmir to Kanyakumari.

Among such achievements, we have not forgotten the countless efforts made by Dr. S.R. Ranganathan, the father of Library and Information Science in India for his great contributions not only the classifications and cataloguing but also promoting the library professionals as a noble professions in India.

Therefore, in this chapter we have been considered various important points and questions about the library and society and other questions with answer related to the topic.

Important Points

- The public library is the local gateway to knowledge that provides lifelong learning of the individual and social groups.
- Intellectual freedom is the core responsibility of the library and information profession.
- The principal responsibility of library professionals is to privacy of users rights in terms of information sought, received, borrowed or accessed.
- Library collections in the different countries characterized their cultural identities.
- According to the IFLA/UNESCO Public Library Manifestation, the·librarian is an active intermediary between users and resources.

- In 2001, IFLA celebrated 75th anniversary.
- The most vital role of national library is to coordinating the network of other kinds of libraries throughout the country along with collecting materials and making them availability in terms of library networks.
- The local center of information where making all kinds of knowledge and information are available to its users is public library.
- Documents collection and preservation of national publishing output of the country is an important service of national library.
- Copyright conditions are most relevant for online availability nowadays.
- There are two ways to make accessible of digital materials; first is made accessible online if it is in the public domain and second is make explicit consent of the rights' holders.
- Due to technology expansion in our society, we create a 21st century black hole in the collection of knowledge.
- Public libraries provide services free of charge to anyone who wishes to use them.
- Library Consortia either of a particular type or in a particular subject.
- IFLA/UNESCO Public Library Manifesto was published in 1994.
- Libraries face real challenges in coping with the transition to the digital age.
- For libraries, the digital age is characterized by graphic user interface, digital data transmission and access with efficient way as well as data dissemination of all clienteles.
- Library is a well effective planning and strategy for handling of information explosion from universe of knowledge.
- Information security, copyrights, and information privacy are most vital challenging issues faced by the libraries in digital age.
- The advents of digital computers including computer networks and Internet are the starting point of digital age.
- The purpose of libraries is not just to create rich collections but also to organize, preserve and make knowledge accessible.
- In modern IT era, the challenge to modern societies is that the basic resource, knowledge is developing from information in very individual, and unpredictable process.
- Library is a well acknowledge social agency.
- According to the UNESCO, without public library support, there can be no true democracy, no real freedom of mind, or of body.
- Public libraries are common man's university.
- The hub of learning source of knowledge society is the academic libraries.
- The central repository of intellectual assets of nation is the national libraries.
- The special libraries emphasize unit of information or location of information rather than complete document.

- The services of special library are surrounded for specific type of users in terms of research institutions, academic professionals or specific subject oriented institutions.
- The highly specialized users are the clienteles of special libraries.
- There are two groups in our society; first is the digital world immigrant and second is the digital world native.
- The digital world native people born after the expansion of Information, Communication and Technology (ICT).
- The repository role of libraries is to storage and management of society's documents by collecting, conserving, and describing the document created by humanity.
- The information role of libraries is to dissemination of collected information.
- To assist the formal and informal learning and accelerate the education in society is the education role of libraries.
- Libraries are characterized as social institutions in the dynamic environment.
- According to J.H. Shera, the library as a wide part of a social system created by people, naming libraries as social institutions for the needs of the society.
- Formal education is the hierarchically structured and chronologically graded education system running from primary level to the higher level.
- Education from mass media or market place is an informal education.
- Any organized educational activity outside the formal system of education is known as non-formal education.
- Library is the main resource for non-formal education.
- Public library facilitates informal self-education of all people in the society or community.
- The history of the libraries can be traced to human efforts in the document collection.
- For successful implementation of a non-formal education system, the development of sound public library system is an essential pre-requisite entity.
- Public library should be suited at central area in the society or community.
- The college library (also school library) should be located at prominent place in the college/school where the student will take easy notice of it.
- The geographical location of the university library is an important factor in terms of library services for all clienteles.
- Articles in periodicals are the example of micro-document.
- The third law of library science (Every Book its Reader) can be satisfied through an open system of library.
- The APUPA pattern for helpful sequence of documents can be implemented of fourth law of library science (Save the Time of the Reader).
- Weeding out of books is not meaning the discarding of books from library; instead it means the removal of the book from a library where their relevance has ceased in order to make room for current and relevant books.

- A systematic removal of resources from a library based on elected criteria is known as weeding out.
- In knowledge society, the library never ceases to grow.
- In 1930, S.R. Ranganathan drafted a Model Library Act, presented at the First All-Asia Educational Conference, held at Banaras.
- In 1948, the Government of India appointed a committee to examine the provision for the National Central Library.
- In 1948, the Government of India passed the Imperial Library Act and by this act the Imperial Library of Calcutta became the National Library of India.
- Under the chairmanship of D.M. Sen, the Model Library Bill was drafted in 1963.
- The Delivery of Books Act (Public Libraries Act) was passed by Indian parliament in 1954 and it was further amended as the Delivery of Books and Newspaper (Public Libraries) Amendment Act 1956 to include serials as well.
- Raja Rammohun Roy Library Foundation was established by the Government of India in 1972 for promoting library movement in the country.
- Raja Rammohun Roy National Agency for ISBN is responsible for ISBN registration in the country.
- Raja Rammohun Roy National Agency for ISBN is working under the Ministry of Human Resource Development (MHRD), Department of Higher Education, Book Promotion and Copyright Division.
- Library legislation is an instrument for development of public libraries in a planned manner.
- According to the UNESCO recommendation, the public libraries should be created under clear mandates of law for nationwide provision of libraries services.
- In India, the first well-known committee on regional libraries is the Library Development Committee, Mumbai in 1939-40 under the chairmanship of A.A.A. Fayzee.
- The National Knowledge Commission (NKC) was constituted on 13 June 2005 to creation, management, use and application of knowledge institutions and services in the country.
- Library and information services are fundamental to the goals of creating, disseminating, optimally utilizing and preserving knowledge.
- The National Assessment and Accreditation Council (NAAC) was established in 1994 by the UGC.
- The first Curriculum Development Committee (CDC) in Library and Information Science was appointed by the UGC under the chairmanship of P.N. Kaula in 1990.
- The second Curriculum Development Committee (CDC) in Library & Information Science was constituted by the UGC under the chairmanship of C.R. Karisiddappa in 2000.
- On 30 January 1903, the Imperial Library was opened for public use which was noticed in Gazette of India.

- The set up of Delhi Public Library and the INSDOC were the joint efforts and assistance of Government of India and UNESCO.
- To preserve and make known the nation's cultural heritage in its multiple forms is the one of the objective of National Policy on Library and Information System.
- The National Policy on Library and Information System covers the academic library system, public library system, national library system and bibliographical service, special libraries and information system, library professionals issues and their implementations and financial support to libraries.
- Libraries associated with educational institutions are known as academic libraries.
- Two or more libraries engaged in a common pattern of information exchange through communications for some functional purpose is known as library network.
- The main purpose of any library network is to provide network-based services to readers (users), bibliographic information service, document delivery services, and human resource development.
- In IT era, the library network is a way with cooperative manner where members or users can access the library resources on electronic gadgets through telecommunication linking.
- The study of the recording and retrieval of information according to the user's needs, and dissemination of information on the basis of any pattern for the clienteles is known as documentation science.
- According to the UNESCO, the public library is the local gateway to knowledge, provides a basic condition for lifelong learning, independent decision-making and cultural development of the individual and social groups.
- The public library is the local center for information, making all kinds of knowledge and information readily and freely available to its users.
- According to the UNESCO, the public library should be accessible for all, regardless of age, race, sex, religion, nationality, language or social status.
- Local cess, endowments, donations are the main sources of income of public libraries.
- A public library does not charge its users any fee for any of its services.
- Adequate public library service is a basic input for the social, political and economic development of a country.
- The activities and accounts of the public library system shall be open to public inspection, supervision and as per official audit rules.
- A federal country like Indi needs a two-tier public library system in a state, that is, one at the State level as an apex body and the other at the District level for spreading its activities to the village level with necessary infrastructure.
- The main source for public library fund is library cess.
- According to state policy for library and information services, the public libraries in a developing society should preserve cultural heritage, provide access to all forms of

cultural expression, make efforts for foster inter-cultural dialog, favour cultural diversity and support oral tradition.

- In 1989, the Model Public Library and Information Services Act (Revised in 1995) was sponsored by Indian Library Association (ILA).
- The basic provision of any public library system are free access to readings and learning materials, advisory board to provide guidelines to policy-making, establishment of institutional structure, finance and recruiting.
- The UNESCO Public Library Manifestation (1994), emphasizes that public library is the responsibility of local and national authorities. It must be supported by specific legislation and financed by national and local government.
- The development of the public libraries is the responsibility of the State Government.
- Special library deals with a limited field of knowledge and provided by a learned society, research organizations, government departments, and specialized educational institutions.
- The special libraries first began to appear in the United States of America (USA) in the early decades of the 20th century.
- According to S.R. Ranganathan, the special library is a specialist library to supply detailed information regarding some subject field—scientific, technical and otherwise.
- In most of the special libraries, periodicals provide the most updated information.
- At the minimum level, a special library disseminates information and materials acquired by them, answer reference questions, direct users needing details on research information to appropriate source and handless routing of periodicals to keep their users informed of current developments in the field.
- At the intermediate level, a special library offers complex literature searches in specific fields, compiles extensive retrospective bibliographies, select and transfers relevant research materials in anticipation of demand, produces current awareness bulletins in specific disciplines, SDI services based on group or individual profiles.
- At the higher level, a special library offers highly specialized consolidation and repackaging services which involve analysis, synthesis and evaluation of information and present them in a form required by users.
- A centre designed especially for storing, processing and retrieving information for dissemination at regular intervals, on demands or selectively according to express needs of users is known as information centre.
- Information centre can be grouped as Data Center, Information Analysis Center, and Information Dissemination Centers.
- An Information Analysis Center provides assistance to a community of users and not just assistance to in-house personnel.
- A process to repackage the analysis of consolidated information in specific form which is more suitable and usable for library users is known as information repackaging.

- Current Awareness Services (CAS) playing a major role in repackaging of information and providing current, new repackaged information to the user in the library.
- Repackaging of information in digital form is the rearrangement or restoring of information on physical media (electronic media) in which information has been presented in computerized form in terms of understandable, readable and easily accessible to users.
- The aim of repackaging is to enhance the acceptance and use of information products and the assimilation and recall of their contents.
- In the past, the library system and services were developed based on literary warrant rather than users warrant.
- The library users can be grouped into following categories according to their information approach:
    - ⇒ **Potential users:** Those who may not or who seldom use library services or one who needs information which can be provided by specific services.
    - ⇒ **Expected users:** One who is known to have the intention of using certain information services.
    - ⇒ **Actual users:** One who has actually used an information services regardless of whether he/she derived advantages from it or not.
    - ⇒ **Beneficiary users:** One who derives measurable advantages from information services.
- According to S.R. Ranganathan, the user groups may be divides into freshman, ordinary inquirer, specialist inquirer, and general reader.
- The major objective of library and information system in a society is to satisfy the information needs of users.
- User education is concern with educating the users in the use of the library with a view to enable them to derive maximum benefit from the materials kept in the library.
- According to Jacques Tacatlian, "User education is to include any effort or programme which will guide and instruct existing and potential users in the recognition and formulation of their information needs, in the effective and efficient use of information services and their assessment."
- Nancy Fjallbrant and Ian Malley said that user education is "concerned with the whole information and communication process and one part of this involves the total interaction of the user with the library. This should be continuous process starting with school and public libraries and with possibilities of extension into academic and specialized libraries."
- According to Thomas G. Kirk planning of user education programme requires four things, namely (i) orientation, (ii) bibliographic instruction, (iii) course in literature search, and (iv) seminar.

- Library orientation or user orientation towards the library has to do with adjusting the new library users to the library and to enable library users to become skilled at finding information and thus foster feelings of confidence and independence.
- Library orientation programme includes introduction to library building, library catalogues and their tools, how to access information through e-catalogue, how to set search criteria on web-OPAC, introduction to various information sources, and exposing to various organizational tools in the library.
- Orientation is a process of familiarizing the library to library users.
- User orientation, library orientation programme, library instruction, user instruction, and information literacy are all the synonyms of user education.
- In lecture method of user education, the librarian address the users about library collections, arrangement of documents, library services, library rules and regulations, etc.
- The process of supplying the relevant documents on a specific topic to the user is known as Document Delivery Service.
- Resource sharing was previously known as library cooperation.
- The mutual sharing of resources by libraries to serve user's needs in most effective way is known as resource sharing.
- A librarian should not discriminate between or against library users is the part of code of ethics of library professionals.
- Indian Library Association (ILA) was founded in 1933 at Calcutta (now Kolkata).

QUESTIONS

1. Library is a well acknowledge
(A) Social agency
(B) Government agency
(C) Commercial agency
(D) Communication agency

2. "Without public library support, there can be no true democracy, no real freedom of mind or of body", who defined it
(A) S.R. Ranganathan (B) Melvil Dewey
(C) UNESCO (D) IFLA

3. The interval of 'Information Age' is generally in
(A) Thousands of year
(B) Centuries
(C) Decades
(D) Incalculable

4. The common man's university is a/an
(A) Academic libraries
(B) Public libraries
(C) Special libraries
(D) Research libraries

5. The hub of learning is
(A) Public libraries
(B) National libraries
(C) Special libraries
(D) Academic libraries

6. According to the IFLA, there should be one public library for every...........people.

(A) 1500 (B) 1800
(C) 2200 (D) 3000

7. Which of the following is the National Library in India?
(A) National Library, Kolkata
(B) Khudabaksh Oriental Library, Patna
(C) National Science Library, New Delhi
(D) All of the above

8. The local gateway to knowledge is
(A) Public library (B) National library
(C) Special library (D) Academic library

9. In which year UNESCO presented IFLA/UNESCO Public Library Manifesto?
(A) 1986 (B) 1989
(C) 1991 (D) 1994

10. Which of the following library will establish under the state enabling laws to serve a community, or region?
(A) Academic library (B) Special library
(C) Public library (D) National library

11. A classroom-based education provided by trained teachers is called
(A) Formal education (B) Informal education
(C) Both (A) and (B) (D) Only (A)

12. A user will get some education from library is called
(A) Formal education (B) Informal education
(C) Only (B) (D) Both (A) and (B)

13. Which of the following is the example of Informal education?
(A) Visiting to museums
(B) Listening to radio broadcasting
(C) Reading journals or magazines
(D) All of the above

14. Education from distance learning programs is the type of
(A) Formal education
(B) Informal education
(C) Non-Formal education
(D) All of the above

15. A well structured education system running from schools to universities, with academic studies and varieties of specialized programs is called
(A) Formal education system
(B) Informal education system
(C) Non-Formal education system
(D) All of the above

16. According to the Census 2011, the literacy rate of male and female in India is
(A) Male = 82.14%, Female = 65.46%
(B) Male = 75.33%, Female = 55.45%
(C) Male = 72.34%, Female = 58.56%
(D) Male = 71.45%, Female = 55.67%

17. According to the Census 2011, the overall literacy rate of India is
(A) 79.34% (B) 65.43%
(C) 69.23% (D) 74.04%

18. A kind of society where information and knowledge are central instruments
(A) Computer Society
(B) Digital Library Society
(C) E-Resource Sharing Society
(D) Information Society

19. The cause of changing contexts of information in modern society is
(A) Advancement of computer technologies
(B) More information demanding society
(C) Awareness for getting new information
(D) All of the above

20. In modern societies, human activities is organized through
(A) Information Technology
(B) Cyber Science
(C) Institutions
(D) E-commerce

21. In which year S.R. Ranganathan was enunciated Five Laws of Library Science?

(A) 1926 (B) 1928
(C) 1930 (D) 1933

22. 'Every Book its Reader' is the......of Library Science.

(A) First Law (B) Second Law
(C) Third Law (D) Fourth Law

23. Which one is the Second Law of Library Science?

(A) Save the Time of the Reader
(B) Every Book its Reader
(C) Books are for use
(D) Every Reader his/her Book

24. From Five Laws of Library Science, the term 'Book' means

(A) Library materials
(B) Knowledge and Information
(C) Knowledge
(D) Information

25. From Five Laws of Library Science, the term 'Reader' means

(A) Users of library's book
(B) Users of library's consortia
(C) Users of e-catalogues
(D) All of the above

26. Third Law of Library Science i.e. Every Book its Reader can be implemented through

(A) Open access system in library
(B) Resource sharing between libraries
(C) Display of new books in library
(D) All of the above

27. From Fifth Law of Library Science i.e. Library is a Growing Organism, the literally meaning of 'organism' is

(A) Library is an institutional organism
(B) In library, books are grow continuously
(C) Library is a living institutional organism
(D) All of the above

28. Which method is applied for weeding out of books?

(A) Useful books are added in place of unwanted books
(B) Discarding the books from shelves
(C) Replacing of irrelevant books with relevant books
(D) Both (A) and (C)

29. The book titled *Five Laws of Library Science* was published in

(A) 1935 (B) 1933
(C) 1931 (D) 1936

30. Right information to the right user is nearest to

(A) Information are for use
(B) Every users his/her information
(C) Every information its user
(D) Save the time of the user

31. Which of the following example shows that library is a growing organism?

(A) Growth of documents
(B) Expansion of library services
(C) Development of multilingual library website
(D) All of the above

32. A collaborate effort for information exchange among libraries is called

(A) Library cooperation
(B) Resource sharing
(C) Library networking
(D) All of the above

33. UAP stands for

(A) Uniform Access Principle
(B) User Account Protection
(C) Universal Access Principle
(D) Universal Availability of Publications

34. Match the following:

LIST-I	LIST-II
(1) UBC	(i) 1986
(2) UNISIST	(ii) 1973

(3) DELNET (iii) 1971
(4) CALIBNET (iv) 1988

Codes:

	(1)	(2)	(3)	(4)
(A)	(i)	(iv)	(ii)	(iii)
(B)	(iv)	(iii)	(i)	(ii)
(C)	(iii)	(i)	(iv)	(ii)
(D)	(ii)	(iii)	(iv)	(i)

35. The Cataloguing in Publication (CIP) programme was initiated by
(A) CILIP (B) FID
(C) LOC (D) IFLA

36. Which of the following project is associated with Library of Congress (LOC)?
(A) OCLC (B) MARC
(C) MODS (D) All of the above

37. MARC developed by
(A) Henriette Avram (B) H.P. Luhan
(C) William Ewart (D) Philippe Dreyfus

38. The Dublin Core Metadata Element Set has ....properties for resource description.
(A) 14 (B) 12
(C) 19 (D) 15

39. SRW, SRU, and CQL are promulgated by
(A) LOC (B) IFLA
(C) UNESCO (D) ISO

40. XML stands for
(A) Extensible Markup Language
(B) Express Markup Language
(C) Extensible Multimedia Language
(D) Express Multimedia Language

41. ISBD is maintained by
(A) LOC (B) IFLA
(C) CILIP (D) UNESCO

42. Which of the following is the information retrieval protocol?
(A) ANSI/NISO Z39.50
(B) ISO 23950
(C) Both (A) and (B)
(D) Only (A)

43. The term 'Prenatal Cataloguing' was coined by
(A) C.A. Cutter (B) H.M. Fussler
(C) Paul Otlet (D) S.R. Ranganathan

44. Which of the following was associated with Public Libraries Act, 1850 of United Kingdom?
(A) William Ewart
(B) Joseph Brotherton
(C) Chartist Edward Edwards
(D) All of the above

45. Who was the Chairman of Reviewing Committee for National Library in India (in 1968)?
(A) V.S. Jha (B) S.R. Ranganathan
(C) C.D. Deshmukh (D) K.P. Sinha

46. Which of the following is the National Library of United Kingdom?
(A) British Library
(B) London Library
(C) CILIP
(D) Library of Birmingham

47. In which year British Library was founded?
(A) 1845 (B) 1890
(C) 1973 (D) 1941

48. Prior to 1972, the National Library of United Kingdom was the part of
(A) British Museum
(B) Old Royal Library
(C) University Library of Limerick
(D) London Library

49. In UK, Thomas Bray was closely associated with establishment of
(A) Wales Library (B) British Library
(C) London Library (D) Parish Library

50. One of the notable librarians who was worked in New York TMCA

(A) Reuben B. Poole (B) George Birbeck
(C) W.H. Smith (D) Thomas Bray

51. Which of the following is true?
(A) In Social Library, the main aim is education, and information is subsidiary aim
(B) In Scientific Library, the main aim is information, and education is subsidiary aim
(C) Museum Library is a kind of Special Library
(D) All of the above

52. The accepted aim of library is
(A) Education (B) Recreation
(C) Preservation (D) All of the above

53. Library Association, UK is now
(A) LAUK (B) CILIP
(C) ABLISS (D) ASLIB

54. In 1915, Adam Report (W.G.S. Adam) was associated with
(A) Public Library System
(B) National Library System
(C) Academic Library System
(D) Special Library System

55. In which year British Government published Parry's Committee report?
(A) 1958 (B) 1962
(C) 1967 (D) 1977

56. Match the following:

LIST-I	LIST-II
(1) Adams Report	(i) 1959
(2) McColvin Report	(ii) 1927
(3) Roberts Report	(iii) 1942
(4) Kenyon Report	(iv) 1915

Codes:

	(1)	(2)	(3)	(4)
(A)	(i)	(iii)	(ii)	(iv)
(B)	(iv)	(iii)	(i)	(ii)
(C)	(ii)	(i)	(iii)	(iv)
(D)	(iv)	(i)	(iii)	(ii)

57. In USA, which of the following place is associated with establishing of first public library?
(A) New York (B) Chicago
(C) Boston (D) Oklahoma City

58. The founder person who was associated with establishing of public library in USA
(A) Robert Keayne (B) Bernard Bailyn
(C) Andrew Camegie (D) Douglas Raber

59. The National Library of Russia was established in
(A) 1806 (B) 1785
(C) 1795 (D) 1802

60. Arrange in ascending order according to their year of established
(i) Imperial Library, India
(ii) British Library, UK
(iii) Library of Congress, USA
(iv) Boston Public Library, USA

Codes:

(A)	(i)	(iii)	(iv)	(ii)
(B)	(iv)	(ii)	(iii)	(i)
(C)	(i)	(iv)	(ii)	(iii)
(D)	(iii)	(iv)	(i)	(ii)

61. In USA, Benjamin Franklin was a pioneer person for founding of
(A) National Library (B) Public Library
(C) Social Library (D) Special Library

62. The National Library of Russia is located at
(A) Saint Petersburg (B) Moscow
(C) Samara (D) Surgut

63. In which year ASLIB was established?
(A) 1924 (B) 1932
(C) 1935 (D) 1940

64. ASLIB stands for
(A) Association for Information Management
(B) Association for Special Libraries and Information Board

(C) Association for Special Libraries and Industrial Bureaux
(D) Association for Special Libraries and International Bureaux

65. The *Journal of Documentation* has been published since

(A) 1941 (B) 1945
(C) 1947 (D) 1949

66. Imperial Library, Kolkata was formally opened to the public on

(A) 29 March 1903 (B) 30 January 1903
(C) 29 April 1905 (D) 29 January 1905

67. Who was the first Librarian of Imperial Library?

(A) John Macfarlane
(B) J.K. Gates
(C) L.J. Strauss
(D) Herman M. Wiseman

68. Who was the first Indian Librarian of Imperial Library?

(A) Hari Nath De
(B) P.K. Rath
(C) Gopal Rao Ekbote
(D) Velaga Venkatappaiah

69. The first Librarian of National Library, Kolkata

(A) R.R. Shaw (B) R. Satyanarayana
(C) D. Moghdam (D) B.S. Kesavan

70. The National Library, Kolkata was opened to the public on

(A) 1 March 1953 (B) 12 April 1956
(C) 15 July 1953 (D) 1 February 1953

71. The first official Website of the National Library, Kolkata was launched on

(A) 26 January 2005
(B) 23 January 2002
(C) 22 February 2002
(D) 22 April 2004

72. Resource Sharing encompasses

(A) Cataloguing
(B) Manpower
(C) Bibliographical database
(D) All of the above

73. Advantage of Resources Sharing Network is

(A) Avoiding duplication
(B) Flow of information among libraries
(C) Controlling of bibliographic literature due to knowledge explosion
(D) All of the above

74. In the context of network based resource,........allows users to access web resources in a defined subject area.

(A) Search Engines
(B) Subject Gateways
(C) Data Warehouse (DW)
(D) All of the above

75. Match the following:

LIST-I	LIST-II
(1) JANET	(i) India
(2) CANARIE	(ii) UK
(3) INFLIBNET	(iii) USA
(4) NLR	(iv) Canada

Codes:

	(1)	(2)	(3)	(4)
(A)	(iv)	(ii)	(i)	(iii)
(B)	(iii)	(ii)	(i)	(iv)
(C)	(ii)	(iv)	(i)	(iii)
(D)	(ii)	(iii)	(i)	(iv)

76. Which of the following is an online Union Catalogue for Indian Universities?

(A) IndCat (B) Shodhganga
(C) UGC-INFONET (D) CANARIE

77. In which year, UGC-INFONET Digital Library Consortium was formally launched?

(A) 1998 (B) 2000
(C) 2003 (D) 2005

78. Who is developed Online Copy Catalogue System (OCS) for promoting cooperative cataloguing in India?

(A) INFLIBNET (B) DELNET
(C) ERNET (D) ISI, Bengaluru

79. DELNET stands for

(A) Delhi Library Network
(B) Developing Library Network
(C) Digital and Electronic Library Network
(D) Departmental Library Network

80. The SOUL stands for

(A) Software for University Libraries
(B) Software for University Linking
(C) Software for Operating of University Libraries
(D) System & Operation of University Libraries

81. The first version of SOUL software was released during CALIBER.............

(A) 2000 (B) 2005
(C) 2006 (D) 2007

82. 'National Library for the Blind and Physically Handicapped' is located at

(A) Kolkata (B) Ahmedabad
(C) Dehradun (D) New Delhi

83. In India, N-LIST executed by

(A) UGC-INFONET (B) INFLIBNET
(C) INDEST-AICTE (D) All of the above

84. DELNET was originally started as the project of

(A) National Informatics Centre (NIC)
(B) Education and Research Network (ERNET)
(C) India International Centre (IIC)
(D) SAARC Documentation Centre

85. Among these, the domain registration organization in India is

(A) INFLIBNET (B) DELNET
(C) ERNET (D) UGC-INFONET

86. With the help of.........we can link e-documents for e-Resource sharing.

(A) Tag (B) Hyperlink
(C) Search Engine (D) Blog

87. Which of the library software is developed specially for the university libraries by the INFLIBNET?

(A) e-Granthalaya (B) GreenStone
(C) SOUL (D) SANJAY

88. Which of the following is the feature of SOUL software?

(A) UNICODE based multilingual support
(B) Complaint to MARC21, AACR-II
(C) Support data exchange through ISO-2709 standard
(D) All of the above

89. A Web tool that automatically sends updates information whenever we post a new article.

(A) RSS Feeds (B) Subject gateway
(C) Blog (D) HTML element

90. In Internet, the RSS stands for

(A) Really Simple Syndication
(B) Real Service Syndication
(C) Route Service Selection
(D) Real Service Syndication

91. Library service that helps eligible patrons obtain materials which are unavailable in the consortium libraries.

(A) Interlibrary Loan (ILL)
(B) Interlibrary Resource Sharing (ILRS)
(C) Document Delivery Service (DDS)
(D) All of the above

92. The Farmington Plan is associated with

(A) Library Cooperation
(B) Library Classification
(C) Indexing
(D) Library Legislation

93. Which of the following is ASLIB publication?

(A) *Journal of Documentation*
(B) *Performance Measurement and Metrics*
(C) *Records Management Journal*
(D) All of the above

94. The frequency of publication of *Journal of Documentation* is
(A) Monthly (B) Bimonthly
(C) Quarterly (D) Biannually

95. The frequency of publication of *Program: Electronic Library and Information System* (an ASLIB publication) is
(A) Monthly (B) Bimonthly
(C) Quarterly (D) Biannually

96. CILIP is formed by the merger of
(A) Library Association and Institute of Information Scientist
(B) British Association of Picture Libraries and Agencies
(C) British and Irish Association of Law Libraries
(D) All of the above

97. CILIP hosts a conference every two years under the title.........
(A) Umbrella
(B) International Summit
(C) International Symposium
(D) Way to Library

98. The International Association of School Librarianship (IASL) was founded in
(A) Kingston, Jamaica
(B) Chicago, USA
(C) Paris, France
(D) Dublin, Ireland

99. United States National Agricultural Library (NAL) was established in
(A) 1858 (B) 1862
(C) 1877 (D) 1892

100. Which of the following organization is associated with Cataloguing-in-Publication (CIP) program?
(A) Library of Congress
(B) American Library Association
(C) National Library of Finland
(D) National Library of Jamaica

101. Who was the founder of Library of Congress?
(A) John Adams
(B) Thomas Jefferson
(C) Amiens Cathedral
(D) Melvil Dewey

102. In which year, the Cyber Law, Information Technology Act is introduced in India?
(A) 1996 (B) 1998
(C) 2004 (D) 2000

103. A discipline dealing with what is good or bad, right or wrong with moral duty
(A) Ethics (B) Demography
(C) Anthropology (D) Cognitive Science

104. Which of the following is professional ethics in Librarianship?
(A) Protect to each library user's rights to privacy
(B) Privacy of user's database search records
(C) Privacy of user's borrowed documents details
(D) All of the above

105. In India, a serious discussion about professional ethics in Librarianship was discussed on
(A) IASLIC Conference, 1984
(B) CALIBER, 2005
(C) CALIBER, 2006
(D) 38th ILA, 1992

106. Which of the following was the founder member of IASLIC?
(A) J. Saha (B) A.K. Mukherjee
(C) G.B. Ghosh (D) All of the above

107. Who was the first president of IASLIC?

(A) J. Saha (B) S.L. Hora
(C) G.B. Ghosh (D) A.K. Mukherjee

108. The frequency of publication of *IASLIC Bulletin* is
(A) Monthly (B) Bimonthly
(C) Quarterly (D) Biannually

109. Indian Library Association (ILA) was founded at
(A) New Delhi (B) Mumbai
(C) Kolkata (D) Ahmedabad

110. Indian Statistical Institute (ISI), Kolkata was founded by
(A) P.C. Mahalanobis
(B) A.K. Mukherjee
(C) S.N. Das
(D) J. Saha

111. After reconstruction of UNESCO-PGI, the new name is
(A) UNESCO-IFAP (B) UNESCO-UNDP
(C) UNESCO-PGII (D) UNESCO-UDI

112. In UNESCO-IFAP, here IFAP stands for
(A) Information For All Programme
(B) Information For All Public
(C) Information For All People
(D) Information For All Persons

113. Which of the following was the first chairman of UGC?
(A) C.D. Deshmukh (B) D.S. Kothari
(C) R.C. Mehrotra (D) P.N. Kaula

114. Which of the following committee recommended that passing a national qualifying test such as 'National Eligibility Test (NET)' for recruitment of Assistant Librarians?
(A) D.S. Kothari Committee
(B) R.C. Mehrotra Committe
(C) P.N. Kaula Committee
(D) B.L. Mungekar Committee

115. In which year UGC constituted CDC on Library and Information Science?
(A) 1987 (B) 1990
(C) 1994 (D) 1995

116. Who was the chairperson of CDC on Library and Information Science in 1990?
(A) P.N. Kaula (B) R.C. Mehrotra
(C) B.L. Mungekar (D) D.S. Kothari

117. The first convention of CALIBER 2003 was held at
(A) New Delhi (B) Ahmedabad
(C) Mumbai (D) Hyderabad

118. The first convention of PLANNER 2003 was held at
(A) North-Eastern Hill University, Shillong
(B) Manipur University, Manipur
(C) Assam University, Silchar
(D) University of Hyderabad, Hyderabad

119. In which year UGC constituted a Committee on the National Network System?
(A) 1991 (B) 1994
(C) 1996 (D) 1988

120. The first PhD in Library & Information Science in India was awarded in
(A) 1950 (B) 1953
(C) 1955 (D) 1964

121. Which of the following is the main promoter of public libraries in India?
(A) INFLIBNET (B) DELNET
(C) UGC (D) RRRLF

122. Arrange the States Public Library Act according to their passing year in ascending order
(i) Goa Public Libraries Act
(ii) Odisha Public Libraries Act
(iii) Andhra Pradesh Public Libraries Act
(iv) West Bengal Public Libraries Act

Codes:

(A) (i)	(iii)	(iv)	(ii)
(B) (ii)	(iii)	(i)	(iv)

(C) (iii) (iv) (ii) (i)
(D) (iii) (iv) (i) (ii)

123. In which year Parliament of India passed the 'Delivery of Books (Public Library Act)'?
(A) 1950 (B) 1952
(C) 1954 (D) 1958

124. In 1850, which country passed the world's first Public Library Act?
(A) Australia
(B) South Africa
(C) Great Britain
(D) United States of America

125. Which of the following Princely state in India was passed the Public Library Act in 1945?
(A) Gwalior Princely State
(B) Rajgarh Princely State
(C) Aundh Princely State
(D) Kolhapur Princely State

126. After Independence, the first State in India had passed the Public Library Act
(A) Karnataka (B) Maharashtra
(C) Andhra Pradesh (D) Tamil Nadu

127. AGRIS is maintained by
(A) FAO (B) IFAD
(C) WHO (D) IAEA

128. Which of the following is an International System for Agriculture Science & Technology database?
(A) AGRIS (B) INIS
(C) DEVSIS (D) Both (A) and (C)

129. Which of the following is the global movement dedicated to open agriculture knowledge?
(A) CIARD (B) INIS
(C) DEVIS (D) All of the above

130. Which of the following is the multilingual controlled vocabulary covering agriculture knowledge?
(A) AGROVOC (B) NNDC
(C) DEVIS (D) Both (A) and (B)

131. Which of the following is an International Information System for the development sciences?
(A) DEVSIS (B) AGRIS
(C) INIS (D) UNISIST

132. Which of the following is not belongs to co-sponsoring organization of DEVSIS?
(A) IDRC (B) ILO
(C) UNDO (D) IFLA

133. A thesaurus keyword 'ETDE' is related to which of the Global Information System?
(A) AGRIS (B) DEVSIS
(C) INIS (D) METADEX

134. UNESCO/PGI was established in
(A) 1978 (B) 1980
(C) 1984 (D) 1987

135. Which of the following is the constituent unit of NASSDOC?
(A) ICSSR (B) NISCAIR
(C) CCRT (D) NISER

136. *Guide to Indian Periodical Literature: Social Sciences and Humanities* has been published since
(A) 1964 (B) 1968
(C) 1971 (D) 1974

137. Which of the following is NASSDOC's database tool?
(A) INSSPEL (B) IIRC
(C) ADRDA (D) INTRAH

138. AGRINDEX, a monthly printed bibliography of AGRIS ceased in
(A) 1995 (B) 1997
(C) 1999 (D) 2002

139. NISSAT programme was launched by
(A) DSIR (B) DRDO
(C) ICAR (D) ICMR

140. The operational periods of NISSAT was
(A) 1977 – 2002 (B) 1978 – 2000
(C) 1976 – 2002 (D) 1978 – 2005

141. Which of the following library house-keeping softwares was developed collaboration with DESIDOC and NISSAT?
(A) SANJAY (B) eGranthalaya
(C) IDAMS (D) SOUL

142. Indian Science Abstracts (ISA) has been published since
(A) 1960 (B) 1962
(C) 1965 (D) 1968

143. Indian Science Abstracts (ISA) is a bibliographical database, published by
(A) ISI, Kolkata (B) NISCAIR
(C) DRDO (D) DSIR

144. DESIDOC started functioning in 1958 as
(A) Information Scientific Bureau (ISB)
(B) Scientific Information Bureau (SIB)
(C) Scientific Information Centre (SIC)
(D) Scientific & Technological Center (STC)

145. At present, DESIDOC is a division of
(A) NISCAIR
(B) DRDO
(C) ISI, Bengaluru
(D) ISI, Kolkata

146. The frequency of publication of *DESIDOC Journal of Library & Information Technology (DJLIT)* is
(A) Monthly (B) Quarterly
(C) Bimonthly (D) Biannually

147. In which year Khuda Bakhsh Oriental Public Library, Patna was officially opened for public?
(A) 1891 (B) 1895
(C) 1897 (D) 1899

148. Rampur Raza Library, Rampur was founded by
(A) Nawab Faizullah Khan
(B) Nawab Sirazullah Khan
(C) Nawab Bakhsh Khan
(D) Ali Ahmad Khan

149. The National Education Commission (1964-66) popularly known as
(A) Kothari Commission
(B) Radhakrishnan Commission
(C) Mehrotra Commission
(D) Rastogi Commission

150. Which Commission stated that 'the university library is the heart of all university's work'?
(A) Rastogi Commission
(B) Mehrotra Commission
(C) Radhakrishnan Commission
(D) Kothari Commission

151. Which of the following year, UNESCO declared as an 'International Literacy Year'?
(A) 1988 (B) 1990
(C) 1994 (D) 1996

152. The most popular method of imparting user education is
(A) Library rules (B) Orientation
(C) Staff introduction (D) Procedures

153. For 'orientation' we can introduce a new user through
(A) Layout of library building
(B) Library collections
(C) Location of various sections
(D) All of the above

154. Which of the following is the input area in a library?
(A) Acquisition
(B) Registration
(C) Cataloguing Cards and Accessions list
(D) All of the above

155. Which of the following is a Communication Barrier?

(A) Internet (B) Language
(C) Noise (D) Outdated software

156. According to S.R. Ranganathan, which of the following is the source for books selection?
(A) Bibliographies
(B) Readers suggestions
(C) Review column in newspapers and periodicals
(D) All of the above

157. In which year, the term 'Information Science' is introduced in Knowledge Organization?
(A) 1955 (B) 1957
(C) 1959 (D) 1962

158. Match the following:

LIST-I	LIST-II
(1) Collection Development: The Selection of Materials for Libraries	(i) W.C.B. Sayers
(2) Library Administration: Theory and Practice	(ii) William A. Katz
(3) Library Manual	(iii) R.L. Mittal
(4) A Manual of Classification for Librarian and Bibliographies	(iv) S.R. Ranganathan

Codes:

	(1)	(2)	(3)	(4)
(A)	(ii)	(iii)	(i)	(iv)
(B)	(i)	(iii)	(iv)	(ii)
(C)	(ii)	(iii)	(iv)	(i)
(D)	(ii)	(iv)	(i)	(iii)

159. Match the following:

LIST-I	LIST-II
(1) INDEST-AICTE Consortium	(i) 2004
(2) UGC-INFONET Consortium	(ii) 2001
(3) CSIR E-Journal Consortium	(iii) 2005
(4) MCIT Library Consortium	(iv) 2003

Codes:

	(1)	(2)	(3)	(4)
(A)	(iii)	(i)	(iv)	(ii)
(B)	(iv)	(i)	(ii)	(iii)
(C)	(iii)	(ii)	(i)	(iv)
(D)	(i)	(ii)	(iii)	(iv)

160. Peter Lazer's Report was related to the 'Information Policy of'.......
(A) USA (B) UK
(C) New Zealand (D) Australia

161. The term 'Invisible College' was coined by
(A) D' Solla Price
(B) E. Garfield
(C) Henry La Fontaine
(D) S.C. Bradford

162. The term 'fair use' is most relevant to
(A) Copyright
(B) Web Access
(C) Physical damage of books
(D) Classification of books in well manner

163. American Documentation Institute (ADI) was founded by
(A) Watson Davis (B) J.H. Shera
(C) H.P. Luhn (D) William A. Katz

164. In which year 'Centre for Documentation and Communication Research (CDCR)' was founded?
(A) 1950 (B) 1955
(C) 1958 (D) 1960

165. Which of the following is the founder member of CDCR along with J.H. Shera?

(A) James W. Perry (B) Alan Kent
(C) C.E. Shannon (D) Both (A) and (B)

166. The book titled *Introduction to Library Science: Basic Elements of Library Service* was written by

(A) J.H. Shera (B) William A. Katz
(C) Allan Kent (D) James W. Perry

167. In which year United States Congress passed the Public Law 480 (Wheat Loan Educational Exchange Programme)?

(A) 1945 (B) 1948
(C) 1951 (D) 1960

168. Which of the following is the Library Consortia in India?

(A) UGC-INFONET (B) INDEST
(C) FORSA (D) All of the above

169. FORSA stands for

(A) Forum of Resource Sharing in Astronomy/ Astrophysics
(B) Forum of Resource Sharing in Astrology
(C) Forum of Research and Scientific Associations
(D) Forum of Resource Sharing among Associations

170. Which of the following books was written by J.H. Shera?

(A) *Sociological Foundation of Librarianship*
(B) *Libraries and the Organization of Knowledge*
(C) *The Classified Catalog: Basic Principles and Practice*
(D) All of the above

171. Assertion (A): The basic purpose of resource sharing is to pool the resources among the group of libraries.

Reason (R): The economy of worldwide now grows, but library budget is not enough for rich collections.

(A) Both (A) and (R) are true
(B) (A) is true, but (R) is false
(C) Both (A), and (R) are false
(D) Only (A) is true

172. Assertion (A): As librarian, we should protect library user's rights to privacy and confidentiality in terms of document borrowed and information sought.

Reason (R): Librarianship is also a profession; therefore we should be followed professional ethics.

(A) Both (A) and (R) are false
(B) Only (A) is true
(C) Both (A) and (R) are true
(D) Only (R) is true

173. Assertion (A): For spreading of knowledge and information to our society, library's professional associations is necessary.

Reason (R): Without this we cannot economically strong as European contries.

(A) Both (A) and (R) are true
(B) Both (A) and (R) are false
(C) (A) is true, but (R) is false
(D) (A) is false, but (R) is true

174. Assertion (A): In IT era, a new society is now exist where knowledge is an essential parameter for day-to-day working.

Reason (R): At present, knowledge society already accepts the importance of IT and their services.

(A) Both (A) and (R) are true
(B) (A) is true, but (R) is false
(C) (A) is false, but (R) is true
(D) Both (A) and (R) are false

ANSWERS KEYS

1. (A) 2. (C) 3. (C) 4. (B)
5. (D) 6. (D) 7. (D) 8. (A)
9. (D) 10. (C) 11. (D) 12. (C)
13. (D) 14. (C) 15. (A) 16. (A)
17. (D) 18. (D) 19. (D) 20. (C)
21. (B) 22. (C) 23. (D) 24. (B)
25. (D) 26. (D) 27. (D) 28. (D)
29. (C) 30. (C) 31. (D) 32. (D)
33. (D) 34. (D) 35. (C) 36. (D)
37. (A) 38. (D) 39. (A) 40. (A)
41. (B) 42. (C) 43. (D) 44. (D)
45. (A) 46. (A) 47. (C) 48. (A)
49. (D) 50. (A) 51. (D) 52. (D)
53. (B) 54. (A) 55. (C) 56. (B)
57. (C) 58. (A) 59. (C) 60. (D)
61. (C) 62. (A) 63. (A) 64. (A)
65. (B) 66. (B) 67. (A) 68. (A)
69. (D) 70. (D) 71. (C) 72. (D)
73. (D) 74. (B) 75. (C) 76. (A)
77. (C) 78. (A) 79. (B) 80. (A)
81. (A) 82. (C) 83. (D) 84. (C)
85. (C) 86. (B) 87. (C) 88. (D)

89. (A) 90. (A) 91. (D) 92. (A)
93. (D) 94. (B) 95. (C) 96. (A)
97. (A) 98. (A) 99. (B) 100. (A)
101. (A) 102. (D) 103. (A) 104. (D)
105. (A) 106. (D) 107. (B) 108. (C)
109. (C) 110. (A) 111. (A) 112. (A)
113. (A) 114. (B) 115. (B) 116. (A)
117. (B) 118. (A) 119. (D) 120. (A)
121. (D) 122. (D) 123. (C) 124. (C)
125. (D) 126. (D) 127. (A) 128. (A)
129. (A) 130. (A) 131. (A) 132. (D)
133. (C) 134. (C) 135. (A) 136. (A)
137. (A) 138. (A) 139. (A) 140. (A)
141. (A) 142. (C) 143. (B) 144. (B)
145. (B) 146. (C) 147. (A) 148. (A)
149. (A) 150. (C) 151. (B) 152. (B)
153. (D) 154. (D) 155. (C) 156. (D)
157. (C) 158. (C) 159. (B) 160. (B)
161. (A) 162. (A) 163. (A) 164. (B)
165. (D) 166. (A) 167. (C) 168. (D)
169. (A) 170. (D) 171. (A) 172. (C)
173. (C) 174. (A)

CHAPTER

3 Information Sources and Services

INTRODUCTION

In any types of libraries, there are three fundamental functions, acquiring, organizing, and disseminating the information. Among three functions, the third function is the reference services. Reference services is directly related to the user's assistance for his/her desired documents, information and other types of queries related to the user's needs. In academic libraries especially university libraries and the research libraries, references services is one of the most important service among other services.

However, each and every document in a library is the study materials, but these materials are not same kinds in the view of their content. Some documents are original works, some are bibliographies of these works, and some documents are encyclopedias related to the specific subjects or general topics and also a number of others documents related to the broad descriptions of universe of knowledge. The division of these documents in library on the basic of their content and format is the kind of information sources as Primary, Secondary and Tertiary sources of information.

Therefore, in this chapter we will discuss make important points and questions about the information sources and services with plenty of questions and their answer.

IMPORTANT POINTS

- Knowledge is organized body of information or the comprehension and understanding, consequent on having acquired an organized body of facts.
- The growth of information beyond a manageable limit is known as information explosion.
- Information is made up of symbolic as well as descriptive elements, communicating knowledge.
- Data is an unorganized piece of information.
- Knowledge is an organized body of information that can be used as the basis of further knowledge.
- A society where all activities are centered on information as a basic unit is known as Information Society.

- A period predominantly centered on information activities when large amounts of information are widely available to many people is known as Information Age.
- The synonyms of Information Age are Computer Age, Digital Age, Cyber Age and New Media Age.
- The beginning period of Information Age was about 1975 when vast amounts of information are instantaneously transmitted in various sectors as well as information-based industries were established in that period.
- Information is power and an essential entity for decision-making.
- The most important aspect in the reference work refers to the reference questions with their corresponding reference sources.
- Information Sources can be in print, non-print, electronic media or e-formats.
- The books which are used to answer immediate questions of users are known as Reference Books.
- Reference Books are not borrowed for use out of the library because they are uses as brief consultation rather than for continuous reading.
- Primary Sources are original information sources on which other research studies are based.
- Primary Sources report a discovery or share new information.
- Primary Sources present information in its original form and not interpreted or evaluated by others.
- Primary Sources present first-hand accounts and information related to any subject.
- Literary manuscripts, biological records and evidence, eyewitness, diaries, autobiography, patents, technical reports, interviews, lab notebooks, surveys, e-mail communication, audio and video recording, etc. are the examples of Primary Sources.
- Primary Sources are original documents that have not been filtered through interpretation or evaluation by others or any second party.
- The Primary Sources are very large in number and can be usually accessed by the help of some Secondary Sources like an indexing services or an abstracting services.
- Secondary Sources were created by someone who did not experience first-hand or did not participate in the events or conditions being researched.
- A Secondary Source interprets and analyzes Primary Sources.
- Secondary Sources are not evidence, but rather commentary on and discussion of evidence.
- Secondary Sources analyze, interpret, evaluate, describe and also discuss the evidence provided by Primary Sources.
- Textbooks, encyclopedias, journal articles, dictionaries, directories, handbooks, public opinions, reviews, bibliographies, commentaries, websites materials, histories, etc. are the examples of Secondary Sources.

- The individual collections or an agency for purpose other than those of a particular research study is the example of secondary data.
- In Secondary Sources, original information is selected, modified and rearranged in a suitable format for the purpose of easy location by the users.
- The Primary Sources are very large in number and can be usually with the help of some Secondary Sources like a bibliography, an indexing service or an abstracting service.
- Tertiary Sources consist of Primary and Secondary Source information which has been collected and distilled.
- Tertiary Sources are intended only to provide an overview of what the topic includes its basic terminology, and often references for further reading.
- Tertiary Sources present summaries of or an introduction to the current state of research on a topic, summarize or condense information from Primary and Secondary Sources.
- Tertiary Sources provide overview of topics by synthesizing information gathered from other resources.
- Tertiary Sources provide a list of Primary and Secondary Sources of more extensive information.
- Bibliography of bibliographies, almanacs, encyclopedias, fact books, pathfinders, dictionaries, Wikipedia and similar user-contributed online encyclopedias, reference materials, digests, indexes, abstracts, guide books, etc. are the example of Tertiary Sources.
- Sometimes, it is difficult to differentiate between Primary, Secondary and Tertiary Sources of information, for example an autobiography is a Primary Source whereas a biography written by other person is a Secondary Source.
- Abstracts and indexes provide citations to documents dealing with specific topics in a field of knowledge.
- Indexes provide the essential bibliographic information needed to identify an article or other publications and usually include information about the author of the work, the source journal or other publication, volume, issue and pagination.
- Abstracting tools include the same key elements but also a summary of the work usually written by the author or sometimes generated by the reviewer where an author did not submit one.
- An index is a Secondary Source if it is used to locate Primary Sources.
- Indexing and Abstracting periodicals are categorized as Secondary publications.
- Any source not falling in the category of Primary and Secondary is a Tertiary Sources.
- Invisible Web is the term used for a specific condition when information available on the World Wide Web but can't found by any general-purpose search engines.

- EMBASE, MEDLINE/PubMed, Scopus, Population Index, Sociological Abstracts, Web of Science, NTIS, NLM Gateway, PAIS International, POPLINE, PsycINFO, SARAI, UNESBIB, INDMED, Open Index Initiative (India), Science Citation Index, UNICORN, CINAHL, etc. are the examples of online Bibliographic Databases.
- Reference Services help the user define and identify his query correctly and it helps the library patron to get access to the information that they needed.
- There are two kinds of reference services; Ready Reference Service and Long Range Reference Service.
- Referral Services do not provide the user with the documents or information actually needed for his query but refer him to the sources such as secondary publications, information units, professional organizations, research institutes, etc. and tell him where to find them.
- In SDI (Selective Dissemination Service), the user profile comprises of a set of Key Words organized as rigorously as the system permits which describe the subjects of interest of the user.
- Literature Search Service is considered as an extension of reference service.
- Document Delivery Service (DDS) is concerned with the supply of document to the user on demand either in original or its photocopies irrespective of the location and form of original document.
- Document Delivery Service (DDS) is a restrictive service and is usually constrained by the provisions of copyright and intellectual property rights.
- Reference Sources are designed to be consulted rather than read through.
- Reference materials/documents can be arranged alphabetically, subject-wise, topic-wise or any chronological order.
- For getting information related to formulas, tables, or how to do it related query we can access Handbooks and Manuals.
- The Directories are helpful for getting information about the names and addresses of people, organizations, institutions, companies, etc.
- Dictionaries can be categorized by abridge, unabridged, bilingual and multilingual.
- Encyclopedia can be categorized into two types; General Encyclopedias and Subject Encyclopedias.
- An Encyclopedia is a systematic summary of the knowledge that is most significant to mankind.
- General Encyclopedias usually arrange article alphabetically by topic.
- Subject Encyclopedias generally assume some prior knowledge of the subject and there is no general rule for how their topics are arranged.
- An almanac containing factual information related to astronomical data, statistical information, facts about the countries, events and statistics usually published every year and it may be categorized as General Almanac and Subject Almanac.

- Handbooks provide facts, terms, concepts, movements, short instructions, etc. of a topic.
- Manuals provide detailed instructions on a particular subject mostly related to how to do something or how something works.
- Bibliographies are sometimes referred to as Guides to the Literature.
- In reference services, the tools that provide direct and factual answers for who, when, what, and where questions is known as Ready Reference Tools.
- What is the email id of INFLIBNET Director is the example of Ready Reference query.
- Almost reference sources such as Directories, Almanacs, Yearbooks, Handbooks, Manuals, etc. are the examples of Ready Reference Tools.
- Modern almanac serves as compendia of current and retrospective statistics and facts.
- Yearbooks focus on the events and information of previous year facts but it can provide more detailed information on events than an almanac.
- According to S.R. Ranganathan, the Ready Reference Service is reference service finished or replied in a very short time in a minute if possible.
- Ready Reference queries are always fact-finding queries.
- Referral Centers provides sources of information whereas Libraries provide not only sources of information but also documents as well as the needed information.
- According to William A. Katz, reference service is a behind the scene activities of the reference library in the selection, acquisition and maintenance of library stock and its careful recording and administration.
- Long Range Reference Service research level questions are those that require extended searches, perhaps over several hours, or days, and sometimes, even longer periods, on continuing basis.
- Reference functions can be described in types; Responsive and Anticipatory services.
- Responsive Services are those that are provided in response to requests for assistance in finding answers to specific questions.
- Anticipatory Services are those that are offered in anticipation of demands and most documentation and information services are fall under this service.
- Abstracting service, Current Awareness Service (CAS), Bibliographic Compilations on specific topics, Newspaper Clipping service, Indexing services, etc. are the examples of Anticipatory Service.
- Literature Search is a kind of Long Range Reference Service where the search has to be more exhaustive, both in depth and extent.
- Compendex is the computerized version of the Engineering Index (Ei).
- Engineering Index was renamed Ei Compendex.
- Ei Compendex (Compendex) is the broadest and most comprehensive bibliographic engineering database and it is now published by Elsevier.

- Compendex stands for COMPuterized ENgineering inDEX.
- National Union Catalogue of Scientific Serials in India (NUCSSI) is the first indigenous database that serves as an ideal tool to access Journal holdings information maintained by NISCAIR.
- In present Information Age, the information becomes a resource as well as a commodity therefore, it's handling and processing also becomes a main activity nowadays.
- The development and generation of information is dependent on the access, location and dissemination of the relevant documents.
- A bibliography is different from catalogues and index.
- An Analytical Bibliography deals with the study and detailed description of documents with physical characteristics of documents, history of the documents as physical entities.
- The Descriptive Bibliography deals with the material conditions of documents that means full name of the author, the exact title of the work, the date and place of publication, typographical details, illustrations and price details, etc.
- The Enumerative Bibliography deals with the enumeration and classification of books and taking care of the assembling of bibliographical entries into logical and useful arrangement for study and research.
- The largest group of Enumerative Bibliography is the Subject Bibliography form.
- The National Bibliographies are serial publications that are current and attempt to list the publication of a particular country.
- According to S.R. Ranganathan, National Bibliographies serve cultural, economic and social purposes.
- According to S.R. Ranganathan, a bibliography to be universal (Universal Bibliographies) when it includes all published materials, whether books or part of them or periodicals or articles in them or combination of them, on all subjects, in all languages, in all countries, at all times.
- The term Bibliographic Control refers to the operations by which recorded information is organized, arranged or location of information sources according to established standards and thereby made readily retrieval.
- The key factors in Bibliographic Control are subject, form, place, time, scope, and the amount of details given in the individual entries.
- The Universal Bibliographic Control (UBC) programme sponsored by IFLA in 1974.
- An Enumerative Bibliography covers both Primary as well as Secondary works.
- The complete list of all the works or writing of an author is known as Author Bibliography.
- A Retrospective Bibliography provides a list of documents or part of documents published in previous years as distinct from a current bibliography or in other ways a bibliography whose scope is restricted to materials published in the past, sometimes within a specific period of the past.

- The INPADOC (International Patent Documentation) center was founded in 1974 by an agreement between the Austrian Patent Office and the World Intellectual Property Organization (WIPO) for providing patent information service worldwide.
- INPADOC is an international patent collection and its database is publically accessible.
- The headquarters of WIPO is located at Geneva.
- Espacenet (or esp@cenet) is a free online service for searching patents and patent applications.
- Espacenet was developed by the European Patent Office (EPO) in 1998.
- DWPI (Derwent World Patents Index) is a database containing patent applications and patents information source.
- In India, the Patent head office is located at Kolkata with branch offices at Chennai, Mumbai and Delhi.
- Government of India, Ministry of Commerce and Industry, Department of Industrial Policy and Promotion established the Patent Information System (PIS) in the year 1980.
- Indian Patent Office publishes the patent journal on every week Friday and also published Patent Office Journal year-wise from Patent Office Kolkata.
- According to the ISO (International Organization for Standardization), a Standard is a document that provides requirements, specifications, guidelines or characteristics that can be used consistently to ensure that materials, products, processes and services are fit for their purpose.
- Maps, Atlases, Globes, Gazetteers and Travel Guides are the examples of Geographical References Sources.
- There are two categories of Biographical Information Sources; Current and Retrospective Biographical Information sources.
- Statistical Sources are a category belonging to the Primary Source.
- The Statistical Abstracts of British India originally launched in 1863.
- The Central Statistical Organization (CSO) of India is responsible for coordination of statistical activities in India, and evolving and maintaining statistical standards.
- The CSO is located in Delhi.

QUESTIONS

1. Which of the following is/are information source?
(A) Books
(B) Websites
(C) Conference Proceedings
(D) All of the above

2. *Encyclopedia of Associations* has been published since
(A) 1956 (B) 1959
(C) 1962 (D) 1967

3. *The Statesman's Yearbook* is published by

(A) Random House
(B) Pearson
(C) Oxford University Press
(D) Palgrave Macmillan

4. The author of *Encyclopedia of Computer Science and Technology* is
(A) Harry Henderson (B) Peter Achebe
(C) Martin Amis (D) Paul Bailey

5. The first edition of *The World Almanac* was published in
(A) 1868 (B) 1872
(C) 1874 (D) 1878

6. *University Handbook: India* is published by
(A) AIU (B) UGC
(C) ILA (D) INFLIBNET

7. Frequency of publication of *University News* is
(A) Weekly (B) Monthly
(C) Quarterly (D) Bimonthly

8. *Current Biography* has been published since
(A) 1936 (B) 1940
(C) 1942 (D) 1945

9. The frequency of publication of *Current Biography* is
(A) Monthly (B) Quarterly
(C) Bimonthly (D) Biannual

10. The *International Encyclopedia of the Social Sciences* was first published in
(A) 1966 (B) 1968
(C) 1970 (D) 1975

11. The *Encyclopedia of the Social Sciences* was first published in
(A) 1930 (B) 1934
(C) 1938 (D) 1944

12. Which of the following was the first editor of *Encyclopedia of Philosophy*?
(A) Paul Edwards (B) Dan Brown
(C) William Boyd (D) Emily Bronte

13. Which of the following information sources is original according to its content?
(A) Primary Source (B) Secondary Source
(C) Tertiary Source (D) All of the above

14. Autobiography is a/an
(A) Primary Source (B) Secondary Source
(C) Tertiary Source (D) Both (B) and (C)

15. Biography is a/an
(A) Primary Source (B) Secondary Source
(C) Tertiary Source (D) All of the above

16. Which of the following is the Secondary Source of information?
(A) Abstracts (B) Yearbooks
(C) Bibliographies (D) All of the above

17. Which of the following is the Tertiary Source of information?
(A) Bibliography
(B) Autobiography
(C) Gazetteers
(D) Bibliography of bibliographies

18. A...........is a document which was written during the time under study.
(A) Primary Source (B) Secondary Source
(C) Tertiary Source (D) All of the above

19. Creative works like poetry, drama, music, art are the example of
(A) Primary Source (B) Secondary Source
(C) Tertiary Source (D) Both (B) and (C)

20. Research data and surveys are the example of
(A) Primary Source (B) Secondary Source
(C) Tertiary Source (D) All of the above

21. Which of the following is Primary Source of information?
(A) Original photographs
(B) Speeches
(C) Letters
(D) All of the above

22. A Secondary Source can be interpreted and analyzed from...........

(A) Primary Source (B) Secondary Source
(C) Tertiary Source (D) None of the above

23. Which of the following is Secondary Source of information?

(A) Textbooks (B) Criticisms
(C) Magazine articles (D) All of the above

24. 'A book about the effects of HIV on human body' is a

(A) Primary Source (B) Secondary Source
(C) Tertiary Source (D) None of the above

25. Match the following:

	LIST-I		LIST-II
(1)	World Communication: Threat or Promise	(i)	A. Panizzi
(2)	Documentation: its Scope and Limitation	(ii)	J.D. Brown
(3)	Manual of Library Economy	(iii)	Colline Chery
(4)	British Museum Code	(iv)	J.H. Shera

Codes:

	(1)	(2)	(3)	(4)
(A)	(iii)	(iv)	(ii)	(i)
(B)	(ii)	(iv)	(iii)	(i)
(C)	(iii)	(ii)	(iv)	(i)
(D)	(ii)	(iii)	(iv)	(i)

26. A kind of information source that provides an overview or summary of a topic and does not included analysis or critique.

(A) Primary Source (B) Secondary Source
(C) Tertiary Source (D) All of the above

27. Almanac is a/an

(A) Primary Source (B) Secondary Source
(C) Tertiary Source (D) None of the above

28. Wikipedia articles is the example of

(A) Primary Source (B) Secondary Source
(C) Tertiary Source (D) All of the above

29. Which of the following is the Primary Source of information?

(A) *A Physics Textbook*
(B) *Oxford Dictionary*
(C) *Indian National Bibliography*
(D) *Diary of Anna Frank*

30. *The Indian National Bibliography* (*INB*) has been published in........Indian languages.

(A) 13 (B) 12
(C) 11 (D) 14

31. Who was the first director of Indian National Scientific Documentation Centre (INSDOC)?

(A) B.S. Kesavan (B) S.R. Ranganathan
(C) Hari Nath De (D) John Macfarlane

32. Which of the following was the father of *Indian National Bibliography* (*INB*)?

(A) B.S. Kesavan (B) S.R. Ranganathan
(C) Annie Proulx (D) Michelle Paver

33. In which year 'International Conference on National Bibliographic Services (ICNBS)', Copenhagen was held?

(A) 1994 (B) 1996
(C) 1998 (D) 2000

34. There are three parts of *INB*, which of the following is not?

(A) Classified (B) Author & Title
(C) Subject Index (D) Citation Index

35. In Classified part of *INB*, entries are arranged according to

(A) Colon Classification
(B) Dewey Decimal Classification
(C) Universal Decimal Classification
(D) Library of Congress Classification

36. In *INB*, which method is used for Subject Heading?

(A) Sears List of Subject Headings
(B) Library of Congress Subject Headings
(C) Chain Procedure
(D) Canadian Subject Headings

37. What is frequency of publication of *INB*?
(A) Quarterly (B) Bimonthly
(C) Monthly (D) Annually

38. The last print edition of *Encyclopedia Britannica* was
(A) 10th (B) 12th
(C) 14th (D) 15th

39. In which year *Encyclopedia Britannica* was stopped to print version?
(A) 2008 (B) 2009
(C) 2010 (D) 2011

40. In which year, the first online version of *Encyclopedia Americana* was introduced?
(A) 1997 (B) 1999
(C) 2001 (D) 2004

41. How many volumes are consist in 2005 edition of *Encyclopedia Americana*?
(A) 25 (B) 29
(C) 30 (D) 32

42. The first edition of *Encyclopedia Americana* was published in
(A) 1826 (B) 1829
(C) 1832 (D) 1838

43. ....are designed to be used in finding immediate answer of question, rather than for whole book reading.
(A) Immediate Books
(B) User Oriented Books
(C) Universal Books
(D) Reference Books

44. Which of the following reference source we can get some information about medieval India?
(A) Directory (B) Yearbook
(C) Encyclopedia (D) Abstract

45. Which of the following is true?
(A) Reference books kept separately in library
(B) Reference Section in a library is generally located at Input area
(C) Reference Sources can help the users for getting immediate information
(D) All of the above

46. A kind of Reference Source that included information such as weather forecast, farmers planting date, astronomical information
(A) Yearbook (B) Directory
(C) Almanac (D) Dictionary

47. A kind of Reference Source that holding a comprehensive summary of knowledge
(A) Almanac (B) Yearbook
(C) Encyclopedia (D) Dictionary

48. A branch of knowledge that studies the development of linguistics
(A) Lexicon (B) Seismography
(C) Cosmography (D) Somatology

49. The literally meaning of Encyclopedia is
(A) All branches of knowledge
(B) Comprehensive summary of information
(C) A particular branch of knowledge
(D) All of the above

50. The first known *Encyclopedia* was written by
(A) Antonius (B) Archelaus
(C) Aristotle (D) Atticus

51. How many volumes in print version of 15th edition of *Encyclopedia Britannica*?
(A) 29 (B) 31
(C) 32 (D) 33

52. In 15th edition of *Encyclopedia Britannica*, how many volumes consists in Micropaedia part?
(A) 11 (B) 10
(C) 12 (D) 14

53. In 15th edition of *Encyclopedia Britannica,* how many volumes consist in Macropaedia part?

(A) 18 (B) 19
(C) 20 (D) 21

54. Which part of *Encyclopedia Britannica* is the Outline of Knowledge?

(A) Micropaedia (B) Macropaedia
(C) Propaedia (D) None of the above

55. The *Encyclopedia Britannica* was first published in

(A) 1768 (B) 1777
(C) 1789 (D) 1791

56. The first edition of the *Encyclopedia Britannica* was published and printed at

(A) Manchester (B) Bristol
(C) Edinburg (D) Boston

57. Which of the following is the Subject Encyclopedia?

(A) *Encyclopedia of Psychology*
(B) *Encyclopedia of Physics*
(C) *Encyclopedia of Science & Technology*
(D) All of the above

58. Which of the following is the General Encyclopedia?

(A) *Encyclopedia Americana*
(B) *Collier's Encyclopedia*
(C) *Oxford Illustrated Encyclopedia*
(D) All of the above

59. The literally meaning of bibliography is

(A) Book publishing (B) Book sorting
(C) Book witting (D) Book querying

60. The first edition of *The World Book Encyclopedia* was published in

(A) 1917 (B) 1919
(C) 1921 (D) 1925

61. Which of the following is the Citation Style?

(A) MLA Citation (B) Harvard Citation
(C) APA Citation (D) All of the above

62. The Reader's Guide to Periodical Literature is published by

(A) Oxford University Press
(B) McMillan
(C) H.W. Wilson
(D) McGraw-Hill

63. The coverage area of *McGraw-Hill Encyclopedia of World Biography* is

(A) Biography (B) Autobiography
(C) Both (A) and (B) (D) Only (A)

64. *International Who's Who* is published by

(A) H.W. Wilson
(B) McGraw-Hill
(C) Europa
(D) Oxford University Press

65. The 168th edition of *Who's Who* was published in

(A) 2012 (B) 2013
(C) 2014 (D) 2015

66. *India Who's Who* is published by

(A) INFA
(B) Cambridge University Press, India
(C) National Book Trust
(D) McMillan India

67. Which of following is the Ready References Source?

(A) Almanac (B) Yearbooks
(C) Directories (D) All of the above

68. Which of the following is true?

(A) Indexes usually provide a bibliographic details without summary
(B) Abstracts offer a brief summary of documents content
(C) Handbook is the example of Ready Reference Sources
(D) All of the above

69. Which of the following is the example of public copyright license?
(A) Creative Commons (CC)
(B) Copyright Record (CR)
(C) World Copyright (WC)
(D) All of the above

70. The Creative Commons (CC) was founded in
(A) 1995 (B) 1999
(C) 2001 (D) 2004

71. How many types of licenses are used in Creative Commons (CC)
(A) 5 (B) 6
(C) 7 (D) 8

72. In Creative Commons (CC), BY+SA means
(A) Attribution + ShareAll
(B) Attribution + ShareAlike
(C) Attribution + ShareAlone
(D) Attribution + ShareAsia

73. In Creative Commons (CC), which license ensured the remix, tweak and build upon our work in non-commercial as long as we can count own credit
(A) CC BY-ND (B) CC BY-NC
(C) CC BY-NC-SA (D) CC BY-NC-ND

74. Chemical Abstracts Service (CAS) is the division of
(A) American Science Society
(B) American Chemical Society
(C) International Science Society
(D) International Chemical Society

75. Which of the following is Non-documentary References source?
(A) Institutional Resource
(B) Human Resource
(C) Mass Media
(D) All of the above

76. A kind of bibliography that examines the physical characteristics of documents such as signatures, water marks, etc.
(A) Analytical Bibliography
(B) Enumerative Bibliography
(C) Descriptive Bibliography
(D) Historical Bibliography

77. Which of the following is Subject Bibliography?
(A) Indian National Bibliography (INB)
(B) Indian Books in Print
(C) British National Bibliography (BNB)
(D) DBLP

78. Who developed the 'Science and the Social Sciences Citation Index'?
(A) Institute for Scientific Information
(B) Institute of Bibliographical Information
(C) UNESCO
(D) IFLA

79. Institute for Scientific Information (ISI) was founded by
(A) Albert Camus (B) Chris Ware
(C) Eugene Garfield (D) William Gibson

80. Coverage area of Science Citation Index is
(A) Science (B) Medicine
(C) Technology (D) All of the above

81. *Arts and Humanities Citation Index* has been published since
(A) 1972 (B) 1975
(C) 1978 (D) 1979

82. Which of the following is the multidisciplinary Citation Index?
(A) Science Citation Index (SCI)
(B) Social Sciences Citation Index (SSCI)
(C) Arts and Humanities Citation Index (A&HC)
(D) All of the above

83. Indian Citation Index (ICI) was launched in
(A) October 2009 (B) November 2010
(C) October 2010 (D) January 2010

84. Which of the following is a free access bibliographic database search engine?

(A) Web of Science (B) Scopus
(C) Inspec (D) INSPIRE-HEP

85. Google Scholar is the example of
(A) A General Search Engine
(B) Indexing and Citation Database
(C) Web Protocol
(D) Communication Protocol

86. Who was the first editor of *Annals of Library and Information Science*?
(A) S.R. Ranganathan
(B) Vishwanatha Sastri
(C) P.K. Srivasan
(D) M.A. Gopinath

87. In which year 'Annals of Library Science' was expanded to 'Annals of Library Science and Documentation'?
(A) 1960 (B) 1964
(C) 1967 (D) 1969

88. Which of the following is not associated with NISCAIR?
(A) National Science Library
(B) National Science Digital Library
(C) National Union Catalogue
(D) National Medical Library

89. Which of the following is an open-access indexing/abstracting database?
(A) LISTA (B) e-Base
(C) e-Access (D) BOOK-index

90. Which of the following is the measurement tool for contextual citation impact by weighting citation based on the total number of citations received by a journal in a subject field?
(A) SJR (B) SNIP
(C) IPP (D) All of the above

91. Which of the following is the publication of RRRLF?
(A) *Indian Libraries: Trends and Perspectives*
(B) *Directory of Indian Public Libraries*
(C) *Granthana: Indian Journal of Library Studies*
(D) All of the above

92. *Indian Library Science Abstract* (ILSA) is published by
(A) ILA (B) DELNET
(C) IASLIC (D) NISCAIR

93. *Cataloging & Classification Quarterly* is published by
(A) McGraw-Hill (B) Taylor & Francis
(C) McMillan (D) H.W. Wilson

94. *The Library Quarterly* is published by
(A) McGraw-Hill
(B) University of Chicago Press
(C) H.W. Wilson
(D) McMillan

95. *Journal of Information & Knowledge Management* is published by
(A) McMillan
(B) World Scientific
(C) Oxford University Press
(D) McGraw-Hill

96. Which of the following was the first president of ISKO?
(A) Ingetraut Dahlberg
(B) Scott Adams
(C) Russell Baker
(D) Steve Ballmer

97. *Transinformacao* has been published from
(A) Brazil (B) United Kingdom
(C) Australia (D) New Zealand

98. *The Grey Journal* has been published from
(A) Japan (B) China
(C) United States (D) Netherlands

99. *International Journal of Information Science and Management* has been published from

(A) United States of America
(B) Sri Lanka
(C) Iran
(D) Australia

100. The subject scope of *Scriptorium* journal is
(A) Bioinformatics
(B) Classification
(C) Cataloging
(D) Mediaeval manuscript

101. *Quaerendo* journal is published by
(A) Oxford University Press
(B) H.W. Wilson
(C) Brill Academic Publisher
(D) McMillan

102. In which year LIBER was founded?
(A) 1965 (B) 1968
(C) 1971 (D) 1975

103. The journal *Asian Libraries* is merged into
(A) *New Library World*
(B) *ASLIB Proceedings*
(C) *IFLA Journal*
(D) *International Journal of Library and Information Science*

104. *UNESCO Journal of Information Science Librarianship and Archives Administration* formerly published as
(A) UNESCO Bulletin for Librarianship
(B) UNESCO Bulletin for Archives
(C) UNESCO Bulletin for Libraries
(D) UNESCO Bulletin for Information Science & Archives

105. Which of the following database covering peer review biomedical journals published from India?
(A) IndMED (B) BioIND
(C) MEDIndia (D) IndiaMED

106. Which of the following is the founder of OCLC?
(A) Frederick Gridley Kilgour
(B) Edward Abbey
(C) Fred Allen
(D) Tori Amos

107. Who is responsible for compilation and selling of INB?
(A) CRL, Kolkata
(B) NISCAIR, New Delhi
(C) INFLIBNET, Ahmedabad
(D) RRRLF, Kolkata

108. Who is the publisher of *Index Indiana*?
(A) NISCAIR, New Delhi
(B) CRL, Kolkata
(C) IASLIC, Kolkata
(D) RRRLF, Kolkata

109. The first issue of *Index Indiana* was published in
(A) 1972 (B) 1975
(C) 1977 (D) 1978

110. The Central Reference Library is located at
(A) New Delhi (B) Kolkata
(C) Mumbai (D) Chennai

111. CRL functioning under
(A) Ministry of Culture
(B) Ministry of Finance
(C) Ministry of Human Resource Development
(D) Ministry of Information and Broadcasting

112. The Legal Deposit Libraries Shared Cataloguing Programme (LDLSCP) is specially for
(A) INB (B) BNB
(C) SLNB (D) Both (A) and (B)

113. Which of the following is related to the BNB MARC?
(A) United Kingdom MARC
(B) British MARC
(C) Both (A) and (B)
(D) BNBMARC

114. *The Sri Lanka National Bibliography* (SLNB) has been published since
(A) 1971 (B) 1974
(C) 1976 (D) 1978

115. In which year, Delivery of Books (Public Libraries) Act was introduced?
(A) 1950 (B) 1952
(C) 1954 (D) 1957

116. The literally meaning of Legal Deposits is
(A) Printers and Publishers deliver their copies to the National Library
(B) Printer and Publishers deliver their copies to the Legal Deposit Libraries
(C) Both (A) and (B)
(D) Only (A)

117. According to the UNESCO/IFLA definition, the "National Imprint" means
(A) The products of the national publishing industry
(B) Book printing industries
(C) Book deliver industries
(D) Books for all

118. The IFLA WLIC 2013 was held in
(A) South Africa
(B) United States of America
(C) Singapore
(D) Switzerland

119. The *Current Biography* is published by
(A) H.W. Wilson
(B) McGraw-Hill
(C) McMillan
(D) Oxford University Press

120. The 'Publishers' Weekly' was founded by
(A) Wendell Berry (B) Ken Bevel
(C) Peter Benenson (D) Frederick Leypoldt

121. Frederick Leypoldt was a/an
(A) Cataloguer (B) Classifier
(C) Bibliographer (D) Conservator

122. Who says "Bibliographical control is a form of power and power to obtain the knowledge recorded in written form"?
(A) Patrick Wilson (B) James Boswell
(C) David Bowie (D) Elena Bonner

123. The database of Indian Patent Information Retrieval Systems (IPAIRS) is a/an
(A) Primary Source (B) Secondary Source
(C) Tertiary Source (D) None of the above

124. Letter written by Pd. Jawaharlal Nehru is the example of
(A) Primary Source (B) Secondary Source
(C) Tertiary Source (D) None of the above

125. The .mp4 file format of film 'Guide' is the example of
(A) Primary Source
(B) Secondary Source
(C) Tertiary Source
(D) None of the above

126. The biography of the director of film *Guide* is the example of
(A) Primary Source (B) Secondary Source
(C) Tertiary Source (D) None of the above

127. Which of the following year IFLA sponsored the Universal Bibliographic Control (UBC) programme?
(A) 1971 (B) 1974
(C) 1976 (D) 1978

128. In amendment Act in 1956 (Delivery of Books Act 1954), included material is/are
(A) Periodicals (B) Newspaper
(C) Both (A) and (B) (D) Only (A)

129. The total number of National Depositor Library in India is
(A) 1 (B) 3
(C) 4 (D) 5

130. Which of the following library is the National Depositor Library in India?

(A) National Library, Kolkata
(B) Central Library, Mumbai
(C) Delhi Public Library
(D) All of the above

131. Which of the following library is not a National Depositor Library in India?
(A) Raza Library, Rampur
(B) Connemara Public Library, Chennai
(C) Khuda Bakhsh Oriental Library, Patna
(D) Both (A) and (C)

132. The International Standard Bibliographic Description (ISBD) is a set of rules produced by
(A) LOC (B) ASLIB
(C) IFLA (D) ALA

133. An Enumerative bibliography covers
(A) Primary works (B) Secondary works
(C) Both (A) and (B) (D) Only (B)

134. Which of the following was printed version of MEDLINE database?
(A) Index Medicus (B) Medicus list
(C) Medicus Index (D) Medicus data

135. The last issue of *Index Medicus* was published in
(A) 2002 (B) 2004
(C) 2006 (D) 2007

136. The subject coverage of 'Biological Abstracts' is
(A) Botany (B) Biochemistry
(C) Toxicology (D) All of the above

137. A kind of information source that provides specifications, guidelines, service instructions.
(A) Index (B) Patents
(C) Standards (D) Trade catalogue

138. The earlier name of Bureau of Indian Standards (BIS) was
(A) Indian Standards Institution
(B) Indian Institute for Trade Mark
(C) Indian Institute for Quality Control
(D) None of the above

139. In which year Patent Information System (PIS) was set up at Nagpur?
(A) 1978 (B) 1980
(C) 1984 (D) 1985

140. *Cumulative Book Index* has been published since
(A) 1898 (B) 1900
(C) 1903 (D) 1908

141. INPADOC was founded by
(A) World Intellectual Property Organization (WIPO)
(B) Universal Postal Union (UPU)
(C) International Organization for Standardization (ISO)
(D) International Electrotechnical Commission (IEC)

142. Which of the following was the editor of *Chambers World Gazetteer: An A to Z of Geographical Information*?
(A) George Eliot
(B) Gillian W. Flynn
(C) David Munro
(D) Thomas S. Frank

143. The *Imperial Gazetteer of India* was first published in
(A) 1881 (B) 1883
(C) 1885 (D) 1887

144. How many volumes were published in first edition of *Imperial Gazetteer of India*?
(A) 7 (B) 8
(C) 9 (D) 10

145. Which of the following is a Travel Guide?
(A) *Imperial Gazetteer of India*
(B) *Swamy's Handbook*
(C) *World of Learning*
(D) *Fodor's Guide to India*

146. Which of the following has been published *International Who's Who* since 2000?

(A) Europa Publication
(B) Routledge
(C) Oxford University Press
(D) H.W. Wilson

147. Match the following:

LIST-I	LIST-II
(1) *Derwent World Patent Index*	(i) 1968
(2) *INPADOC*	(ii) 1935
(3) *International Who's Who*	(iii) 1975
(4) *International Encyclopedia of the Social Science*	(iv) 1972

Codes:

	(1)	(2)	(3)	(4)
(A)	(i)	(ii)	(iv)	(iii)
(B)	(iii)	(iv)	(ii)	(i)
(C)	(ii)	(iv)	(i)	(iii)
(D)	(iii)	(i)	(ii)	(iv)

148. Which of the following is the publisher of *Cumulative Book Index*?

(A) Oxford University Press
(B) McGraw-Hill Publication
(C) H.W. Wilson
(D) McMillan

149. Statistical sources of information is a/an

(A) Primary Source (B) Secondary Source
(C) Tertiary Source (D) None of the above

150. Which of the following was the editor of *ALA Glossary of Library and Information Science*?

(A) Heartsill Young (B) John P. Banville
(C) Jane S. Austen (D) Martin N. Amis

151. Which of the following is the Primary Sources of information?

(A) Autobiographies (B) Letters
(C) Biography (D) Both (A) and (B)

152. The 'Statistical Abstract of the Indian Union' has been published since

(A) 1950 (B) 1952
(C) 1954 (D) 1958

153. Which of the following is the Secondary Sources of information?

(A) Indexes (B) Abstracts
(C) Journal articles (D) All of the above

154. The word 'Index' is derived from the Latin word

(A) Indicare (B) Inanis
(C) Informatio (D) Iuxta

155. An index can be arranged

(A) Alphabetical (B) Chronological
(C) Geographical (D) All of the above

156. According to the ALA Glossary of Library & Information Science, an index can be

(A) Abbreviate (B) Accurate
(C) With criticism (D) Both (A) and (B)

157. Indexing services can be included

(A) Bibliographical details
(B) Abstract of the document
(C) Only (A)
(D) Both (A) and (B)

158. Which of the following is the quality of an abstract?

(A) Indexes
(B) Bibliographical description
(C) Most recent information
(D) All of the above

159. 'Science Citation Index' was created by

(A) Eugene Garfield (B) Philip M. Dick
(C) David S. Sedaris (D) Anne W. Enright

160. The 'Science Citation Index' is originally produced by

(A) Institute for Scientific Information
(B) American Library Association
(C) IFLA
(D) UNESCO

161. The 'Social Science Citation Index' was developed by
(A) American Library Association
(B) Institute for Scientific Information
(C) Canadian Library Association
(D) IFLA

162. The *Arts and Humanities Citation Index* is published by
(A) Institute for Scientific Information
(B) Thomas Scientific
(C) Canadian Library Association
(D) CILIP

163. *Forthcoming International Conference on Military Science & Technology* (FICMST) is published by
(A) DESIDOC (B) NASA
(C) ISRO (D) BARC

164. The first edition of *Encyclopedic Dictionary of Mathematics* was appeared in
(A) 1972 (B) 1974
(C) 1977 (D) 1979

165. The book titled *Documentation and its Facets* was written by
(A) S.R. Ranganathan (B) William A. Katz
(C) C.A. Cutter (D) J.D. Brown

166. Who is the author of book, *New Trends in Biology Teaching*?
(A) UNESCO
(B) William S. Gibson
(C) David T. Grossman
(D) IFLA

167. Technically 'collection of information (data) from different sources and putting them together' is called
(A) Receiving and Compiling
(B) Receiving and Abstracting
(C) Repackaging
(D) Receiving and Indexing

168. The science of compiling of dictionary is called
(A) Lexicography (B) Etymology
(C) Ornithology (D) Morphology

169. The term 'Thesaurus' was coined by
(A) Peter Mark Roget
(B) Thomas F. Frank
(C) James S. Frey
(D) Sigmund S. Freud

170. The *Encyclopedic Dictionary of Mathematics* is prepared by
(A) Mathematical Society of Japan
(B) Mathematical Association of America
(C) Chinese Mathematical Society
(D) Canadian Mathematical Society

171. The first edition of *Roget's International Thesaurus* was published in
(A) 1848 (B) 1850
(C) 1852 (D) 1854

172. *Oxford Dictionary of Quotations* is the example of
(A) Subject dictionary (B) General dictionary
(C) Special dictionary (D) Either (A) or (C)

173. Dictionaries can be evaluated through
(A) Size and appearance
(B) Binding and print quality
(C) Price
(D) All of the above

174. The book titled *Introduction to Reference Work* was written by
(A) S.R. Ranganathan
(B) William A. Katz
(C) C.A. Cutter
(D) Thomas H. Hardly

175. Which of the following is less important for the purpose of evaluation of an Encyclopedia?

(A) Authority (B) Arrangement
(C) Treatment (D) Size

176. Which of the following is the Ready Reference Source?

(A) Yearbooks (B) Directories
(C) Almanac (D) All of the above

177. *A Bibliography of Dictionaries and Encyclopedias in Indian Languages* is published by

(A) National Library, Kolkata
(B) NISCAIR, New Delhi
(C) DELNET, New Delhi
(D) IASLIC, Kolkata

178. With the help of 'Handbook', we can get

(A) Astronomical information
(B) Bibliographical information
(C) A sort information related to the facts
(D) All of the above

179. *Universities Handbooks* is published by

(A) IASLIC, Kolkata
(B) Association of Indian Universities (AIU), New Delhi
(C) Delhi University, New Delhi
(D) Jawaharlal Nehru University, New Delhi

180. Match the following:

LIST-I	LIST-II
(1) First edition of International Who's Who	(i) United Nations
(2) Current Biography	(ii) McGraw-Hill
(3) Introduction to Reference Work	(iii) H.W. Wilson
(4) New Trends in Biology Teaching	(iv) Europa

Codes:

	(1)	(2)	(3)	(4)
(A)	(iv)	(ii)	(iii)	(i)
(B)	(iv)	(i)	(iii)	(ii)
(C)	(i)	(ii)	(iii)	(iv)
(D)	(iv)	(iii)	(ii)	(i)

181. Which of the following is the e-tool for reference services?

(A) Online database access
(B) Online Catalogue
(C) e-bibliographies
(D) All of the above

182. Match the following:

LIST-I	LIST-II
(1) MEDLARS	(i) 1976
(2) MEDOC	(ii) 1879
(3) POPLINE	(iii) 1969
(4) EXCERPTA	(iv) 1970

Codes:

	(1)	(2)	(3)	(4)
(A)	(i)	(ii)	(iv)	(iii)
(B)	(ii)	(iv)	(i)	(iii)
(C)	(ii)	(iii)	(i)	(iv)
(D)	(ii)	(i)	(iv)	(iii)

183. Which of the following is related to the bibliographic database for Life Science and Biomedical information?

(A) MEDLARS (B) MEDOC
(C) NIMH (D) NTIS

184. Match the following:

LIST-I	LIST-II
(1) POPLINE	(i) Scientific and Technical
(2) MEDLARS	(ii) Population, Reproductive and Health

(3) NTIS (iii) Agriculture, Animal and Plant Science

(4) AGRICOLA (iv) Life Science and Biomedical

Codes:

	(1)	(2)	(3)	(4)
(A)	(ii)	(iv)	(i)	(iii)
(B)	(i)	(iv)	(iii)	(ii)
(C)	(ii)	(i)	(iii)	(iv)
(D)	(i)	(iv)	(ii)	(iii)

185. Which of the following is the online version of MEDLARS?
(A) MEDLINE (B) ONLINEMED
(C) e-MEDLINE (D) e-MEDLARS

186. The *Index Medicus* is published by
(A) National Library of Medicine, USA
(B) Canadian Health Libraries Association
(C) Medical Library Association, Chicago
(D) British Medical Association, UK

187. Which of the following is a free search engine for accessing MEDLINE database?
(A) PubMed (B) e-Med
(C) e-MEDLINE (D) e-Access

188. In which year PubMed was released?
(A) 1993 (B) 1996
(C) 1998 (D) 2000

189. Which of the following is the search engine for Medical and Health database?
(A) PubMed (B) Entrez
(C) Twease (D) All of the above

190. Which of the following was first editor of *Index-Catalogue*?
(A) John Shaw Billings
(B) Mark T. Haddon
(C) Joseph S. Heller
(D) Chloe J. Hooper

191. Which of the following is a digitized version of printed *Index-Catalogue*?
(A) IndexCat (B) e-Index
(C) ONLINEINDEX (D) e-Cat

192. Which of the following is a Toxicity Bibliography database?
(A) TOXBIB (B) TXBIB
(C) BIBTOX (D) e-TXBIB

193. Match the following:

LIST-I	LIST-II
(1) *McGraw-Hill Encyclopedia of World Biography*	(i) 1968
(2) *Who's Who*	(ii) 1969
(3) *India Who's Who*	(iii) 1973
(4) *Encyclopedia of Library and Information Science*	(iv) 1849

Codes:

	(1)	(2)	(3)	(4)
(A)	(iv)	(i)	(ii)	(iii)
(B)	(iii)	(iv)	(ii)	(i)
(C)	(iv)	(ii)	(i)	(iii)
(D)	(iii)	(i)	(ii)	(iv)

194. Which of the following is the example of Union Catalogue?
(A) WorldCat (B) Copac
(C) Amicus (D) All of the above

195. Which of the following was the first journal published in India?
(A) Asiatic Researches (B) Asia Records
(C) India's Researches (D) Asia Researches

196. Match the following:

LIST-I	LIST-II
(1) Conference on the Improvement of Bibliographical Service	(i) 1998
(2) International Congress on National Bibliographic	(ii) 2010

(3) International Conference on National Bibliographic Service (iii) 1950
(4) ASLIB: Translating and the Computer 30th Conference (iv) 1977

Codes:

	(1)	(2)	(3)	(4)
(A)	(iv)	(ii)	(i)	(iii)
(B)	(iii)	(iv)	(i)	(ii)
(C)	(i)	(iii)	(iv)	(ii)
(D)	(iv)	(i)	(ii)	(iii)

197. 'A paperless society is one in which written documents are replaced by electronic communication and storage', concept originated by
(A) F.W. Lancaster (B) Bill Gates
(C) Mark Zuberkar (D) Sergey Brin

198. Which of the following is true for Data Center?
(A) It vary both in scope and size
(B) Data collects from different sources
(C) Data can be accessed without any Internet connection
(D) Both (A) and (B)

199. Which of the following is false for Clearing House?
(A) It works as central agency for documents collection and distribution
(B) It may be performed the function of a Referral Centre
(C) It works as an information gathering networks
(D) All above are true

200. 'Research and Information System for Developing Countries (RIS)' is located at
(A) Kolkata (B) New Delhi
(C) Bengaluru (D) Hyderabad

201. Online Copy Catalogue System (OCS) is associated with
(A) DELNET (B) INFLIBNET
(C) NML (D) NISCAIR

202. IndCat: Online Union Catalogue of Indian Universities is associated with
(A) INFLIBNET (B) NML
(C) NISCAIR (D) DESIDOC

203. Literature reviews are.........of information
(A) Primary Source (B) Secondary Source
(C) Tertiary Source (D) All of the above

204. International Development Research Centre (IDRC) is located in
(A) USA (B) Canada
(C) Australia (D) Japan

205. Which of the following services is given by an Information Center?
(A) Lending of Books
(B) Referral Services
(C) Current Awareness Services (CAS)
(D) All of the above

206. Which of the following is the national level Information Centre in India?
(A) NISCAIR (B) DESIDOC
(C) ICAR (D) All of the above

207. In which year National Standard Reference Data System (NSRDS) was established?
(A) 1963 (B) 1965
(C) 1967 (D) 1970

208. National Institute of Standards and Technology (NIST) is an agency of
(A) USA, Department of Commerce
(B) UK, Department for Education
(C) Australia, Department of Education
(D) Canada, Department of National Defence

209. Which of the following is the parent organization of CODATA?
(A) ICSU (B) IFLA
(C) LOC (D) CILIP

210. Which of the following is a professional organ of NSSO?

(A) Survey Design and Research Division (SDRD)
(B) Society for Technical Communication (STC)
(C) Institution of Engineering and Technology (IET)
(D) Indian Chemical Society (ICS)

211. Which of the following is true for Referral Centers?

(A) Provide document services those related to the Secondary Source of information
(B) It does not provide technical details in answer to inquirer
(C) It work simply as the 'information desk' without any bibliographic assistance
(D) Both (B) and (C)

212. The book titled *Handbook for Information Systems and Services* was written by

(A) Pauline A. Cochrane
(B) Martin M. Amis
(C) Diana S. Athill
(D) Enid Y. Blyton

213. India International Centre (IIC) is located at

(A) Bengaluru (B) Hyderabad
(C) Kolkata (D) New Delhi

214. In which year 'UNESCO Symposium on Information Analysis and Consolidation' was held in Colombo, Sri Lanka?

(A) 1975 (B) 1978
(C) 1999 (D) 2001

215. *Brazilian Journal of Information Science* (BRAJIS) has been published since

(A) 2001 (B) 2004
(C) 2006 (D) 2008

216. Which of the following is true?

(A) Packaging of information is physical recording
(B) Repackaging of information is rearrangement of information according to the users' requirement
(C) Information consolidation activity is the example of information repackaging
(D) All of the above

217. India-ASEAN News on Agriculture and Forestry Newsletter is published by

(A) Indian Council of Agricultural Research (ICAR), New Delhi
(B) Assam Agriculture University, Assam
(C) Indian Agricultural Research Institute (IARI), New Delhi
(D) Central Agricultural University, Manipur

218. Which of the following is true?

(A) Information sources are related to library & information science
(B) Information resources are related to information & communication technologies
(C) Documentation Centers are able to repackaging of information
(D) All of the above

219. Information sources can be categorized according to

(A) Their types (B) Their contents
(C) Their media (D) All of the above

220. Which of the following is a non-Documentary Source of Information?

(A) CD/DVD-ROM (B) Databases
(C) e-books (D) Common men

221. The modern printing machine was developed in

(A) Australia (B) United Kingdom
(C) Germany (D) China

222. Which of the following is the Cyber media?

(A) Web pages (B) e-periodicals
(C) Blogs (D) All of the above

223. The term Cyberspace is coined by

(A) William Gibson (B) Paul S. Auster
(C) Tim Berners-Lee (D) William F. Blake

224. IFLA was founded in
(A) Edinburgh, Scotland
(B) Basel, Switzerland
(C) Milan, Italy
(D) Melbourne, Australia

225. In which year NISSAT programme was closed?
(A) 1998 (B) 2000
(C) 2002 (D) 2007

226. Which of the following is a nodal department for granting reorganization to in-house R&D units in industries, scientific and industrial research organizations in India?
(A) DSIR (B) NISSAT
(C) NISCAIR (D) RRRLF

227. Which of the following is a national level linkage network provided by NIC?
(A) NICNET (B) DELNET
(C) ERNET (D) INFLIBNET

228. In which year NIC introduced 'IT in villages to exchange of information among agencies'?
(A) 1984 (B) 1986
(C) 1989 (D) 1991

229. The Centre for DNA Fingerprinting and Diagnosis (CDFD) is located at
(A) New Delhi (B) Ahmedabad
(C) Hyderabad (D) Kolkata

230. In which year Environmental Information System (ENVIS) was established?
(A) 1980 (B) 1982
(C) 1985 (D) 1988

231. Which of the following is established by UGC as National Facilities Centre?
(A) Western Regional Instrumentation Centre, Mumbai University
(B) Crystal Growth Centre, Anna University
(C) IUCHSS, Indian Institute of Advanced Study, Shimla
(D) All of the above

232. *Kriti Rakshana* (a bimonthly publication of National Mission for Manuscripts, India) has been published since
(A) 1997 (B) 2000
(C) 2003 (D) 2005

233. Central Institute of Indian Languages (CIIL) is located at
(A) New Delhi (B) Mysore
(C) Kolkata (D) Hyderabad

234. The CIIL library was established in
(A) 1967 (B) 1970
(C) 1973 (D) 1976

235. Which of the following is the Global Information System?
(A) ASTINFO (B) INIS
(C) INFOTERRA (D) All of the above

236. ASTINFO was established in
(A) 1978 (B) 1980
(C) 1983 (D) 1988

237. Which of the following is the UNEP's Global Environmental Information Exchange Network?
(A) INFOTERRA (B) INIS
(C) MEDLARS (D) ASTINFO

238. Match the following:

LIST-I	LIST-II
(1) INIS	(i) 1974
(2) INSPEC	(ii) 1970
(3) AGRIS	(iii) 1977
(4) INFORTERRA	(iv) 1967

Codes:

	(1)	(2)	(3)	(4)
(A)	(i)	(iii)	(ii)	(iv)
(B)	(i)	(iv)	(ii)	(iii)

(C) (ii) (iv) (i) (iii)
(D) (ii) (i) (iv) (iii)

239. AGRIS was started by
(A) FAO, United Nations
(B) IAEA, Austria
(C) Institute of Food and Agricultural Sciences, United States
(D) ICAO, Korea

240. INSPEC is produced by
(A) Institution of Electrical Engineers (IEE)
(B) International Atomic Energy Agency (IAEA)
(C) UNESCO
(D) Library of Congress

241. IndMED (Indian MEDLARS) centre set-up at
(A) NIC (B) ICMR
(C) Both (A) and (B) (D) AIIMS, New Delhi

242. Medicinal & Aromatic Plants Information Services (MAPIS) system is associated with
(A) IFLA (B) NISCAIR
(C) LOC (D) AGRIS

243. Which of the following is the national centre in India of ISSN international center?
(A) RRRLF, Kolkata
(B) NSL, New Delhi
(C) INFLIBNET, Ahmedabad
(D) DELNET, New Delhi

244. Which of the following is the database of Indian Social Science Periodical Literature?
(A) INSSPEL (B) arXiv
(C) AULIMP (D) Inspec

245. In which year DESIDOC became a self-accounting unit of DRDO?
(A) 1960 (B) 1965
(C) 1970 (D) 1975

246. In which year UNESCO established the Communication and Information Sector (CI)?
(A) 1980 (B) 1988
(C) 1990 (D) 1992

247. UNESCO Network of Associated Libraries (UNAL) was established in
(A) 1988 (B) 1990
(C) 1992 (D) 1995

248. IASLIC Newsletter has been published since
(A) 1962 (B) 1966
(C) 1968 (D) 1970

249. Which of the following is U.S. National Library of Medicine's automated interlibrary loan system?
(A) MEDLINE (B) DOCLINE
(C) e-ILL (D) US-ILL

250. The Research Library Group (RLG) was founded by
(A) Columbia University
(B) Harvard University
(C) Yale University
(D) All of the above

251. In which year RLG was founded?
(A) 1970 (B) 1972
(C) 1974 (D) 1986

252. The purpose of Content Analysis is
(A) Critically analyzed the content of Primary documents
(B) Useful for creating Secondary Sources of information
(C) To developed value-added information services for the users
(D) All of the above

253. Concordance means
(A) Etymology of the words
(B) Synonymous of the words
(C) An alphabetical index to author works with the places of location
(D) Further explanations of idioms

254. Which of the following is the Content Analysis tool?

(A) Indexing Services
(B) Concordance
(C) Abstracting Services
(D) All of the above

255. Which of the statement is true for Boolean Operators?
(A) AND decrease the number of results
(B) OR increase the number of results
(C) NOT reduce the number of results
(D) All of the above

256. The Boolean Operators formulated by
(A) George Boole (B) John Boole
(C) Jeffrey Boole (D) William Boole

257. Institute for Scientific Information (ISI) is located at
(A) Philadelphia (B) New York
(C) The Hague (D) Edinburgh

258. Which of the following is the founder of Science, Social Science and Humanities Citation Indexing?
(A) Eugene Garfield
(B) Simon J. Gray
(C) Thomas S. Hardy
(D) David T. Harsent

259. 'ISI Web of Science' was launched in
(A) 1990 (B) 1992
(C) 1995 (D) 1997

260. The term 'Webometrics' is coined by
(A) Tomas C. Almind and Peter Ingwersen
(B) Damon G. Galgut and Simon Garfield
(C) David S. Grossman and David J. Harsent
(D) Joseph H. Heller and John T. Grisham

261. Who introduced the 'Web Impact Factor (WIF)'?
(A) Joseph H. Heller
(B) David S. Grossman
(C) Peter Ingwersen
(D) David J. Harsent

262. 'ISI Web of Knowledge' was launched in
(A) 1992 (B) 1999
(C) 2001 (D) 2005

263. An entry in a bibliography (or footnote) that refers to an earlier work of some kind is called
(A) Citation (B) List of References
(C) Page Footer (D) Both (A) and (B)

264. The term 'Bibliometrics' is coined by
(A) Alan Pritchard (B) Frank M. Miller
(C) Alan Moore (D) Alice M. Minro

265. Which algorithm is used by Google search engine to ranking the websites in their search engine results?
(A) PageRank (B) Teoma
(C) Poison Words (D) SALSA algorithm

266. The book titled *Handbook for Information Systems and Services* is published by
(A) IFLA
(B) UNESCO
(C) Oxford University Press
(D) McMillan

267. Match the following:

LIST-I	LIST-II
(1) Information Today & Tomorrow	(i) ISI Web of Knowledge
(2) Kriti Rakshana	(ii) Informatics (India) Ltd.
(3) Open J-Gate	(iii) NISSAT
(4) Current Contents Connect (CCC)	(iv) NAMAMI

Codes:

	(1)	(2)	(3)	(4)
(A)	(iv)	(i)	(iii)	(ii)
(B)	(iii)	(iv)	(ii)	(i)
(C)	(i)	(iv)	(iii)	(ii)
(D)	(iv)	(ii)	(i)	(iii)

268. Match the following:

LIST-I	LIST-II
(1) Science Citation Index	(i) 2006
(2) Social Science Citation Index	(ii) 1963
(3) Arts and Humanities Citation Index	(iii) 1978
(4) Open J-Gate	(iv) 1973

Codes:

	(1)	(2)	(3)	(4)
(A)	(ii)	(iv)	(iii)	(i)
(B)	(i)	(ii)	(iii)	(iv)
(C)	(iv)	(ii)	(i)	(iii)
(D)	(iii)	(i)	(iv)	(ii)

269. Which of the following is true?
(A) Tables of contents, indexes, cumulative indexes are information sources aid
(B) Primary information is getting accessed through the Secondary Sources of information
(C) Ulrich's Periodicals Directory is the example of Tertiary Source of information
(D) All of the above

270. Which of the following can be developed library classification scheme on the basis of principle of universe of knowledge.
(A) Classifier
(B) Classificationist
(C) Reference Librarian
(D) Web Librarian

271. Melvil Dewey, S.R. Ranganathan, and Henry E. Bliss are known as
(A) Classificationist (B) Classifier
(C) Cataloguer (D) Developer

272. In which year S.R. Ranganathan coined the term 'Librametrician'?
(A) 1945 (B) 1947
(C) 1949 (D) 1951

273. Which of the following is the information generator?
(A) Authors (B) Researchers
(C) Judges (D) All of the above

274. Which of the following is the synonym of 'Expert System'?
(A) Knowledge-Based System
(B) Intelligent System
(C) Knowledge System
(D) All of the above

275. Which following is the freely accessible web resource search engine?
(A) Google Scholar (B) CiteSeerX
(C) getCITED (D) All of the above

276. Assertion (A): In modern days, Knowledge-Based Organization is an essential entity.

Reason (R): Knowledgeable employees are necessary for any Management Information System (MIS)-based organization.
(A) Both (A) and (R) are true
(B) (A) is true, but (R) is false
(C) (A) is false, but (R) is true
(D) Both (A) and (R) are false

277. Assertion (A): World Wide Web (WWW) now changed the importance of library in our society.

Reason (R): Users generally hits the websites for their desired information.
(A) Both (A) and (R) are true
(B) (A) is true, but (R) is false
(C) (A) is false, but (R) is true
(D) Both (A) and (R) are false

278. Assertion (A): Due to emerging of ICT in libraries, the physical location of information resources may be less important in coming years.

Reason (R): In paperless societies, users want to access locators rather than resources location.

(A) Both (A) and (R) are false
(B) (A) is true, but (R) is false
(C) Both (A) and (R) are true
(D) (A) is false, but (R) is true

279. Assertion (A): Referral centre works as an intermediary, for querying concerning scientific and technical subjects as well as knowledge sharing among users.

Reason (R): NISCAIR is a Referral Centre.

(A) Both (A) and (R) are true
(B) (A) is true, but (R) is false
(C) (A) is false, but (R) is true
(D) Both (A) and (R) are false

280. Assertion (A): Information Center will not work properly without the existence of traditional library concept.

Reason (R): Traditional libraries are less important as comparison with Digital libraries in current IT era.

(A) Both (A) and (R) are false
(B) Both (A) and (R) are true
(C) (A) is true, but (R) is false
(D) (A) is false, but (R) is true

281. Assertion (A): Library services are totally different as comparison with information services.

Reason (R): Without technical works of documents, information centers will not able to give full services like library.

(A) Both (A) and (R) are false
(B) Both (A) and (R) are true
(C) (A) is true, but (R) is false
(D) (A) is false, but (R) is true

282. Assertion (A): Information is not static pattern and also not a common physical format.

Reason (R): Repackaging of information is an essential activity under information consolidation.

(A) Both (A) and (R) are true
(B) Both (A) and (R) are false
(C) (A) is true, but (R) is false
(D) (A) is false, but (R) is true

Answers Keys

1. (D)	2. (A)	3. (D)	4. (A)	49. (D)	50. (C)	51. (C)	52. (C)
5. (A)	6. (A)	7. (A)	8. (B)	53. (B)	54. (C)	55. (A)	56. (C)
9. (A)	10. (B)	11. (A)	12. (A)	57. (D)	58. (D)	59. (C)	60. (A)
13. (A)	14. (A)	15. (B)	16. (D)	61. (D)	62. (C)	63. (C)	64. (C)
17. (D)	18. (A)	19. (A)	20. (A)	65. (D)	66. (A)	67. (D)	68. (D)
21. (D)	22. (A)	23. (D)	24. (B)	69. (A)	70. (C)	71. (C)	72. (B)
25. (A)	26. (C)	27. (C)	28. (C)	73. (C)	74. (B)	75. (D)	76. (A)
29. (D)	30. (D)	31. (A)	32. (A)	77. (D)	78. (A)	79. (C)	80. (D)
33. (C)	34. (D)	35. (B)	36. (C)	81. (B)	82. (D)	83. (A)	84. (D)
37. (C)	38. (D)	39. (C)	40. (A)	85. (B)	86. (A)	87. (B)	88. (D)
41. (C)	42. (B)	43. (D)	44. (C)	89. (A)	90. (D)	91. (D)	92. (C)
45. (D)	46. (C)	47. (C)	48. (A)	93. (B)	94. (B)	95. (B)	96. (A)

97. (A)	98. (D)	99. (C)	100. (D)
101. (C)	102. (C)	103. (A)	104. (C)
105. (A)	106. (A)	107. (A)	108. (B)
109. (C)	110. (B)	111. (A)	112. (B)
113. (D)	114. (B)	115. (C)	116. (C)
117. (A)	118. (C)	119. (A)	120. (D)
121. (C)	122. (A)	123. (B)	124. (A)
125. (A)	126. (B)	127. (B)	128. (C)
129. (C)	130. (D)	131. (D)	132. (C)
133. (C)	134. (A)	135. (B)	136. (D)
137. (C)	138. (A)	139. (B)	140. (A)
141. (A)	142. (C)	143. (A)	144. (C)
145. (D)	146. (B)	147. (B)	148. (C)
149. (A)	150. (A)	151. (D)	152. (A)
153. (D)	154. (A)	155. (D)	156. (D)
157. (C)	158. (D)	159. (A)	160. (A)
161. (B)	162. (B)	163. (A)	164. (C)
165. (A)	166. (A)	167. (C)	168. (A)
169. (A)	170. (A)	171. (C)	172. (D)
173. (D)	174. (B)	175. (D)	176. (D)
177. (A)	178. (C)	179. (B)	180. (D)
181. (D)	182. (D)	183. (A)	184. (A)
185. (A)	186. (A)	187. (A)	188. (B)
189. (D)	190. (A)	191. (A)	192. (A)
193. (B)	194. (D)	195. (A)	196. (B)
197. (A)	198. (D)	199. (D)	200. (B)
201. (B)	202. (A)	203. (B)	204. (B)
205. (D)	206. (D)	207. (A)	208. (A)
209. (A)	210. (A)	211. (D)	212. (A)
213. (D)	214. (B)	215. (C)	216. (D)
217. (A)	218. (D)	219. (D)	220. (D)
221. (C)	222. (D)	223. (A)	224. (A)
225. (C)	226. (A)	227. (A)	228. (B)
229. (C)	230. (B)	231. (D)	232. (D)
233. (B)	234. (B)	235. (D)	236. (C)
237. (A)	238. (C)	239. (A)	240. (A)
241. (C)	242. (B)	243. (B)	244. (A)
245. (C)	246. (C)	247. (B)	248. (B)
249. (B)	250. (D)	251. (C)	252. (D)
253. (C)	254. (D)	255. (D)	256. (A)
257. (A)	258. (A)	259. (D)	260. (A)
261. (C)	262. (C)	263. (D)	264. (A)
265. (A)	266. (B)	267. (B)	268. (A)
269. (D)	270. (B)	271. (A)	272. (C)
273. (D)	274. (D)	275. (D)	276. (A)
277. (C)	278. (C)	279. (A)	280. (C)
281. (B)	282. (A)		

CHAPTER

4 Reference, Information and Referral Services

INTRODUCTION

When we have got information from anywhere, technically, there are the information sources. These sources may be books, journals, dictionaries, indexes, abstracts, speeches, pictures, people and also websites. In Library & Information Science these are not just an information source but also the categories of information sources which means whether they are authoritative sources of information, current literature, bibliographical information, referral sources of information or any other categories.

From these categories, library services will be able to right information to right user at the right time according to the users' demands. Translation and Reprographic services are one of the most popular services under Reference Services especially for Research Libraries.

Therefore, in this chapter we have listing sufficient number of important point and questions with their answer according to the demandable pattern of said examinations.

IMPORTANT POINTS

- A group of persons such as researchers, inventors, innovators, authors, writers, planners, policy-makers, etc. are known as Information Generators.
- A group of persons whose jobs require the gathering of information and report them through appropriate channels is known as Information Gatherers.
- Newspaper reporters, correspondents, journalists, compilers of reference sources such as bibliographers, encyclopaedists, etc. are the example of Information Gatherers.
- The Information Gatherer acts as an intermediary between the user and information sources on the Internet.
- A group of persons who are involved in giving a shape of collected information for ease of use in other users is known as Information Processors.
- Newspaper editors, editors in publishing houses, journal editors, etc. are the examples of Information Processors.
- A group of persons who are involved in disseminating information or knowledge that is already collected and available in some form is known as Information Disseminators.
- Documentalists, publishers, consultants, information specialists, teachers, advertisers, etc. are the examples of Information Disseminators.

- A group of persons who are involved in creating tools for information storage and retrieval is known as Information Retrievers.
- Classifier, cataloguers, indexers, abstractors, reference officers, etc. are the example of Information Retrievers.
- Information Generators by their nature of work, produce Primary Literature.
- Information Gatherers operate mostly in the designing and production of Secondary Information.
- In ICT, the Information Technologists requires knowledge of computers, technology, and database and network security and their role as an Information System Managers.
- Reference Service is providing in libraries, directing the enquirer to a document available in the library and Referral Service provides only source to information.
- Referral Services directs enquirers to a source of information which may be either a directory of an organization or an individual expert.
- According to the Harrod's Librarians' Glossary, a Referral Centre is an organization for directing researchers for information and data to appropriate sources, such as libraries, information evaluation centres, documents and documentation centres and individuals and a Referral Centre does not supply data or documents that carry the required information.
- Library stocks Primary, Secondary and Tertiary literature whereas Referral Centre stocks only access tools, such as literature or source directories, guides and lists.
- Referral Centre provides only sources of information whereas Library provides not only sources of information but also documents carrying the required information and very often the needed information also.
- There is no bibliographical service in Referral Centre.
- INFOTERRA network is a Referral Service established by the United Nations Environment Programme (UNEP).
- INFOTERRA began to function in 1976 and it does not collect and disseminate information but sources of information.
- Mass Media means technology that is intended to reach a mass audience and there are two vital components of mass communication; first is the physical media and second is the contents carried by the media for communication.
- These two components of mass communication can be categorized into five types as print, radio, regular broadcast television, cable television and telecommunications such as the Internet or satellite services.
- Mass Media is defined as a type of communication that uses technology to simultaneously reach a wide audience.
- Mass Media is primarily a one-way form of communication, with the audience having limited or no means to respond to the information it receives.
- Electronic Media is media that requires an electronic device to receive and therefore, radio, television and Internet are the examples of this media.

- Daily newspapers, weekly, fortnightly, monthly magazines, journals or any printed mass communication is known as Print Media.
- As information resources, the Mass Media carries the contents contemporary events and activities which are vital interest to every citizen.
- Modern society is a society of institutions and it is rapidly transforming into a Knowledge Society.
- Knowledge Based Economy (KBE) is a system of consumption and production that is based on intellectual capital.
- In Information Age, the primary goal of management is to develop the intellectual capital.
- Data centre is an instructional mechanism where data collected from different sources by different methods and data stored for future purpose and make available to those who require it.
- Referral Centres provide switching mechanism among different types of Information Institutions.
- A central agency for collection, classification and distribution of information is known as Clearing Houses.
- Most Clearing Houses have information gathering networks to acquire documents in their subject areas.
- A kind of information agent that can autonomously search, gather and integrate information on behalf of a user is known as Information Broker.
- Information Filter is a system that removes redundant or unwanted information from an information stream using automated or computerized methods prior to presentation to the users.
- Internal Communication is the process of exchanging information among the people of different level or internal participants with the organization.
- External Communication is an informal exchange of information and message between an organization and other organizations.
- The main purpose of Internal Communication is to exchange information of various departments and division of the organization.
- The coverage of External Communication is broad with external bodies that mean it focuses on audience outside the organization as users, consumers or any clienteles.
- Individual who maintain consistent, ongoing contact outside their organizations, who know the way in which outsiders differ in their perspective from their own organizational colleagues, and who are able to translate between the two systems is known as Technological Gatekeeper.
- The Technological Gatekeeper receives information from a wide variety of sources external to his organization and acts as an information source for his colleagues in his group.

- Technological Gatekeepers are different from Invisible College.
- Invisible Colleges are concerned with the flow of information among different individuals in different institutions, in different countries and even using different languages at a time.
- Technological Gatekeepers concerned with the flow of information inside an organization.
- The term Invisible College was first used in seventeenth century European when the Royal Society of London was founded. Members of this early Royal Society of Scientists did not belong to a formal institution, but referred to themselves as an invisible college due to their geographical closeness and regular meetings based on shared scientific interest.
- Information Centres operate at various levels which can be international, or global, regional, national or local levels.
- The National Science Library, Canada formerly known as the Canada Institute for Scientific and Technical Information (CISTI), began in 1924 as the library of the National Research Council of Canada (NRC).
- The NRC library took on the role of National Science Library, Canada unofficially in 1957 and became the official National Science Library, Canada in 1966.
- The description of the characteristics of data is called metadata.
- A discipline which is to define what data are available and where they can be found with addition to defining controls and quality mechanism is known as Data Resource Management (DRM).
- In 1963, the National Standard Reference Data System (NSRDS) was established in USA.
- CODATA provide scientists and engineers with access to international data activities for increased awareness, direct cooperation and new knowledge.
- In India, Council of Scientific and Industrial Research (CSIR), Indian Council of Agricultural Research (ICAR), Indian Space Research Organization (ISRO), Defence Research and Development Organization (DRDO), Indian Council of Medical Research (ICMR), etc. are the National Data Centres.
- National Sample Survey Office (formerly known as National Sample Survey Organization (NSSO)) was established in 1950.
- National Reference Centre, Library of Congress was established in 1963.
- The United Nations Development Programs (UNDP) Special Unit for Technical Cooperation Among Development Countries (SU/TCDC) was launched the WIDE Initiative (Web of Information for Development) in 2000.
- SU/TCDC, established within UNDP by the United Nations General Assembly in 1974.
- CODATA is an interdisciplinary Scientific Committee of the International Council for Science (ICSU), which works to improve the quality, reliability, management and accessibility of data of importance to all fields of science and technology.

- ICSU was founded in 1931 to promote international scientific activity in the different branches of science and its application for the benefit of humanity.
- According to the UNESCO, the Information Consolidation Activities is used to define the responsibilities exercised by individuals, departments or organizations for evaluating and compressing relevant documents in order to provide definite user groups with reliable and concise new body of knowledge.
- According to Tefco Saracevic and J. Wood, the Consolidated Information is public knowledge specifically selected, analyzed, evaluated, and possibly restructured and repackaged for the purpose of serving some of the immediate decisions, problems and information needs of a defined clientele or social group.
- The process of merging of information from one or more sources and presenting in a new arrangement tailored to the requirement of a specific clientele is known as Consolidation of Information.
- The most important consolidation function is evaluation that means the retaining of reliable information only.
- A formal structured organization unit specially established for the purpose of acquiring, selecting storing, retrieving, evaluating, analyzing, and synthesizing a body of information in a clearly defined specialist field or pertaining to a specified mission with the intent of compiling, digesting, repackaging and presenting pertain information in a form most authoritative, timely, and useful to a society of peer and management is known as Information Analysis Centre (IAC).
- The IAC Centres are committed to provide users timely, authoritative, evaluated, information in most convenient and usable form.
- Information resource can be categorized into; Documentary Sources, Institutional Sources, and Human Sources.
- The information sources that are in the form of documents are known as documentary sources of information.
- Documentary Sources are Primary, Secondary and Tertiary Sources.
- The Primary and Secondary Sources contain information on a subject and Tertiary Sources are used as an aid for selection of Primary, Secondary, Institutional, as well as Human Sources.
- According to Tefco Saracevic and J. Wood, the Packaging of information is physical recording, arrangement and presentation of information on a given medium and in a given form and Repacking of information is arrangement of physical media and/or form in which information has been presented, which is tailored to the requirement of a specific clientele.
- The aim of repacking is to enhance the acceptance and use of information products and the assimilation and recall of their contents.
- Repacking depends on the target audience.
- The Communication is a process by which information is transferred through a given channel from a source or a sender to a destination or recipient.

- Diffusion is a specific type of communication of a special interest in the context of consolidated information and it is communication process by which a new idea or an innovation spreads among the members of a social group or among a defined social group.
- Individuals or groups of individual performing Information Consolidation Activities would each constitute an Information Consolidation Unit (ICU).
- A process of ascertaining and appraising the intrinsic merit, validity and reliability of information conveyed, comparison of information on the same topic from a variety of source is known as Evaluation of Information.
- Information sources are related to library and information science, and information resources are related to information and communication technologies.
- Information sources can be categorized according to types, contents and media.
- Treatise is a kind of documentary source of information which is a long and serious piece of writing on a particular subject and it is considered as a secondary source of information.
- Prolegomena to Library Classification by S.R. Ranganathan is a book but it is also a treatise on classification theory and an influence source of information on the subject.
- A monograph is documentary source of information that presents a detailed study on a single subject, or a specialist work of writing on a single subject or an aspect of a subject, usually by a single author.
- A monolingual dictionary explains the meaning of word in the language that we are learning that means we can get the meaning, definition, explanation, etc. of a word in the same language in which the dictionary is written.
- The Longman Dictionary of Contemporary English was published in 1978 and it is a monolingual dictionary.
- A thesaurus is a documentary source of information which allows a person to look up groups of synonyms and related concepts.
- Thesaurus is not a dictionary as much as it does not use as meaning, explanation, definition, etc., of a word, instead it uses what is best suited word in a particular context.
- The first general thesaurus in English was compiled by Peter Mark Roget and is popularly known as Roget's Thesaurus and WorldNet is the another example of general thesaurus in English language.
- In Information Retrieval (IR) system, the thesaurus is a set of items (phrases or words) plus a set of relations between these items.
- The second type of thesauri is IR-oriented and phrase-based like INSPEC, LCSH, MeSH and they usually contain relations between thesaurus item such as BT (Broader Term), NT (Narrow Term), UF (Used For), and RT (Related to), and can be either general or specific, depending on the needs of thesaurus constrictions and this is known as Information Retrieval Thesaurus.

- A handbook is a guide or list of instructions on one particular subject and it is a kind of documentary source of information.
- Manual refers specifically to a reference document which provides detailed information about operation and maintenance of a product.
- Handbook offers guidelines for a number of situations whereas Manual explains how to use a product and also talking about a list of instructions for doing something.
- A kind of documentary source of information that contains a list of documents arranged in some logical order is known as Bibliography.
- Who is Who are biographical dictionaries which provides biographical information about various persons who are living.
- India Who's Who is a national biographical dictionary which published since 1969.
- A gazetteer is a geographical dictionary of place names and other geographical entities with descriptive, statistical, economical, geographical and historical information.
- According to the Harrod's Librarians' Glossary, a periodical is a publication with a distinctive title which appears at stated or regular intervals, without prior decision as to when the last issue shall appear.
- According to the UNESCO, a publication will be called a periodical if it constitutes one issue in a continuous series under the same title, published at regular or irregular intervals, over an indefinite period, individual issues in the series being numbered consecutively or each issue being dated.
- The term journal is a synonym and serial a near synonym of the term periodical.
- Periodicals can be categorized as Primary, Secondary, and Tertiary sources of information.
- Generally, the primary periodicals publish original contributions in the form of research articles.
- General topics periodicals, indexing and abstracting are known as secondary periodicals.
- Periodicals that publish review articles are categorized as tertiary periodicals.
- In academia, the Festschrift is a collection of writings published in honour of a learned person especially an academic.
- The information sources that are not in the form of documents are known as non-documentary sources.
- An imaginary place where data, messages, audio and video or any hypertext information are exist in digital form is known as cyberspace.
- Internet is a non-documentary source of information.
- Hypertext is the example of electronic media.
- Hypermedia is a system where various forms of information as data, text, graphics, audio, video elements are linked together by a hypertext code or programme.
- Optical media refers to discs that are read by a laser, therefore CD-ROM, CD-R, CD-RW, DVD-ROM, DVD-R, DVD-RW and Blu-ray are the examples of such media.

- Magnetic media refers to any storage medium that uses magnetic pattern to record information and hard disk and magnetic tapes are the examples of such media.
- A URL (Universal Resource Locator) specifies the address of various network resources on the Internet more commonly it is the address of a web page.
- A URI (Uniform Resource Identifier) is used to identify a name or resource on the Internet that means it specify that where an identified resource is available and it determined the retrieving mechanism from resources.
- On Internet, URL and URI are not identical in terms of working procedures.
- On August 15, 1995, Videsh Sanchar Nigam Limited (VSNL) launched public Internet access in India.
- Regional Network for the Exchange of Information and Experience in Science and Technology for Asia and Pacific Region (ASTINFO), a UNESCO programme relating to information exchange and experience in the science and technology among countries in Asia and Pacific region and it was established in 1983.
- An association of a group of libraries who partner to coordinate activities, share resources to achieve mutually the common object is known as Library Consortium.
- A specially designed website that often serves as the single point of access for information is known as Web Portal and it is capable of handling both structured and unstructured information.
- The UGC-INFONET Digital Consortium has been merged into e-Shodh Sindhu Consortium since 31st December, 2015.
- The e-Shodh Sindhu Consortium is forming after merging of three consortia namely UGC-INFONET Digital Library Consortium, NLIST and INDEST-AICTE Consortium.
- Boolean Search allow the users to combine words and phrases using the words AND, OR, NOT (known as Boolean Operators) to limit, broaden, or define our search criteria.
- The AND operator allows user to combine two or more search terms and it will retrieve all those terms (documents) that contain all the constituent terms and this operator narrows a search by combining terms.
- The OR operator broadens a search that allows user to combine two or more search terms that contain either one or all the constituent terms.
- The NOT operator allows the user to specify those terms that they do not want to occur in retrieved records that means it will narrow a search by excluding certain search terms.
- Among three, the Boolean Search operator OR is the default setting of any search engine.
- However, NEAR, SAME are also search operators which can be used to combine terms in order to broaden or narrow retrieval.
- One who designs and builds up a scheme of library classification on sound principles is a classificationist.

- The term librametrics was coined by S.R. Ranganathan in 1949 and it is a discipline that measures library activities, library collections and quite often entails mathematical and statistical applications in library and information science.
- Librametricians are the sources of information relating to quantitative studies of various library objects and activities.

Questions

1. The book titled *Documentation* was written by

(A) S.C. Bradford

(B) William F. Burroughs

(C) Lewis S. Carroll

(D) Raymond F. Carver

2. Which of the following is true?

(A) Information source is the store/location where information is kept

(B) Information resource is information source, organized as an intuitional manner like library

(C) Current Awareness Service (CAS) is the example of anticipatory services

(D) All of the above

3. Which of the following is information source?

(A) Encyclopedia (B) Dictionary

(C) Yearbook (D) All of the above

4. Which of the following is on-demand service?

(A) Reference services

(B) Referral services

(C) Document delivery services

(D) All of the above

5. Transfer of information to someone with appropriate source of information is called

(A) Reference service

(B) Referral service

(C) User Interface service

(D) All of the above

6. Which of the following is information service?

(A) SDI

(B) Translation service

(C) Reprography service

(D) All of the above

7. Which of the following is In-House service of CAS?

(A) Notifying the receipts of new arrivals

(B) Currently received documents displaying

(C) Notifications according to the user profiles

(D) Both (A) and (B)

8. Which of the following is true?

(A) Referral centre provides only enquiry services

(B) Referral centre stored and organized Primary, Secondary and Tertiary Sources of information

(C) Referral centre provides Bibliographic Services

(D) Only (A)

9. Institute for Scientific Information (ISI), Philadelphia is a kind of institute

(A) Public information centre

(B) Semi-public information centre

(C) Private information centre

(D) None of the above

10. The International Translation Centre (ITC) formerly known as

(A) European Translation Centre, Delft

(B) World Translation Center, Atlanta

(C) Interpreting and Translating Centre, Adelaide

(D) Institute of Linguists, London

11. World Translation Index (WTI) is published by
(A) International Translation Centre, Delft
(B) World Translation Center, Adelaide
(C) National Translation Centre, Chicago
(D) IFLA, The Hague

12. The 'National Translation Centre for Humanities' is located at
(A) Chicago (B) New York
(C) Milan (D) Venice

13. European Translation Centre (ETC), Delft was established in
(A) 1955 (B) 1958
(C) 1960 (D) 1962

14. In which year ETC changed the name as International Translation Centre (ITC)?
(A) 1964 (B) 1968
(C) 1970 (D) 1975

15. World Translation Index (WTI) has been published since
(A) 1975 (B) 1978
(C) 1980 (D) 1983

16. In which year International Serials Data System (ISDS) was established by UNISIST?
(A) 1960 (B) 1965
(C) 1971 (D) 1976

17. In which year 'ISSN International Centre' was officially founded?
(A) 1972 (B) 1976
(C) 1978 (D) 1980

18. International Serials Data System (ISDS) was established at
(A) Paris (B) Philadelphia
(C) Atlanta (D) Chicago

19. In which year OCLC (Ohio College Library Centre) renamed as Online Computer Library Centre (OCLC)?
(A) 1970 (B) 1975
(C) 1981 (D) 1985

20. In which year IFLA adopted the International Standard Bibliographic Description (ISBD)?
(A) 1969 (B) 1971
(C) 1974 (D) 1978

21. How many alphanumeric characters in International Standard Music Number (ISMN)?
(A) 9 (B) 11
(C) 13 (D) 18

22. The International Standard Text Code (ISTC) was developed under the direction of
(A) ISO (B) OCLC
(C) IFLA (D) ISDS

23. The Development Science Information System (DEVSIS) was launched in
(A) 1970 (B) 1972
(C) 1974 (D) 1978

24. DEVSIS was launched by
(A) IDRC, Canada (B) IFLA, The Hague
(C) FAO, Rome (D) UNESCO, Paris

25. In which year FAO headquarters moved to the Rome from Washington, DC?
(A) 1951 (B) 1953
(C) 1958 (D) 1960

26. Which of the following is the publisher of INSPEC?
(A) Institute of Engineering and Technology (IET), London
(B) Massachusetts Institute of Technology (MIT), Massachusetts
(C) University of California, Berkeley
(D) University of Joseph Fourier, Grenoble

27. NISSAT was established under which Five-Year Plan?
(A) Third Five-Year plan
(B) Fourth Five-Year Plan
(C) Fifth Five-Year Plan
(D) Sixth Five-Year Plan

28. The Library and Information Service Division of Bhabha Atomic Research Centre was established in

(A) 1962 (B) 1965
(C) 1968 (D) 1970

29. National Centre for Science Information (NCSI) is an information centre of

(A) Indian Institute of Science (IIS), Bengaluru
(B) Indian Institute of Technology (IIT), Kharagpur
(C) Indian Institute of Technology (IIT), Kanpur
(D) Indian Institute of Technology (IIT), Mumbai

30. Who says "Reference Service as the behind-the-scene activities of the reference library in the selection, acquisition and maintenance of library stock and its careful recording and administration"?

(A) H.P. Luhn (B) William A. Katz
(C) Donald Davinson (D) Henry E. Bliss

31. For literature references, the probable reference source is

(A) Bibliographies (B) Indexes
(C) Abstracts (D) All of the above

32. Information about formula, tables and how-to-do-it, can be obtained from

(A) Almanacs
(B) Reviews
(C) Handbooks and Manuals
(D) Bibliographies

33. The information about scholarly works can be obtained from

(A) Almanacs (B) Reviews
(C) Criticism (D) Both (B) and (C)

34. Which of the following is the Responsive Service of Reference Service?

(A) CAS
(B) Ready Reference Service
(C) Indexing Service
(D) Both (A) and (B)

35. Which of the following is the Anticipatory Service of Reference Service?

(A) Bibliographic Compilation
(B) News Clipping Service
(C) Indexing Service
(D) All of the above

36. The National Union Catalogue of Scientific Serials in India (NUCSSI) is maintained by

(A) NISCAIR, New Delhi
(B) DELNET, New Delhi
(C) IIS, Bengaluru
(D) ISI, Kolkata

37. Which of the following was the founder of public library movement in United States of America?

(A) Samuel Swett Green
(B) Peter S. Harris
(C) William A. Katz
(D) Jane S. Austen

38. *The Reader's Guide to Periodical Literature* is published by

(A) H.W. Wilson
(B) McMillan
(C) Oxford University Press
(D) McGraw-Hill Publication

39. *The World Book Encyclopedia* is currently published by

(A) World Book, Inc.
(B) Thomson Reuters
(C) Penguin Random House
(D) Harper Collins

40. Which of the following is Fact Source?

(A) Manuals (B) Yearbooks
(C) Almanac (D) All of the above

41. *Dictionary of American Slang* is published by

(A) Harper Collins
(B) McGraw-Hill Publication

(C) Wolters Kluwer
(D) Oxford University Press

42. *The World Atlas of the World* is currently published by
(A) RELX Group (B) Scholastic
(C) Harper Collins (D) Holtzbrinck

43. Which one is the most important feature for Ready Reference Sources?
(A) Authority (B) Format
(C) Purpose (D) Timeliness

44. A type of bibliography that concerned the physical description of the book is called
(A) Subject bibliography
(B) Analytical bibliography
(C) Textual bibliography
(D) Both (A) and (C)

45. *Guide to Reference Books* (11th edition) is edited by
(A) Robert Balay (B) Nicola S. Barker
(C) Enid T. Blyton (D) William Z. Blake

46. *Guide to Reference Books* (9th edition) is edited by
(A) Eugene P. Sheehy (B) Stewart Brand
(C) Paul S. Auster (D) Jane Y. Austen

47. *Guide to Reference Books* is published by
(A) American Library Association
(B) Harper Collins
(C) Oxford University Press
(D) McGraw-Hill

48. The review *Booklist* is published by
(A) Thomson Reuters
(B) RELX Group
(C) Wolters Kluwer
(D) American Library Association

49. The review *Book Review Digest* is published by
(A) American Library Association
(B) H.W. Wilson
(C) Oxford University Press
(D) McMillan

50. The frequency of publication of *Book Review Index* is
(A) Tri-annual (B) Bi-annual
(C) Monthly (D) Weekly

51. Which of the following is the author/contributor of U.S. National Union Catalogue (NUC)?
(A) Library of Congress
(B) American Library Association
(C) Special Library Association
(D) Both (A) and (B)

52. Which of the following was the author of *A World Bibliography of Bibliographies*?
(A) Theodore Besterman
(B) Emily D. Dickinson
(C) Colum F. McCann
(D) Daniel D. Defoe

53. *Book Review Index* has been published since
(A) 1965 (B) 1968
(C) 1974 (D) 1976

54. Match the following:

LIST-I	LIST-II
(1) International Serials Data System (ISDS) Bulletin	(i) 1895
(2) The Reader's Guide to Periodical Literature	(ii) 1905
(3) The Times Atlas of the World	(iii) 1974
(4) Booklist	(iv) 1901

Codes:

	(1)	(2)	(3)	(4)
(A)	(i)	(iii)	(ii)	(iv)
(B)	(iii)	(iv)	(i)	(ii)

(C) (iv) (i) (iii) (ii)
(D) (ii) (i) (iv) (iii)

55. The online version of *Applied Science and Technology Index* has been published since
(A) 1981 (B) 1983
(C) 1985 (D) 1989

56. The first ALA conference was held in
(A) 1885 (B) 1876
(C) 1879 (D) 1881

57. At present 'ALA Bulletin' is published under the title of
(A) *American Libraries Magazine*
(B) *American Libraries Bulletin*
(C) *The Bulletin of ALA*
(D) *ALA Bulletin and News*

58. In which year ALA Bulletin was renamed as *American Libraries Magazine*?
(A) 1970 (B) 1973
(C) 1976 (D) 1980

59. Which of the following is the author of book titled *Familiar Quotations*?
(A) John Bartlett (B) Martin M. Amis
(C) Philip J. Ardagh (D) Jane J. Austin

60. *The Encyclopedia Britannica* has been published since
(A) 1768 (B) 1770
(C) 1772 (D) 1776

61. In which year, the online version of the Encyclopedia Americana was launched?
(A) 1994 (B) 1997
(C) 2000 (D) 2002

62. Which of the following was the scholar's edition of Encyclopedia Britannica?
(A) 7th (B) 9th
(C) 11th (D) 14th

63. The first edition of *World Book Encyclopedia* was published in
(A) 1914 (B) 1917
(C) 1919 (D) 1922

64. At present, the *World Book Encyclopedia* is published in..........volumes.
(A) 20 (B) 22
(C) 24 (D) 26

65. Which of the following is a home and school encyclopedia?
(A) *Encyclopedia Britannica*
(B) *Reader's Encyclopedia*
(C) *Compton's Encyclopedia and Fact-Index*
(D) *Chamber's Encyclopedia*

66. Which of the following is single volume encyclopedia?
(A) *The New Columbia Encyclopedia*
(B) *The Random House Encyclopedia*
(C) *Chamber's Encyclopedia*
(D) Both (A) and (B)

67. Who says "an encyclopedia collect all knowledge scattered over the face of the earth...."?
(A) Denis Diderot
(B) Dante K. Alighieri
(C) Peter S. Ackroyd
(D) Martin M. Amis

68. Which of the following is true?
(A) General Encyclopedia attempting to cover all fields of knowledge
(B) Subject Encyclopedia limits its scope either a narrow or broad field of interest
(C) Handbook is a collection of a miscellaneous group of facts centered on one central subject
(D) All of the above

69. *Encyclopedia of Education* is published by
(A) Macmillan Reference
(B) Thomson Reuters
(C) McGraw-Hill Education
(D) Harper Collins

70. *Cassell's Encyclopedia of World Literature* has been published since

(A) 1950 (B) 1953
(C) 1956 (D) 1960

71. Which of the following is the Ready Reference Source?

(A) Handbooks (B) Directories
(C) Yearbooks (D) All of the above

72. Which of the following is an important reference source for getting information related to the recent development?

(A) Yearbooks (B) Almanacs
(C) Directories (D) Handbooks

73. Whitaker's Almanack is published from

(A) UK (B) USA
(C) Australia (D) Switzerland

74. In which year, 149th edition of Statesman's Yearbook was published?

(A) 2008 (B) 2010
(C) 2012 (D) 2015

75. Who was the first editor of Statesman's Yearbook?

(A) Frederick Martin (B) John Paxton
(C) Barry Tuner (D) Mortimer Epstein

76. *The International Year Book and Statesman's Who's Who* has been published since

(A) 1950 (B) 1953
(C) 1955 (D) 1958

77. *Yearbook of the United Nations* has been published since

(A) 1946 (B) 1948
(C) 1950 (D) 1951

78. Frequency of publication of *UN Chronicle* is

(A) Monthly (B) Quarterly
(C) Annually (D) Weekly

79. *Yearbook of International Organizations* is published by

(A) UIA (B) IFLA
(C) CILIP (D) UNESCO

80. In which year, Union of International Associations (UIA) was founded?

(A) 1903 (B) 1905
(C) 1907 (D) 1912

81. UIA was founded by

(A) Henri La Fontaine
(B) Paul Otlet
(C) The 1913 Nobel peace prize laureate
(D) All of the above

82. *Guinness World Record* has been published since

(A) 1951 (B) 1955
(C) 1958 (D) 1959

83. The editor of *CRC Handbook of Chemistry and Physics* (95th edition) is

(A) William M. Haynes
(B) Martin M. Amis
(C) Alexander S. Harris
(D) W.H. Auden

84. The first edition of *Webster's Biography Dictionary* was published in

(A) 1955 (B) 1961
(C) 1965 (D) 1967

85. *Handbook of Pseudonyms and Personal Nicknames* (Volume 1) is edited by

(A) Harold S. Sharp
(B) Enid S. Blyton
(C) Jeffrey Y. Brown
(D) Gordon S. Burn

86. *Who Was When?: A Dictionary of Contemporaries* is published by

(A) Oxford University Press
(B) H.W. Wilson
(C) RELX Group
(D) Harper Collins

87. The first publication place of *Who's Who* was

(A) Great Britain (B) Australia
(C) USA (D) Switzerland

88. Which of the following is Retrospective Biographical Source?

(A) Encyclopedia of World Biography
(B) Dictionary of Scientific Biography
(C) Dictionary of National Biography
(D) All of the above

89. *World Authors* has been published since

(A) 1971 (B) 1975
(C) 1978 (D) 1981

90. *World Authors* is published by

(A) H.W. Wilson
(B) Oxford University Press
(C) Cambridge University Press
(D) McGraw-Hill

91. The *Webster's New International Dictionary of the English Language* has been published since

(A) 1898 (B) 1905
(C) 1909 (D) 1915

92. *Books In Print* is published by

(A) H.W. Wilson
(B) R.R. Bowker
(C) Cambridge University Press
(D) Simon & Schuster

93. *International Maps and Atlas in Print* is published by

(A) R.R. Bowker (B) Wolters Kluwer
(C) Scholastic (D) Holtzbrinck

94. The 14th edition of *The Times Comprehensive Atlas of the World* is published in

(A) 1999 (B) 2005
(C) 2010 (D) 2014

95. *The Times Comprehensive Atlas of the World* is published by

(A) Harper Collins
(B) H.W. Wilson
(C) Informa Plc
(D) Cambridge University Press

96. In India, which of the following is the parent body for publishing of map of India?

(A) Survey of India
(B) National Informatics Centre (NIC)
(C) Bureau of Indian Standards (BIS)
(D) National Remote Sensing Centre, Hyderabad

97. *Columbia Lippincott Gazetteer of the World* is published by

(A) Columbia University Press
(B) Oxford University Press
(C) H.W. Wilson
(D) Harper Collins

98. *Webster's New Geographical Dictionary* is published by

(A) Merriam Webster
(B) Columbia University Press
(C) McGraw-Hill
(D) H.W. Wilson

99. Who characterized the reference process as 'complex associative series of linkages, or event'?

(A) J.H. Shera (B) William A. Katz
(C) Alan Rees (D) S.R. Ranganathan

100. Which of the following is the probable principal retrieval key for bibliographic data?

(A) Author
(B) Title
(C) Name of the publisher
(D) Both (A) and (B)

101. Which of the following is online digital library database for education research and information?

(A) ERIC (B) DERIC
(C) EDIC (D) E-EDU

102. Facet of documentation is/are
(A) Abstracting Service
(B) Document Reproduction Service
(C) Translation Service
(D) All of the above

103. Which of the following is the example of documentation list?
(A) Index to periodicals
(B) Abstracting journals
(C) Index to Newspapers
(D) All of the above

104. Which indexing system is used by the BNB for Subject Heading?
(A) COMPASS (B) LCSH
(C) POPSI (D) KWIC

105. Which of the following is an advanced form of Chain Procedure?
(A) PRECIS (B) POPSI
(C) KWIC (D) KWOC

106. POPSI is developed by
(A) IFLA (B) DESIDOC
(C) DRTC (D) UNESCO

107. KWIC stands for
(A) Key Word In Context
(B) Key Word Index Context
(C) Key Word Index Control
(D) Key Word Index Coordinate

108. The term KWIC was coined by
(A) H.P. Luhn (B) J.H. Shera
(C) Paul Otlet (D) G. Bhattacharya

109. Who developed the KWPSI (Word/Phrase Subject Index)?
(A) G. Vladutz (B) E. Garfield
(C) H.P. Luhn (D) Both (A) and (B)

110. The KWPSI is based on noun phrase entries algorithmically from
(A) Subject (B) Title
(C) Class Number (D) Book Number

111. LCSH stands for
(A) Library of Congress Subject Headings
(B) Library of Congress Systematic Headings
(C) Library of Congress Subject Helping
(D) Library of Congress Subject Hierarchy

112. Which of the following is the example of Indexing System?
(A) LCSH (B) PRESIS
(C) Chain Procedure (D) All of the above

113. TABLEDEX indexing method is developed by
(A) C.N. Mooers (B) E. Garfield
(C) Robert S. Ledley (D) H.P. Luhn

114. 'Social Sciences Citation Index (SSCI)' was started in
(A) 1965 (B) 1970
(C) 1973 (D) 1975

115. Arts & Humanities Citation Index (A&HCI) has been published since
(A) 1975 (B) 1982
(C) 1985 (D) 1987

116. *Science Citation Index* (SCI) has been published since
(A) 1960 (B) 1963
(C) 1965 (D) 1970

117. Which of the following index has been published by Institute for Scientific Information (ISI)?
(A) Science Citation Index (SCI)
(B) Social Sciences Citation Index (SSCI)
(C) Arts & Humanities Citation Index (A&HCI)
(D) All of the above

118. Which of the following is the citation index database?
(A) PsycINFO (B) APA
(C) e-INFO (D) e-CIT

119. LCSH is an example of
(A) Library Classification Scheme

(B) Library Cataloguing Rules
(C) Subject Indexing Language
(D) Reprography

120. 'PsycINFO' has been published since
(A) 1965 (B) 1967
(C) 1970 (D) 1973

121. Which of the following was the founder of 'Coordinating Indexing Method'?
(A) M. Taube (B) D. Austin
(C) J.O. Kaiser (D) S.R. Ranganathan

122. Which of the following is Pre-Coordinate Indexing System?
(A) PRECIS (B) POPSI
(C) Chain Indexing (D) All of the above

123. Uniterm Indexing System is the example of
(A) Pre-Coordinate Indexing
(B) Post-Coordinate Indexing
(C) Both (A) and (B)
(D) Facets Indexing

124. Which of the following keyword or term is not associated with Chain Indexing?
(A) Sought (B) Unsought
(C) False (D) True

125. Who categorized the two component terms 'Concrete' and 'Process' in indexing system?
(A) J.O. Kaiser (B) H.P. Luhn
(C) M. Taube (D) D. Austin

126. In which year COMPASS was introduced in place of PRECIS in BNB?
(A) 1990 (B) 1992
(C) 1994 (D) 1999

127. COMPASS stands for
(A) Computer Aided Subject System
(B) Computer Pre-Access Subject System
(C) Computer Post-Access Subject System
(D) Computer Programming Access Subject System

128. Which of the following is the founder of 'American Documentation Institute'?
(A) Wastson Davis
(B) J.O. Kaiser
(C) Robert Proctor
(D) Belinda B. Bauer

129. Who was the founder of 'Modular Contents Analysis Abstracts'?
(A) F.W. Lancaster (B) S. Herner
(C) D. Austin (D) Both (A) and (B)

130. TOXLINE is compiled by
(A) US National Library of Medicine
(B) Cambridge Information Group
(C) Excerpta Medica
(D) CILIP

131. *Guide to Indian Periodical Literature* is published by
(A) Indian Documentation Service
(B) DELNET
(C) ILA
(D) IASLIC

132. *Poole's Index to Periodical Literature* has been published since
(A) 1802 (B) 1805
(C) 1808 (D) 1810

133. *Indian Science Abstracts* is published by
(A) ILA (B) IASLIC
(C) NISCAIR (D) ISI, Kolkata

134. *World Trans Index* has been published since
(A) 1978 (B) 1982
(C) 1984 (D) 1986

135. Match the following:

LIST-I	LIST-II
(1) INIS	(i) 1926
(2) INFOTERRA	(ii) 1970
(3) ASTINFO	(iii) 1983
(4) BIOSIS Preview	(iv) 1977

Codes:

	(1)	(2)	(3)	(4)
(A)	(ii)	(iv)	(iii)	(i)
(B)	(i)	(ii)	(iii)	(iv)
(C)	(ii)	(i)	(iv)	(iii)
(D)	(iv)	(iii)	(i)	(ii)

136. The *Roster of Indian Scientific and Technical Translators* was published by
(A) INSDOC (B) IASLIC
(C) ILA (D) RRRLF

137. National Commission on Libraries and Information Science (NCLIS) is an agency of the.........
(A) US Government
(B) Australian Government
(C) UK Government
(D) German Government

138. In 1962, who developed the DIALOG language?
(A) Roger K. Summit (B) Thomson K.
(C) Phyllis E. Worden (D) Denis Ritchie

139. In which year DIALOG Information Service was launched?
(A) 1966 (B) 1968
(C) 1970 (D) 1975

140. Investigations related to users' opinion, willingness, etc. are referred to as
(A) Technical study (B) User study
(C) Scientific study (D) Database study

141. Which of the following is the subjective aspect of Information System?
(A) Users' opinion (B) Feelings
(C) Willingness (D) All of the above

142. Users' information behaviour has two aspects, which of the following?
(A) Verbal and Actual
(B) Local and National
(C) Communicated and Non-communicated
(D) Offline and Online

143. Match the following:

LIST-I	LIST-II
(1) MLA International Bibliography	(i) 1949
(2) Columbia Lippincott Gazetteer of the World	(ii) 1952
(3) Webster's Geographical Dictionary	(iii) 1963
(4) ERIC	(iv) 1966

Codes:

	(1)	(2)	(3)	(4)
(A)	(iii)	(ii)	(i)	(iv)
(B)	(i)	(iii)	(ii)	(iv)
(C)	(iv)	(i)	(ii)	(iii)
(D)	(i)	(iv)	(ii)	(iii)

144. Match the following:

LIST-I	LIST-II
(1) Systematic Indexing	(i) 1974
(2) Relational Indexing	(ii) 1898
(3) LCSA	(iii) 1950
(4) PRECIS	(iv) 1911

Codes:

	(1)	(2)	(3)	(4)
(A)	(i)	(iii)	(iv)	(ii)
(B)	(iv)	(iii)	(ii)	(i)
(C)	(iii)	(i)	(ii)	(iv)
(D)	(i)	(iv)	(iii)	(ii)

145. In which year POPSI was developed?
(A) 1978 (B) 1981
(C) 1984 (D) 1989

146. Match the following:

LIST-I	LIST-II
(1) Chain Indexing	(i) J.O. Kaiser
(2) Systematic Indexing	(ii) J.E.L. Farradane
(3) Relational Indexing	(iii) E.J. Coates
(4) Subject Indexing	(iv) S.R. Ranganathan

Codes:

	(1)	(2)	(3)	(4)
(A)	(iv)	(i)	(ii)	(iii)
(B)	(iv)	(ii)	(i)	(iii)
(C)	(iv)	(iii)	(ii)	(i)
(D)	(iv)	(i)	(iii)	(ii)

147. Match the following:

LIST-I	LIST-II
(1) PRECIS	(i) G. Bhattacharyya
(2) POPSIS	(ii) M. Taube
(3) Uniterm Indexing	(iii) D. Austin
(4) Headings and Canons	(iv) S.R. Ranganathan

Codes:

	(1)	(2)	(3)	(4)
(A)	(iii)	(i)	(ii)	(iv)
(B)	(i)	(iii)	(ii)	(iv)
(C)	(ii)	(iv)	(i)	(iii)
(D)	(ii)	(i)	(iii)	(iv)

148. *Mathematical Reviews* is published by
(A) American Mathematical Society
(B) Association of Mathematical Society of America
(C) Royal Society of United Kingdom
(D) Australian Mathematical Society

149. For the purpose of observations, the users behaviour can be studied at the
(A) Periodical Room
(B) Catalogue Section
(C) Acquisition Section
(D) Both (A) and (B)

150. Which of the following is Bibliographic Service?
(A) Current Awareness Service (CAS)
(B) Literature Searching Service
(C) Indexing Service
(D) All of the above

151. Which of the following is culmination of information service?
(A) Reference Service
(B) Translation Service
(C) Reprography Service
(D) Document Delivery Service

152. Which of the following is true for Literature Search Service?
(A) It is a long range reference service
(B) Search will be more exhaustive
(C) Encyclopedias make as useful reference
(D) All of the above

153. For literature search, which of the following information source is an important tool?
(A) Primary Sources
(B) Secondary Sources
(C) Tertiary Sources
(D) All of the above

154. *Mathematical Reviews* has been published since
(A) 1935 (B) 1940
(C) 1944 (D) 1965

155. *Guide to Indian Periodical Literature* has been published since
(A) 1964 (B) 1968
(C) 1970 (D) 1976

156. In which year 'International Translation Centre' was established?
(A) 1960 (B) 1962
(C) 1967 (D) 1978

157. *World Encyclopedia of Library and Information Service* has been published since
(A) 1932 (B) 1945
(C) 1969 (D) 1993

158. Match the following:

LIST-I	LIST-II
(1) NISCAIR	(i) France
(2) VINITI	(ii) Canada
(3) CISTI	(iii) India
(4) INIST	(iv) Russia

Codes:

	(1)	(2)	(3)	(4)
(A)	(iii)	(iv)	(ii)	(i)
(B)	(iii)	(i)	(ii)	(iv)
(C)	(iii)	(iv)	(i)	(ii)
(D)	(iii)	(ii)	(i)	(iv)

159. Efficiency of the Document Delivery Service is determined by

(A) Level of satisfaction

(B) Cost of service

(C) Speed of services

(D) All of the above

160. Match the following:

LIST-I	LIST-II
(1) INIS	(i) Life Science Information System
(2) INFOTERRA	(ii) Science & Technology Information System
(3) ASTINFO	(iii) Environment Information System
(4) BIOSIS Preview	(iv) Nuclear Information System

Codes:

	(1)	(2)	(3)	(4)
(A)	(iv)	(iii)	(ii)	(i)
(B)	(i)	(ii)	(iii)	(iv)
(C)	(ii)	(i)	(iii)	(iv)
(D)	(iv)	(i)	(ii)	(iii)

161. KBE stands for

(A) Knowledge Based Economy

(B) Knowledge Based Entity

(C) Knowledge Budget Economy

(D) Knowledge Based Environment

162. LCSA stands for?

(A) Library of Congress Subject Authorship

(B) Library of Congress Subject Authority

(C) Library of Congress Systematic Authorship

(D) Library of Congress Subject Automation

163. John Crerar Library is located at

(A) Chicago (B) London

(C) Paris (D) Rome

164. The first edition of *Harrod's Librarians' Glossary* was published in

(A) 1938 (B) 1945

(C) 1960 (D) 1976

165. Which of the following is the father of reference service?

(A) Samuel Swett Green

(B) Melvil Dewey

(C) Paul J. Bailey

(D) William A. Katz

166. *International Encyclopedia of Information and Library Science* is edited by

(A) John Feather

(B) Rodney Paul Sturges

(C) Paul J. Bailey

(D) Both (A) and (B)

167. The first edition of *Dorland's Illustrated Medical Dictionary* was published in

(A) 1890 (B) 1895

(C) 1899 (D) 1910

168. In which year DESIDOC was started as Scientific Information Bureau (SIB)?

(A) 1955 (B) 1958

(C) 1960 (D) 1965

169. SAARC Documentation Centre (SDC) is located at

(A) New Delhi (B) Dhaka

(C) Islamabad (D) Colombo

170. *Bharat Ki Sampada* is published by

(A) NISCAIR

(B) DESIDOC

(C) ICAR

(D) Indian Agricultural Research Institute, New Delhi

171. *International Encyclopedia of Information and Library* has been published since
(A) 1997 (B) 1999
(C) 2001 (D) 2004

172. Which of the following is the Global Information System?
(A) AGRIS (B) DEVSIS
(C) INFOTERRA (D) All of the above

173. In India, which of the following is the National Center for INIS?
(A) BARC's Library & Information Center
(B) NISCAIR's Library
(C) IISc's Library
(D) Roja Muthiah Research Library, Chennai

174. Which of the following is the UNESCO Network System?
(A) ORBICOM
(B) UNAL
(C) APIN
(D) All of the above

175. In which city, Machine Translation (MT) system was demonstrated in first time?
(A) New York (B) London
(C) Washington (D) Paris

176. Indian Scientific Translators Association (ISTA) was established in
(A) 1958 (B) 1962
(C) 1965 (D) 1972

177. International Translation Day is celebrating each year on
(A) 15 July (B) 25 August
(C) 30 September (D) 17 December

178. Reference sources may overlaps on
(A) Secondary sources (B) Tertiary sources
(C) Both (A) and (B) (D) Only (A)

179. The Impact Factor was devised by
(A) Eugene Garfield (B) Elana R. Broch
(C) C. Hoeffel (D) S.P. Lock

180. Entries as a list of references at the end of an article, chapter, URL, etc. called
(A) Citation (B) Bibliography
(C) Class Number (D) Book Number

181. Which of the following is the quantitative measurement tool for quality and quantity of attention in terms of articles downloading, citation of scholarly work and information spreading from social media platform?
(A) Impact Factor (B) Altmetics
(C) Citation Analysis (D) h-index

182. CSIR Research Output Citation Index is based on
(A) Science Citation Index
(B) Chemistry Citation Index
(C) Arts and Humanities Citation Index
(D) Music Citation Index

183. In Chemical Abstract Service of Chemical Abstracts, 'keyword Indexes' are arranged according to the
(A) Alphabetical order
(B) Classified order
(C) Alphanumerical order
(D) Both (A) and (C)

184. BASIC Subject Index is related to
(A) Chemical abstracts
(B) Biological abstracts
(C) Electrical & Electronic abstracts
(D) Physics abstracts

185. The original Impact Factor (IF) is developed by
(A) ISI (B) IFLA
(C) UNESCO (D) LOC

186. Which of the following is not a formal communication channel?
(A) Technological Gatekeepers
(B) Scientist
(C) Researchers
(D) Management Experts

187. For Information Filtering, which of the following logic we have used?
(A) Boolean Logic
(B) Probability Logic
(C) Indexing Logic
(D) Physiological Logic

188. Which of the following is the Automated Information Intermediaries?
(A) Search engine
(B) Knowledge-based systems
(C) Artificial Intelligence software
(D) All of the above

189. Reprographies and their services originally popular in
(A) Netherlands (B) Germany
(C) Italy (D) France

190. The First International Congress on Reprography was held in
(A) 1960 (B) 1963
(C) 1965 (D) 1972

191. Which of the following was the venue of 1st International Congress on Reprography?
(A) Cologne, Germany
(B) Rome, Italy
(C) UK, Birmingham
(D) Australia, Brisbane

192. The process of document miniaturization is called
(A) Indexing (B) Abstracting
(C) Micrographic (D) Preservation

193. In which year United Kingdom passed the Copyright Act?
(A) 1970 (B) 1972
(C) 1975 (D) 1978

194. The Indian Copyright Act is based on
(A) British Copyright Act
(B) American Copyright Act
(C) Australian Copyright Act
(D) Netherlands Copyright Act

195. The venue of 3rd International Congress on Reprography (held in 1971) was
(A) London, United Kingdom
(B) Brussels, Belgium
(C) Milan, Italy
(D) Paris, France

196. The venue of 2nd International Congress on Reprography (held in 1967) was
(A) Cologne, Germany
(B) Moscow, Russia
(C) Brussels, Belgium
(D) Milan, Italy

197. International Council for Reprography was established in
(A) 1969 (B) 1972
(C) 1975 (D) 1977

198. Diazography is related to
(A) Reprography
(B) Digitalization
(C) Abstracting
(D) Indexing

199. Who established the French Academy of Sciences?
(A) Cardinal Richelieu
(B) William M. Blake
(C) William H. Boyd
(D) W.H. Auden

200. In which year INSPEC was published 'Science Abstracts' in first time?
(A) 1895 (B) 1898
(C) 1905 (D) 1910

201. Match the following:

LIST-I	LIST-II
(1) Applied Science and Technology Index	(i) 1947
(2) Biography Index	(ii) 1969
(3) Humanities Index	(iii) 1946

(4) Library and Information Science Abstracts		(iv) 1958	

Codes:

	(1)	(2)	(3)	(4)
(A)	(i)	(iv)	(iii)	(ii)
(B)	(ii)	(i)	(iv)	(iii)
(C)	(iii)	(i)	(ii)	(iv)
(D)	(iv)	(iii)	(i)	(ii)

202. Match the following:

LIST-I	LIST-II
(1) *Index Medicus*	(i) 1860
(2) *ALA Bulletin*	(ii) 1931
(3) *Keesings's Contemporary Achieves*	(iii) 1907
(4) *Chamber's Encyclopedia*	(iv) 1879

Codes:

	(1)	(2)	(3)	(4)
(A)	(iv)	(ii)	(i)	(iii)
(B)	(iv)	(iii)	(ii)	(i)
(C)	(iii)	(i)	(ii)	(iv)
(D)	(i)	(iii)	(ii)	(iv)

203. 'Royal Society of Chemistry' was established in

(A) 1841 (B) 1843
(C) 1845 (D) 1865

204. *British Education Index* has been published since

(A) 1951 (B) 1954
(C) 1958 (D) 1965

205. Commonwealth Agriculture Bureaux (CAB) was established in

(A) 1910 (B) 1915
(C) 1918 (D) 1922

206. Commonwealth Agriculture Bureaux (CAB) is presently known as

(A) CABI (B) CABL
(C) CABM (D) CAAB

207. Which of the following is the Research and Education Network of United Kingdom?

(A) JANET (B) BANET
(C) UKNET (D) EUNET

208. Match the following:

LIST-I	LIST-II
(1) *New International Encyclopedia*	(i) 1926
(2) *Whitaker's Almanac*	(ii) 1864
(3) *Statesman's Year Book*	(iii) 1902
(4) *Europa World Year Book*	(iv) 1868

Codes:

	(1)	(2)	(3)	(4)
(A)	(iii)	(iv)	(ii)	(i)
(B)	(iii)	(i)	(ii)	(iv)
(C)	(i)	(iv)	(iii)	(ii)
(D)	(ii)	(i)	(iv)	(iii)

209. BIOSIS stands for

(A) Bioscience Information Systems
(B) Bibliographical System for Biosciences
(C) Bioscience Information Services
(D) Biological Information Systems

210. Information from meetings, seminars and symposiums is the

(A) Primary source of information
(B) Secondary source of information
(C) Tertiary source of information
(D) None of the above

211. Match the following:

LIST-I	LIST-II
(1) Encyclopedia of Associations	(i) 1948
(2) UN Chronicle	(ii) 1964
(3) Yearbook of International Organizations	(iii) 1975

(4) Chamber's Biographical Dictionary (iv) 1897

Codes:

	(1)	(2)	(3)	(4)
(A)	(iii)	(ii)	(i)	(iv)
(B)	(i)	(iii)	(ii)	(iv)
(C)	(iv)	(ii)	(iii)	(i)
(D)	(i)	(iii)	(iv)	(ii)

212. Cambridge Scientific Abstracts was founded in the late

(A) 1920's era (B) 1930's era
(C) 1940's era (D) 1950's era

213. In which year Internet Database Service was launched by Cambridge Science Abstracts?

(A) 1994 (B) 1996
(C) 1998 (D) 2001

214. In which year 'The Royal Society Scientific Information Conference' was held?

(A) 1945 (B) 1948
(C) 1950 (D) 1955

215. Assertion (A): In IT era, Information & Referral (I & R) service is expected to provide information to the users 24 hours per day.

Reason (R): I & R is a direct responsive service.

(A) Both (A) and (R) are true
(B) Both (A) and (R) are false
(C) (A) is true, but (R) is false
(D) (A) is false, but (R) is true

216. Assertion (A): The growing popularity of Google and other search engines, information finding is now quite simple.

Reason (R): At present, the reference libraries are not valuable in current scenario of information seeking behaviour of users.

(A) Both (A) and (R) are false
(B) Both (A) and (R) are true
(C) (A) is false, but (R) is true
(D) (A) is true, but (R) is false

217. Assertion (A): With the help of the Citation Analysis, we can easily analyzed impact factor of scholarly articles among researchers.

Reason (R): h-Index is one of the specific methods that utilized citation analysis for determining an individual impact.

(A) Both (A) and (R) are false
(B) (A) is true, but (R) is false
(C) (A) is false, but (R) is true
(D) Both (A) and (R) are true

218. Assertion (A): Few decades ago, the Reference Services were commonly called 'Computer-Based-Reference-Service'.

Reason (R): After emerging of the Internet and web based services in libraries; the Reference Services are known as 'Online Search Service'.

(A) Both (A) and (R) are true
(B) Both (A) and (R) are false
(C) (A) is true, but (R) is false
(D) (A) is false, but (R) is true

219. Assertion (A): Research Libraries provides broad-based community information for their users through automated system.

Reason (R): There is no need to Reference Librarians in Research Libraries because users are capable to find-out his/her desired documents.

(A) Both (A) and (R) are true
(B) Both (A) and (R) are false
(C) (A) is true, but (R) is false
(D) (A) is false, but (R) is true

220. Assertion (A): Scopus is a citation database containing abstracts and peer-reviewed academic journal articles.

Reason (R): Academic institutions should be subscribed such type of citation database.

(A) Both (A) and (R) are true
(B) Both (A) and (R) are false
(C) (A) is true, but (R) is false
(D) (A) is false, but (R) is true

221. Assertion (A): General search engines are not fair in terms of displaying web references because they tie-up the business firms and can manipulate the search results.

Reason (R): Search engines rank the web pages based on its popularity not its quality.

(A) Both (A) and (R) are true
(B) Both (A) and (R) are false
(C) (A) is true, but (R) is false
(D) (A) is false, but (R) is true

222. Assertion (A): DRTC was established in Bengaluru as a research and training centre of Indian Statistical Institute (ISI) in 1962.

Reason (R): Due to foreign pressure, such kind of research intuitions was established in our country.

(A) Both (A) and (R) are true
(B) Both (A) and (R) are false
(C) (A) is false, but (R) is true
(D) (A) is true, but (R) is false

ANSWERS KEYS

1. (A)	2. (D)	3. (D)	4. (D)
5. (B)	6. (D)	7. (D)	8. (D)
9. (C)	10. (A)	11. (A)	12. (A)
13. (C)	14. (D)	15. (B)	16. (C)
17. (B)	18. (A)	19. (C)	20. (B)
21. (C)	22. (A)	23. (C)	24. (A)
25. (A)	26. (A)	27. (C)	28. (C)
29. (A)	30. (B)	31. (D)	32. (C)
33. (D)	34. (D)	35. (D)	36. (A)
37. (A)	38. (A)	39. (A)	40. (D)
41. (A)	42. (C)	43. (D)	44. (B)
45. (A)	46. (A)	47. (A)	48. (D)
49. (B)	50. (A)	51. (D)	52. (A)
53. (A)	54. (B)	55. (B)	56. (B)
57. (A)	58. (A)	59. (A)	60. (A)
61. (B)	62. (B)	63. (B)	64. (B)
65. (C)	66. (D)	67. (A)	68. (D)
69. (A)	70. (B)	71. (D)	72. (A)
73. (A)	74. (C)	75. (A)	76. (B)
77. (A)	78. (B)	79. (A)	80. (C)
81. (D)	82. (B)	83. (A)	84. (B)
85. (A)	86. (B)	87. (A)	88. (D)
89. (B)	90. (A)	91. (C)	92. (B)
93. (A)	94. (D)	95. (A)	96. (A)
97. (A)	98. (A)	99. (A)	100. (D)
101. (A)	102. (D)	103. (D)	104. (B)
105. (B)	106. (C)	107. (A)	108. (A)
109. (D)	110. (B)	111. (A)	112. (D)
113. (C)	114. (C)	115. (A)	116. (B)
117. (D)	118. (A)	119. (C)	120. (B)
121. (A)	122. (D)	123. (B)	124. (D)
125. (A)	126. (A)	127. (A)	128. (A)
129. (D)	130. (A)	131. (A)	132. (A)
133. (C)	134. (A)	135. (A)	136. (A)
137. (A)	138. (A)	139. (A)	140. (B)
141. (D)	142. (A)	143. (A)	144. (B)
145. (C)	146. (A)	147. (A)	148. (A)
149. (D)	150. (D)	151. (D)	152. (D)
153. (B)	154. (B)	155. (A)	156. (A)
157. (D)	158. (A)	159. (D)	160. (A)
161. (A)	162. (B)	163. (A)	164. (A)
165. (A)	166. (D)	167. (A)	168. (B)
169. (A)	170. (A)	171. (A)	172. (D)
173. (A)	174. (D)	175. (A)	176. (B)
177. (C)	178. (C)	179. (A)	180. (A)
181. (B)	182. (A)	183. (A)	184. (B)
185. (A)	186. (A)	187. (A)	188. (D)
189. (A)	190. (B)	191. (A)	192. (C)

193. (A)	194. (A)	195. (A)	196. (A)
197. (A)	198. (A)	199. (A)	200. (B)
201. (D)	202. (B)	203. (A)	204. (B)
205. (A)	206. (A)	207. (A)	208. (A)
209. (C)	210. (A)	211. (A)	212. (D)
213. (A)	214. (B)	215. (A)	216. (D)
217. (D)	218. (A)	219. (C)	220. (A)
221. (A)	222. (D)		

CHAPTER

5 Organization of Information and Knowledge

Introduction

Knowledge Organization (KO) or Information Organization (IO) has been an important part in Library & Information Science curriculum. In this discipline, various activities such as Classification and Cataloguing of documents according to the various schemes, database activities for physical document as well as e-documents, managing of bibliographic record according to various methods such as ISBN, ISSN, MARC, etc., arrangement of documents according to the users' friendly manner are working.

All these activities are done a well-defined classification and cataloguing rules as well as canons and the principles. Classification and the Cataloguing of the documents are very fundamental technical works in any types of library. The various computerized cataloguing integrated software are available now for centralized storing of bibliographical records for the purpose of data storing, searching and also accessing.

In early curriculum in this subject areas emphasized the cataloguing, resource description and classification as depth curriculum but nowadays, the scenario has been changed. Presently, we have studies, how to create metadata structures and how to access these structures and how to organized e-documents or e-resources in the field of Knowledge Organization or Information Organization.

Thus, in this respect we will take consideration of various related important points and questions and their answer according to the latest pattern in above said topic.

Important Points

- The term Classification is a derivation from the Latin word 'classi(s)' which connotes Grouping.
- Thesauri and Subject Heading Systems are the examples of Alphabetical Indexing Languages.
- In knowledge organization and information retrieval, the term aboutness was first coined by Robert Fairthorne in 1969 and he categorized it into two types; intentional aboutness and extensional aboutness.
- Intentional aboutness is the author's views and intentions of what a document is about, and extensional aboutness which is the document aboutness as reflected semantically by actual units and parts of the text.

- According to S.R. Ranganathan, the subject is an organized or systematized body of ideas, whose extension and intention are likely to fall coherently within the field of interest and comfortably within the intellectual competence and the field of inevitable specialization of a normal individual.
- S.R. Ranganathan is the first person to whom the credit goes for enunciating, propounding, describing, and analyzing Normative Principles of cataloguing and these principles are developed on the basis of scientific method.
- There are three terms used by S.R. Ranganathan for denoting normative principles; Law, Canon, and Principles.
- In Library & Information Science, the law tells us what we have to do and what not to do.
- The Canon means a general principle or standard by which judgments may be formed in cataloguing. For example, the Canon will works for drafting of Catalogue Code including the formulation of each rule, a suitable guidance for day-to-day technical works of documents, and interpretation of the rules to meet new situations brought out by particular document.
- S.R. Ranganathan enunciated canon in Classified Catalogue Code and discuss in his book *Headings and Canons* published in 1953.
- Principles have been used to the varying extent by the frames of Classification and the Cataloguing and regulate the procedures and methods.
- S.R. Ranganathan's *Classified Catalogue Code* with Additional Rules for Dictionary Catalogue (CCC) was published in 1934 and the Normative Principles of Cataloguing first time were included in *Theory of Library Cataloguing* published in 1938 and at that time there are six canons were introduced and in later editions, canons were elaborated and at present there are nine canons in Normative Principles of Cataloguing.
- Canon of Ascertainability prescribes the use of the title page and overflow pages as the main source of cataloguing information for the choice and rendering of the Heading of the Main Entry and specific added entries.
- Canon of Prepotence is used in arrangement of entries and this canon decide the position of an entry among the various entries in a catalogue and maximum potency is given to the Leading Section of the library catalogue.
- Canon of Sought Heading prescribes that Main Entry and Added Entries heading should be chosen based upon the possibilities of the users' approaches to the library catalogue.
- Canon of Individualization reveals that appropriate individualizing elements should be added for the name of any entity—be it of a person, a geographical entity, a corporate body, a series, a document, a subject, or a language—used as the Heading of a catalogue entry should be made to denote one and only one entity which helps in easy identification and remove confusion.
- Canon of Consistence recommend that a catalogue code should be framed in such a manner that all the added entries of a document to be consistent with its Main Entry,

the entries of all documents should be consistent with one another in certain essential points such as choice of headings, and style of writing the heading and the other sections.

- Canon of Currency implies that current terminologies should be used to denote a subject of a catalogue entry that means Subject in a Class Index Entry of a Classified Catalogue and in a Subject Entry of a Dictionary Catalogue should be the one in current usage.
- Canon of Context prescribe that, the rules of catalogue code should be formulated in the context of the nature of the cataloguing features of the book, prevent in the mode of book production and therefore, the rules should be amended and revised from time to time to keep step with the changes in the context.
- Canon of Permanence prescribes that no element in an entry the heading in particular, should be subjected to change by the rules of a catalogue code except the rules themselves are changed in response to the Canon of Context.
- Canon of Recall Value is the ninth additional canon enunciated by S.R. Ranganathan in Classified Catalogue Code in 1969. This canon helps in choosing heading for the catalogue entry and rendering style and it directs that the entry element and rendering style to be chosen should be the one having highest probability of beings called back to memory by a majority of the readers. This canon is called master canon.
- The Canon of Relevance of the Theory (1938) was renamed as Canon of Sought Heading in *Headings and Canons* published in 1953.
- CCC and AACR-II both satisfy the Canon of Prepotence.
- The Association for Library Collections and Technical Services (ALCTS) is a division of the American Library Association (ALA) and it was created in 1957.
- The basic tool for organizing and exploring the documents which stored in a library is Library Classification.
- Classification is a procedure of grouping similar items and objects and is essential in formulating groups that known as classifying which results in Classification.
- The most important part for any library organization is Classification and it also known as Foundation of Librarianship.
- Classification deals with assigning codes notation representing the subject of the Universe of Knowledge, other words, it determines the subject of an information source and allocation of notation by which that information is shelved in the library.
- Cataloguing deals with physical description of information source called bibliographic description.
- Classification involves systematic grouping of information sources by subject contents and translation of the subjects into codes of ordinal numbers.
- For knowledge organization, the Classification Schemes are the main tool in classifying information sources.

- A classification scheme consist three parts; schedule, notation, and index.
- The schedule contains the list of all the Main Classes and Sub-Classes of the scheme.
- The notation is a symbol in a definite order representing subjects and their list in the schedule.
- The index is an alphabetical list of subject terms in the schedule with their corresponding notation.
- In bibliographic control, the access-point provision refers to designating selected elements in the representation that the user can use as means to gain entry to the representation.
- A Library Catalogue is a kind of bibliographic record and it differs from a bibliography or a periodical index.
- Library Catalogues are multiple-access point which means that they offer many ways or access points to retrieve a particular catalogue record.
- The chief access point is the Main Entry in the catalogue record.
- Before appearance of Card Catalogue, most library catalogues were in book form, either printed or loose-leaf.
- The establishment and maintenance of consistent form of terms—names, subjects, and titles that can be used as headings in the bibliographic records of the library catalogue is known as Authority Control.
- The purpose of Authority Control is to make sets of objects.
- Sir Anthony Panizzi formulated the ninety-one rules for compiling the catalogue of the British Museum.
- The most important events in the evolution of cataloguing codes tool place in 1961 when International Conference on Cataloguing Principles was held in Paris from October 9 to October 18, 1961 under the auspicious of the IFLA and it is known as Paris Principles.
- International Meeting of Cataloguing Experts was held in Copenhagen in 1969 and at this meeting, an international working group was established for the purpose of developing a standard order and content for descriptive monographic material.
- The term Universal Bibliography originally meant an attempt of creating a complete World Bibliography.
- Any document would be only be catalogued once in its country of origin, and in that records then be available for the use of any library in the world, theoretical called as Universal Bibliographic Control (UBC) and this concept introduced by IFLA in 1970s era.
- The British Museum Cataloguing Rules also known as Panizzi's ninety-one rules.
- The Jewett's Rules code contains thirty-three rules.
- The first edition of the Cutter's Rules for a Dictionary Catalogue was appeared in 1876.

- Copy Cataloguing is the process of editing a pre-existing bibliographic record instead of creating a completely new record from scratch that means it is the process of building upon original cataloguing and it involves matching an established bibliographic record, examples are the OCLC WorldCat Catalogue or Library of Congress Catalogue which hold millions of catalogue MARC and others standards, with an exact duplicate item described to be added into a collection.
- The Original Cataloguing is to do the cataloguing in-house from scratch.
- Copy Cataloguing occurs when library personnel use pre-existing cataloguing information.
- In Information Technology (IT) era, the pre-existing cataloguing information are available electronically through the communication mediums.
- The correct original cataloguing is a complicated and time-consuming process that is bound by many rules.
- At present, the OCLC is the most common vendor for Copy Catalogue records.
- An important component of the cooperative cataloguing activities worldwide is the Programme for Cooperative Cataloguing (PCC).
- PCC is an international cooperative effort aimed at expanding access to library collections by providing useful, timely, and cost-effective cataloguing that meets mutually accepted standards of libraries around the world.
- The Library of Congress was established the Cataloguing-in-Publication (CIP) Programme in 1971.
- The Electronic Cataloguing-in-Publication (ECIP) partnership programme was introduced in 1999.
- Online Computer Library Centre (OCLC) was founded by Frederick G. Kilgour in 1967 as consortium of forty-nine academic libraries in the state of Ohio.
- The principle objective of OCLC was resource sharing and reduction of per-unit library costs and it began operation in 1971.
- In 2005, the OCLC Open WorldCat programme was launched for freely accessible of library records worldwide through web interface.
- The MARC structure was adopted as a national standard (ANSI Standard Z39.2) in 1971 and as an international standard (ISO standard 2709) in 1973.
- The MARC Advisory Committee known as MAC previously known as MARBI.
- The Library of Congress is responsible for the maintenance and publication of the MARC21 formats.
- MARC21 is the current version of MARC.
- In MARC records, the bibliographic data of a catalogued item has been divided logically into fields.
- In MARC records, each field is represented by a three digits code called Tags which can be unique.

- A Field is subdivided into Subfields and each type of data within the Field is called a Subfield and each Subfield is associated with Subfield Code. For example, in Title Statement (245), the Subfields Codes are
  - ⇒ $a—Title Proper.
  - ⇒ $h—Medium (often used for non-book media).
  - ⇒ $p—Name of Part/Section of a work.
  - ⇒ $b—Remainder of title (Subtitle, etc.).
  - ⇒ $c—Remainder of title-page transcription/statement of responsibility.
- In MARC records, a Tag is always a three digit code, for example tag 020 represents ISBN and tag 100 represents a Personal Name fields.
- In MARC records, Indicators supply information about the field for indexing, display, or other system functions and it is the convention to represent a blank or undefined indicator (either Indicator 1 or Indicator 2 or both) position by the character # (hash) and each Indicator value is a number from 0 to 09.
- In MARC records, some tags are NR (No Repeated), for example 100 Main Entry—Personal Name Tag and some are R(Repeated), for example 020 International Standard Book Number (ISBN).
- The basic divisions of the MARC21 bibliographic records (tags) are:

0XX	Control information, Numbers, Codes.
1XX	Main Entry.
2XX	Titles, Edition, Imprint (in general, the title, statement of responsibility, edition, and publication information).
3XX	Physical Description, etc.
4XX	Series Statements.
5XX	Notes.
6XX	Subject Added Entries.
7XX	Added Entries other than Subject or Series.
8XX	Series Added Entries (other authoritative forms).
9XX	Left for locally-defined users, such as local barcode numbers.

- The tags used more frequently are:

010	Marks the Library of Congress Control Number (LCCN)

020	Marks the International Standard Book Number (ISBN)
100	Marks a Personal Name Main Entry (Author)
130	Main Entry-Uniform Title
245	Marks the Title Information (which includes the Title, other title information, and the statement of responsibility.
260	Marks the Publication Information.
300	Marks the Physical Description.
490	Marks the series Statement.
520	Marks the annotation or summary note.
650	Marks a topical Subject Headings.
700	Marks a Personal Name Added Entry (Joint author, Editor or Illustrator).

- There are three main sections in MARC21 Records; the Leader, the Directory, and the Fields.
- The Leader fixed at twenty-four characters (position 0-23) is the first field in a MARC record.
- The Directory is a computer-generated index to the location of the control and data filed within a record and it begins at record position 24.
- The Fields contain the essence of the record, that is Cataloguing, Authority, Classification, or Holding Data and each field is identified by a three-character numeric tag stored in the directory.
- MARCXML is an XML Schema based on the Common MARC21 Standard and it was developed by the Library of Congress.
- UNIMARC is an international standard maintained by the IFLA to facilitate the international exchange of data in machine readable form between national bibliographic agencies.
- In Library & Information Science, the metadata is structure information that describes, explains, locates, or makes it easier to retrieve and manage information resources.
- Metadata Schemas are sets of metadata elements designed for a specific purpose, such as describing a particular type of information resource.
- At present there are fifteen metadata elements in Dublin Core and these are Title, Creator, Subject, Description, Publisher, Contributor, Date, Type, Format, Identifier, Source, Language, Resource, Coverage, and Rights.

- All Dublin Core elements are optional and all are repeatable and elements may be presented in any order.
- Metadata Object Description Schema (MODS) is an XML based metadata schema for creating original resource description records that consists of selected data from the MARC21 Bibliographic Format.
- The standard of MODS is maintained by the Network Development and MARC Standard Office of the Library of Congress.
- MODS was published in 2002 and the current version is 3.6 that was released in 20th June, 2016.
- The Metadata Authority Description Schema (MADS) is an XML schema for an authority element set that may be used to provide metadata about agents (people, organizations), events and terms (topics, geographic, genres, etc.).
- The standard of MADS is maintained by the MODS/MADS Editorial Committee with the Network Development and MARC Standards Office.
- BIBFRAME (Bibliographic Framework) is an initiative to evolve bibliographic description standards to a linked data model, in order to make bibliographic information more useful both within and outside the library committee and it was designed to replace the MARC Standards.
- BIBFRAME 2.0 organize bibliographic information into three core level of abstraction; Work, Instance, and Item.
- The BIBFRAME vocabulary consists of RDF Classes and Properties.
- Dublin Core Metadata Initiative (DCMI) is an open forum that oversees the continuing development of the Dublin Core metadata standards.
- Dublin Core was published as ISO Standard 15836 in February 2009.
- The Encoded Archival Description (EAD) is a standard for describing and encoding finding aids for archival materials and it began in 1993 at the University of California, Berkeley.
- Visual Resources Association Core Categories (VRA Core Categories) or VRA Core is a data standard for the description of works of visual culture as well as the images that document them and standard is hosted by the National Development and MARC Standard Office of the Library of Congress.
- Online Information Exchange (ONIX) is an international metadata standard designed specifically to support electronic commerce applications.
- The Text Encoding Initiative (TEI) is an international project to develop guidelines for making up electronic text such as novels, plays and poetry, primarily to support research in the humanities.
- The Metadata Encoding and Transmission Standards (METS) was developed to fill the need for a standard data structure for describing complex digital library objects.

- Resource Description and Access (RDA) is a standard for descriptive cataloguing, providing instructions and guidelines on formulating bibliographic data and it was released in 2010.
- RDA is the successor to Anglo-American Cataloguing Rules Second Edition (AACR-II).
- RDA does not provide guidelines for the presentation of data in a record structure, instead it provides a set of guidelines and instructions on formulating data to support resource discovery.
- RDA can be utilized in FRBR and FRAD.
- The Resource Description Framework (RDF) is a family of World Wide Web consortium (W3C) specifications originally designed as a metadata model and it has come to be used as a general method for information that is implemented in Web Resources, using a variety of syntax notations and data serializations formats.
- RDF was adopted as a W3C recommendation in 1999.
- The RDF data model is based on Entity-Relationship Diagrams and it is based upon the idea of making statement about resources in the form of Subject, Predicate, and Object Expression.
- An Entity-Relationship Diagram/Model describes inter-related things of interest in a specific domain of knowledge and it was developed by Peter Chen in 1976.
- In cataloguing, the Authority Control means establishing a recognized form for an entity name and using that form whenever the name is needed as an access point in a bibliographic records.
- Common Communication Format (CCF) is a structure format for creating bibliographical records and for exchanging records between groups of information agency and libraries developed by UNESCO.
- The first edition of CCF was published in 1984 under the editorship of Peter Simmons and Alan Hopkins and its second edition was published in 1988 in two volumes called CCF/B and CCD/F.
- The International Standard Bibliographic Description (ISBD) is a set of rules produced by the IFLA to create a bibliographic description in a standard, human-readable form for library catalogue.
- The ISBD defines nine areas of description and each area except 7, is composed of multiple elements with structured classifications and all the nine areas are described as:

0	Content form and media type.
1	Title and statement of responsibility area.
2	Edition area.

3	Material or type of resource specific area (for example, the scale of a map or the numbering of a periodical).
4	Publication, Production, Distribution, etc. area.
5	Physical description (for example, number of pages in a book or number of CDs is issued as a unit) area.
6	Series and Multipart monographic resource area.
7	Notes area.
8	Resource identification and terms of availability area such as ISBN, ISSN.

- The first of the ISBDs was the International Standard Bibliographic Description for Monographic Publications (ISBD(M)), which appeared in 1971.
- The Standard Bibliographic Description for Serials (ISBD(S)) was published in 1974.
- The types of resources covered by the ISBD including Cartographic resources, electronic resources, moving images, multimedia resources, notated music resources, printed texts, sound recordings, and still images.
- The ISBD formats conform to AACR-II Rules.
- The IFLA's First International Meeting of Experts on a International Cataloguing Code (IME ICC) was held in July 28-30, 2003 in Frankfurt, Germany.
- Functional Requirements for Bibliographic Records (FRBR) is a conceptual Entity-Relationship model developed by the IFLA to describe entities, relationships, and attributes (metadata of bibliographic data).
- FRBR is a 1998 recommendation of the IFLA to restructure catalogue databases to reflect the conceptual structure of information sources.
- FRBR model is significant because it is separate from specific cataloguing standards such as AACR and ISBD.
- In FRBR, the Entities are defined in three groups as:

⇒ **Group 1**
  * **Work** – a creative piece
  * **Expression** – the realization of a work
  * **Manifestation** – the embodiment of work
  * **Item** – a single exemplar of a manifestation

⇒ **Group 2**
  * Person
  * Corporate Body

⇒ **Group 3**
  * Concepts

  * Objects
  * Events
  * Places

- The FRBR bibliographic model utilize through metadata standards rather than MARC.
- The Group 1 entities of FRBR are Work, Expression, Manifestation, and Item (WEMI) and they represent the products of intellectual or artistic Endeavour.
- The Group 2 entities of FRBR are Person, and Corporate Body that are related to Group 1 entities through specific relationships.
- The Group 3 entities of FRBR are the subjects of works. These can be Concepts, Objects, Events, Places, and any of the Group 1 or Group 2 entities or both groups along with Group 3 entities.
- The Joint Steering Committee for Revision of the Anglo-American Cataloguing Rules (JSC) is using FRBR not only to update terminology, but also to re-examine and improve the traditional linking devices of uniform titles in light of FRBR.
- FRBR is a conceptual model, RDA is a content standard (as is AACR-II), and MARC is a communication format, therefore, they are not the same thing.
- In field level, the MARC fields are containers for content whereas RDA describes content to be recorded that sometimes ends up in different fields.
- There is no Main Entry and no Entry Under a Heading in RDA.
- CONSER (Conversion of Serials) is a cooperative online serials cataloguing programme of Library of Congress.
- Cataloguing Cultural Objects (CCC) is the first data content standards specifically intended for cataloguing of cultural heritage materials and their images.
- Z39.50 is an ANSI/NISO standard for information storage and retrieval protocol for bibliographic records across entire computer network systems and it enables information seekers to search different systems on a network or the Internet through the user interface. But this protocol is not used by the general Internet search engines (because they use http).
- The ISO Inter-Library Loan Protocol (ISO ILL) was developed to provide uniform procedures when accessing a library across a network to order copy or loan material, and for carrying out the administrative tasks involved in loan management.
- SRU (Search/Retrieval via URL) is a standard synchronous search protocol for Internet search queries, utilizing CQL (Contextual Query Language), a standard syntax for representing queries.
- SRW (Search/Retrieval Web Service) is a web service for search and retrieval and it provides a SOAP interface to queries, to augment the URL interface provided by its companion protocol SRU.
- SRU/SRW services are easy to implement compare to Z39.50 because they are web-based protocols.

- Standards of SRW, SRU, and CQL are promulgated by the Library of Congress.
- The OpenURL is a standardized format for encoding the metadata package within a Uniform Resource Locator (URL), intended to identify about an information object.
- The OpenURL provides a mechanism for encoding a citation for an information resource (bibliographic resource) as a URL.
- An OPAC (Online Public Access Catalogue) is an online bibliography of a library collection that is available to the public.
- OPAC is the advance form of conventional Card Catalogue that means it always provide Author, Title, Subject, ISBN, ISSN, and also Call Numbers of documents and with the help of Boolean Operators and keywords OPAC can be limited the search results.
- The Web OPAC an OPAC that allows users to interface the library collections through web interface from anywhere in the world and in any time.
- A Web OPAC is a Graphical User Interface (GUI), which uses the World Wide Web (WWW) protocol to act as an OPAC.
- A classification which is not provided enough details and meets the requirement of the small libraries is described Broad Classification and Riders International Classification and early editions of the DDC are broad classification.
- A classification which is provided maximum details and meets the requirement of the special libraries for documentation works is described Depth Classification.
- Depth or Special Classification schedules are detailed organizations to classify micro literatures such as periodicals, articles, dissertations, patents, standards, abstracts, indexes pertaining to a narrow subject field.
- The word Bibliographic Classification is also used for depth classification.
- Bibliographic Classifications are library classification systems where schedule designed to organize micro literature in the form of bibliographies and indexes.
- Arranges knowledge on the basis of evaluating and classify thoughts, concepts and ideas is known as Knowledge Classification.
- A Book Classification is based on systems and principles that means it is a device for the arrangement of books and other macro documents through subject or form in a logical order.
- The Dewey Decimal Classification (DDC) was intended to be a Book Classification, whereas the Universal Decimal Classification (UDC) was intended to be a Bibliographic Classification.
- Aristotle divided knowledge into ten categories viz. Substance, Quantity, Quality, Relation, Place, Time, Situation, State, Action and Passion.
- Library classification systems are broadly divided into two categories; Enumerative System and Faceted System.

- An Enumerative System is designed as a library classification system which systematically enumerated (lists) all subjects of past, present and anticipated future divided into disciplines, main classes and their subdivisions.
- Arrangement of documents is based on mutually exclusive facets or categories which reflect the various aspects of a subject is known as Faceted System and facets must be homogenous or should be of the same category.
- The first truly faceted classification schedule was Colon Classification, which was first published in 1933.
- Knowledge has been divided into major regions described Disciplines.
- In library classification, the Main Class is conventional but extremely cohesive region of knowledge.
- According to S.R. Ranganathan, there are three kinds of subjects, namely, Basic Subjects, Compound Subjects, and Complex Subjects.
- In library classification, the subject of the document is translated into a Class Number with the help of a Notation.
- A freely faceted classification based on postulates and principles for analysis and synthesis of the subjects, and where there is no rigid, predetermined formula for the compound subjects going with a basic subject is known as Analytico-Synthetic Classification.
- In library classification, the supplementary facets schedules which is used for construction of class numbers with Main Class and their isolates known as Common Auxiliaries or Common Isolates.
- In Universal Decimal Classification (UDC), the common isolates are known as Auxiliaries.
- In Dewey Decimal Classification (DDC), the Relative Index forming a very important part of the whole work has been considered as the heart of the scheme from the beginning of this classification scheme and it is called "Relative" because it shows the connection between subjects and the disciplines in which they appear.
- In Dewey Decimal Classification (DDC), subjects are listed alphabetically in the Relative Index.
- In Dewey Decimal Classification (DDC), a note instructing the classifier about the location of interrelated topics is known as Class-elsewhere note.
- In Dewey Decimal Classification (DDC), a note that identifies topics that is equivalent to the whole of the class under which the note appears in known as Class-here note.
- A Complex Subject is a subject that has more than one characteristic. For example, "unemployed carpenters" is a complex subject because it has more than one characteristic (employment status and occupation).
- The main objective of a library catalogue is to inform the availability or non-availability of a particular reading material in the library.

- Trade Catalogues comprises entries arranged in an alphabetical order of authors and titles, under broad subject groups and are not expected to meet the different approaches of users, as library catalogue is expected to do.
- If the catalogue represents the collection of two or more libraries, the catalogue is termed as Union Catalogue.
- A designation for a class of materials added in cataloguing according to AACR-II following the title to specify the physical medium category is known as General Material Designation (GMD).
- In an alphabetical subject catalogue, entries are made under the name of the specific subject of documents.
- According to S.R. Ranganathan, a specific subject of a document as that division of knowledge whose intention and extension are equal to its thought contents.
- An Alphabetico-Classed Catalogue provides alphabetically arranged broad subject headings with alphabetically arranged subdivisions.
- Leading Section is the part of catalogue entry that forms the first part which determines its filling position in the catalogue.
- There are five entries in Classified Catalogue Code (CCC) viz. Main Entry, Cross Reference Entries, Class Index Entries, Book Index Entries, Cross Reference Index Entries.
- The sections of the Main Entry in the Classified Catalogue Code (CCC) are listed at Chapter MB and there are six sections in Main Entry.
- In Classified Catalogue Code (CCC), the very first section of the Main Entry is known as the Leading Section and it occupied by the Call Number of a document.
- There are ten rules in the Classified Catalogue Code (CCC) regulating the choice and form of Pseudonyms.
- A.C. Foskett divides indexing system in two groups, viz., Derived Indexing and Assigned Indexing.
- Derived Indexing Systems derive their information for indexing from the document.
- In Assigned Indexing systems, the index terms are assigned by the indexer to documents for the purpose of storage and retrieval of information.
- In indexing system, the Syntactic Relation refers to the citation order of concepts in index statement whereas, the Semantic Relationship refers to the hierarchical and affinitive or associative relationships of concepts.
- The tools that used for indexing are known as Indexing Language and it include Classification System, Subject Headings Lists, Thesauri, Thesaurofacet, and Classaurus.
- The term Thesaurofacet was coined by J. Aitchison as the combination of a Facet Classification (Analytico-Synthetic Classification) and Thesaurus for covering engineering and related scientific, and management subjects for both Pre-coordinate and Post-coordinate Indexing System.

- Sears List of Subject Headings (SLSH), Library of Congress Subject Headings (LCSH), Medical Subject Headings (MESH), Subject Headings in Engineering (SHE), and Public Affairs Information Service (PAIS) are the famous and widely used Subject Headings lists in knowledge and information organization.
- In Social Sciences, the Public Affairs Information Service (PAIS) Subject Headings List is widely used.
- Content Analysis is a multi-discipline subjects concerning, in Library & Information Science, the content analysis means to organize the content of documents intellectually, irrespective of their physical form, so that the users get easy access to their source of information.
- The word Index comes from the Latin word indicaire meaning to point out or to guide.
- The verbal representation of the subject contents of a document is known as Index whereas Class Number helps to arrange the documents on shelves according to the documents and arrangement of the documents on shelves is in a near neighborhood relation according to the APUPA pattern.
- Derived Indexing also known as Natural Language Indexing (NLI) because it uses the same language as that used by the author.
- Assigned Indexing is based on conceptual analysis of terms and words.
- The citation order of classification schemes reflects the characteristics of syntax of an indexing language.
- The primary purpose of Subject Headings in the catalogue is to provide subject access to information.
- The Subject Headings Lists show the semantic aspects of the indexing language through See and See Also references.
- Thesaurus is an example of an indexing language providing vocabulary control for indexing and information searching.
- Subject Headings Lists were developed to suit the subject catalogue useful for pre-coordinating indexing system, whereas, Thesaurus has been developed in the context of post-coordinating indexing system.
- Classaurus is one of the control vocabulary device, developed by G. Bhattacharyya for POPSI Indexing system.
- The technique of using controlled language to describe terms in an information storage and retrieval system is known as Vocabulary Control.
- Universal Decimal Classification (UDC) is an Analytico-Synthetic Classification Scheme, where the concepts can be broken down into simple concept (analyzed) and then combined (synthesized).
- In order to preserve the precise meaning, and enable accurate parsing of Complex UDC class number, a number of Connecting Symbols are made available, and these Common Auxiliary Signs are:

Symbol	Purpose	Associated with
+	Addition Coordination	Table 1a
/	Consecutive extension	Table 1a
:	Simple relation	Table 1b
::	Order-fixing	Table 1b
[ ]	Sub-grouping	Table 1b
*	Introduce non-UDC notation	Table 1h
A/Z	Direct alphabetical specification	Table 1h

- List of Common Auxiliaries and their purpose in UDC:

Symbol	Purpose	Associated with
=...	Common auxiliaries of language	Table 1c
(0...)	Common auxiliaries of form	Table 1d
(1/9)	Common auxiliaries of place	Table 1e
(=...)	Common auxiliaries of human ancestry, ethnic grouping and nationality	Table 1f
"..."	Common auxiliaries of time	Table 1g
-0...	Common auxiliaries of general characteristics: Properties, Materials, Relations/Processes and Persons	Table 1k
-02	Common auxiliaries of properties	Table 1k
-03	Common auxiliaries of materials	Table 1k
-04	Common auxiliaries of relations, processes and operations	Table 1k
-05	Common auxiliaries of persons and personal characteristics	Table 1k (this is repeated)

- In UDC, Special Auxiliaries are not listed at one place in schedule like Common Auxiliaries due to their local recurrent characteristics and most special auxiliaries are enumerative and they are applicable only where they are indicated that means they cannot be used as independent numbers.
- There are three kinds of notations used in Special Auxiliaries in UDC viz. Hyphen Series (-1/-9), Point-nought Series (.01/.09) and Apostrophe Series ('1/'9).

- The Hyphen Series (-1/-9) indicate elements, components, properties and other details of the subject denoted by the main number to which they serve.

  For example,

  535 Optics, Light

  -1 Infra-red rays

  -2 Spectrums

  -3 Ultra-violet rays
- The Point-nought Series (.01/.09) provides sets and subsets of recurrent concepts, like aspect studies, processes, operations, plant and equipments.

  For example,

  591 General Zoology. Animal Biology

  .04 Physical and physic-chemical factors.

  .05 Metabolism.
- The Apostrophe Series ('1/'9) are most of the time synthetic or integration in function and denote compound subjects by compound notation.

  For example,

  547 Organic Chemistry

  547.29'26 Carboxy-acid esters
- The Citation Order of UDC is Things → Kind → Part → Material → Property → Process → Operation → Agent → Space → Time.
- There are five new notations has been added in Colon Classification 7th Edition as + (plus), = (equal to), " (double inverted comma), * (asterisk), and & (ampersand).
- There are 74 notational digits (60 semantics and 14 indicator) has been used in Colon Classification 7th Edition.

QUESTIONS

1. The journal *Knowledge Organization* is published by

(A) ISKO (B) IFLA

(C) ALA (D) CILIP

2. In which year 'International Society for Knowledge Organization (ISKO)' was founded?

(A) 1989 (B) 1999

(C) 2001 (D) 2003

3. *Knowledge Organization* has been published since

(A) 1971 (B) 1974

(C) 1976 (D) 1979

4. *Knowledge Organization* formerly known as

(A) International Classification

(B) The Classification Journal

(C) Document Management

(D) Journal for Classification

5. Which of the following country is not officially recognized national chapters of ISKO?

(A) India (B) Canada
(C) United Kingdom (D) Australia

6. ISKO was founded by
(A) Ingetraut Dahlberg
(B) William G. Boyd
(C) Dan B. Brown
(D) Nicola S. Barker

7. Subject Bundle is commonly known as
(A) Cluster (B) Fission
(C) Denudation (D) Loose Assemblage

8. Which of the following was the first scholar of Book Classification?
(A) Francis Bacon (B) H.E. Bliss
(C) J.D. Brown (D) S.R. Ranganathan

9. According to G.W.F. Hegel, Universe of Ideas has four successive divisions as Idea, Imperfect Idea, Essence and.......
(A) Being (B) Philosophy
(C) Psychology (D) Poetry

10. The term 'Modes of Formation of Subjects' is coined by
(A) W.C.B. Sayers (B) J.D. Brown
(C) H.E. Bliss (D) S.R. Ranganathan

11. The 22nd edition of DDC was brought out in the year
(A) 2001 (B) 2003
(C) 2005 (D) 2009

12. Francis Bacon divided the Universe of Ideas into three successive groups namely History, Poesy and.......
(A) Psychology (B) Philosophy
(C) Medicine (D) Religion

13. Library Classification Schemes can be categorized as
(A) Enumerative (B) Hierarchical
(C) Faceted (D) All of the above

14. In DDC, the index is known as
(A) Relative Index
(B) Book Index
(C) Classification Index
(D) Alphabetical Index

15. Which of the following is keyword based information retrieval tool?
(A) KWIC (B) KWOC
(C) Both (A) and (B) (D) Only (A)

16. The term 'Tacit Knowledge' was first introduced by
(A) Michael Polanyi (B) K. Thomas
(C) J.M. John (D) J.E. Hunter

17. Which of the following knowledge can be articulated, codified, accessed as well as verbalized?
(A) Tacit Knowledge
(B) Explicit Knowledge
(C) Externalized Knowledge
(D) Both (B) and (C)

18. Which of the following is associated with Cutter Number?
(A) It is used for assigning the Author Numbers
(B) Beginning with first letter of the author's name
(C) Used in Library of Congress Classification for assigning Book Number
(D) All of the above

19. Threefigure Tables is used in
(A) Cutter Number
(B) Cutter-Sanborn Number
(C) Colon Classification
(D) All of the above

20. Encyclopedia is the example of
(A) Tacit Knowledge
(B) Explicit Knowledge
(C) Externalized Knowledge
(D) Artificial Knowledge

21. Which of the following was the designer of Sears List of Subject Headings (SLSH)?
(A) Minnie Earl Sears (B) Marc K. Sears
(C) Peggy S. Sears (D) Hans A. Sears

22. A kind of vocabulary control device 'Classaurus' is developed by
(A) G. Bhattacharyya, DRTC
(B) Ingetraut Dahlberg, ISKO
(C) Ralph Munn, ALA
(D) H.P. Luhn, IBM

23. In which year Charles C. Jewett was published a catalogue code rules for the Smithsonian Institute?
(A) 1854 (B) 1858
(C) 1860 (D) 1862

24. Which of the following notation is used for 'See reference' in SLSH?
(A) X (B) XX
(C) X0 (D) X00

25. In CCC, Class Index Entries are derived from
(A) Book Number (B) Title
(C) Class Number (D) Both (B) and (C)

26. In CCC, the maximum information about a document is store in
(A) Main Entry
(B) Class Index Entries
(C) Book Index Entries
(D) Cross Reference Index Entries

27. Which of the following is the official bi-monthly journal of *ISKO*?
(A) Knowledge Organization
(B) Knowledge and Society
(C) Journal for Knowledge Organization
(D) Knowledge, Society and Organization

28. Which of the following is the Enumerative Subject Headings?
(A) LCSH (B) SLSH
(C) Chain Procedure (D) Both (A) and (B)

29. Library of Congress Subject Headings (LCSH) originally published in
(A) 1976 (B) 1978
(C) 1980 (D) 1985

30. In CCC, which of the following notation is used for abnormal size of book in Book Number?
(A) Underline
(B) Overline
(C) Both Underline and Overline
(D) Circle

31. PRECIS Indexing System is developed by
(A) Derek Austin (B) H.P. Luhn
(C) M. Dykstra (D) Both (B) and (C)

32. What of the following sequence is true for CCC?
(A) Leading Section->Heading Section->Title Section->Note Section->Accession Section->Tracing Section
(B) Heading Section->Leading Section-> Title Section->Note Section->Accession Section->Tracing Section
(C) Heading Section->Leading Section->Note Section->Title Section->Accession Section->Tracing Section
(D) Leading Section->Heading Section->Note Section->Title Section->Accession Section->Tracing Section

33. Subject Headings for Children Materials (SHCM) is published by
(A) UNESCO (B) IFLA
(C) ALA (D) CILIP

34. The chain of POPSI is represented the Mode of
(A) Indexing Analysis
(B) Abstracting Analysis
(C) Facet Analysis
(D) Both (A) and (C)

35. The Selective Listing In Combination (SLIC) Indexing System was developed by

(A) J.P. Sharp (B) H.P. Luhn
(C) Derek Austin (D) Ralph Munn

36. How many canons are existed in cataloguing?

(A) 7 (B) 8
(C) 9 (D) 10

37. How many canons are presented by S.R. Ranganathan in Classification?

(A) 35 (B) 43
(C) 48 (D) 52

38. Which of the following is not the Canon of Cataloguing?

(A) Canon of Prepotence
(B) Canon of Sought Heading
(C) Canon of Currency
(D) Canon of Locality

39. Which of the Classification Scheme was developed by F. Rider?

(A) Expansive Classification
(B) Bibliographic Classification
(C) International Classification
(D) Subject Classification

40. A catalogue system where all the entries are arranged in a single alphabetical sequence is called

(A) Dictionary Catalogue
(B) Classified Catalogue
(C) Alphabetical Catalogue
(D) Sequence Catalogue

41. Which of the following is associated with cataloguing?

(A) H.W. Acomb
(B) Margrett Mann
(C) S.R. Ranganathan
(D) All of the above

42. Which of the following is the indexing system?

(A) COMPASS (B) SCISEARCH
(C) PRECIS (D) All of the above

43. Who says "Catalogue is a list of books which is arranged on some definite plan"?

(A) S.R. Ranganathan (B) J.D. Brown
(C) C.A. Cutter (D) W.C.B. Sayers

44. In Chain Procedure, the missing isolate in a chain is called

(A) Sought Link (SL)
(B) Unsought Link (UL)
(C) Missing Link (ML)
(D) False Link (FL)

45. In thesauri when only one term to denote a concept for indexing is called

(A) Vertical Thesauri
(B) Controlled Thesauri
(C) Context Thesauri
(D) Conventional Thesauri

46. A/an..................as ultimate unit record in a catalogue or documentation list.

(A) List (B) Entry
(C) Array (D) Index

47. In first time, who made the Cataloguing rules?

(A) C.A. Cutter (B) S.R. Ranganathan
(C) A. Pannizi (D) W.C.B. Sayers

48. In first time, who made the basic rules for Cataloguing?

(A) S.R. Ranganathan
(B) C.A. Cutter
(C) A. Pannizi
(D) J.D. Brown

49. In CC6, how many Main Classes?

(A) 40 (B) 42
(C) 44 (D) 45

50. Who says "Cataloguing is sometimes science and sometimes art"?

(A) S.R. Ranganathan
(B) Margaret Mann
(C) H.W. Acomb
(D) Seymour Lubetzky

51. In Chain Procedure, which of the following notation will create False Link (FL)?
(A) : (B) .
(C) , (D) All of the above

52. The Working Group on Functional Requirements and Numbering of Authority Records (FRANAR) was established in
(A) 1996 (B) 1999
(C) 2001 (D) 2003

53. The literally meaning of 'Modes of Formation of Subjects' is
(A) Analysis of subject
(B) Evolution of new subjects
(C) Class Number of new subjects
(D) Alphabetization of new subject

54. Which of the following is not associated with Three Planes?
(A) Idea Plane
(B) Verbal Plane
(C) Notational Plane
(D) Systematic Plane

55. Which of the following is the example of Post-Coordinate Indexing System?
(A) Uniterm Indexing System
(B) Peek-a-boo
(C) Systematic Indexing
(D) Both (A) and (B)

56. The TRAC (an information retrieval computer language) is developed by
(A) Calvin Northrup Mooers
(B) Eugene Garfield
(C) Charlotte D. Mooers
(D) John Vincent Atanasoft

57. Which of the following is true?
(A) AACR-I provided 'statement of authorship'
(B) AACR-II provides 'statement of responsibility'
(C) In RDA, there is no 'rule of three' like AACR-II
(D) All of the above

58. Which of the following was developed the MARC in 1960?
(A) Henrietta Avram (B) Charles Bachman
(C) Andrew Barto (D) Gordon Bell

59. The literally meaning of 'Epistemology' is
(A) Theory of knowledge
(B) Evolution of knowledge
(C) Processing of knowledge
(D) All of the above

60. ....was designed to replace the MARC standards
(A) BIBFRAME (B) MIBFRAME
(C) MARCFRAME (D) EMRACFRAME

61. Which of the following is the example of Search Strategy?
(A) Boolean Search (B) Keyword Search
(C) Proximity Search (D) All of the above

62. Who was the founder of American Classification System?
(A) Melvil Dewey (B) W.C.B. Sayers
(C) Margaret Mann (D) H.E. Bliss

63. In AACR-II, if place of publication is not available, we can write
(A) [s.l.] (B) [s.n.]
(C) [s.m.] (D) [n.p]

64. Which one is correct for 'third indention' in AACR-II?
(A) 9 spaces from left margin
(B) 13 spaces from left margin
(C) 15 spaces from left margin
(D) 18 spaces from left margin

65. The contraction for pseudonym in CCC is

(A) Pseud (B) Pseudo
(C) Psue (D) Psuedy

66. BIBFRAME is associated with
(A) PDF (B) RDF
(C) RTA (D) JTA

67. Which of the following was drafting the 'Dictionary Catalogue'?
(A) S.R. Ranganathan
(B) C.A. Cutter
(C) Margaret Mann
(D) W.C.B. Sayers

68. In which year MARC 21 was developed?
(A) 1997 (B) 1999
(C) 2001 (D) 2002

69. In AACR-II, the Title and the Statement of Responsibility are rendering on which section of Catalogue Card?
(A) Leading Section (B) Heading Section
(C) Note Section (D) Both (A) and (B)

70. Who introduced the term 'Bibliographic Coupling'?
(A) M.M. Kessler (B) B. Jarneving
(C) T.S. Kuhn (D) A.F.J. Van Raan

71. Match the following:

LIST-I	LIST-II
(1) Classification: Theoretical and Practical	(i) B.C. Vickery
(2) Manual for Classification for Librarians and Bibliographers	(ii) E.C.Richardson
(3) Primer of Book Classification	(iii) W.H. Phillips
(4) Classification and Indexing in Science	(iv) W.C.B. Sayers

Codes:

	(1)	(2)	(3)	(4)
(A)	(ii)	(iv)	(iii)	(i)
(B)	(iii)	(i)	(ii)	(iv)
(C)	(i)	(ii)	(iv)	(iii)
(D)	(ii)	(i)	(iii)	(iv)

72. Which of the following is true for FRBR?
(A) It is a conceptual model
(B) It is not a new cataloguing standard
(C) It is not new cataloguing rules
(D) All of the above

73. The basic structure of DDC was adapted from...........Classification System
(A) William Torrey Harris
(B) Marcel Proust
(C) David Hume
(D) Wallace Breem

74. The term "Descriptor" in Information Science was used by
(A) Calvin Mooers
(B) B. Eddison
(C) A. Thomas
(D) F.W. Lancaster

75. Match the following:

LIST-I	LIST-II
(1) Classification: Theoretical and Practice	(i) J.D. Brown
(2) Manual of Library Economy	(ii) H.W. Parker
(3) Modern Outline of Library Classification	(iii) J. Mills
(4) Library Classification	(iv) E.C.Richardson

Codes:

	(1)	(2)	(3)	(4)
(A)	(iv)	(i)	(iii)	(ii)
(B)	(i)	(iv)	(ii)	(iii)
(C)	(iv)	(ii)	(i)	(iii)
(D)	(ii)	(iv)	(iii)	(i)

76. Match the following:

LIST-I	LIST-II
(1) 7th edition of Colon Classification	(i) 1940

(2) Subject Classification (ii) 1987
(3) Bibliographic Classification (iii) 1906
(4) Library of Congress Classification (iv) 1897

Codes:

	(1)	(2)	(3)	(4)
(A)	(ii)	(i)	(iii)	(iv)
(B)	(ii)	(iii)	(i)	(iv)
(C)	(iii)	(i)	(ii)	(iv)
(D)	(iii)	(iv)	(i)	(ii)

77. Match the following:

LIST-I	LIST-II
(1) Subject Classification	(i) C.A. Cutter
(2) Bibliographic Classification	(ii) J.D. Brown
(3) Expansive Classification	(iii) H.E. Bliss
(4) Library of Congress Classification	(iv) Herbert Putnam

Codes:

	(1)	(2)	(3)	(4)
(A)	(ii)	(iii)	(i)	(iv)
(B)	(i)	(ii)	(iii)	(iv)
(C)	(i)	(iii)	(ii)	(iv)
(D)	(iv)	(ii)	(i)	(iii)

78. Match the following:

LIST-I	LIST-II
(1) Organization of Knowledge in Libraries	(i) H.E. Bliss
(2) Manual of Library Classification and Shelf Arrangement	(ii) J.D. Brown
(3) Grammar to Classification	(iii) W.C.B. Sayers
(4) Classification and Communication	(iv) S.R.Ranganathan

Codes:

	(1)	(2)	(3)	(4)
(A)	(i)	(ii)	(iii)	(iv)
(B)	(iii)	(ii)	(i)	(iv)
(C)	(i)	(iii)	(ii)	(iv)
(D)	(ii)	(i)	(iii)	(iv)

79. In which year IFLA recommended the FRBR?

(A) 1988 (B) 1990
(C) 1993 (D) 1996

80. An indexing method, where search term is determined by the indexer rather than by the Searcher called

(A) Post-Coordinate Indexing
(B) Pre-coordinate Indexing
(C) Analytical Indexing
(D) Parallel Indexing

81. Match the following:

LIST-I	LIST-II
(1) S.R. Ranganathan	(i) 1851
(2) J.D. Brown	(ii) 1870
(3) H.E. Bliss	(iii) 1862
(4) Melvil Dewey	(iv) 1892

Codes:

	(1)	(2)	(3)	(4)
(A)	(iv)	(iii)	(ii)	(i)
(B)	(iv)	(i)	(ii)	(iii)
(C)	(iv)	(ii)	(iii)	(i)
(D)	(iv)	(iii)	(i)	(ii)

82. Match the following:

LIST-I	LIST-II
(1) ALA Cataloguing Rules for Author and Title Entries (2nd edition)	(i) 1978
(2) AACR-I	(ii) 1967
(3) International Conference on Cataloguing Principles (Paris)	(iii) 1949
(4) AACR-II	(iv) 1961

Codes:

	(1)	(2)	(3)	(4)
(A)	(iii)	(ii)	(iv)	(i)
(B)	(i)	(ii)	(iv)	(iii)
(C)	(ii)	(iv)	(iii)	(i)
(D)	(iv)	(ii)	(iii)	(i)

83. In which year ISBD(G) was developed?
(A) 1977 (B) 1980
(C) 1983 (D) 1988

84. The term 'Thesaurus' in Information Retrieval (IR) is coined by
(A) Helen Brownson (B) L.M. Chan
(C) D.J. Foskett (D) D. Austin

85. Who formulated the term 'Criteria' in Library Classification?
(A) E.C. Richardson (B) H.E. Bliss
(C) W.C.B. Sayers (D) S.R. Ranganathan

86. Which of the following is the editor of ALA Cataloguing Rules for Author and Title Entries (2nd edition)?
(A) W.C.B. Sayers (B) Clara Beetle
(C) H.E. Bliss (D) J.D. Brown

87. Charles C. Jewett followed..........on his Cataloguing Rules.
(A) C.A. Cutter (B) J.D. Brown
(C) W.C.B. Sayers (D) John Dury

88. Which one is serves as a single framework for the description of all types of published media?
(A) ISBD(G) (B) ISBD(M)
(C) ISBD(A) (D) ISBD(S)

89. In which year Classification Research Group (CRG) was established in United Kingdom?
(A) 1945 (B) 1948
(C) 1952 (D) 1960

90. In Chain Procedure, which of the following link is used for Class Index Entry?
(A) False Link (B) Sought Link
(C) Unsought Link (D) Missing Link

91. Match the following:

LIST-I	LIST-II
(1) ISBD Area 1	(i) Material or type of resource specific area
(2) ISBD Area 2	(ii) Title and statement of responsibility area
(3) ISBD Area 3	(iii) Note area
(4) ISBD Area 7	(iv) Edition area

Codes:

	(1)	(2)	(3)	(4)
(A)	(iii)	(ii)	(i)	(iv)
(B)	(ii)	(iv)	(i)	(iii)
(C)	(i)	(ii)	(iii)	(iv)
(D)	(iv)	(i)	(ii)	(iii)

92. Colon Classification was first appeared in
(A) 1928 (B) 1931
(C) 1933 (D) 1935

93. In which year ALA List of Subject Headings was first published?
(A) 1892 (B) 1895
(C) 1897 (D) 1899

94. After 1 January 2007, how many digits in ISBN?
(A) 10 (B) 12
(C) 13 (D) 15

95. Each ISBN consists of................elements and each section is separated by space or hyphen.
(A) 4 (B) 5
(C) 6 (D) 8

96. How many digits in ISSN?
(A) 6 (B) 7
(C) 8 (D) 10

97. In first time who practically used the thesaurus in Information Retrieval (IR) system?
(A) H.P. Luhn (B) Helen Brownson
(C) Du Pont (D) D.J. Foskett

98. The headquarters of ISSN International Centre is located at

(A) Paris (B) Brussels
(C) Madrid (D) Athens

99. Which of the following is the National Center in India for assigning ISSN?

(A) National Science Library, New Delhi
(B) National Library, Kolkata
(C) Raja Rammohun Roy Library Foundation, Kolkata
(D) DRTC, Bengaluru

100. Who developed the FAST (Faceted Application of Subject Terminology)?

(A) OCLC (B) IFLA
(C) UNESCO (D) CILIP

101. In which plane we can assign 'Isolate Number' of a document?

(A) Idea (B) Verbal
(C) Notational (D) Any level of plane

102. Universe of Knowledge has.........number of entities.

(A) Finite (B) Infinite
(C) Knowing (D) Fixed

103. In.............S.R. Ranganathan was appointed first librarian of the University of Madras?

(A) 1922 (B) 1924
(C) 1926 (D) 1929

104. When man observed a nascent thought in his mind and yet not expressed in any form of expression is called

(A) Idea Plane (B) Verbal Plane
(C) Notational Plane (D) Any of the above

105. Universe of Knowledge is

(A) Continuum (B) Infinite
(C) Multidimensional (D) All of the above

106. The subject 'Mathematics' is the example of

(A) Compound Specific Subject
(B) Complex Specific Subject
(C) Both (A) and (B)
(D) Simple Specific Subject

107. The Step-0 is called

(A) Raw Title (B) Kernel Title
(C) Analyzed Title (D) Expressive Title

108. Which one is odd?

(A) Umbral (B) Penumbral
(C) Alien (D) Align

109. According to 'Palmer', the wholeness of any subject is

(A) Time (B) Space
(C) Energy (D) Personality

110. In CC6, Human Body of Main Class 'Medicine' is a/an

(A) Personality Facet (B) Energy Facet
(C) Matter Facet (D) Space Facet

111. In CC6, Author of Main Class 'Literature' is a/an

(A) First Level Personality [P1]
(B) Second Level Personality [P2]
(C) Third Level Personality [P3]
(D) Fourth Level Personality [P4]

112. Level does not exist in which category?

(A) Personality [P] (B) Space [S]
(C) Time [T] (D) Energy [E]

113. Which Classification Scheme was used Common Isolates in first time?

(A) Colon Classification
(B) Universal Decimal Classification
(C) Expensive Classification
(D) Dewey Decimal Classification

114. Which of the following Common Auxiliaries is not associated with UDC?

(A) Common Auxiliaries of Language
(B) Common Auxiliaries of Form

(C) Common Auxiliaries of Time
(D) Common Auxiliaries of Literature

115. In UDC, the connecting symbol for Common Auxiliaries of Language is
(A) (=...) (B) " "
(C) :: (D) =...

116. In CC6, notational symbol for bibliography is
(A) b (B) c
(C) f (D) a

117. In CC6, Personality PCI generally added after
(A) Time Facet (B) Space Facet
(C) Energy Facet (D) Matter Facet

118. In UDC, which of the following notation representing 'Asia'?
(A) 3 (B) 4
(C) 5 (D) 6

119. British Museum Code was published in?
(A) 1841 (B) 1845
(C) 1847 (D) 1856

120. According to CC6, which of the following notation represent Commonwealth Nations?
(A) 1N42 (B) 1N48
(C) 1N52 (D) 1N54

121. The American Library Association (ALA Rules) Codes for Cataloguing was published in
(A) 1945 (B) 1949
(C) 1951 (D) 1956

122. According to CC6, which of the following notation represent Hindi Speaking countries?
(A) 1(P152) (B) 1(Q152)
(C) 1(Y152) (D) 1(U152)

123. In CC6, the Public Time is represent through
(A) Roman Capital letter
(B) Roman Small letter
(C) Numerical only
(D) All of the above

124. In CC6, which of the following notation represent Ayurveda System of treatment?
(A) LM (B) LL
(C) LD (D) LB

125. Which of the following is 'Specials' according to CC6?
(A) L9C (B) C9B2
(C) E9G (D) All of the above

126. In CC6, the notation for Super Imposition Relation is
(A) & (B) :
(C) – (D) >

127. Who says "a notation is a series of symbols or shorthand signs"?
(A) W.C.B. Sayers (B) S.R. Ranganathan
(C) Margaret Mann (D) H.E. Bliss

128. The Anglo-American Code (Join-Code) for Cataloguing was published in
(A) 1906 (B) 1908
(C) 1912 (D) 1914

129. Which of the following is an empty digit in CC?
(A) 9 (B) 7
(C) 6 (D) 5

130. Which of the following connecting symbol has been used in ACI in CC6?
(A) ;
(B) :
(C) '
(D) Without any connecting symbol

131. International Federation of Classification Societies (IFCS) was founded in
(A) 1982 (B) 1985
(C) 1988 (D) 2000

132. Which of the following Medical Subject Headings is maintained by the U.S. National Library of Medicine?
(A) MeSH (B) USeH
(C) SMeH (D) NLeH

133. Which of the following digits is used in Mixed Notation System?
(A) Numbers (B) Alphabet
(C) Alphanumerical (D) All of the above

134. Which of the following is a specialized classification scheme for Law?
(A) Moys Classification Scheme
(B) NLM Classification Scheme
(C) Harvard-Yenching Classification Scheme
(D) Library of Congress Classification Scheme

135. In which year, Resource Description and Access (RDA) was released?
(A) 2002 (B) 2005
(C) 2008 (D) 2011

136. RDF stands for
(A) Resource Description Framework
(B) Resource Described Framework
(C) Resource Description Frequency
(D) Resource Description Format

137. Which of the following Subject Headings is widely used in academic library?
(A) Sears List of Subject Headings (SLSH)
(B) Library of Congress Subject Headings (LCSH)
(C) Faceted Application of Subject Terminology (FAST)
(D) MeSH Subject Headings

138. What was the profession of both Henri La Fontaine and Paul Otlet?
(A) Lawyer (B) Translator
(C) Doctor (D) Teacher

139. Which of the following is a common problem of Colon Classification Scheme?
(A) Language
(B) Not according to Universe of Knowledge
(C) Mixed notation system
(D) Lack of update

140. The word 'Concept' is derived from Latin word
(A) Conceptum (B) Concent
(C) Concrew (D) Compusion

141. The reason based knowledge was discussed in first time by
(A) Plato (B) Aristotle
(C) Aesara (D) Alexinus

142. Which logic has starts from unknown and proceeds from general to particular?
(A) Deductive Logic (B) Inductive Logic
(C) Abductive Logic (D) Defeasible Logic

143. The word 'Epistemology' is derived from the Greek words
(A) Episteme and Logos
(B) Emporeutic and Logos
(C) Empery and Logos
(D) Emotivism and Logos

144. The term 'Epistemology' was first used by the
(A) Plato (B) Aristotle
(C) J.F. Ferrier (D) Alexinus

145. Which of the following statements is false according to the fundamental principles of Universe of Knowledge?
(A) Number of known entities are finite
(B) Number of unknown entities are infinite
(C) It is not continuous like time
(D) Expanding in one direction

146. In first time, the mapping of Universe of Knowledge in scientific order was crystallized by
(A) S.R. Ranganathan (B) E.C. Richardson
(C) Melvil Dewey (D) H.E. Bliss

147. Among these, which of the following Main Class of CC6 is most abstract?
(A) Chemistry (B) Biology
(C) Physics (D) Mathematics

148. Which of the following is correct order of decreasing concreteness?
(A) PMEST (B) PEMST
(C) TSEMP (D) EMPST

149. Wall-Picture Principle is associate with
(A) Principle of Facet Sequence
(B) Principle of Decreasing Extension
(C) Principle of Consistent Sequence
(D) Principle of Alphabetical Sequence

150. Which of the following Classification Schemes was developed as individual Classes by different group of specialists?
(A) Subject Classification
(B) Expansive Classification
(C) Bibliographic Classification
(D) Library of Congress Classification

151. Which of the following was associated with development of Library of Congress Classification Scheme?
(A) J.C.M. Hanson (B) Charles Martel
(C) W.T. Harris (D) Both (A) and (B)

152. Which of the following Classification Schemes is used only English alphabets for Main Classes notation?
(A) Expansive Classification
(B) Subject Classification
(C) Bibliographic Classification
(D) All of the above

153. Rider's International Classification Scheme is developed by
(A) Fremont A. Rider
(B) Douglas H. Rider
(C) Dan M. Rider
(D) Rosenfeld M. Rider

154. Which of the following is false?
(A) The main context of Universe of Knowledge is Knowledge Classification
(B) Book Classification is based on any System
(C) Knowledge Classification can be renowned through personal theories
(D) Knowledge Classification is a single dimension

155. The book titled *The Manual of Library Classification and Shelf Arrangement* was written by
(A) J.D. Brown (B) H.W. Parker
(C) W.I. Fletcher (D) S.R. Ranganathan

156. In Universe of Knowledge, 'Subjects of study' is a/an
(A) Finite Universe (B) Infinite Universe
(C) Fixed Universe (D) Both (A) and (C)

157. Which of the following is the Canonical Class of Main Class Physics in CC6?
(A) Light (B) Magnetism
(C) Heat (D) All of the above

158. In CC6, which of the following is a/an example of 'Systems'?
(A) Homeopathy Treatment
(B) Child Medicine
(C) Dry Farming
(D) Large Scale Industry

159. In CC6, Child Psychology is a/an
(A) Basic Subject
(B) Compound Subject
(C) Complex Subject
(D) Combined Subject

160. In CC6, 'Comparative Study of Indian and American Constitutions' is the example of
(A) Basic Subject
(B) Compound Subject
(C) Combined Subject
(D) Complex Subject

161. Who says "classification is the arranging of things according to likeness and unlikeness..."?
(A) Margaret Mann (B) J.D. Brown
(C) H.W. Parker (D) S.R. Ranganathan

162. Language that represents specific subject or thought in a classification scheme is called
(A) Natural Language
(B) Artificial Language

(C) Intelligent Language
(D) Knowledge Language

163. The father of modern library classification is
(A) S.R. Ranganathan
(B) Melvil Dewey
(C) J.D. Brown
(D) H.E. Bliss

164. How many parts are exist in Call Number?
(A) Two (B) Three
(C) Four (D) Five

165. Among Five Laws of Library Science, which law advocates the classification of documents?
(A) First Law (B) Second Law
(C) Fourth Law (D) All Five Laws

166. Guinn-Brown Scheme was developed in
(A) 1894 (B) 1896
(C) 1898 (D) 1910

167. Which of the following is not belongs to the Postulation Approach?
(A) Idea plane (B) Verbal plane
(C) System plane (D) Notational plane

168. August Comte's Philosophy of Mode of Thinking is based on
(A) Speculative Mode of Thinking
(B) Positivistic Mode of Thinking
(C) Tenacious Mode of Thinking
(D) Authority Mode of Thinking

169. A systematized body of ideas is called
(A) Knowledge (B) Subject
(C) Universe (D) Entity

170. Relay Research means
(A) Fresh but continuous from previous thought
(B) Fresh and without continuous from previous thought
(C) Research will be continue without discussing of new problem
(D) New problem never discussing in this research

171. Which of the following plane is determining the subjects' formation and their representation in Library Classification scheme?
(A) Idea plane (B) Verbal plane
(C) Notational plane (D) Intellectual plane

172. Which of the following is false in Attributes of Universe of Subjects?
(A) Dynamic Continuum
(B) Finiteness
(C) Grafting
(D) Proliferation

173. A subject is a/an.......................body of knowledge
(A) Organized (B) Unorganized
(C) Unstructured (D) Both (A) and (B)

174. Relay Research is like a
(A) Spiral movement
(B) Linear movement
(C) Vertical movement
(D) Horizontal movement

175. Which of the following edition of Colon Classification Scheme is the Analytico-Synthetic Scheme?
(A) 1st (B) 6th
(C) 7th (D) All editions of CC

176. Who founded the UDCC (UDC Consortium)?
(A) FID (B) IFLA
(C) LOC (D) UNESCO

177. Which of the following statements is true in context of CCC?
(A) Classified part is the notation entry part
(B) Book Number is entered on the Leading Line
(C) Both classified and alphabetical cataloguing are possible
(D) All of the above

178. Since.........., the ownership of UDC is transfer from FID to UDCC.
(A) 1 January 1992 (B) 12 April 1994
(C) 20 May 1995 (D) 1 January 1996

179. In which year, the Main Class 4 was cancelled from UDC Scheme?
(A) 1960 (B) 1963
(C) 1967 (D) 1971

180. In which year Classification Research Group (CRG) issued a manifesto, "The need for a faceted classification as the basis for all methods of information retrieval"?
(A) 1948 (B) 1950
(C) 1953 (D) 1955

181. In 1905, the first international edition of UDC was published in which language?
(A) English (B) Spanish
(C) French (D) German

182. Which edition of DDC was the origin of UDC?
(A) 4th (B) 5th
(C) 6th (D) 7th

183. Which of the following version of Colon Classification is considered as Freely Faceted Scheme?
(A) Version 1 (B) Version 2
(C) Version 3 (D) Both (A) and (B)

184. The first edition of UDC was published under the title of
(A) Handbook to the Universal Bibliographic Repertory
(B) Manual of Universal Classification System
(C) Handbook to the Universal Decimal Classification
(D) Manual of Universal Bibliographic Repertory

185. At present, the maintainer agency of UDC is
(A) FID (B) UDCC
(C) LOC (D) IFLA

186. Which of the following is the first complete version of Analytico-Synthetic Classification Scheme?
(A) CC (B) DDC
(C) UDC (D) LOC

187. According to S.R. Ranganathan, which of the plane is paramount?
(A) Idea Plane (B) Verbal Plane
(C) Notational Plane (D) All of the above

188. According to AACR-II, which of the following is/are corporate body?
(A) Business firms (B) Associations
(C) Governments (D) All of the above

189. In which year emptying digit was postulated by S.R. Ranganathan?
(A) 1958 (B) 1960
(C) 1963 (D) 1965

190. According to AACR-II, which of the following is correct form of Heading?
(A) India. Department of Social Welfare
(B) India. Parliament. Lok Sabha
(C) India. Lok Sabha
(D) Both (A) and (B)

191. The nature of Universe of Subject is a/an
(A) Static (B) Dynamic
(C) Systematic (D) Linear

192. Who enunciated the library classification theory in first time?
(A) E.C. Richardson
(B) J.D. Brown
(C) S.R. Ranganathan
(D) E. Wyndham Hulme

193. Who referred to as the first grammarian of library classification?
(A) J.D. Brown (B) E.C. Richardson
(C) W.C.B. Sayers (D) S.R. Ranganathan

194. According to CCC, which of the following is correct form of Heading?

(A) INDIA, FINANCE (Ministry of-)
(B) INDIA, Finance (Ministry of-)
(C) India, Finance (Ministry of-)
(D) India, Finance (MINISTRY OF-)

195. The first edition of Prolegomena to Library Classification was published in
(A) 1934 (B) 1937
(C) 1940 (D) 1941

196. According to CCC, which one is true, if source of real name of authors is getting outside of book?
(A) Single Thought, Psued, (i.e. Mukesh Kumar and Rahim Alam)
(B) Single Thought, Psued, [i.e. Mukesh Kumar and Rahim Alam]
(C) SINGLE THOUGHT, Psued, [i.e. Mukesh Kumar and Rahim Alam]
(D) SINGLE THOUGHT, Psued, (i.e. Mukesh Kumar and Rahim Alam)

197. Which of the following is paramount?
(A) Laws of Library Science
(B) Canons
(C) Principles
(D) Postulates

198. From which edition of Colon Classification, the number 9 has been used as an empty or sectorizing digit?
(A) First edition (B) Second edition
(C) Third edition (D) Sixth edition

199. In which year S.R. Ranganathan decided that two distinctive symbols for Space and Time Isolates?
(A) 1952 (B) 1954
(C) 1963 (D) 1969

200. In CC6, the notations for Posteriorising Common Isolates is/are
(A) Roman capital letters
(B) Roman small letters
(C) Indo-Arabic numerals
(D) Both (B) and (C)

201. Which of the following digit represents as mother country for Space Isolate in CC?
(A) 2 (B) 3
(C) 5 (D) 6

202. In Colon Classification, notation for favoured language is
(A) = (B) ---
(C) + (D) *

203. Which of the following is not exists in context of basic laws of library science?
(A) Law of Impartiality
(B) Laws of Symmetry
(C) Laws of Osmosis
(D) Laws of Capacity

204. Which of the following canon is not favoured by S.R. Ranganathan?
(A) Canon of relatively
(B) Canon of hierarchy
(C) Canon of non-hierarchy
(D) Canon of mixed notation

205. Which of the following library classification scheme theoretically follow the Principle of Later-in-Evolution?
(A) CC (B) DDC
(C) UDC (D) All of the above

206. In Main Class 'Library Science', category of libraries under Personality[P] Isolate are arranged according to the
(A) Decreasing Quantitative Sequence
(B) Increasing Quantitative Sequence
(C) Mixed Quantitative Sequence
(D) Both (B) and (C)

207. The term 'literary warrant' is coined by
(A) S.R. Ranganathan
(B) B.S. Wynar
(C) E.C. Richardson
(D) E. Wyndham Hulme

208. Which of the following canon is/are formulated by S.R. Ranganathan for working at Verbal Plane?
(A) Canon of Context
(B) Canon of Enumerative
(C) Canon of Currency
(D) All of the above

209. In UDC, which of the following notation is representing 'India'?
(A) 540 (B) (540)
(C) (94) (D) 530

210. Which of the following is an ordinal value, but not semantic value in CC6?
(A) 9 (B) 91
(C) ZA (D) ZZA

211. Which of the following will increase the capacity of an array?
(A) Faceted Notation
(B) Non-Faceted Notation
(C) Retroactive Notation
(D) Sector Notation

212. Match the following:

LIST-I	LIST-II
(1) Zoology	(i) 512
(2) Diseases	(ii) 616
(3) Algebra	(iii) 590
(4) Biochemistry	(iv) 572

Codes:

	(1)	(2)	(3)	(4)
(A)	(ii)	(iii)	(i)	(iv)
(B)	(ii)	(iv)	(iii)	(i)
(C)	(iii)	(ii)	(i)	(iv)
(D)	(iii)	(i)	(ii)	(iv)

213. The total capacity of an array of Indo-Arabic numerals, Roman capital and Roman small letters in CC6 are
(A) 47 (B) 56
(C) 67 (D) 77

214. In which year S.R. Ranganathan formulated the Wall-Picture Principle?
(A) 1956 (B) 1958
(C) 1962 (D) 1965

215. The notation for Agglomeration Device is
(A) Asterisk (*) (B) Plus (+)
(C) Both (A) and (B) (D) Only (B)

216. In UDC, the works of specific authors in Main Class 'Literature' are arranged through
(A) Alphabetical Device
(B) Classic Device
(C) Numerical Device
(D) Chronological Device

217. In which year, the Madras Library Association started an annual titled 'Memoirs'?
(A) 1935 (B) 1939
(C) 1941 (D) 1943

218. Which of the following notation is used for making of Environment Compound Basic Subject?
(A) Hyphen (-) (B) Plus (+)
(C) Asterisk (*) (D) Division (/)

219. Which of the following fundamental category is self-explanatory?
(A) Personality [P] (B) Space [S]
(C) Time [T] (D) Both (B) and (C)

220. 'Method of Residues' is used for manifestation of
(A) Personality [P] (B) Matter [M]
(C) Energy [E] (D) Space [S]

221. The abridge edition BS 1000A of UDC was first published in
(A) 1943 (B) 1945
(C) 1948 (D) 1952

222. Which of the following is the definitive and authorized version of the UDC?
(A) UDCMRF (B) UDCMYDATA
(C) UDCDATA (D) UDCCONSORTIA

223. In which of the following isolate, there is no possibility of levels?
(A) Personality (B) Matter
(C) Energy (D) Space

224. Which of the following Relational Database Management System is supported by UDCMRF?
(A) mySQL (B) MS SQL 2005
(C) Oracle 10g (D) DB2

225. In which year Melvil Dewey introduced the principle of division by transfer in literature, history and philosophy?
(A) 1874 (B) 1876
(C) 1888 (D) 1891

226. From which edition of *Colon Classification*, inverted comma used as an indicator digit for Time facet?
(A) 3rd edition (B) 4th edition
(C) 5th edition (D) 6th edition

227. Which of the following fundamental category is mandatory for making any Class Number in Colon Classification?
(A) Personality (B) Matter
(C) Energy (D) Time

228. The first International Medium Edition (IME) of UDC was published in
(A) 1984 (B) 1987
(C) 1989 (D) 1991

229. The Second International Medium Edition (IME) of UDC was published in
(A) 1991 (B) 1993
(C) 1995 (D) 1999

230. Who says "Bibliographical control is a form of power,............knowledge recorded in written form".
(A) Patrick Wilson (B) Charles Jewett
(C) James Wilson (D) Albert Blor

231. In UDC, the Main Class 4 is merged into which Main Class?
(A) 3 Social Service (B) 7 Arts
(C) 8 Language (D) Geography

232. The frequency of International conference of ISKO is?
(A) Every year
(B) Every two years
(C) Every two and half years
(D) Every three years

233. The 14th International ISKO conference will be held in
(A) 2016, Brazil (B) 2017, Italy
(C) 2018, Germany (D) 2019, Poland

234. Match the following:

	LIST-I		LIST-II
(1)	10th International ISKO conference	(i)	Canada
(2)	11th International ISKO conference	(ii)	Italy
(3)	12th International ISKO conference	(iii)	India
(4)	13th International ISKO conference	(iv)	Poland

Codes:

	(1)	(2)	(3)	(4)
(A)	(i)	(ii)	(iii)	(iv)
(B)	(ii)	(iii)	(i)	(iv)
(C)	(iv)	(i)	(ii)	(iii)
(D)	(iii)	(ii)	(i)	(iv)

235. The first International ISKO conference was held in
(A) Germany, 1990 (B) Italy, 1992
(C) Denmark, 1994 (D) Austria, 1994

236. How many times India hosted the ISKO International conference?
(A) Only one (B) Two times
(C) Three times (D) Never

237. According to CC6, which one is a Personality facet in Main Class Biology?

(A) Tissue (B) Morphology
(C) Metabolism (D) Microscopy

238. The indicator digit for Space Isolate in UDC is

(A) * (B) ()
(C) [ ] (D) { }

239. Which of the following library classification scheme is the founder of modern library classification?

(A) Dewey Decimal Classification
(B) Colon Classification
(C) Subject Classification
(D) Bibliographic Classification

240. Which of the following is the example of Freely Faceted Classification scheme?

(A) Colon Classification Ed 3
(B) Bibliographic Classification Ed 1
(C) Bibliographic Classification Ed 2
(D) Subject Classification

241. Which of the following are the hosted cities of ISKO International Conference in India?

(A) Chennai and Mysore
(B) New Delhi and Mysore
(C) Hyderabad and Kolkata
(D) Mumbai and Kolkata

242. The UNISIST (United Nations International Scientific Information System) programme was started in

(A) 1967 (B) 1971
(C) 1973 (D) 1976

243. Which of following years India hosted International ISKO Conference?

(A) 1992 and 2012 (B) 1994 and 2012
(C) 1992 and 2010 (D) 1992 and 2008

244. The indicator digit for Phase Relation in UDC is

(A) : (B) { }
(C) [ ] (D) &

245. Which of the following was the first President of ISKO?

(A) Ingetraut Dahlberg
(B) Ama Bontemps
(C) Audre Lorde
(D) Margaret A. Edwards

246. Which of the following year and place, Library Research Group (LRC) was founded by S.R. Ranganathan?

(A) 1951, Delhi (B) 1952, Chennai
(C) 1951, Kolkata (D) 1950, Bangalore

247. In CC6, the indicator digit of Intra-Facet Phase Relation for Comparison is

(A) b (B) m
(C) p (D) w

248. Among these, who was the teacher of S.R. Ranganathan?

(A) E.C. Richardson (B) J.D. Brown
(C) E.W. Hulme (D) W.C.B. Sayers

249. The article titled "Organization of Knowledge and the System of Science" was written by

(A) E.C. Richardson
(B) W.C.B. Sayers
(C) H.E. Bliss
(D) S.R. Ranganathan

250. Which of the following development stage of General Theory of Library Classification regarded as Dynamic Theory of Library Classification?

(A) Stage 1 (B) Stage 2
(C) Stage 3 (D) Stage 4

251. In UDC, Common Isolates are known as

(A) System (B) Canonical
(C) Auxiliaries (D) Methods

252. The connecting symbol for Time Isolate in UDC is

(A) Single inverted comma
(B) Double inverted comma

(C) Two double inverted comma
(D) Plus sign

253. At present, the maintainer agency of DDC is
(A) OCLC (B) DeweyConsortia
(C) LOC (D) ALA

254. Which of the following is the root expression of word 'catalogue'?
(A) Ketalogos (B) Katalogos
(C) Kotalogos (D) Kitalogos

255. The 15th abridge edition of *DDC* was published in
(A) 2008 (B) 2010
(C) 2012 (D) 2014

256. The meaning of 'Intra' is/are
(A) Within (B) Without
(C) Excluding (D) Both (A) and (B)

257. In *DDC* 23rd edition, the Ethnic and National Groups is enumerated under the
(A) Table 3rd (B) Table 4th
(C) Table 5th (D) Table 6th

258. Which of the following is a Compound Subject?
(A) Chemistry (B) Psychology
(C) Lung diseases (D) Economics

259. There are.......volumes in 23rd edition of DDC.
(A) 2 (B) 3
(C) 4 (D) 5

260. The first librarianship school in Columbia University was founded by Melvil Dewey in.......
(A) 1887 (B) 1889
(C) 1892 (D) 1894

261. In 23rd edition of *DDC*, the Relative Index is enumerated in
(A) Volume 1 (B) Volume 2
(C) Volume 3 (D) Volume 4

262. In which year, first abridge edition of *DDC* was published?
(A) 1895 (B) 1915
(C) 1926 (D) 1929

263. Which of the following notations is not used in Common Auxiliaries in UDC?
(A) : (Colon) (B) * (Asterisk)
(C) ; (Semicolon) (D) A/Z (Alphabet)

264. The notation for Special Auxiliaries in UDC is/are
(A) .0 (Point naught) (B) '(Apostrophe)
(C) - (Hyphen) (D) All of the above

265. Which of the following Tables is not enumerated in 22nd edition of *DDC*?
(A) Table 4 (B) Table 5
(C) Table 6 (D) Table 7

266. In 23rd edition of *DDC*, the organization of knowledge from 000 to 599 is enumerated which of the following volume?
(A) Volume 1 (B) Volume 2
(C) Volume 3 (D) Volume 4

267. In 23rd edition of *DDC*, the organization of knowledge from 600 to 999 is enumerated which of the following volume?
(A) Volume 1 (B) Volume 2
(C) Volume 3 (D) Volume 4

268. The online version of *DDC* is now available under
(A) WebDewey (B) OnlineDewey
(C) DDCOnline (D) DeweyOnline

269. The Class Number of 'Data Processing in Computer Science' in DDC is?
(A) 002 (B) 003
(C) 004 (D) 010

270. The Citation Order of UDC is
(A) Class Number + Special Auxiliaries + Common Auxiliaries
(B) Class Number + Common Auxiliaries + Special Auxiliaries

(C) Common Auxiliaries + Class Number + Special Auxiliaries
(D) Special Auxiliaries + Class Number + Common Auxiliaries

271. 'Anesthesiology' is obtained from which of the following subject formation?
(A) Distillation (B) Fusion
(C) Fission (D) Both (B) and (C)

272. Which of the following notations has been used as Facet Indicator in Standard Subdivision of DDC?
(A) 0 (B) [
(C) {} (D) +

273. BSO stands for
(A) Broad System of Ordering
(B) Basic System of Ordering
(C) Bilingual System of Ordering
(D) Broad System of Ontology

274. Library of Congress Classification was invented by
(A) Herbert Putnam (B) H.E. Bliss
(C) J.D. Brown (D) W.C.B. Sayers

275. Which of the following is the Class Number for 'Metaphysics' in DDC?
(A) 100 (B) 120
(C) 130 (D) 110

276. Which of the following is the Common Isolates in UDC?
(A) Common and Special Auxiliaries
(B) Common and System Auxiliaries
(C) System and Special Auxiliaries
(D) Common and Form Auxiliaries

277. From which edition of DDC, Common Isolates know as Standard Subdivisions?
(A) 15th (B) 17th
(C) 18th (D) 20th

278. In DDC, which of the following Tables is used for Space Isolate?
(A) Table 2 (B) Table 3
(C) Table 4 (D) Table 5

279. Which one of the following is not belongs to Basic Laws for library classification?
(A) Law of Interpretation
(B) Law of Osmosis
(C) Law of Symmetric
(D) Law of Meaningfulness

280. Which of the following is the example of Compound Subject?
(A) History
(B) Psychology
(C) Psychology of child
(D) Physics

281. The subject 'Astrophysics' is the example of
(A) Distillation (B) Fission
(C) Fusion (D) Cluster

282. What was the term for 'Agglomeration' used by S.R. Ranganathan in earlier?
(A) Partial Comprehension
(B) Full Comprehension
(C) Dynamic Comprehension
(D) Subject Bundle

283. Dichotomy means division into
(A) One (B) Two
(C) Ten (D) More than ten

284. In which year Sears List of Subject Headings was first appeared?
(A) 1921 (B) 1923
(C) 1925 (D) 1931

285. Who compiled famous 91 Rules for Library Catalogue?
(A) Anthony Panizzi (B) Donald J. Lehnus
(C) C.A. Cutter (D) S.R. Ranganathan

286. In which year Charles Cutter's Rules for Printed Dictionary Catalogue was published?
(A) 1869 (B) 1872
(C) 1876 (D) 1879

287. In ISBD, there are....areas of bibliographic description

(A) 7 (B) 8
(C) 9 (D) 12

288. Which of the following are associated with *AACR-II*?

(A) Michael Gorman and Paul Walter Winkler
(B) Michael Gorman and John Adamaris
(C) Charlie Winkler and Daniel Paul
(D) Alexander Paul and William Alfie

289. In which year *AACR-II* (Revised) edition was published?

(A) 1978 (B) 1988
(C) 1990 (D) 1991

290. Which of the following is the publisher of *AACR-II*?

(A) American Library Association
(B) Canadian Library Association
(C) Chartered Institute of Library and Information Professionals (UK)
(D) All of the above

291. Which of the following is considered to be the first major cataloguing code?

(A) Rules for the Compilation of the Catalogue by Anthony Panizzi
(B) Rules for a Printed Dictionary Catalogue by C.A. Cutter
(C) Anglo-American Cataloguing Rules–I
(D) Classified Catalogue Code by S.R. Ranganathan

292. In which year, Resource Description and Access (RDA) was released?

(A) May 2008 (B) June 2008
(C) June 2010 (D) April 2012

293. Which of the following statements is true?

(A) In cataloguing, S.R. Ranganathan used the word 'book' not 'work'
(B) Seymour Lubetzky inspired the 'work' not 'book'
(C) Cutter's Rules for Cataloguing became the basic rules for the Dictionary Catalogue
(D) All of the above

294. In which year FRBR metadata model for information object recommended by IFLA?

(A) 1996 (B) 1998
(C) 2001 (D) 2005

295. Which of the following is now successor of AACR-II?

(A) RDA (B) FRBR
(C) DOI (D) RFID

296. Which of the following keyword is used for Author (in AACR-II) in RDA?

(A) Creator (B) Interior
(C) Philosopher (D) Compiler

297. Which of the following cataloguing works are compiled by publisher itself?

(A) Cataloguing-In-Publishing (CIP)
(B) Prenatal Cataloguing
(C) Commercial Cataloguing
(D) Both (A) and (B)

298. Common Communication Format (CCF) is developed by

(A) UNESCO (B) IFLA
(C) LOC (D) CILIP

299. In CCC, which of the following is the authentic source for Main Entry?

(A) Title page
(B) Overflow pages
(C) Anywhere in the book
(D) Both (A) and (B)

300. In which year S.R. Ranganathan enunciated Canon of Recall Value?

(A) 1964 (B) 1966
(C) 1969 (D) 1971

301. Which of the following cannons suggests that bibliographic information should be collected from the title page of book?

(A) Canon of Ascertainability
(B) Canon of Individualization
(C) Canon of Contests
(D) Canon of Consistency

302. The first edition of *Common Communication Format* (CCF) was published in
(A) 1982 (B) 1984
(C) 1987 (D) 1989

303. The..........in CCF is a table, containing a variable number of fourteen-characters entries.
(A) Directory (B) File
(C) Node (D) Workplace

304. Which of the following is true?
(A) FRBR is based on Entity-Relationship model
(B) AACR-II is the single flat record concept
(C) Sears List of Subject Headings is the example of enumerative lists
(D) All of the above

305. The first edition of Classified Catalogue Code with Additional Rules for Dictionary Catalogue Code was appeared in
(A) 1931 (B) 1934
(C) 1936 (D) 1938

306. Which of the following is the corporate author?
(A) An organization
(B) A government body
(C) An association
(D) All of the above

307. In CCF, the Directory Entry is divided into five parts, which of the following is the first part?
(A) Segment Identifier
(B) Occurrence Identifier
(C) Length of Datafield
(D) Tag

308. Which of the following MARC Tag is locally-defined-fields?
(A) 1XX (B) 5XX
(C) 7XX (D) 9XX

309. Who maintain the standard of Z39.50 protocol?
(A) IFLA (B) CILIP
(C) LOC (D) UNESCO

310. How many sections in Main Entry in CCC?
(A) 4 (B) 5
(C) 6 (D) 7

311. In which chapter of CCC, the rules for rendering of Series Entry are discussed?
(A) JA6 (B) JF5
(C) JC (D) FH

312. Match the following:

LIST-I	LIST-II
(1) Pseudonymous Works	(i) PF4
(2) Corporate Authorship	(ii) FF31
(3) Composite Works	(iii) FC6
(4) Multivolume Book	(iv) FC32

Codes:

	(1)	(2)	(3)	(4)
(A)	(iv)	(ii)	(iii)	(i)
(B)	(iii)	(iv)	(i)	(ii)
(C)	(i)	(iii)	(ii)	(iv)
(D)	(iv)	(ii)	(i)	(iii)

313. In *AACR-II*, cataloguing of non-book materials such as Braille, Microfilm, Motion pictures, etc. are described under
(A) General Material Designation (GMD)
(B) Non-Book Materials (NBM)
(C) E-book Materials (EBM)
(D) E-Documents Materials (EDM)

314. BIBFRAME (Bibliographic Framework) is a data model for bibliographic description, developed by
(A) LOC (B) UNESCO
(C) IFLA (D) CILIP

315. Which of the following schema is the XML based metadata bibliographic description?

(A) MODS (B) XOBIS
(C) METS (D) All of the above

316. The Filing Rules of CCC is based on
(A) Class Number (B) Book Number
(C) Both (A) and (B) (D) Only (A)

317. In CCC, the rules for Filing of Entries in Classified Part are discussed in.....chapter.
(A) EG (B) EH
(C) FC32 (D) PF4

318. Which of the following is the Subject Headings tool?
(A) Library of Congress List of Subject Headings
(B) Canadian Subject Headings
(C) Chain Procedure
(D) All of the above

319. What is the length of Occurrence Identifier in CCF directory?
(A) 1 character
(B) 3 characters
(C) 5 characters
(D) More than 5 characters

320. In CCC, in which section we have entered Main Entry?
(A) Leading Section (B) Heading Section
(C) Title Section (D) Notes Section

321. In CCC, in which section we have entered Cross Reference Entries?
(A) Leading Section (B) Heading Section
(C) Notes Section (D) Title Section

322. In CCC, in which section we have entered Book Index Entries?
(A) Leading Section (B) Heading Section
(C) Title Section (D) Notes Section

323. The Canadian Subject Headings (CSH) is a list of subject headings in the.....
(A) Medical Science
(B) Library & Information Science
(C) English Language
(D) Astrophysics

324. In cataloguing, which of the following 'level' is provide minimum bibliographic information for Main Entry?
(A) First level (B) Second level
(C) Third level (D) None of the above

325. The physical description about a document in cataloguing is called
(A) Collation (B) Copy Right
(C) Author Name (D) Collaborator Name

326. In *AACR-II*, which of the following indention has been used for rendering of Title Proper?
(A) First indention (B) Second indention
(C) Third indention (D) None of the above

327. Which of the following is correct order for description in *AACR-II*?
(A) Full stop, space, dash and space
(B) Dash, space, full stop and space
(C) Space, dash, full stop and space
(D) Space, full stop, space and dash

328. Which of the following entry is the Classified Part of CCC?
(A) Main Entry
(B) Cross Reference Entries
(C) Class Index Entries
(D) Both (A) and (B)

329. Which of the following entry is the Alphabetical Part of CCC?
(A) Class Index Entries
(B) Book Index Entries
(C) Cross Reference Index Entries
(D) All of the above

330. Any additional useful information about the document is entered in
(A) Heading Section (B) Tracing Section
(C) Note Section (D) Leading Section

331. In Dictionary Catalogue, the Tracing Section in Main Entry is placed in
(A) First paragraph
(B) Second paragraph
(C) Last paragraph
(D) Any place in Main Entry

332. In *AACR-II*, which of the following is the punctuation for GMD?
(A) () (B) [ ]
(C) { } (D) < >

333. In *AACR-II*, how many spaces in third imaginary indention in Main Entry?
(A) 12 (B) 14
(C) 16 (D) 18

334. Which of the following chapter of CCC is describing the rules for rendering of Main Entry?
(A) MB (B) FQ
(C) FC (D) FD

335. Pseudonym-Real Name Entry is the example of
(A) Book Index Entry
(B) Cross Reference Entry
(C) Cross Reference Index Entry
(D) Class Index Entry

336. In *AACR-II*, GMD stands for
(A) General Material Designation
(B) General Matter Designation
(C) General Material Description
(D) Group of Material Description

337. In *AACR-II*, which of the following punctuation is used for Parallel Title?
(A) = (B) +
(C) [ ] (D) { }

338. Which of the following term is used by S.R. Ranganathan for Cataloguing-in-Publication (CIP)?
(A) Pre-Natal Cataloguing
(B) Prewritten Cataloguing
(C) Cataloguing Before Publishing (CBP)
(D) PreBook Cataloguing

339. In which year UNIMARC Bibliographic format was proposed by IFLA?
(A) 1975 (B) 1977
(C) 1979 (D) 1982

340. In CCC, the Call Number is written........ vertical on the Leading line.
(A) From the First
(B) From the Second
(C) From the Third
(D) From Second to First

341. Which of the following is the Subject Entry in CCC?
(A) Main Entry
(B) Class Index Entry
(C) Cross Reference Entries
(D) All of the above

342. Which of the following entry we can create through Chain Procedure?
(A) Cross Reference Entries
(B) Book Index Entries
(C) Class Index Entries
(D) Both (A) and (B)

343. In 1969, which of the following place hosted the International Meeting of Cataloguing Experts (IMCE)?
(A) Copenhagen (B) Paris
(C) Milan (D) New York

344. Which Boolean Operator excluded the term(s) from our search string?
(A) AND (B) OR
(C) NOT (D) NOR

345. AACR-II code consists............of description.
(A) First Level (B) Second Level
(C) Third Level (D) Fourth Level

346. In which level of description in *AACR-II*, we can render Parallel Title?
(A) First Level (B) Second Level
(C) Third Level (D) Any Level

347. How many description areas of Main Entry in *AACR-II* (revised ed.)?
(A) 6 (B) 7
(C) 8 (D) 10

348. Which of the following is associated with 'All-The-Book-Plan Card Services' in 1953?
(A) Library of Congress
(B) UNESCO
(C) American Library Association
(D) Boston Public Library

349. The Library of Congress National Program for Acquisitions and Cataloguing (NPAC) has been operate since
(A) 1963 (B) 1966
(C) 1972 (D) 1975

350. Pre-Natal-Cataloguing is associated with
(A) S.R. Ranganathan (B) LOC
(C) C.C. Jewett (D) IFLA

351. Which of the following is associated with Library of Congress?
(A) Cataloguing-In-Source
(B) Cataloguing-In-Publication
(C) Pre-Natal Cataloguing
(D) Both (A) and (B)

352. Which of the following is true?
(A) In Dictionary Catalogue, entries are arranged according to the Class Number
(B) In Dictionary Catalogue, subjects are entered their Class Number
(C) No APUPA pattern is possible according to the given schedule in Dictionary catalogue
(D) All of the above

353. In which year American National Union Catalogue Pre-1956 Imprints (NUC) was completed?
(A) 1956 (B) 1978
(C) 1981 (D) 1985

354. Which of the following is the largest electronic Union Catalogue database?
(A) WorldCat (B) Copac
(C) Amicus (D) OAIster

355. In Classified Catalogue Code (CCC), Cross Reference Index Entries is the part of
(A) Classified Part
(B) Alphabetical Part
(C) Universal Part
(D) Book Part

356. 'Dictionary of Mathematics', here 'dictionary' in CC is a/an
(A) Standard Isolate
(B) Special Isolate
(C) Common Isolate
(D) None of the above

357. What will be the Main Class of title 'Prevention of Social Evils' in CC6?
(A) S (B) Y
(C) T (D) U

358. Match the following:

LIST-I	LIST-II
(1) WorldCat	(i) University of Michigan, USA
(2) Copac	(ii) Library and Archives, Canada
(3) Amicus	(iii) Research Libraries, UK
(4) OAIster	(iv) OCLC, USA

Codes:

	(1)	(2)	(3)	(4)
(A)	(iv)	(iii)	(ii)	(i)
(B)	(iv)	(i)	(ii)	(iii)
(C)	(iv)	(ii)	(i)	(iii)
(D)	(iv)	(iii)	(i)	(ii)

359. Which of the following is true for Centralized Cataloguing?

(A) Cost of cataloguing can be minimized
(B) Duplication of work can be maximized
(C) Catalogue Codes may be varied
(D) Both (A) and (B)

360. Which of the following is the ultimate Macro Subject?
(A) Physics (B) History
(C) History of India (D) Both (A) and (B)

361. With the help of............a catalogue card will informed equivalent terms or information related to the users desired documents.
(A) Book Index Entries
(B) Class Index Entries
(C) Cross Reference Index Entries
(D) Cross Reference Entries

362. Which of the following notation is used for Intra-Facet Phase Relation?
(A) j (B) m
(C) r (D) All of the above

363. Which of the following Library Classification Scheme is associated with UNIMARC?
(A) UDC (B) DDC
(C) LCC (D) All of the above

364. Which of the following is the editor of 23rd edition of DDC?
(A) Benjamin A. Custer
(B) John P. Comaromi
(C) John S. Mitchell
(D) Winter E. Mathews

365. Which of the following DDC edition was published under John S. Mitchell editorship?
(A) 21st (B) 22nd
(C) 23rd (D) All of the above

366. The 23rd edition of DDC was published in
(A) 2004 (B) 2009
(C) 2011 (D) 2013

367. In which year 'Dewey for Windows' was developed by OCLC Forest Press?
(A) 1994 (B) 1996
(C) 1998 (D) 2000

368. The online version of DDC (Web Dewey) has been available from......edition.
(A) 20th (B) 21st
(C) 22nd (D) 23rd

369. Which of the following is the first book written by S.R. Ranganathan?
(A) *Philosophy of Library Classification*
(B) *Prolegomena to Library Classification*
(C) *Five Laws of Library Classification*
(D) *Classification and Communication*

370. Which of the following device will increase the capacity of an array with the aid of an empty digit?
(A) Classical Device
(B) Chronological Device
(C) Sector Device
(D) Enumeration Device

371. *A Dictionary of Documentation Terms* was written by
(A) Frank S. Wagner
(B) W.C.B Sayers
(C) J.D. Brown
(D) S.R. Ranganathan

372. Which of the following is a scholarly society devoted to the theory and practice of knowledge organization?
(A) CILIP (B) ISKO
(C) ALA (D) UNESCO

373. In which year *A Dictionary of Documentation Terms* was published in first time?
(A) 1955 (B) 1960
(C) 1965 (D) 1968

374. What is the MARC Tag for Subject Headings?

(A) 3XX (B) 4XX
(C) 5XX (D) 6XX

375. The central core facet of any subject in CC is........

(A) Matter (B) Energy
(C) Space (D) Personality

376. Match the following:

LIST-I	LIST-II
(1) 0XX	(i) Physical description
(2) 1XX	(ii) Titles, edition, imprint
(3) 2XX	(iii) Main entry
(4) 3XX	(iv) Control information, number, code

Codes:

	(1)	(2)	(3)	(4)
(A)	(iv)	(iii)	(ii)	(i)
(B)	(i)	(ii)	(iii)	(iv)
(C)	(iii)	(ii)	(iv)	(i)
(D)	(iii)	(iv)	(ii)	(i)

377. Which of the following notation is used for Speciator Kind 2 in CC7?

(A) Hyphen (-) (B) Comma (,)
(C) Colon (:) (D) Semi Colon (;)

378. Match the following:

LIST-I	LIST-II
(1) 4XX	(i) Other added entries and linking entries
(2) 5XX	(ii) Series Statements
(3) 7XX	(iii) Notes
(4) 8XX	(iv) Series added entries

Codes:

	(1)	(2)	(3)	(4)
(A)	(iv)	(i)	(iii)	(ii)
(B)	(iii)	(i)	(ii)	(iv)
(C)	(ii)	(iii)	(i)	(iv)
(D)	(i)	(iii)	(iv)	(ii)

379. Which of the following is render under the Cross Reference Index Entry?

(A) Generic Name Entry
(B) Pseudonym Real Name Entry
(C) Editor of Series Entry
(D) All of the above

380. Which of the following is the example of Physical Form of library catalogue?

(A) Bound Register Form
(B) Sheaf Form
(C) Card Form
(D) All of the above

381. Which of the following is the markup-language that defines the set of rules for document encoding in a common format for both human and machine readable?

(A) XML (B) XHTML
(C) SML (D) Both (A) and (B)

382. Assertion (A): In Physical Form of catalogue, Card Form is very popular among various forms of catalogue.

Reason (R): In 12.5 × 7.6 cm card size, we can constantly update and also it is flexible in keeping.

(A) Both (A) and (R) are true
(B) Both (A) and (R) are false
(C) (A) is true, but (R) is false
(D) (A) is false, but (R) is true

383. Assertion (A): In Enumerative Classification Systems, it is not possible to accommodate new subjects due to their rigid structure.

Reason (R): Enumerative Classification Systems are based on an explicit theory guided by principles and postulates.

(A) Both (A) and (R) are true
(B) Both (A) and (R) are false
(C) (A) is false, but (R) is true
(D) (A) is true, but (R) is false

384. Assertion (A): According to the theory of library classification, isolate facets cannot form a subject unless these are attached to a Basic Subject.

Reason (R): Because that, every Compound Subject has a Basic facet.
(A) Both (A) and (R) are false
(B) Both (A) and (R) are true
(C) (A) is true, but (R) is false
(D) (A) is false, but (R) is true

385. Assertion (A): Descriptive cataloguing is the process of identifying and describing the bibliographic information of the documents such as title, author name, imprint, etc.
Reason (R): AACR-II is the example of descriptive cataloguing.
(A) Both (A) and (R) are true
(B) Both (A) and (R) are false
(C) (A) is true, but (R) is false
(D) (A) is false, but (R) is true

386. Assertion (A): Other than Library Science, the Idea and Verbal Planes are studies as a discipline.
Reason (R): Idea, Verbal and the Notational planes in Library Science are necessary for systematic arrangement of knowledge.
(A) Both (A) and (R) are false
(B) Both (A) and (R) are true
(C) (A) is false, but (R) is true
(D) (A) is true, but (R) is false

387. Assertion (A): Accession register cannot serve as a finding tool for documents available in library as library catalogue.
Reason (R): For finding particular bibliographic information such as title, author name, even subjects, the entire accession register will be search serially.
(A) (R) is false, but (A) is true
(B) (R) is true, but (A) is false
(C) Both (A) and (R) are false
(D) Both (A) and (R) are true

388. Assertion (A): Empty device is an unlimited addition of numbers in a schedule which represent coordinates ideas.
Reason (R): These digits in a schedule do not have semantic value, but possesses ordinal value.
(A) Both (A) and (R) are true
(B) Both (A) and (R) are false
(C) (A) is false, but (R) is true
(D) (A) is true, but (R) is false

389. Assertion (A): The International Standard Bibliographic Description (ISBD) is a set of rules produced by the IFLA.
Reason (R): The main purpose of ISBD is to provide a standard form of bibliographic description that could be used to exchange bibliographic records internationally.
(A) Both (A) and (R) are false
(B) Both (A) and (R) are true
(C) (A) is false, but (R) is true
(D) (A) is true, but (R) is false

390. Assertion (A): If two or more libraries wish to exchange bibliographic records with one another, it is necessary to follow a common standard format of bibliographic records.
Reason (R): CCF would be an effective format for such exchange of bibliographic records.
(A) Both (A) and (R) are true
(B) Both (A) and (R) are false
(C) (A) is true, but (R) is false
(D) (A) is false, but (R) is true

391. Assertion (A): For information retrieval of bibliographic description from different sources, a standard principle and formula should be maintained to all clienteles that associated with each other.
Reason (R): Z39.50 is an international standard protocol used by network computer systems for information retrieval and worked as a common gateway between clientele.
(A) Both (A) and (R) are true
(B) Both (A) and (R) are false

(C) (A) is true, but (R) is false
(D) (A) is false, but (R) is true

392. Assertion (A): The Classified Catalogue is a kind of subject catalogue, displaying entries according to the Class Number of documents.

Reason (R): Classified Catalogue has two parts, one is Classified part and second is the Alphabetical part and Classified Catalogue Code (CCC) is the example of Classified Catalogue.

(A) Both (A) and (R) are false
(B) Both (A) and (R) are true
(C) (A) is true, and (R) is false
(D) (A) is false, and (R) is true

393. Assertion (A): In Dictionary catalogue, entries such as author, title, subjects, series, etc. and their parts are arranged in one general alphabet.

Reason (R): *AACR-II* is the example of Dictionary catalogue, where entries are arranged in alphabetical order.

(A) Both (A) and (R) are true
(B) Both (A) and (R) are false
(C) (A) is false, but (R) is true
(D) (A) is true, but (R) is false

394. Assertion (A): According to S.R. Ranganathan, there is no need of physical descriptions of documents such as size of work, number of pages, illustration, etc. for cataloguing.

Reason (R): However, Series Notes, Pseudo Series Note, Change of the Title Note, etc. can be entered in Notes section in CCC.

(A) Both (A) and (R) are true
(B) Both (A) and (R) are false
(C) (A) is true, but (R) is false
(D) (A) is false, but (R) is true

Answers Keys

1. (A)	2. (A)	3. (B)	4. (A)	65. (A)	66. (B)	67. (A)	68. (B)
5. (D)	6. (A)	7. (A)	8. (A)	69. (A)	70. (A)	71. (A)	72. (D)
9. (A)	10. (D)	11. (B)	12. (B)	73. (A)	74. (A)	75. (A)	76. (B)
13. (D)	14. (A)	15. (C)	16. (A)	77. (A)	78. (A)	79. (A)	80. (B)
17. (B)	18. (D)	19. (B)	20. (B)	81. (A)	82. (A)	83. (A)	84. (A)
21. (A)	22. (A)	23. (B)	24. (A)	85. (A)	86. (B)	87. (A)	88. (A)
25. (C)	26. (A)	27. (A)	28. (D)	89. (C)	90. (B)	91. (B)	92. (C)
29. (B)	30. (C)	31. (A)	32. (A)	93. (B)	94. (C)	95. (B)	96. (C)
33. (C)	34. (C)	35. (A)	36. (C)	97. (C)	98. (A)	99. (A)	100. (A)
37. (B)	38. (D)	39. (C)	40. (A)	101. (C)	102. (B)	103. (B)	104. (A)
41. (D)	42. (D)	43. (C)	44. (C)	105. (D)	106. (D)	107. (A)	108. (D)
45. (B)	46. (B)	47. (C)	48. (B)	109. (D)	110. (A)	111. (C)	112. (D)
49. (B)	50. (C)	51. (D)	52. (B)	113. (C)	114. (D)	115. (D)	116. (D)
53. (B)	54. (D)	55. (D)	56. (A)	117. (B)	118. (C)	119. (A)	120. (B)
57. (D)	58. (A)	59. (A)	60. (A)	121. (B)	122. (A)	123. (A)	124. (D)
61. (D)	62. (A)	63. (A)	64. (C)	125. (D)	126. (C)	127. (A)	128. (B)

129. (A) 130. (D) 131. (B) 132. (A)
133. (D) 134. (A) 135. (C) 136. (A)
137. (A) 138. (A) 139. (D) 140. (A)
141. (A) 142. (A) 143. (A) 144. (C)
145. (D) 146. (B) 147. (D) 148. (A)
149. (A) 150. (D) 151. (D) 152. (D)
153. (A) 154. (D) 155. (A) 156. (B)
157. (D) 158. (A) 159. (B) 160. (D)
161. (A) 162. (B) 163. (B) 164. (B)
165. (D) 166. (A) 167. (C) 168. (B)
169. (B) 170. (A) 171. (C) 172. (B)
173. (A) 174. (A) 175. (D) 176. (A)
177. (D) 178. (A) 179. (B) 180. (D)
181. (C) 182. (B) 183. (C) 184. (A)
185. (B) 186. (A) 187. (A) 188. (D)
189. (C) 190. (D) 191. (B) 192. (B)
193. (C) 194. (A) 195. (B) 196. (C)
197. (A) 198. (A) 199. (C) 200. (D)
201. (A) 202. (B) 203. (D) 204. (C)
205. (D) 206. (A) 207. (D) 208. (D)
209. (B) 210. (A) 211. (D) 212. (C)
213. (B) 214. (C) 215. (C) 216. (A)
217. (B) 218. (A) 219. (D) 220. (A)
221. (C) 222. (A) 223. (C) 224. (A)
225. (B) 226. (D) 227. (A) 228. (B)
229. (B) 230. (A) 231. (C) 232. (B)
233. (A) 234. (A) 235. (A) 236. (B)
237. (A) 238. (B) 239. (A) 240. (C)
241. (A) 242. (B) 243. (A) 244. (A)
245. (A) 246. (A) 247. (B) 248. (D)
249. (C) 250. (B) 251. (C) 252. (C)
253. (A) 254. (B) 255. (C) 256. (A)
257. (C) 258. (C) 259. (C) 260. (A)
261. (D) 262. (A) 263. (C) 264. (D)
265. (D) 266. (B) 267. (C) 268. (A)
269. (C) 270. (A) 271. (A) 272. (A)
273. (A) 274. (A) 275. (D) 276. (A)
277. (B) 278. (A) 279. (D) 280. (C)
281. (C) 282. (A) 283. (B) 284. (B)
285. (A) 286. (C) 287. (C) 288. (A)
289. (B) 290. (D) 291. (A) 292. (C)
293. (D) 294. (B) 295. (A) 296. (A)
297. (D) 298. (A) 299. (D) 300. (C)
301. (A) 302. (B) 303. (A) 304. (D)
305. (B) 306. (D) 307. (D) 308. (D)
309. (C) 310. (C) 311. (D) 312. (B)
313. (A) 314. (A) 315. (D) 316. (C)
317. (A) 318. (D) 319. (A) 320. (A)
321. (A) 322. (B) 323. (C) 324. (A)
325. (A) 326. (B) 327. (A) 328. (D)
329. (D) 330. (C) 331. (C) 332. (B)
333. (C) 334. (A) 335. (C) 336. (A)
337. (A) 338. (A) 339. (B) 340. (A)
341. (D) 342. (C) 343. (A) 344. (C)
345. (C) 346. (B) 347. (C) 348. (A)
349. (B) 350. (A) 351. (D) 352. (C)
353. (C) 354. (A) 355. (B) 356. (C)
357. (B) 358. (A) 359. (A) 360. (D)
361. (C) 362. (D) 363. (D) 364. (C)
365. (D) 366. (C) 367. (B) 368. (C)
369. (C) 370. (C) 371. (A) 372. (B)
373. (B) 374. (D) 375. (D) 376. (A)
377. (A) 378. (C) 379. (D) 380. (D)
381. (D) 382. (A) 383. (D) 384. (B)
385. (A) 386. (B) 387. (D) 388. (A)
389. (B) 390. (A) 391. (A) 392. (B)
393. (A) 394. (A)

CHAPTER

6 Library Management

INTRODUCTION

The term management is multi-discipline and very broad in the sense of common using. Management is applying in every fields of activity such as finance management, personnel management, resource management, etc. in same case; library is a physically existing entity and also covered under educational, social, academic, institutional, etc. Therefore, all activities related to the smoothly and successfully working of any library are surrounded with some norms and principles and overall these control activity is governed under library management.

In library management, discussing areas are very broad and comparatively very exhaustive in the sense of general principles, scientific principles, library personnel, documents delivery, physical location of library, users as well staff covering areas, etc. From Taylor to Barnard principles in terms of their views related to the common as well as scientific principles of management and in various activities like library house-keeping, and the principles of materials selection of Drury, Dewey, McColvin and Ranganathan are discuss under the library management.

Thus, above said thought and concepts, we will take plenty of questions with their answer according to the latest examinations pattern related to the library management.

IMPORTANT POINTS

- Figurehead, leader, and liaison are the three interpersonal role of manager.
- Monitor, disseminator, and spokesperson are the three informational role of the manager.
- Entrepreneur, disturbance handler, resource allocator and negotiator are the four decisional role of the manager.
- Henry Mintzberg has identified the above ten managerial roles for any organization.
- Among various information systems, Decision Support System (DSS) is relatively a low-volume data and analytical model system as data inputs.
- In management, MBO stands for Management By Objectives.
- MBO was first popularized by Peter Drucker in 1954 in his book *The Practice of Management*.
- In MBO, the managers and employees work together to set and monitor goals for a specific period of time with a clear understanding of their roles and the responsibilities.

- In MBO, managers focus on the result, not the activity and it appropriate for knowledge-based-enterprises.
- Library is a peoples' organization and basically a non-profit organization.
- The school of management theory can be divided into three parts, viz., Classical Management Theory, Neo-Classical Theory and Modern Management Theory.
- According to Total Quality Management Approach, the quality tends to increase and costs fall over time, when people and organizations focus primarily on quality and it defined as Quality = Result of work efforts/Total Costs.
- There are three levels of management generally found in an organization, viz. Top-Level, Middle-Level and Low-Level Management.
- The Top-Level Management responsible for planning, evaluation, policy-making and resource mobilization.
- The Middle-Level Management responsible for executing organizational plans, execution of activities and monitoring.
- The Low-Level Management focuses on controlling and directing as well as routine tasks.
- Planning is the primary function or first function of the management and logically precedes the execution of all other managerial functions.
- SWOT stands for Strengths, Weaknesses, Opportunities, and Threats.
- The concept of Unity of Command is a classical principle of management theory and it provides that an employee is responsible to only one supervisor and it is the one among fourteen principles of Henry Fayol.
- A type of organization where rules established by an organization to govern procedures and operation is called Formal Organization.
- The MIS (Management Information System) broadly refers to a computer based system that provides well structured information for decision-making as well as planning and control processes, performance appraisal of different units and individuals.
- Ideally, a library should be centrally located so that it is easily accessible to its clientele.
- The stack rooms issue and return counter, public catalogue and Web-OPAC terminals constitute the Circulation Area.
- The storage spaces for the various types of documents kept in a library is known as Stacks.
- The reading room in a library should be located nearest to the document collection concerned.
- Classification and Cataloguing of the documents are the technical processing done by the Technical Section in a library after acquisition process.
- A property counter is generally placed near the Issue Counter, where the readers can leave their personal belongings before going inside the library.

- Macro-Document usually a work expressing macro thought is embodied into a document all by itself, therefore, book, monograph, thesis, dissertation, report, etc. are the examples of macro-document.
- Micro-Document usually a work expressing micro thought is not embodied into a document all by itself and several micro documents are embodied in one and the same document, therefore, periodical is macro document but each article in it is micro-document.
- Library catalogues, reading lists, bookseller's catalogue, subject catalogues, etc. are the examples of secondary bibliographies.
- Acquisition work comprises three distinct functions, viz., selection, procurement and accessioning.
- The acquiring of current issues of periodicals and newspapers is not done by Acquisition Department instead, it done by the Periodical Department.
- The principle "The best reading for the largest number at the least cost" is associated with Melvil Dewey.
- Library documents are entered in the Accession Register date-wise according to their receipt in the library, however, all purchased books are entered in the order of the bills as their purchased.
- According to Leslie Gillert and Jan Wright, "NBM (Non-Book Materials) have increased the range and means of obtaining and exploiting information for teaching, learning and research purposes, but to separate books from NBM is to divide information into false compartments. Hence, it is essential that books and non-book can be jointly identified and located to meet particular needs."
- For periodical processing, the Three Card System introduced by S.R. Ranganathan and in this system three different card of the size 5 × 3 is maintained for each periodical.
- Register Card, Check Card and the Classified Index Card are three kinds of cards in Three Card System.
- Vocabulary Control Device is a tool that consist Classification Schemes, Cataloguing Codes, Subject Headings Lists, Thesauri, etc.
- In periodical processing, the Rounding off Work consists of sending reminders to the publishers/suppliers of non-receipt of current or back issues, or other related issues such as title page, contents, index, defective, duplicate issues of periodicals.
- The basic tool in classifying documents is the Classification Scheme.
- The translating the specific subject of a document into an artificial language of ordinal numbers is called Library Classification.
- In library cataloguing, the Authority Control is a process for organizing bibliographic information consist a series of decisions made by a library staff and the main objective of this control is to maintain a controlled vocabulary in the catalogue.

- There are different kinds of authority files, including the Name Authority File consist an alphabetical list of personal, geographic, corporate and conference names that are found in a library catalogue and used...as main, added, analytical, or subject entries.
- Browne and Newark Charging Systems were two popular and widely practiced systems of issue and return of documents in libraries.
- The Browne Charging System was devised by Nine E. Browne.
- User Registration is the very first step for running circulation system.
- The Day Book, Ledger System and Dummy System are associated with the Circulation System.
- In circulation system in library, the Charging is the issue of books (documents) which are presented at the circulation counter to users.
- Discharging is the work of securing books (documents) borrowed from users.
- In circulation work, books are kept on reserve for users, that have already been issued is known as Holds.
- In an open access library system, users should able to browse, choose and select the documents (books) on their interest.
- The process of examining and checking the new books for proper pagination, completeness, illustrations, etc. are known as Collation.
- Basically there are three types of financial support is to be given by libraries (i) Recurring Grant, (ii) Non-Recurring Grant, and (iii) Ad hoc Grant.
- The Recurring Grants are generally given for the purchase of books and periodicals.
- The Non-Recurring Grants are given for specific purposes such as construction of library building, purchase of library equipments, furniture and ICT software and hardware equipments.
- The Ad hoc Grant is given on special recommendations for special purchases.
- Library cess, government grants, subscriptions, and government as well as public endowment are the main sources of public library revenue.
- The special libraries get their financial assistance from respective parent organizations.
- The Kothari Education Commission (1964-66) recommended that, a university should spend each year approx. ₹ 25 for each student and ₹ 300 per teacher.
- Library is growing institution as well as permanent bodies; therefore, library expenditure is recurring in nature.

QUESTIONS

1. A person who is responsible to all activities of an organization at any level is a/an

(A) Manager (B) Supervisor

(C) Auditor (D) None of the above

2. The bottom level of manager that observes the efforts of those who actually perform the work

(A) Middle Managers

(B) Operational Managers

(C) Top Management
(D) None of the above

3. Which of the following country was used 'Newark System' in first time?
(A) USA (B) UK
(C) Australia (D) India

4. Which of the following is belongs to Operational Managers?
(A) First Line Manager
(B) Supervisor
(C) Top Manager
(D) Both (A) and (B)

5. Entering of Call Number on the books is known as
(A) Accessing (B) Marking
(C) Pointing (D) Quoting

6. In library, return of books is called
(A) Charging (B) Discharging
(C) Entry (D) Recording

7. Which of the following 'Charging System' is most popular?
(A) Browne Charging System
(B) Newark Charging System
(C) Gaylord Charging System
(D) Both (A) and (B)

8. The.................responsible to develop implementations strategies, execution of activities, monitoring and supervisions determined by Top Management.
(A) Middle Manager
(B) Operational Manager
(C) Supervisor
(D) None of the above

9. The term 'Loose Leaf Books' is used in
(A) Recording receipt of periodicals
(B) Reading point of book
(C) Classification of ILL books
(D) Preservation of books

10. Which of the following is the main focus of Drury's Book Selection Principle?
(A) Management (B) Staffs
(C) Reader (D) ILL

11. Match the following:

LIST-I		LIST-II
(1) Living With Books	(i)	Arlene G. Taylor
(2) Developing Library and Information Center Collection	(ii)	Robert N. Broadus
(3) Selecting Materials for Libraries	(iii)	G. Edward Evans
(4) The Organization of Information	(iv)	Helen E. Haines

Codes:

	(1)	(2)	(3)	(4)
(A)	(iv)	(iii)	(ii)	(i)
(B)	(i)	(iii)	(ii)	(iv)
(C)	(ii)	(iii)	(i)	(iv)
(D)	(iv)	(i)	(ii)	(iii)

12. ....is the formal line of authority which moves from highest to lowest rank in a straight line.
(A) Unit Chain
(B) Scalar Chain
(C) Procedure Chain
(D) Demanding Chain

13. The term 'Taylorism' is associated with
(A) Scientific Management
(B) Bureaucratic Management
(C) Human Relational Management
(D) All of the above

14. Which of the following is associated with Classical Management Theory?
(A) Henri Fayol
(B) F.W. Taylor
(C) Max Weber
(D) All of the above

15. Henri Fayol was belongs to which country?
(A) French (B) USA
(C) Australia (D) UK

16. In Bureaucracy Theory of Management, which of the following legitimate authority is described by Wax Weber?
(A) Traditional Authority
(B) Charismatic Authority
(C) Rational-Legal Authority
(D) All of the above

17. Which of the following is the Neo-Human Relational Theory?
(A) Maslow
(B) McGregor (Theory X and Theory Y)
(C) Linkert
(D) All of the above

18. A type of 'System', where information and their resources are free for users is called
(A) Closed System
(B) Open System
(C) Focal System
(D) Associated System

19. Decision based on the situation at hand rather than a 'one size fits all' is a
(A) System Theory
(B) Contingency Theory
(C) Chaos Theory
(D) Theory X and Theory Y

20. Who developed the Management By Objectives (MBO)?
(A) Peter Drucker
(B) Max Weber
(C) Douglas McGregor
(D) A.M. Henderson

21. The book titled *Work and Motivation* was written by
(A) Victor H. Vroom
(B) Frederick Herzberg
(C) Abraham H. Maslow
(D) Douglas McGregor

22. The book titled *The Theory of Social and Economic Organization* was written by
(A) Max Weber
(B) A.M. Henderson
(C) Douglas McGregor
(D) Both (A) and (B)

23. The book titled *The Motivation to Work* was written by
(A) Frederick Herzberg
(B) Bernard Mausner
(C) Barbara Snyderman
(D) All of the above

24. ....determines the objective, policies and plans of the organization.
(A) Supervisor
(B) Operational Manager
(C) Top Manager
(D) None of the above

25. In India, the main financial source for University Library is
(A) Library cess (B) UGC grant
(C) Students fee (D) University grant

26. Which of the following are the three managerial skills that able to translate knowledge into action for desired result and the performance?
(A) Technical, Human and Conventional skills
(B) Technical, Human and Knowledge skills
(C) Technical, Human and Conceptual skills
(D) Technical, Logical and Conversation skills

27. In which year, Zero Based Budgeting was introduced?
(A) 1965 (B) 1968
(C) 1970 (D) 1972

28. Through.........skill, a person interacts with others very effectively.

(A) Human (B) Technical
(C) Conceptual (D) None of the above

29. CPM (Critical Path Method) was developed by
(A) Morgan R. Walker
(B) James E. Kelley
(C) F.P. Brooks
(D) Both (A) and (B)

30. ....are abilities and knowledge to perform specialized tasks in terms of knowledge, process and method.
(A) Technical skills (B) Conceptual skills
(C) Artificial skills (D) Both (B) and (C)

31. What is the standard depth of Pigeon Hole?
(A) 26 cm (B) 28 cm
(C) 30 cm (D) 32 cm

32. ....deals with thought, ideas and abstract relationship that realized abstracts or general ideas for applying specific situation.
(A) Human skills (B) Conceptual skills
(C) Technical skills (D) Artificial skills

33. The book titled *The Practice of Management* was written by
(A) Peter F. Drucker
(B) John A. Drucker
(C) S.R. Ranganathan
(D) Henri Fayol

34. Which of the following statements is true?
(A) Technical skill is most important for supervisor level
(B) Human skills are important at every level in the organization
(C) Lower level managers focus on controlling and directing
(D) All of the above

35. The book titled *Management Techniques for Librarian* was written by
(A) G. Evans (B) S.R. Ranganathan
(C) J.D. Brown (D) H.E. Bliss

36. The book titled *Management Techniques for Librarian* was originally published in
(A) 1971 (B) 1976
(C) 1978 (D) 1981

37. Which of the following statements is true?
(A) Technical skills are less important as the manager move up to the middle and top level
(B) Conceptual skill is important as manager moves up the levels of management
(C) Both (A) and (B)
(D) None of the above

38. Which of the following was the author of book *Library Manual*?
(A) S.R. Ranganathan
(B) J.D. Brown
(C) H.E. Bliss
(D) Margaret Mann

39. According to the basic principle of management, the five basic managerial functions are
(A) Planning, Organizing, Staffing, Directing, Coordinating and Controlling.
(B) Planning, Ordering, Staffing, Directing, Coordinating and Controlling.
(C) Planning, Ordering, Staffing, Directing, Coordinating and Commanding.
(D) Planning, Organizing, Staffing, Directing, Cooperating and Controlling,

40. The four managerial functions that defined by the 'Newman' and 'Summer' are
(A) Organizing, Planning, Leading and Controlling
(B) Organizing, Planning, Learning and Coordinating
(C) Organizing, Planning, Leading and Coordinating
(D) Observing, Planning, Learning and Controlling

41. Which of the following principles is used for documents arrangement on the shelves?
(A) Alphabetical order
(B) Numerical order
(C) Alpha-numerical order
(D) Classified order

42. POSDCoRB stands for
(A) Planning, Organizing, Staffing, Directing, Coordinating, Reporting and Budgeting.
(B) Planning, Organizing, Staffing, Directive, Coordinating, Reporting and Budgeting
(C) Processing, Organizing, Staffing, Directing, Coordinating, Reporting and Budgeting
(D) Processing, Observing, Staffing, Directing, Coordinating, Reporting and Budgeting

43. The seven managerial functions (POSDCoRB) was described by
(A) Luther Gulick (B) L. Urwick
(C) Henri Fayol (D) Both (A) and (B)

44. The slogan 'Books for the Millions at their Doorsteps' is associated with
(A) ALA (B) CILIP
(C) RRRLF (D) UNESCO

45. Which of the following five managerial functions defined by the Henri Fayol?
(A) Planning, Operating, Commanding, Coordinating and Controlling
(B) Planning, Organizing, Commanding, Coordinating and Controlling
(C) Planning, Organizing, Commanding, Coordinating and Communicating
(D) Planning, Organizing, Commanding, Coordinating and Consisting.

46. IRRO (Indian Reprographic Rights Organization) is located at
(A) New Delhi (B) Mumbai
(C) Kolkata (D) Bengaluru

47. Match the following:

LIST-I	LIST-II
(1) Acknowledge as 'father of Scientific Management'	(i) Henry L. Gantt
(2) Referred to as 'father of Modern Management Theory'	(ii) Frank and Lillan Gilbreth
(3) Called 'Harmonious Cooperation Labour and Management'	(iii) Fredrick W. Taylor
(4) Focused on the 'Human Aspects of Work and the Understanding of Workers'	(iv) Henri Fayol

Codes:

	(1)	(2)	(3)	(4)
(A)	(i)	(ii)	(iii)	(iv)
(B)	(iii)	(iv)	(i)	(ii)
(C)	(i)	(iii)	(iv)	(ii)
(D)	(iv)	(iii)	(i)	(ii)

48. Match the following:

LIST-I	LIST-II
(1) Unity of command is important	(i) Chaos Theory
(2) Actions are subject to rules	(ii) Theory of Bureaucracy
(3) The future is unknowable	(iii) Scientific Management
(4) Motivation is primarily based on pay	(iv) Management Principles

Codes:

	(1)	(2)	(3)	(4)
(A)	(iv)	(ii)	(i)	(iii)
(B)	(iii)	(i)	(iv)	(ii)
(C)	(i)	(iii)	(ii)	(iv)
(D)	(ii)	(i)	(iii)	(iv)

49. The book titled *The Principles of Scientific Management* was published in

(A) 1911 (B) 1922
(C) 1932 (D) 1934

50. Which of the following is a function of management that arranges peoples and resources to work towards a goal?
(A) Staffing (B) Controlling
(C) Organizing (D) Planning

51. A book published with soft-cover called
(A) Paperback (B) Hardback
(C) Hardbound (D) Both (B) and (C)

52. A book published with rigid protective cover is called
(A) Paperback (B) Protected Edition
(C) Hardcover (D) Preserved Edition

53. .... is measuring and correcting individual and organizational performance to ensure that events conform to plan.
(A) Controlling (B) Organizing
(C) Reporting (D) Budgeting

54. Which of the following is the father of Administrative Management?
(A) Henri Fayol
(B) Fredrick W. Taylor
(C) Henry L. Gantt
(D) Harrington Emerson

55. Which of the following is the father of the Bureaucratic Management Theory?
(A) Harrington Emerson
(B) Henry L. Gantt
(C) Fredrick W. Taylor
(D) Max Weber

56. Which of the following is the father of the System Theory?
(A) Chester Barnard (B) Max Weber
(C) Henry L. Gantt (D) Fredrick W. Taylor

57. The book titled *Functions of the Executive* was written by
(A) Chester Barnard
(B) C. Ray Gullett
(C) Herbert G, Hicks
(D) Susan M. Phillips

58. Which of the following systems is not directly interacting with an environment?
(A) Closed System
(B) Empirical System
(C) Probabilistic System
(D) Open System

59. Match the following:

LIST-I	LIST-II
(1) ISO 9000	(i) Environmental Management
(2) ISO 14000	(ii) Quality Management
(3) ISO 27001	(iii) Social Responsibility
(4) ISO 26000	(iv) Information Security Management

Codes:

	(1)	(2)	(3)	(4)
(A)	(ii)	(i)	(iv)	(iii)
(B)	(iv)	(ii)	(i)	(iii)
(C)	(i)	(iii)	(iv)	(ii)
(D)	(iii)	(ii)	(i)	(iv)

60. What is the exact meaning of Henri Fayol's 'Esprit De Corps'?
(A) Employees should received orders from one superior only
(B) People should be allowed the freedom to propose
(C) Specialization promotes efficiency of the workforce and increased productivity
(D) 'In union there is strength' that emphasizing the need for teamwork

61. Which of the following principle of management emphasized the sociological approach to human relations and management?
(A) Barnard's Principle
(B) Fayol's Principle
(C) Taylor's Principle
(D) Gilbreth's Principle

62. According to C. Barnard, organization is a/an
(A) Executive System
(B) Cooperative System
(C) Non-Cooperative System
(D) Comparative System

63. Library management is under the part of ....management.
(A) Financial (B) Trade
(C) Human (D) Service

64. A specific probability theory used by management to develop the method for handling relationships between centre, unit, event, activities to minimize or avoid delays.
(A) Management Information System (MIS)
(B) Programme Evaluations Reviewing Techniques (PERT)
(C) Operations Research (OR)
(D) Queuing Theory (QT)

65. Flow Process Chart is introduced by
(A) Frank Gilbreth (B) Gray Dessler
(C) D. Smith (D) G.E. Evans

66. In Network analysis techniques, G.E.R.T. stand for
(A) Graphical Evaluation Review Technique
(B) Graphical Evaluation Repeating Technique
(C) Graphical Evaluation Reporting Technique
(D) Graphical Evaluation Reparative Technique

67. Which of the following is related to Fayol's Principles of Management that, "employee should be aware of where they stand in the organization's hierarchy or chain of command"?
(A) Centralization
(B) Order
(C) Scalar chain
(D) Unity of command

68. Which of the following is related to Fayol's principles of management that, 'team with the same objective should be working under the direction of one manager, using one plane'.
(A) Discipline
(B) Unity of Command
(C) Unity of Direction
(D) Equity

69. ASK (Approach, Skill and Knowledge) principle is related to
(A) Cataloguing (B) Classification
(C) Management (D) SDI

70. The book titled *Library Administration* was brought out by S.R. Ranganathan in
(A) 1930 (B) 1933
(C) 1935 (D) 1938

71. The tagline 'Managing Information' is associated with
(A) ASLIB (B) ALA
(C) IFLA (D) CILIP

72. Who introduced the concept of 'Sister Libraries' for improvements of reading habit among children and young adults?
(A) IFLA (B) UNESCO
(C) ALA (D) ASLIB

73. The tagline 'Connecting People and Information' is associated with
(A) UNESCO (B) LOC
(C) SLA (D) ASLIB

74. Which of the following is the example of library cooperation?
(A) Cataloguing (B) Classification
(C) Preservation (D) Resource sharing

75. ....is a continuous efforts by the management as well as employees of a particular organization to ensure long-term customer(user) loyalty and customer(user) satisfaction.
(A) Management Information System (MIS)
(B) Human Resources Development (HRD)

(C) Total Quality Management (TQM)
(D) Quality Assurance (QA)

76. In Total Quality Management (TQM), PDCA stands for
(A) Program, Directing, Controlling, Applying
(B) Program, Determine, Coordinating, Acting
(C) Plan, Do, Check, Act
(D) Progress, Directing, Controlling, Action

77. 'Management By Objectives' (MBO) was popularized by
(A) L. Gulick (B) C. Barnard
(C) F.W. Taylor (D) Peter Drucker

78. According to Edward Evans, the development theory of Management between 1880-1930 eras is called
(A) Synthesis period
(B) Pre-Scientific period
(C) Human Relations period
(D) Scientific-Management period

79. Which of the following is the father of Modern Management theory?
(A) F.W. Taylor (B) C. Barnard
(C) Luther Gulick (D) L. Urwick

80. In Scientific-Management period, the concept fair day's work and fair day's pay was defined by
(A) C. Barnard (B) L. Gulick
(C) C.L. Urwick (D) F.W. Taylor

81. According to Elton Mayo, ...is a human-relation theory between management and workers.
(A) Cooperative (B) Productivity
(C) Controlling (D) Humanism

82. Match the following:

LIST-I	LIST-II
(1) Administration	(i) a right person must be given a right job
(2) Management	(ii) directs and guides the operations of an organization
(3) Theory X and Theory Y	(iii) responsible for the determination of aims of an organization
(4) Order	(iv) Douglas McGregor

Codes:

	(1)	(2)	(3)	(4)
(A)	(iii)	(i)	(iv)	(ii)
(B)	(iv)	(i)	(iii)	(ii)
(C)	(i)	(iii)	(iv)	(ii)
(D)	(iii)	(ii)	(iv)	(i)

83. In Management, term 'School' means
(A) Related to practice
(B) Related to techniques
(C) Related to education
(D) Related to theory and method

84. The Classical School of Management Theory was developed in
(A) UK (B) USA
(C) Italy (D) France

85. Which of the following is the oldest formal school of thought?
(A) Classical School
(B) Behavioral School
(C) Quantitative School
(D) Systems School

86. Which of the following area of study can be grouped under the Classical School?
(A) Scientific Management
(B) Administrative Management
(C) Bureaucratic Management
(D) All of the above

87. The Theory of Classical School of Management had been evolved as a result of
(A) Economic revolution
(B) Social revolution
(C) Cultural revolution
(D) Industrial revolution

88. ....has been considered as the father of the Human Relations Movement, which later became organizational behavior.
(A) C. Barnard
(B) Henri Fayol
(C) Harrington Emerson
(D) Elton Mayo

89. The....................is the result of behavioral sciences into management through in order to solve the problems.
(A) Classical Management Theory
(B) Neo Classical Management Theory
(C) Modern Management Theory
(D) All of the above

90. The.......................highlights the complexity of the organization as well as individuals and the diversity of their need and objects.
(A) Classical Management Theory
(B) Neo Classical Management Theory
(C) Modern Management Theory
(D) All of the above

91. Match the following:

LIST-I	LIST-II
(1) Elements of Administration	(i) C. Barnard
(2) Twelve Principles of Efficiency	(ii) Henri Fayol
(3) General and Industrial Management	(iii) Harrington Emerson
(4) The Functions of Executive	(iv) C. L. Urwick

Codes:

	(1)	(2)	(3)	(4)
(A)	(i)	(iii)	(iv)	(ii)
(B)	(ii)	(iv)	(i)	(iii)
(C)	(iv)	(i)	(iii)	(ii)
(D)	(iv)	(iii)	(ii)	(i)

92. How many rules were setups by Henri Fayol in Principles of Management?
(A) 12 (B) 14
(C) 15 (D) 17

93. Who developed the concept 'Informal Organization'?
(A) Chester Barnard (B) M.P. Follett
(C) Henri Fayol (D) Max Weber

94. Bureaucratic Management is related to the
(A) Ideal form of organization
(B) Management process and principles
(C) Organizational behavior in an organization
(D) Understanding the organizational structure

95. Which of the following techniques is related to the project planning?
(A) Management Information System (MIS)
(B) Strength, Weaknesses, Opportunities and Threats (SWOT)
(C) Critical Path Method (CPM)
(D) All of the above

96. A two dimensional graph where time is depict on the horizontal axis and lists of the part of a programs on the vertical axis is a/an
(A) Pie Chart (B) Bar Chart
(C) Gantt Chart (D) Line Chart

97. ....is a statistical tool that is used for the evaluation and review technique for any project management.
(A) PERT (B) Gantt
(C) Flow diagram (D) Pie

98. The cooperative action of two or more persons or organizations working together to accomplish more than they could work separately is called
(A) Synergism (B) Motivation
(C) Leadership (D) Cooperative

99. Scientific Management is related to the
(A) One best way to do a job
(B) Formulation of rules
(C) Manager and their functions
(D) Division of work

100. A specific type of organization that exists through a network of personal and social relationships without have any own rules and regulations.
(A) Commercial organization
(B) Cooperative organization
(C) Informal organization
(D) Formal organization

101. A/an................is a pictorial presentation of an organization that depict its structure and the relationships.
(A) Gantt Chart
(B) PERT Chart
(C) Flow Chart
(D) Organizational Chart

102. In Organizational Chart, the unbroken line is used for displaying the........
(A) Staff positions
(B) Staff functions
(C) Lines of authority
(D) Staffs duty hour

103. Which of the following is the example of 'Library Cooperation'?
(A) Abstracting (B) Reprography
(C) Resource Sharing (D) Classification

104. Which of the following thought is related to F. Taylor?
(A) To developed Social Groups on the job
(B) The concept of Human Behavior and Motivation
(C) The concept of System School
(D) The principle of Scientific Management

105. Who wrote the book *The Human Side of Enterprise*?
(A) Henri Fayol
(B) C.L. Urwick
(C) Frederick Herzberg
(D) Douglas McGregor

106. The Theory X and Theory Y is related to human behavior, developed by
(A) Peter F. Drucker
(B) Henri Fayol
(C) Edward Evans
(D) Douglas McGregor

107. In Theory X and Theory Y, the 'Theory X' will be represented which of the following?
(A) Assumes that employees are naturally unmotivated and dislike working
(B) This encourage an authoritarian style of management
(C) Both (A) and (B)
(D) None of the above

108. In Theory X and Theory Y, the 'Theory Y' will be represented which of the following?
(A) Assume that employee are ambitious and self-motivated
(B) Take responsibility and are motivated to their goals
(C) Both (A) and (B)
(D) None of these

109. MIS (Management Information System) is related to........
(A) A system which provides information support for decision-making
(B) An integrated system of man and machine for supporting the operations
(C) A computer based Information system for providing information to the people
(D) All of the above

110. Under MIS, a model where all commercial activities are done through online such as marketing, selling, servicing, paying for goods, etc. is called
(A) M-commerce (B) P-commerce
(C) F-commerce (D) E-commerce

111. Which of the following is the physical component for any MIS based system?
(A) Hardware
(B) Software

(C) Communication network
(D) All of the above

112. A 'Green library' also known as.....
(A) Online library
(B) IT based library
(C) AI library
(D) Sustainable library

113. A library designed to minimize negative impact on the natural environment, use of natural construction materials, production of resources like water, paper, etc., and responsible waste disposal recycling is a/an
(A) Yellow library (B) Natural library
(C) Green library (D) White library

114. In library management, PPBS relates to
(A) Budgeting (B) Book accession
(C) Book selection (D) Stock verification

115. Which of the following is the disadvantage of Zero Based Budgeting?
(A) It is a lengthy and also time consuming process
(B) High degree of managerial skills are required
(C) It not ensure optimum use of financial resources
(D) Both (A) and (B)

116. For stamping of book, library stamp put on
(A) Lower half of the half-title page
(B) Lower half of back of the title page
(C) Bottom of the last page of text
(D) All of the above

117. Which of the following is true for the term 'Incunabula'?
(A) Books, pamphlet or other document was printed, and not handwritten
(B) Documents were printed before 1501 A.D.
(C) Documents were printed after 1501 A.D.
(D) Both (A) and (B)

118. The revised version of Maslow's Theory of Motivation is known as
(A) ETG Theory of Motivation
(B) EDG Theory of Motivation
(C) EST Theory of Motivation
(D) ERG Theory of Motivation

119. The ERG Theory of Motivation (revised version of Maslow's Theory) is coined by
(A) Clayton Paul Alderfer
(B) Rusell A. Barkley
(C) Clyde H. Coombs
(D) John Gabrieli

120. In 'ERG Theory of Motivation', ERG stands for
(A) Excellence, Relatedness, and Growth
(B) Existence, Relatedness, and Growth
(C) Existence, Replacement, and Growth
(D) Excellence, Replacement, and Growth

121. David McClelland defined the 'Three Needs Theory of Motivation', these three needs are
(A) Needs for Achievement, Power, and Affiliation
(B) Needs for Achievement, Progress, and Affiliation
(C) Needs for Achievement, Progress, and Activeness
(D) Needs for Achievement, Performance, and Affiliation

122. In India, which type of libraries has fulfilled the UGC's finance assistant?
(A) School libraries
(B) Special libraries
(C) Academic libraries
(D) Public libraries

123. Which of the following types of document is the fundamental and authoritative document?
(A) Secondary Sources
(B) Tertiary Sources

(C) Primary Sources

(D) None of the above

124. Which of the following is a Primary Source of information?

(A) Statistical data after demographics study

(B) Results section in an article

(C) Articles in newspapers

(D) Both (A) and (B)

125. Match the following:

LIST-I	LIST-II
(1) Newton's diary	(i) Secondary sources
(2) Biography of Newton	(ii) Primary sources
(3) Textbook on three famous Newton Laws of motion	(iii) Tertiary sources
(4) An oversized book, too large for normal shelving	(iv) Folio

Codes:

	(1)	(2)	(3)	(4)
(A)	(i)	(ii)	(iii)	(iv)
(B)	(ii)	(i)	(iii)	(iv)
(C)	(iii)	(ii)	(i)	(iv)
(D)	(i)	(iii)	(ii)	(iv)

126. What is the preferred colour for printed catalogue card?

(A) Aero-Blue (B) Bright-Green

(C) Yellow (D) Cream-White

127. The disadvantage of PPBS is/are

(A) It is not able to links planning and budgeting into an integrated system

(B) It is capable only for short-range and single-year planning routine

(C) Massive amount of data and staff skills are required

(D) Both (A) and (B)

128. The stack room, public catalogue, and issue and return counter constitute the..........

(A) Reference Department

(B) Technical Department

(C) Circulation Department

(D) Acquisition Department

129. Area that acquire documents for cataloguing, classification, and bar-coding is called

(A) Reference Section (B) Circulation Section

(C) Technical Section (D) Both (A) and (B)

130. Area that assist the users queries, maintaining reference files, and selecting reference documents is called

(A) Reference section (B) Circulation section

(C) Technical section (D) None of the above

131. 'Mobile Library' is a kind of which service?

(A) Ready Reference Service

(B) Extension Service

(C) Reference service

(D) All of the above

132. ....of the library deals with the purchase of books, day-to-day operations such as placing orders, receiving and entering the books with serial number in the accession register, etc.

(A) Acquisition section

(B) Periodicals section

(C) Technical section

(D) Circulation section

133. Library is derived from the Latin word 'liber' which means

(A) Book (B) Public

(C) Democracy (D) People

134. The syllabus for the M.Lib.Sc. course of Delhi University, originally drawn up by S.R. Ranganathan in

(A) 1947 (B) 1951

(C) 1954 (D) 1958

135. A type of library established for specific groups of users, viz., Scientist, Technologist, Economist, Lawyer, Doctors, etc. is called

(A) Public Library
(B) National Library
(C) Special Library
(D) None of the above

136. The Central Library of Bhabha Atomic Research Centre (BARC) is the example of
(A) Public Library
(B) Special Library
(C) National Library
(D) None of the above

137. The first formal course for training in Librarianship in India started in
(A) 1911 (B) 1920
(C) 1931 (D) 1935

138. The Madras Library Association was founded in
(A) 1921 (B) 1926
(C) 1928 (D) 1932

139. In which year, Madras University was started B.Lib.Sc. degree course in place of one year diploma course of Librarianship?
(A) 1960 (B) 1965
(C) 1967 (D) 1968

140. A specific type of documents in a library which become valueless after a short period of time is called
(A) Enduring documents
(B) Interminable documents
(C) Eternal documents
(D) Ephemeral documents

141. Match the following on the basis of starting of Librarianship courses in different universities in India

LIST-I	LIST-II
(1) Banaras Hindu University	(i) 1947
(2) Delhi University	(ii) 1946
(3) Calcutta University	(iii) 1944
(4) Bombay University	(iv) 1941

Codes:

	(1)	(2)	(3)	(4)
(A)	(i)	(iii)	(iv)	(ii)
(B)	(ii)	(iv)	(iii)	(i)
(C)	(i)	(iv)	(ii)	(iii)
(D)	(iv)	(i)	(ii)	(iii)

142. In which year National Medical Library in India was established?
(A) 1 April 1966 (B) 1 May 1967
(C) 11 April 1968 (D) 12 June 1968

143. After merging of NISCOM and INSDOC, which of following new centre was established on 30th September, 2002.
(A) INFLIBNET (B) NISCAIR
(C) UGC-INFONET (D) DELNET

144. Book, Thesis, Dissertation are the example of
(A) Micro-documents
(B) Macro-documents
(C) Both (A) and (B)
(D) None of the above

145. Article in a periodical is the example of
(A) Macro-document (B) Micro-document
(C) Both (A) and (B) (D) None of the above

146. According to S.R. Ranganathan, the form of documents, viz., writing, typing, printing which are recorded on paper in natural language is called
(A) Neo-Conventional
(B) Conventional
(C) Non-Conventional
(D) Meta-document

147. According to S.R. Ranganathan, audio-video, microforms documents are the example of
(A) Conventional (B) Non-Conventional
(C) Meta-document (D) All of the above

148. Which of the following is true for Meta-document?
(A) Unedited document
(B) Created by the human mind
(C) e-documents
(D) Both (A) and (B)

149. Court decisions, Federal register, Text of legislative bills are the example of
(A) Primary Sources (B) Secondary Sources
(C) Tertiary Sources (D) None of the above

150. Who divided the source of information in two categories: Primary and the Secondary?
(A) C.W. Hanson
(B) Denis Grogan
(C) S.R. Ranganathan
(D) H.P. Luhn

151. On the basis of level of reorganization, Denis Grogan has classified the documents into
(A) Primary
(B) Secondary
(C) Both (A) and (B)
(D) Primary, Secondary and Tertiary

152. Which of the following sentence is true for Primary Source of information?
(A) New knowledge
(B) New interpretation of old knowledge
(C) First published of original research article
(D) All of the above

153. 'Encyclopedia of Religion' is the example of
(A) Primary Source (B) Secondary Source
(C) Tertiary Source (D) None of the above

154. Bibliography of Bibliographies is the example of
(A) Primary Source (B) Secondary Source
(C) Tertiary Source (D) None of the above

155. Conference Proceedings is the example of
(A) Primary Source (B) Secondary Source
(C) Tertiary Source (D) None of the above

156. Patents and Standards are the examples of
(A) Primary Source (B) Secondary Source
(C) Tertiary Source (D) None of the above

157. Yearbooks and Directories are the examples of
(A) Primary Source (B) Secondary Source
(C) Tertiary Source (D) None of the above

158. According to the UNESCO, a book should have at least................pages, exclusive of the cover pages.
(A) 60 (B) 59
(C) 76 (D) 49

159. The Indian Patent Office is administered by the Office of the.....
(A) NISCAIR (B) INFLIBNET
(C) IISER (D) CGPDTM

160. The headquarters of Patent Office of India is located at
(A) Chennai (B) Mumbai
(C) Kolkata (D) New Delhi

161. Which of the following cities is not located the Branch office of Patent Office of India?
(A) Chennai (B) Bengaluru
(C) New Delhi (D) Mumbai

162. Who says "to provide the right book to the right reader at the right time"?
(A) S.R. Ranganathan
(B) L.R. McColvin
(C) Haines
(D) Drury

163. In which year Drury's Principle for book selection was enunciated?
(A) 1930 (B) 1932
(C) 1939 (D) 1942

164. In which year McColvin's Principle for book selection was enunciated?

(A) 1921 (B) 1925
(C) 1932 (D) 1935

165. Which of the following book selection principle advocates the selection only those documents which are demanded by the users for their informational needs?
(A) S.R. Ranganathan's Principle
(B) McColvin's Principle
(C) Drury's Principle
(D) Dewey's Principle

166. Which of the following is the limitation to resource building in a library?
(A) Available space
(B) Resources for document processing
(C) Financial constraints
(D) All of the above

167. Which of the following is the Book Selection tool?
(A) Publishers catalogue
(B) Newspapers
(C) Scientific periodicals
(D) All of the above

168. For formulating the Ranganathan's principles of books selection in a library, which Law of Library Science is helpful?
(A) Books are for use
(B) Every reader his book
(C) Every book its reader
(D) All of the above

169. Which of the following is included in 1956 amendment of Delivery of Books and Newspaper (Public Libraries) Act, 1954 in India?
(A) Musical Sources (B) Newspaper
(C) Periodicals (D) Serials

170. For Acquisition Work, which of the following is necessary?
(A) Selection (B) Procurement
(C) Accessioning (D) All of the above

171. The purpose of.............is to rule out the possibilities of unnecessary duplications of study materials in a library.
(A) Scanning (B) Scrutiny
(C) Recording (D) Cataloguing

172. Who advocate 'Best Reading for the largest number at the least Cost' for Book Selection?
(A) S.R. Ranganathan
(B) Drury
(C) L.R. McColvin
(D) Melvil Dewey

173. In Accession Register, documents are entered in........according to their receipt in the library.
(A) Alphabetical order
(B) Classified order
(C) Date-wise order
(D) Any order

174. According to AACR, which of the following is the Non-Book material?
(A) Graphics materials
(B) Sound recording
(C) Video recording
(D) All of the above

175. The standard size of Accession Register will be
(A) 16" × 15" (B) 14" × 13"
(C) 16" × 13" (D) 13" × 12"

176. For documents management, technical processing of the document consisting
(A) Classification
(B) Cataloguing
(C) Both (A) and (B)
(D) Documents saved in database

177. For technical processing of the documents, which of the following is the vocabulary control device?
(A) Classification Scheme
(B) Catalogue Code

(C) Subject Headings
(D) All of the above

178. 'Browne Charging System' was devised by
(A) J.D. Brown (B) Nina E. Browne
(C) W.C.B. Sayers (D) Both (A) and (B)

179. A library system where books are brought to user from the shelves by the library staffs is called
(A) Open Access (B) Closed Access
(C) Support System (D) Manual System

180. Pamphlets are paper covered materials of fewer than........pages
(A) 35 (B) 45
(C) 50 (D) 57

181. ....is focused on the requirements of the user in library.
(A) SWOT (B) PERT
(C) TQM (D) DFD

182. Library cess is a revenue source specially for
(A) University Library (B) School Library
(C) Public Library (D) Research Library

183. Who evolved the 'Three Cards System' for maintenance of periodicals record in the library.
(A) S.R. Ranganathan
(B) Sanford Berman
(C) C.A. Cutter
(D) J.D. Brown

184. Which one is odd in 'Three Cards System'?
(A) Register Card
(B) Alphabetical Card
(C) Check Card
(D) Classified Index Card

185. Who introduced the 'Newark Charging System' for books issue?
(A) Charles Cutter
(B) J.D. Brown
(C) John Cotton Dana
(D) L.R. McColvin

186. The 'Dictaphone Charging System' is associated with
(A) Automatic Charging System
(B) Audio Charging System
(C) Three Card System
(D) None of the above

187. In first time where 'Dictaphone Charging System' was used?
(A) Library of Congress
(B) IFLA
(C) National Library of Laos
(D) St. Louis Country Public Library

188. For periodicals periodicity, 'Fortnightly' means
(A) Published in every two months
(B) Published in every three months
(C) Published in every month
(D) Published in every two weeks

189. Match the following:

LIST-I	LIST-II
(1) Published in every month	(i) Quarterly
(2) Published in every three months	(ii) Annual
(3) Published in every four months	(iii) Monthly
(4) Published in every year	(iv) Quadrimestre

Codes:

	(1)	(2)	(3)	(4)
(A)	(ii)	(iv)	(i)	(iii)
(B)	(iii)	(ii)	(iv)	(i)
(C)	(iii)	(iv)	(i)	(ii)
(D)	(iii)	(i)	(iv)	(ii)

190. 'Kardex System Method' for recording the receipt of periodicals is made by

(A) Elico Ltd.
(B) Keltron Ltd.
(C) Biocon India Ltd.
(D) Remington Rand of India Ltd.

191. As per General Financial Rules 2005, Govt. of India, the loss of up to......books per 1000 books issued/consulted in a year can be considered reasonable.

(A) 5 (B) 7
(C) 8 (D) 10

192. A book may be withdrawn from the stock register and shelf list, if

(A) Book is outdated
(B) Book is missed in stock verification
(C) Book is unusable due to damage
(D) All of the above

193. 'Checking of Pagination of the books' is called

(A) Collation (B) Counting
(C) Accessing (D) Recoding

194. In which type of budgeting method has propounded by Hoover Commission Report in 1949?

(A) Formula Budgeting
(B) Zero-Based Budgeting
(C) Programme Budgeting
(D) Performance Budgeting

195. The 'Three Card System' is used in

(A) Statistics for periodicals
(B) Book Classification
(C) For making Main Entry
(D) For making User Profiles

196. Which of the following are the elements in Three Card System?

(A) Register Card, Check Card and Main Entry
(B) Register Card, Check Card and Classified Index Entry
(C) Register Card, Check Card and Book Index Entry
(D) Record Card, Check Card and Class Index Entry

197. In library, the term 'Beespeaking' means

(A) Tell about users profile
(B) A kind of open library system
(C) Reservation of the book
(D) Reminding the users

198. What is the meaning of 'Charging' in library management?

(A) Returns of books
(B) Issue of books
(C) Classification of books
(D) Cataloguing of books

199. Planning, Programming, and Budgeting System (PPBS) method of budgeting was first proposed by

(A) Department of Defense (DOD), USA
(B) Department of Energy (DOE), USA
(C) Department of Treasury (DOT), USA
(D) Bank of England, UK

200. A method of budgeting in which all expenses must be justified for each new period.

(A) Programme Budgeting
(B) Formula Budgeting
(C) Planning, Programming, and Budgeting System (PPBS)
(D) Zero-Based Budgeting System (ZBB)

201. Zero-Based Budgeting System (ZBB) was developed by

(A) Peter Pyhrr (B) Paul Samuelson
(C) Milton Friedman (D) James Tobin

202. S.R. Ranganathan has suggested that ....of the total university library budget should be spent on books and others reading materials.

(A) 30% (B) 35%
(C) 55% (D) 40%

203. A chart in which the numerical values of variables are represented by the height or length of lines or rectangle of equal width?

(A) Pie Chart (B) Area Chart
(C) Scatter Chart (D) Bar Chart

204. IPAIRS is a/an

(A) Web portal for Patents Information System, India
(B) Data communication protocol
(C) Indexing System
(D) Language translator software

205. In Newark System, how many registrations files are used?

(A) 2 (B) 4
(C) 5 (D) 7

206. The Wikipedia articles are the example of

(A) Primary Source (B) Secondary Source
(C) Tertiary Source (D) None of the above

207. An analysis tool for audit and analysis of the overall strategic position of any organization and its environment.

(A) SWOT (B) PERT
(C) PEST (D) CPM

208. In SWOT analysis tool, arrival of new technology in our library is

(A) Strengths (S) (B) Weaknesses (W)
(C) Opportunities (O) (D) Threats (T)

209. Who wrote book *The Management of Organization*?

(A) C. Ray Gullett (B) Susan M. Phillips
(C) William M. Pride (D) Herbert G. Hicks

210. In SWOT analysis tool, (O) stands for

(A) Opportunities (B) Organization
(C) Optimistic (D) Objective

211. Browne Charging System is specially used in

(A) Classification (B) Cataloguing
(C) Circulation (D) Book Selection

212. Assertion (A): For library management, the major affecting factors are working environment, technology and psychological characteristics of library staffs.

Reason (R): Modern theory of management emphasis the well structured office environment, and technologies are more important than administration.

(A) Both (A) and (R) are true
(B) Both (A) and (R) are false
(C) (A) is false, but (R) is true
(D) (A) is true, but (R) is false

213. Assertion (A): The main purpose of Management Information System (MIS) are decision-making, planning, and outputting.

Reason (R): The output of MIS is usually in the form of information report.

(A) Both (A) and (R) are true
(B) (A) is true, but (R) is false
(C) (A) is false, but (R) is true
(D) Both (A) and (R) are false

214. Assertion (A): In library, MIS can assist the library staffs, for data analysis, and decision-making.

Reason (R): MIS works as tools, which improved the effectiveness and efficiency of library staff.

(A) Both (A) and (R) are true
(B) Both (A) and (R) are false
(C) (A) is true, but (R) is false
(D) (A) is false, but (R) is true

215. Assertion (A): Management is both a Science and an Art.

Reason (R): Management knowledge constitutes as the Science and managing of knowledge is the Art.

(A) Both (A) and (R) are false
(B) Both (A) and (R) are true
(C) (A) is false, but (R) is true
(D) (A) is true, but (R) is false

ANSWERS KEYS

1. (A)	2. (B)	3. (A)	4. (D)
5. (B)	6. (B)	7. (D)	8. (A)
9. (A)	10. (C)	11. (A)	12. (B)
13. (A)	14. (D)	15. (A)	16. (D)
17. (D)	18. (B)	19. (B)	20. (A)
21. (A)	22. (D)	23. (D)	24. (C)
25. (B)	26. (C)	27. (C)	28. (A)
29. (D)	30. (A)	31. (C)	32. (B)
33. (A)	34. (D)	35. (A)	36. (B)
37. (C)	38. (A)	39. (A)	40. (A)
41. (D)	42. (A)	43. (D)	44. (C)
45. (B)	46. (A)	47. (B)	48. (A)
49. (A)	50. (C)	51. (A)	52. (C)
53. (A)	54. (A)	55. (D)	56. (A)
57. (A)	58. (A)	59. (A)	60. (D)
61. (A)	62. (B)	63. (D)	64. (D)
65. (A)	66. (A)	67. (C)	68. (C)
69. (C)	70. (C)	71. (A)	72. (A)
73. (C)	74. (D)	75. (C)	76. (C)
77. (D)	78. (D)	79. (A)	80. (D)
81. (D)	82. (D)	83. (D)	84. (D)
85. (A)	86. (D)	87. (D)	88. (D)
89. (B)	90. (C)	91. (D)	92. (B)
93. (A)	94. (A)	95. (C)	96. (C)
97. (A)	98. (A)	99. (A)	100. (C)
101. (D)	102. (C)	103. (C)	104. (D)
105. (D)	106. (D)	107. (C)	108. (C)

109. (D)	110. (D)	111. (D)	112. (D)
113. (C)	114. (A)	115. (D)	116. (D)
117. (D)	118. (D)	119. (A)	120. (B)
121. (A)	122. (C)	123. (C)	124. (D)
125. (B)	126. (D)	127. (C)	128. (C)
129. (C)	130. (A)	131. (B)	132. (A)
133. (A)	134. (A)	135. (C)	136. (B)
137. (A)	138. (C)	139. (A)	140. (D)
141. (D)	142. (A)	143. (B)	144. (B)
145. (B)	146. (B)	147. (B)	148. (D)
149. (A)	150. (A)	151. (D)	152. (D)
153. (B)	154. (C)	155. (A)	156. (A)
157. (C)	158. (D)	159. (D)	160. (C)
161. (B)	162. (D)	163. (A)	164. (B)
165. (B)	166. (D)	167. (D)	168. (D)
169. (B)	170. (D)	171. (B)	172. (D)
173. (C)	174. (D)	175. (C)	176. (C)
177. (D)	178. (B)	179. (B)	180. (C)
181. (C)	182. (C)	183. (A)	184. (B)
185. (C)	186. (B)	187. (D)	188. (D)
189. (D)	190. (D)	191. (A)	192. (D)
193. (A)	194. (C)	195. (A)	196. (B)
197. (C)	198. (B)	199. (A)	200. (D)
201. (A)	202. (D)	203. (D)	204. (A)
205. (A)	206. (B)	207. (A)	208. (C)
209. (D)	210. (A)	211. (C)	212. (D)
213. (D)	214. (A)	215. (B)	

CHAPTER

7 Academic Libraries and their Kinds and Services

Introduction

It is a fact that libraries classified according to working structure, pattern, providing services, types of users and their documents utilization in the form of academic library, public library, research library and special library which is founded for special purpose and also special kind of users. Among them, academic libraries are one of the most existing and popular among users. School, college and the universities are existed under the academic libraries. In modern time where information are decentralized and also in dynamic manner, academic libraries play a significant role in the context of academic requirement of students, researchers as well as faculties. In school library system where users are limited and also the service area is not too big as college and university libraries. University library is an important unit for undergraduate and postgraduate students for learning process of their study programme.

Thus, in this chapter, we have been considered in respect of academic library system and their service as according to the present pattern of said examinations.

Important Points

- School, college, university and research libraries are categories under Academic Libraries.
- The primary objective of academic libraries is conservation and preservation of knowledge.
- For the development of the college libraries, report of Library Committee of the University Grants Commission was published in 1965.
- Report of the Radhakrishnan Commission on University Education (1948-49) stated that—"The library is the heart of all university's work, directly so, as regards its research work, and indirectly as regards its educational work which derives its life from research work."
- According to M.A. Gelfand, the function of university library is as a "dynamic instrument of education, to feed the intellect of student, encourage researchers of the faculty and invite all who enter its house to partake fully of its intellectual and cultural contents".

- The University Education Commission (1948-49), under the Chairmanship of Dr. S. Radhakrishnan recommended that 6.25% of sanction of the total budget or ₹ 40 per student made as the annual grant for the university library.
- On 22 July 1988, the Government of India accepted the recommendations of the Mehrotra Committee for the implementation of revised pay scales and qualifications for teachers in universities and colleges.
- A library committee can set up the broad policies for acquisitions, organization, evaluation and weeding out.
- The paternal role of library authorities comprises creating, launching, funding and monitoring of libraries.
- A body which is responsible for library services is known as Library Authority.
- There are four basic requirements for providing library service in any type of library are (a) information, (b) instruction, (c) guidance, and (d) stimulation.
- Reference Service from the library can be defined as "the process of establishing contact between reader and book by personal service".
- How to user interact with our library in first time or for daily routine visiting, the library orientation is the most important imparting method.
- Direct method and Indirect method are two basic categories of library orientation.
- In Direct method, we can assist the users through lecture, guided tour, individual help, practical exercises and demonstration.
- In Indirect method, we can guide the users through audio-video, power point presentations, multimedia animations, printed guide books and self-guided 3D videos.
- Fine on late return of study materials, loss or misuse of books (documents) simply is not considered the source of income of a library, but practically it seem to be pressurized the users to treat well with library books and make availability for other users.
- According to Kothari Commission, the 6.5% to 10% of educational budget is reasonable expenditure on libraries.
- Per Capita Method, Proportional Method, and Method of Details are the methods for measuring financial requirements of a library.
- According to Harrod's Librarian Glossary, the collection development as the process of planning a stock acquisition programme no simple to cater for immediate needs but to build a coherent and reliable collection over a number of years, to meet the objectives of the services.
- For library collection development policy, the weeding out means removing documents which are found not useful or not serviceable from a library.
- There are three possible cases of weeding out of the documents, (a) documents removed completely from library collections, (b) documents may be denoted some other library

where they may be useful, and (c) apply dormitory library policy that means documents kept in a reserve place.

- A proper committee should be established for weeding out the documents in a library, therefore weeding out should not be arbitrary.
- S.R. Ranganathan observes that many of the modern books get out mode in ideas expounded in them within 20 years. After that period such books should not be preserved in library but should be weeded out and written off.
- The weeded out materials such as textbooks completely worn out and they sold like old newspapers.
- For weeded out purpose, the old edition reference materials like dictionaries, encyclopedia, handbooks, yearbooks, etc. may have to be donated to other libraries who are not in a position to buy such costly books.
- According to UGC Committee on University and College Libraries (1965) headed by S.R. Ranganathan, "at least one copy of the weeded out documents should be preserved at a place within a region of the country".
- Weeded out process in a library should be done through concerned library committee or the library authority.
- In university library, the best document arrangement method is subject approach (classified) and open-shelf collection.
- According to C.G. Viswanathan, "Cataloguing and Classification are the twin processes adopted in modern library administration to help readers in locating the desired books and other reading materials quickly and conveniently."
- The main objective of the Reference Librarian is to provide right information to the right user at the right time; therefore, he/she is a mediator between the book and the user.
- Examination books to see that they are in correct order on the shelves is known as shelf checking and shelf tiding, shelf reading, revising shelves and reading shelves are the synonymous terms for this.
- S.R. Ranganathan given the term shelf rectification for the process of restoring order among the book on the shelves.
- The systematic reading the shelves and shelving back the books that are misplaced according to their proper sequence is known as shelf rectification.
- After 1984, the Government of India amended the rule that books, journals, etc. are not "store item", therefore, the stock verification of library materials is separate case as compare with other "store items".
- Before 1984, Government of India treated books, journals, etc., as "store items" which made stock verification essential.

QUESTIONS

1. Which of the following is the best place for answering related to research questions?
(A) Circular Section
(B) Reference Section
(C) Technical Section
(D) Periodical Section

2. Which of the following is the example of academic library?
(A) School (B) College
(C) Research (D) All of the above

3. According to the Kothari Commission (1964-66), the recommendation for.....of education budget for the development of college libraries.
(A) 6.5% to 10% (B) 4% to 9%
(C) 7% to 15% (D) 8% to 14%

4. In which year UGC-INFONET Digital Library Consortium was launched?
(A) 1997 (B) 2000
(C) 2003 (D) 2005

5. The person who responsible for the ongoing design, development and evaluation of the library consortium is called
(A) Web Service Librarian
(B) Web Page Reference Librarian
(C) URL Reference Librarian
(D) Both (B) and (C)

6. Which of the following is the controlled vocabulary specially used for describing of art, architecture, and graphical materials?
(A) TGM (B) AAT
(C) LCSH (D) Both (A) and (B)

7. According to Guy R. Lyle, librarian should spend at least......each week for procedure of book selection.
(A) One day (B) Two days
(C) Three days (D) Four days

8. Who says "Academic library system postulates that there should be library centered education in schools, colleges and universities"?
(A) S.R. Ranganathan (B) D.S. Kothari
(C) P.N. Kaula (D) C.D. Deskmukh

9. Indian Association of Academic Librarians (INDAAL) was established in
(A) 1975 (B) 1978
(C) 1980 (D) 1982

10. Indian Association of Teachers of Library and Information Science (IATLIS) was established at
(A) DRTC, Bengaluru (B) IASLIC, Kolkata
(C) ILA, New Delhi (D) ISI, Bengaluru

11. Which of the following is the primary tool for book selection?
(A) Newspapers ads
(B) Web sites
(C) Publishers' Catalogue
(D) Book reviews

12. Which of the following challenges affecting the management of academic libraries?
(A) Rising of e-research among scholars
(B) Management of e-documents according to the users requirements
(C) Increasing the quantity of research output in digital form
(D) All of the above

13. Medical Library Association of India is located at
(A) New Delhi (B) Kolkata
(C) Bengaluru (D) Mumbai

14. TGM stands for
(A) Thesaurus for Graphics Materials
(B) Thesaurus for General Materials
(C) Tools for Geographical Materials
(D) Tools for Geometrical Materials

15. Match the following:

LIST-I	LIST-II
(1) Book Binding and Book Production	(i) S.R. Ranganathan
(2) Administration of College Library	(ii) M. Dorothy Evans
(3) Library Administration	(iii) Guy R. Lyle
(4) Book Selection	(iv) F.K.W. Drury

Codes:

	(1)	(2)	(3)	(4)
(A)	(iii)	(ii)	(i)	(iv)
(B)	(ii)	(iii)	(i)	(iv)
(C)	(iv)	(ii)	(i)	(iii)
(D)	(ii)	(iii)	(iv)	(i)

16. The UGC Committee on University and College Libraries recommended that......books per thousand issue may be considered a normal loss for a library.

(A) Three (B) Four
(C) Eight (D) Twelve

17. What is SCONUL?

(A) Sub-committee to promote higher education and national libraries in UK
(B) Committee to promote school education system in USA
(C) An open source software for university libraries
(D) A kind of metadata standard

18. In which year 'UGC Review Committee on Library Science in Indian Universities' recommendation was published?

(A) 1963 (B) 1965
(C) 1968 (D) 1971

19. AAT stands for

(A) Art & Architecture Thesaurus
(B) Artificial & Archeological Thesaurus
(C) Art & Archeological Thesaurus
(D) Art & Artificial Thesaurus

20. Match the following:

LIST-I	LIST-II
(1) Role of Academic Library in Education	(i) S.R. Ranganathan
(2) The Public Relation of Academic Libraries	(ii) P.N. Kaula
(3) Library Building: Planning and Designing	(iii) Davis E. Wilson
(4) Library Book Selection	(iv) Abdul Waheed Khan

Codes:

	(1)	(2)	(3)	(4)
(A)	(i)	(iii)	(ii)	(iv)
(B)	(iii)	(i)	(iv)	(ii)
(C)	(iv)	(iii)	(ii)	(i)
(D)	(i)	(iii)	(iv)	(ii)

21. In which year National Committee of Archivists (NCA) was established?

(A) 1950 (B) 1953
(C) 1956 (D) 1958

22. All Bengal School Librarians' Association (ABSLA) was founded in

(A) 1990 (B) 1994
(C) 1998 (D) 2000

23. Bombay Science Librarians' Association (BOSLA) was established in

(A) 1965 (B) 1970
(C) 1975 (D) 1978

24. Which of the following is the graphical interface for Digital Libraries?

(A) GUI (B) ZUI
(C) CUI (D) Both (A) and (B)

25. Society for the Advancement of Library and Information Science (SALIS) is located at

(A) Chennai (B) Bengaluru
(C) Mangalore (D) Madurai

26. Which of the following service is provided by university library?
(A) Reprography service
(B) Inter-Library Loan (ILL) service
(C) Current Awareness Service (CAS)
(D) All of the above

27. ZUI stands for
(A) Zenith User Interface
(B) Zooming User Interface
(C) Zombie User Interface
(D) Both (A) and (B)

28. Which of the following committees considered the pay scale of librarians in colleges and universities?
(A) Mehrotra Committee
(B) D.S. Kothari Committee
(C) P.N. Kaula Committee
(D) G.R. Damodaran Committee

29. In which year UGC was formally established in United Kingdom?
(A) 1917 (B) 1919
(C) 1921 (D) 1934

30. Which of the following is true for Virtual Library (VL)?
(A) It means library without wall
(B) There is no paper-based environment
(C) The resources are available in digital format
(D) All of the above

31. Which of the following is the purpose of preservation of digital documents?
(A) Durability
(B) Intellectual integrity
(C) Maximize the usability
(D) All of the above

32. Apache is a/an
(A) Operating System software
(B) Antivirus software
(C) Plagiarism software
(D) Web server software

33. Which of the following bibliographic metadata follow the OAI-PMH standard?
(A) Dublin Core (B) MARC
(C) RFC (D) All of the above

34. In which committee suggested that 'National Eligibility Test' (NET) is necessary for requirement of lectures and assistant librarians in academic institutions?
(A) D.S. Kothari Committee
(B) P.N. Kaula Committee
(C) Mehrotra Committee
(D) S.R. Ranganathan Committee

35. National University of Educational Planning and Administration (NIEPA) is suited at
(A) Mumbai (B) New Delhi
(C) Kolkata (D) Chennai

36. Which of the following is the Internet Resource Discovery (IRD) tool?
(A) Search Engines (B) Digital Libraries
(C) Java (D) Both (A) and (B)

37. Which of the following is the open source web server?
(A) Apache (B) Xampp
(C) Tornado (D) All of the above

38. Academic libraries are established specifically to
(A) Research (B) Support learning
(C) Teaching (D) All of the above

39. In which year National Council for Teacher Education (NCTE) was established?
(A) 1973 (B) 1975
(C) 1978 (D) 1981

40. The 'IFLA/UNESCO School Library Manifesto: the school library in teaching and learning and learning for all' was published in......

(A) 1992 (B) 1995
(C) 1997 (D) 2000

41. With the help of..................we can know how many books are lost in the library.
(A) Accession Register
(B) Charging
(C) Shelf list
(D) Stock verification

42. Calcutta School Society was established in
(A) 1817 (B) 1819
(C) 1821 (D) 1824

43. ....is a social institution.
(A) Public library (B) Academic library
(C) Research library (D) Both (B) and (C)

44. IASL stands for
(A) International Association of School Librarianship
(B) International Assembly for School Librarianship
(C) International Academy for School Librarianship
(D) International Accreditation of School Librarianship

45. *School Libraries Worldwide* is published by
(A) UNESCO (B) IFLA
(C) IASL (D) CILIP

46. The 81st IFLA General Conference and Assembly (IFLA World Library and Information Congress) was held in
(A) Lyon, France, 2014
(B) Helsinki, Finland, 2012
(C) Cape Town, South Africa, 2015
(D) San Juan, Puerto Rico, 2011

47. The frequency of publication of *School Libraries Worldwide* is
(A) Monthly (B) Quarterly
(C) Half-yearly (D) Annually

48. 'Indira Gandhi Memorial Library' is suited at
(A) University of Hyderabad
(B) University of Mumbai
(C) University of Calcutta
(D) University of Madras

49. Match the following:

	LIST-I		LIST-II
(1)	IFLA WLIC 2016	(i)	Singapore
(2)	IFLA WLIC 2015	(ii)	Lyon, France
(3)	IFLA WLIC 2014	(iii)	Columbus, Ohio, USA
(4)	IFLA WLIC 2013	(iv)	Cape Town, South Africa

Codes:

	(1)	(2)	(3)	(4)
(A)	(iii)	(iv)	(ii)	(i)
(B)	(i)	(ii)	(iii)	(iv)
(C)	(iv)	(iii)	(ii)	(i)
(D)	(ii)	(iii)	(iv)	(i)

50. National Environment Engineering Research Institute (NEERI) Library is located at
(A) New Delhi (B) Hyderabad
(C) Nagpur (D) Mumbai

51. Metadata....is the aggregation of metadata records from multiple providers (sources) into a single database
(A) Harvesting (B) Compiling
(C) Grouping (D) Indexing

52. The book titled *Handbook of Usability Testing: How to Plan, Design, and Conduct Effective Test* (1st edition) was written by
(A) Jeffrey Rubin (B) Kim Goodwin
(C) Warren B. Powell (D) Robbie T. Nakatsu

53. CORBA is a/an
(A) Web browser
(B) Operating System for Server
(C) Linux-based Operating System
(D) Standard architecture for distributed object systems

54. The Board of Education of American Library Association (ALA) was established in
(A) 1920 (B) 1924
(C) 1928 (D) 1932

55. The headquarters of Association of Research Libraries (ARL) is located at
(A) Paris (B) Washington, D.C.
(C) Sydney (D) Milan

56. In which year Association of Research Libraries (ARL) was founded?
(A) 1929 (B) 1932
(C) 1938 (D) 1942

57. Which of the following is the necessary element for a Digital Library?
(A) Collection (B) Technology
(C) Institution (D) All of the above

58. In ancient India, which university became the highest citadel of knowledge in Asia?
(A) Vallabhi University
(B) Takshila University
(C) Nalanda University
(D) Vikramshila University

59. Which of the formula is used for evaluation of web content in terms of web accessing of an academic library?
(A) OWPC
(B) CWPC
(C) Lotka's Law
(D) Both (A) and (B)

60. Which of the following is a Metadata Harvesting protocol?
(A) FAT32 (B) OAI-PMH
(C) OSI (D) OWPC

61. TEI stands for
(A) Text Encoding Initiative
(B) Transfer Encoding Initiative
(C) Textual Encoding Interchange
(D) Text Encoding Interchange

62. OWPC stands for
(A) Online Website Performance Calculation
(B) Offline Website Performance Calculation
(C) Overall Website Performance Calculation
(D) Optimal Website Performance Calculation

63. CWPC stands for
(A) Criteria-wise Website Performance Calculation
(B) Community-wise Website Performance Calculation
(C) Command-wise Website Performance Calculation
(D) Complex-widest Website Performance Calculation

64. Which of the following was associated with blueprint for university education in India in 1885?
(A) Charles Wood (B) James Mill
(C) W.B. Yeats (D) D.A. Malcom

65. As of 23 April 2015, the Ministry of Human Resource Development, Govt. of India has listed ....institutes under the category of Institutes of National Importance (INI)?
(A) 74 (B) 80
(C) 85 (D) 92

66. National Library of China was established in
(A) 1885 (B) 1889
(C) 1903 (D) 1909

67. Which of the following is the second largest Central Government Library after the National Library, Kolkata?
(A) Central Secretariat Library, New Delhi
(B) Raja Rammohan Roy Library Foundation, Kolkata
(C) Khuda Bakhsh Oriental Library, Patna
(D) Connemara Public Library, Chennai

68. Central Secretariat Library, New Delhi formerly known as

(A) Govt. of India Secretariat Central Library, Kolkata
(B) Imperial Secretariat Library, Kolkata
(C) Reference Secretariat Library, Kolkata
(D) Central Secretariat Library, Kolkata

69. Imperial Secretariat Library, Kolkata was established in
(A) 1874 (B) 1888
(C) 1891 (D) 1895

70. In which year Imperial Secretariat Library, Kolkata was shifted to New Delhi at Shastri Bhawan?
(A) 1956 (B) 1969
(C) 1972 (D) 1976

71. In which year National Knowledge Commission (NKC) recommended to setting up the National Mission on Libraries (NML)?
(A) 2007 (B) 2009
(C) 2011 (D) 2012

72. CORBA stands for
(A) Common Object Request Broker Architecture
(B) Classified Object Request Broker Architecture
(C) Common Object Response Broker Architecture
(D) Common Object Request Binary Architecture

73. Match the following:

LIST-I	**LIST-II**
(1) TexShare	(i) India
(2) CALIS	(ii) United Kingdom
(3) RLUK	(iii) USA
(4) INDEST-AICTE	(iv) China

Codes:

	(1)	**(2)**	**(3)**	**(4)**
(A)	(iv)	(ii)	(iii)	(i)
(B)	(iii)	(iv)	(ii)	(i)
(C)	(iv)	(iii)	(ii)	(i)
(D)	(iii)	(ii)	(iv)	(i)

74. Which of the following library consortium established in USA?
(A) GALILIO (B) OhioLink
(C) VIVA (D) All of the above

75. A desktop environment that composed entirely of free and open source software
(A) GNOME (B) Pantheon
(C) Plasma (D) All of the above

76. Which of the following universities was set up on the pattern of the London University?
(A) Calcutta University
(B) Bombay University
(C) Madras University
(D) All of the above

77. HQL stands for
(A) Harvest Query Language
(B) Hypermedia Query Language
(C) Hypertext Query Language
(D) High-level Query Language

78. ....is an international free software community
(A) SDD (B) KDE
(C) TDE (D) HGT

79. Which of the following consortium has been merged into e-ShodhSindu Consortia?
(A) UGC-INFONET (B) INDEST-AICTE
(C) NLIST (D) All of the above

80. Who is the founder of KDE?
(A) Matthias Ettrich (B) John S. Smith
(C) William S. Rocs (D) Parley Smith

81. The..........provides a common framework for data sharing and reusing across the application and also community boundaries.
(A) Semantic Web (B) Analytical Web
(C) Systematical Web (D) All of the above

82. In which year Calcutta University Library was established?
(A) 1870 (B) 1873
(C) 1878 (D) 1880

83. The term 'Semantic Web' is coined by
(A) Tim Berners-Lee
(B) John Allsopp
(C) Thomas S. Straccia
(D) J. Handler

84. In which year Bombay University Library was inaugurated?
(A) 1878 (B) 1880
(C) 1882 (D) 1886

85. Which of the following is the component for Digital Library?
(A) Internet and Intranets
(B) End-user services
(C) Integrated access to information
(D) All of the above

86. Which of the following is the technology for Semantic Web?
(A) RDF (B) Ontology
(C) OWL (D) All of the above

87. OWL stands for
(A) Web Ontology Language
(B) Web Online Language
(C) Web Object Language
(D) Web Optical Language

88. Which of the following was the India's first Education Commission?
(A) Sadler Commission
(B) Hunter Commission
(C) MacDonnell Commission
(D) Mehrotra Committee

89. 'Sadler Commission' also called
(A) Calcutta University Commission
(B) Bombay University Commission
(C) Madras University Commission
(D) Review Committee for the National Library

90. GSDL (Green Stone Digital Library) is developed by the University of Waikato in collaboration with..............
(A) IFLA (B) CILIP
(C) ALA (D) UNESCO

91. Louvre is a/an
(A) Museum Website
(B) Networking model
(C) Protocol for data transfer
(D) Plagiarism software

92. Who says "the word library merely implied a collection of books; it did not matter however where it was housed"?
(A) D.S. Kothari
(B) S.R. Radhakrishnan
(C) A.L. Mudaliar
(D) S. Bashiruddin

93. Which one is recognized as a pioneer of faceted search?
(A) Endeca (B) Wikipedia
(C) Yahoo (D) Google

94. Which of the following is related to the web-based electronic educational technology platform?
(A) SROM (B) SCROM
(C) DEROM (D) TEROM

95. Which of the following was the Chairperson of Commission for University Education (1948-49)?
(A) S. Radhakrishnan
(B) A. Lakshmanswamy Mudaliar
(C) D.S. Kothari
(D) S.D. Deshmukh

96. Which of the following is false related to the special library?
(A) The CAS and SDI services are not provided
(B) Provides index and abstract services

(C) Translation services are not available
(D) Both (A) and (C)

97. Which of the following is responsible for execution of e-ShodhSindhu Consortia?
(A) INFLIBNET (B) AICTE
(C) ILA (D) RRRLF

98. S. Radhakrishnan's Commission recommended that all university libraries should remain open for at least......hours a day for seven days of the week.
(A) 7 (B) 9
(C) 11 (D) 12

99. From 'Book fund', library will purchase
(A) Books (B) Periodicals
(C) Newspapers (D) All of the above

100. SCROM stands for
(A) Sharable Content Object Reference Model
(B) Syntax Content Object Reference Model
(C) Semantic Content Object Reference Model
(D) Systematic Content Object Reference Model

101. Metadata schemes are usually represented as set of.....that form a schema for metadata record.
(A) Tags (B) Queries
(C) Interpreter (D) Compiler

102. In which year Open Archives Initiative (OAI) was launched?
(A) 1997 (B) 1999
(C) 2002 (D) 2004

103. In which year, the University Grants Commission organized a seminar titled "From Publisher to Reader, Work-Flow in University and College Libraries"?
(A) 1955 (B) 1959
(C) 1963 (D) 1968

104. Which of the following is the legal issue for a Digital Library?
(A) Privacy (B) Contracts
(C) Copyright (D) All of the above

105. Which of the following is a gateway of Post Graduate courses established by MHRD, Govt. of India?
(A) e-GatewayPG
(B) e-PG Pathshala
(C) e- PGConsortia
(D) e-PGSubjectGateway

106. Which of the following user education programme is necessary for research scholars in academic library?
(A) Information about literature search
(B) Detail information about bibliographies
(C) Information about e-journals subscription
(D) All of the above

107. CDP stands for
(A) Collection Development Policy
(B) Center Development Policy
(C) Content Development Policy
(D) Cooperation Development Policy

108. The Kothari Commission was appointed in which year?
(A) August 1964 (B) April 1963
(C) July 1964 (D) October 1966

109. Which of the following selection criteria is applicable for CDP in university library?
(A) Currency of information
(B) Treatment of subject according to the syllabus
(C) Local emphasis
(D) Both (A) and (B)

110. Which of the following methods/techniques is applying for user education in academic library?
(A) Orientation week
(B) Messaging alerts method for new coming books
(C) Mobile library
(D) Both (A) and (C)

111. According to the Kothari Commission,...... of University Budget should be allocated for the university library.

(A) 5% (B) 6.5%
(C) 7.5% (D) 9.5%

112. Which of the following common technical issue is related to the Digital Library?

(A) Security
(B) Standards
(C) Infrastructure development
(D) All of the above

113. A kind of library where resources are available only in electronic format and can be accessed in any time of day or night.

(A) Digital Library
(B) Virtual Library
(C) Physical Library
(D) All of the above

114. In India, which of the following universities was constituted a committee for preparing the list of books to be purchased for university library in first time?

(A) Mumbai University
(B) Calcutta University
(C) Madras University
(D) Allahabad University

115. In which year ALA published the 'Code of Ethics and the Library Bill of Rights'?

(A) 1992 (B) 1995
(C) 1999 (D) 2001

116. Which of the following is a conceptual framework for describing and accessing the information about art and architecture works?

(A) CDWA (B) FART
(C) CDMA (D) MART

117. Association of College and Research Libraries (ACRL) is the division of

(A) ALA (B) IFLA
(C) CILIP (D) ASLIB

118. In 1957, University Grants Commission set up the 'Library Committee' under the chairmanship of

(A) S.R. Ranganathan
(B) S. Radhakrishnan
(C) A.L. Mudaliar
(D) D.S. Kothari

119. In which year INDEST Consortium was set up?

(A) 2000 (B) 2003
(C) 2005 (D) 2007

120. CDWA stands for

(A) Categories for the Description of Works of Art
(B) Categories for the Directory of Works of Art
(C) Classification and Description of Works of Art
(D) Cataloguing and Description of Works of Art

121. CCO stands for

(A) Cataloguing Cultural Objects
(B) Cataloguing Computer Objects
(C) Cataloguing Complex Objects
(D) Cataloguing Creative Objects

122. Which of the following is the data standard for description of visual culture and image documents works?

(A) VRA Core
(B) TRA Core
(C) XRA Core
(D) All of the above

123. The current digital era, research library face which type of challenge?

(A) Copyright
(B) Management of e-resources
(C) IT savvy users
(D) All of the above

124. VRA stands for

(A) Virtual Resources Association
(B) Visual Resources Association
(C) Virtual Repository Association
(D) Visual Repository Application

125. In which year VRA was founded?
(A) 1976 (B) 1978
(C) 1982 (D) 1988

126. In which year INDEST Consortium was re-named as INDEST-AICTE Consortium?
(A) 2005 (B) 2006
(C) 2007 (D) 2008

127. Directory of Open Access Journals (DOAJ) was founded in 2003 by
(A) Lars Bjornshauge
(B) Trip A. Allen
(C) Tom A. Anderson
(D) Ryan Allis

128. Which of the following sentences is false for Virtual Libraries?
(A) They exist in cyberspace only
(B) They have no building like traditional library
(C) Documents are available only in digital format and access through Internet
(D) All of the above are true

129. SGML stands for
(A) Standard Generalized Markup Language
(B) Syntax Generalized Markup Language
(C) Semantic Generalized Markup Language
(D) Systematic Generalized Markup Language

130. Which of the following is data standard for archival description?
(A) EAD (B) CDWA
(C) VRA Core (D) All of the above

131. A halfway step towards the fully Digital Library is a/an
(A) Hybrid Library
(B) Harvesting Library
(C) Dynamic Library
(D) Static Library

132. KOS stands for
(A) Knowledge Organization System
(B) Knowledge Optimized System
(C) Knowledge Object System
(D) Knowledge Oriented System

133. ....is the ability of a computer program to understand human speech as it is spoken.
(A) Natural Language Processing (NLP)
(B) Compiling Processing (CP)
(C) Assembling Processing (AP)
(D) Database Processing (DP)

134. Special Libraries Association (SLA)-Asian Chapter was established in
(A) 1997 (B) 1999
(C) 2001 (D) 2003

135. Central Government Library Association (CGLA) was established in
(A) 1998 (B) 2001
(C) 2004 (D) 2006

136. EAD stands for
(A) Encoded Archival Description
(B) Entity Archival Description
(C) Encoded Application Description
(D) Effective Archival Description

137. Who says "a library is like an island in the middle of a vast sea of ignorance"?
(A) Nora Roberts (B) Charles L. Grant
(C) Lemony Snicket (D) Edger A. Poe

138. ERIC stands for
(A) Educational Resources Information Center
(B) Educational Research Information Center
(C) Educational Resources Interlinked Center
(D) Educational Resources International Center

139. Match the following:

LIST-I	LIST-II
(1) Inter-University Centre for Astronomy and Astrophysics (IUCAA)	(i) Pune
(2) Raman Research Institute (RRI)	(ii) Bengaluru
(3) Tata Institute of Fundamental Research (TIFR)	(iii) New Delhi
(4) Indian Agriculture Research Institute (IARI)	(iv) Mumbai

Codes:

	(1)	(2)	(3)	(4)
(A)	(ii)	(i)	(iv)	(iii)
(B)	(i)	(ii)	(iv)	(iii)
(C)	(ii)	(iii)	(iv)	(i)
(D)	(i)	(iii)	(iv)	(ii)

140. Which of the following attributes is related to the Digital Libraries?
(A) E-resources should be accessible from anywhere
(B) Library website should be enabled to locate information
(C) Modern tools should be available for information access
(D) All of the above

141. Which of the following is the best location for University/Central Library?
(A) Any nearer place in university campus
(B) Nearer to hostels campus
(C) Centre of the university campus
(D) Outside of the hostels campus

142. Which of the following search engine is especially for E-Resource?
(A) JSTOR (B) Jurn
(C) Project MUSE (D) All of the above

143. Who says "it is a crime to deny a person a direct access to his document which he alone can find out"?
(A) Melvil Dewey
(B) J.D. Brown
(C) S.R. Ranganathan
(D) W.C.B. Sayers

144. Match the following:

LIST-I	LIST-II
(1) JSTOR	(i) 2009
(2) Jurn	(ii) 1966
(3) Project MUSE	(iii) 1995
(4) ERIC	(iv) 1993

Codes:

	(1)	(2)	(3)	(4)
(A)	(iii)	(i)	(iv)	(ii)
(B)	(i)	(iv)	(iii)	(ii)
(C)	(ii)	(iii)	(iv)	(i)
(D)	(iii)	(iv)	(i)	(ii)

145. In which year first India Public Libraries Conference (IPLC) was organized?
(A) 2008 (B) 2010
(C) 2012 (D) 2015

146. Which of the following was the venue of second India Public Libraries Conference (IPLC)?
(A) Kolkata (B) Bengaluru
(C) New Delhi (D) Hyderabad

147. NASSCOM was established in
(A) 1994 (B) 1998
(C) 1999 (D) 2001

148. Who organized second India Public Libraries Conference?
(A) NASSCOM (B) DELNET
(C) RRRLF (D) Both (A) and (B)

149. Which of the following is the largest database related to education in world-wide?
(A) JSTOR (B) ERIC
(C) Lingbuzz (D) POIESIS

150. Who inaugurated the first INDAAL Conference held at New Delhi

(A) P.N. Kaula (B) Krishan Kumar
(C) H.R. Khanna (D) B.S. Kesavan

151. Which of the following is false for 'Virtual Libraries'?
(A) It is a place but cyberspace
(B) It is an Internet-based environment
(C) It can exist without the existence of Digital Library
(D) Both (A) and (B)

152. According to the library professionals, the Digital Library is
(A) A database records for data processing
(B) An institution and the services-oriented system.
(C) A databank without the concept of library
(D) Digital library exist only in academic library

153. VLE stands for
(A) Virtual Learning Environment
(B) Virtual Literacy Environment
(C) Vector Learning Environment
(D) Virtual Linking Environment

154. Which of the following is a single most vexing barrier to Digital Library environment?
(A) Technical Architecture
(B) Metadata
(C) Copyright
(D) Digitization

155. In which year, UNESCO prepared the Public Library Manifesto in cooperation with IFLA?
(A) 1985 (B) 1988
(C) 1991 (D) 1994

156. Assertion (A): The main objective of an academy library is to serve the needs of the academic community.

Reason (R): Any academic library can be realized only in the context of the academic philosophy of education.
(A) Both (A) and (R) are true
(B) Both (A) and (R) are false
(C) (A) is true, but (R) is false
(D) (A) is false, but (R) is true

157. Assertion (A): Special Library deals with specific kind of users and collections of subject should be maintained according to their requirements.

Reason (R): The main objective of Special Library is to develop current as well as retrospective collections in core subject according to their programs.
(A) Both (A) and (R) are false
(B) Both (A) and (R) are true
(C) (A) is true, but (R) is false
(D) (A) is false, but (R) is true

158. Assertion (A): In Integrated Library Software, information resources should be carefully selected and organized.

Reason (R): Internet is a major source of information but there are no proper methods in terms of selection and classification of documents.
(A) Both (A) and (R) are true
(B) Both (A) and (R) are false
(C) (A) is true, but (R) is false
(D) (A) is false, but (R) is true

159. Assertion (A): From open access journals, we can access and download the desired documents without any payment.

Reason (R): Directory of Open Access Journals (DOAJ) is a platform where we can get URL of open access journals in worldwide.
(A) Both (A) and (R) are true
(B) Both (A) and (R) are false
(C) (A) is true, but (R) is false
(D) (A) is false, but (R) is true

160. Assertion (A): On the basis of services, there is no difference between traditional libraries and Digital Libraries, but management and nature of the documents is not the same.

Reason (R): The Digital Libraries consist of resources in machine-readable form only.
(A) Both (A) and (R) are true
(B) Both (A) and (R) are false
(C) (A) is true, but (R) is false
(D) (A) is false, but (R) is true

161. Assertion (A): Traditionally, the main purpose of establishing a library consortium is to resources sharing among associated libraries and information centers.

Reason (R): In Information Technology (IT) era, there is no need Inter Library Loans (ILL) for resources sharing because e-documents are easily available on the Internet.
(A) Both (A) and (R) are false
(B) Both (A) and (R) are true
(C) (A) is true, but (R) is false
(D) (A) is false, but (R) is true

162. Assertion (A): Library users generally interested in micro level collections, not the macro level.

Reason (R): Library users desired a particular book, article or particular information and they are not interested collections strength of a particular library.
(A) Both (A) and (R) are true
(B) Both (A) and (R) are false
(C) (A) is false, but (R) is true
(D) (A) is true, but (R) is false

163. Assertion (A): The print-based information resources generally regarded as less important but they are more useful than electronic resources.

Reason (R): Among research scholars, the e-resources now very popular because these types of resources are easily handled and also friendly to electronic gadget.
(A) Both (A) and (R) are true
(B) Both (A) and (R) are false
(C) (A) is true, but (R) is false
(D) (A) is false, but (R) is true

164. Assertion (A): In IT era, Digital Library is now appears as an intellectual information center where users and technologies interact to each other.

Reason (R): The existence of traditional libraries now worthless in our society because everything is available on the Internet.
(A) Both (A) and (R) are false
(B) Both (A) and (R) are true
(C) (A) is false, but (R) is true
(D) (A) is true, but (R) is false

165. Assertion (A): Library professionals should be changed their role from traditional librarian to information scientist in present IT era.

Reason (R): 'Everything is available on the web' is a new challenge to the traditional library system.
(A) Both (A) and (R) are true
(B) Both (A) and (R) are false
(C) (A) is true, but (R) is false
(D) (A) is false, but (R) is true

166. Assertion (A): Virtual Library is a parallel library system where multimedia and electronic information resources are assemblage in single place.

Reason (R): Virtual Library has developed with the growth of telecommunication network, especially the Internet.
(A) Both (A) and (R) are false
(B) Both (A) and (R) are true
(C) (A) is true, but (R) is false
(D) (A) is false, but (R) is true

167. Assertion (A): Virtual Library is more than a collection of digitized resources but it encompasses the concept of Digital Library.

Reason (R): Virtual Library is an integrated collection of electronic and multimedia resources.

(A) Both (A) and (R) are true
(B) Both (A) and (R) are false
(C) (A) is true, but (R) is false
(D) (A) is false, but (R) is true

168. Assertion (A): There is no need of technical works for e-documents such as Classifications and Cataloguing in Digital Libraries.

Reason (R): Because Digital Library is implemented through computer programme and software and they are capable of technical works.

(A) Both (A) and (R) are true
(B) Both (A) and (R) are false
(C) (A) is true, but (R) is false
(D) (A) is false, but (R) is true

169. Assertion (A): Digital Libraries will be existed without a Virtual Library but Virtual Libraries does not exist without the Digital Library.

Reason (R): The Digital Libraries follow all criteria of traditional libraries but in e-form.

(A) Both (A) and (R) are true
(B) Both (A) and (R) are false
(C) (A) is true, but (R) is false
(D) (A) is false, but (R) is true

170. Assertion (A): The minimum technical requirement for any Virtual Library is connectivity and if there is no Internet connection then Virtual Library is inaccessible.

Reason (R): The digital divide is a major problem for developing the Virtual Libraries.

(A) Both (A) and (R) are true
(B) Both (A) and (R) are false
(C) (A) is true, but (R) is false
(D) (A) is false, but (R) is true

Answers Keys

1. (B)	2. (D)	3. (A)	4. (C)	65. (A)	66. (D)	67. (A)	68. (B)
5. (A)	6. (D)	7. (A)	8. (A)	69. (C)	70. (B)	71. (B)	72. (A)
9. (B)	10. (A)	11. (D)	12. (D)	73. (B)	74. (D)	75. (D)	76. (D)
13. (A)	14. (A)	15. (B)	16. (A)	77. (A)	78. (B)	79. (D)	80. (A)
17. (A)	18. (B)	19. (A)	20. (C)	81. (A)	82. (B)	83. (A)	84. (B)
21. (B)	22. (A)	23. (B)	24. (D)	85. (D)	86. (D)	87. (A)	88. (B)
25. (A)	26. (D)	27. (B)	28. (A)	89. (A)	90. (D)	91. (A)	92. (D)
29. (A)	30. (D)	31. (D)	32. (D)	93. (A)	94. (B)	95. (A)	96. (D)
33. (D)	34. (C)	35. (B)	36. (D)	97. (A)	98. (D)	99. (D)	100. (A)
37. (D)	38. (D)	39. (A)	40. (D)	101. (A)	102. (B)	103. (B)	104. (D)
41. (D)	42. (B)	43. (A)	44. (A)	105. (B)	106. (D)	107. (A)	108. (C)
45. (C)	46. (C)	47. (C)	48. (A)	109. (D)	110. (D)	111. (B)	112. (D)
49. (A)	50. (C)	51. (A)	52. (A)	113. (B)	114. (B)	115. (B)	116. (A)
53. (D)	54. (B)	55. (B)	56. (B)	117. (A)	118. (A)	119. (B)	120. (A)
57. (D)	58. (C)	59. (D)	60. (B)	121. (A)	122. (A)	123. (D)	124. (B)
61. (A)	62. (C)	63. (A)	64. (A)	125. (C)	126. (A)	127. (A)	128. (D)

129. (A)	130. (D)	131. (A)	132. (A)	153. (A)	154. (C)	155. (D)	156. (A)
133. (A)	134. (B)	135. (C)	136. (A)	157. (B)	158. (A)	159. (A)	160. (A)
137. (C)	138. (A)	139. (B)	140. (D)	161. (C)	162. (A)	163. (A)	164. (D)
141. (C)	142. (D)	143. (C)	144. (A)	165. (A)	166. (B)	167. (A)	168. (B)
145. (D)	146. (C)	147. (B)	148. (D)	169. (A)	170. (A)		
149. (B)	150. (C)	151. (C)	152. (B)				

CHAPTER

8 Library Automation

Introduction

The word 'automation' means a technique, method or system of operating or controlling a process in various disciplines. In electronic environments where various types of devices are working as an integrated mode and a centralized controlling system will control all such types of integrated devices and modules in user-friendly environment. Same things happen in library either conventional or e-libraries. Library automation is the application of ICTs to library operations and services and the library services such as acquisition, cataloguing, indexing and abstracting, and web-based services (OPAC and WebOPAC), etc. are automated by a 'System' called Library Automation System. From data storing to the data retrieving, data accessing to the data mining, whole system is controlled by an integrated library management system and that system not only a computer-based system but also have retrieval protocol, online cataloguing services as well as library administration services.

Thus, according to present trends of ICT in library system, we have been listing lots of questions and their answer exactly same pattern asking in said examinations.

Important Points

- The term automation was first introduced by D.S. Harder in 1936.
- The word automation has been derived from Greek word automose means something, which was power of spontaneous motion or self-movement.
- According to *Encyclopedia of Library and Information Science*, "automation is the technology concerned with the design and development of process and system that minimize the necessity of human intervention in operation".
- According to *Encyclopedia of Library and Information Science*, "library automation is the use of automatic and semiautomatic data processing machines to perform such traditional library activities as acquisitions, cataloguing, and circulation."
- Library automation means the use of ICT (Information Communication and Technology) as an aid for library activities.
- Colvin Mooers coined the term information retrieval and described it as "searching and retrieval of information from storage according to specific subject".
- H.P. Luhn had organized computerized indexes in 1950s.

- In India, the Indian Statistical Institute (ISI), Kolkata was first institute to install a computer system in 1955.
- The Information System (IS) is an organized system for the data storing, organizing, retrieving and report generating according to the specific purpose.
- There are five basic components of an information system: (a) hardware, (b) software, (c) database, (d) network system, and (e) users.
- According to online Britannica, "Information System, an integrated set of components for collecting, storing, and processing data and for providing information, knowledge, and digitals products".
- Management Information System (MIS) is the study of people (users), technology, organizations, and the relationships among them.
- The database is a centralized integration collection of data resources.
- The central repository for all or specific parts of the data that enterprise various sources of data is called data warehouse.
- A data warehouse is a relational database, designed for query processing and data analyzing rather than day-to-day data transactions.
- In relation database, data mining is the process of finding anomalies, data patterns and data correlations within large data sets for forecasting results.
- The System Developing Life Cycle (SDLC) is a term used in information systems and software engineering to describe a process for planning, creating, testing, and deploying an information system.
- There are ten life-cycle phases of SDLC: (a) initiation, (b) system concept development, (c) planning, (d) requirements analysis, (e) design, (f) development, (g) integration and test, (h) implementation, (i) operations and maintenance, and (j) disposition.
- Black-box testing is a method of software testing that examines the functionality of an application without peering into its internal structures or working.
- White-box testing is a method of testing software that tests internal structures or workings of an application.
- The Alpha testing phase is the first phase of software testing and in this phase, the software developers using white-box testing method.
- The second level test after Alpha testing is the Beta testing phase, which begins when the software is almost complete but likely to contain a number of known or unknown bugs.
- Software may be freeware or shareware, both are copyrighted software but freeware refers to copyrighted software that is available free of charge for an unlimited time whereas shareware refers to copyrighted software that is distributed for free but for a particular evaluation period only that means trial period.
- The Open-Source Software (OSS) is a kind of software where source code made available with a license in which the copyright holder provides the rights to study, change, and distribute the software to anyone and for any purpose.

- The Free and Open-Source Software (FOSS) can be classified as both free software and open-source software.
- There are four software release steps, viz.: (a) Pre-Alpha, (b) Alpha, (c) Beta, and (d) Release.
- Pre-Alpha refers to all activities performed during the software project before formal testing.
- In software developing, the step by step instructions that solve a problem are called an algorithm.
- SDLC is an outline of a system development process that keeps develop successful information systems.
- Dynamic memory is difficult to interface with processor because it refreshes periodically.
- A byte consists of eight bits.
- Electronic Delay Storage Automatic Computer (EDSAC) was the first practical general purpose stored program electronic computer.
- CPU register, Cache and main memory (RAM) are the examples of internal memory of computer system.
- The page file or swap file is used in Virtual Memory (VM).
- Programs larger than the main memory size can be run through Virtual Memory.
- Data redundancy and inconsistency, and data isolation are two main disadvantages of File System as compare to Database Management System (DBMS).
- W3C stands for World Wide Web Consortium.
- The tar command on Linux is often used to create .tar.gz or .tgz archive files.
- A compress or Archive file is any file that contains one or more files or directory that is smaller than their original file size.
- The .zip, .rar, .arj, .tar.gz, .tgz are the examples of compress files.
- Knowledge Retrieval (KR) focuses on the knowledge level and KR models are based on the computational reasoning technique developed in Artificial Intelligence (AI).
- Information Retrieval (IR) focuses on the documents level and web search engines are very effective IR models for finding the relevant documents or web pages.
- A bibliographic information retrieval system, searches can be divided into two ways: (a) known entity search, and (b) unknown entity search.
- The bibliographic information such as author name, title, publisher name, ISBN, ISSN, edition, etc. are the examples of known entity search.
- When the users not aware about any relevant information related to his/her documents is known as unknown entity search.
- Hierarchical, Network, and Relational are three types of data model of Database Management System (DBMS).

- In hierarchical database model, data is organized tree-like structure where one parent record and many children and one-to-one and one-to-many relationships can be allowed.
- The network data model also tree-like structure but it allows multiple parent and childs record and one-to-one, one-to-many and many-to-many relationship can be allowed.
- In relational model of DBMS, the data and their relationships are represented by collection of inter-related tables.
- In relational model, each table is group of column and rows, where column represents attributes or fields of an entity and rows represents set of records of particular database.
- A single row of a table, which contains a single record for the database relation is called a tuple.
- The Relational Database Management System (RDBMS) is a database management system based on relational model introduced by E.F. Codd.
- Procedural query language consist a set of queries that instruct the DBMS for performing various transactions in the sequence to meet the user request.
- Relational algebra is a procedure query language relational and algebra in DBMS has six fundamental operations, viz.: (a) selection, (b) project, (c) Cartesian product, (d) union, (e) set-difference, and (f) join.
- RAID (Redundant Array of Inexpensive Disks) now Redundant Array of Independent Disks is a data storage virtualization technology that combines multiple physical disk drive components into a single logical unit for the purpose of data redundancy and performance improvement of secondary storage of computer system. There are seven levels of RAID from RAID 0 to RAID 6.
- A binary search (or half-interval search) is a search algorithm which finds the position of a target value within a sorted array and it compares the target value to the middle element of the array.
- In data structure, a linked list is a linear collection of data elements, called node and each node linked to other node as previous and next address of node by means of a pointer.
- There are four relationships will made among records in DBMS, viz.: (a) one-to-one (1:1), (b) one-to-many (1:n), (c) many-to-one (n:1), and (d) many-to-many (n:m).
- There are seven basic logic gates, viz.: (a) AND, (b) OR, (c) XOR, (d) NOT, (e) NAND, (f) NOR, and (g) XNOR.
- The basic element for building a digital circuit is logic gate.
- The binary condition of logic gate (true or false or 1 or 0) is depends on the voltage value of digital circuits. In most logic gates, the low state is approximately zero volts (0 V), while the high state is approximately five volts positive (+5 V), however, the low state and high state voltage are depends on hardware configuration of computer's motherboard.

- A Network Card or Network Interface Card (NIC) is an electronic device (hardware) that connects a computer to a computer network usually a Local Area Network (LAN) and in modern days some network cards do not use a cable to connect to the network, but an antenna, and wireless LAN or Wi-Fi and Bluetooth, are wireless network card.
- A common pathway for data transmission from one component to another or data communication path between components is known as Bus.
- The Open Systems Interconnection (OSI) model is reference model for how different applications can be communicated over a network without regard to their underlying internal structure and technology.
- There are seven layers in OSI model, viz.: (a) application layer, (b) presentation layer, (c) session layer, (d) transport layer, (e) network layer, (f) data link layer, and (g) physical layer.
- The physical layer is the layer of low-level networking equipment, such as hubs, cabling, and repeaters.
- For node-to-node data transfer, the data-link layer is used and responsible for error free data transfer from one to another, over the physical layer.
- The network layer divides the outgoing messages into packets and assembles the all incoming packets into messages to further transmission.
- The main function of transport layer is to be transmit the entire message from source node to destination node and ensures that whole message from network layer arrives intact and also in-order.
- The session layer controls the communications between computer, which means it establishes, manages and terminates the connections between the local and remote applications.
- The presentation layer ensures that the data communications passing according to appropriate file format as per recipient requirement and this layer provides independence from data encryption (data representation) by translating between application and network formats.
- The highest layer is application layer and this layer closet to the end user, in the sense of both OSI application and the user interact directly with software application.

QUESTIONS

1. Which of the following is/are advantage of library automation?

(A) Redundancy of bibliographical records will be minimized

(B) Resource sharing in entire library network is possible

(C) Real time system improved the users service

(D) All of the above

2. Kiosk is a/an

(A) Operating System

(B) Web browser

(C) Programming language
(D) Database Management Software

3. Libman is developed by
(A) Data Pro-Consultancy Service
(B) IFLA
(C) UNESCO
(D) ILA

4. SOUL is developed by
(A) INFLIBNET (B) NISCAIR
(C) IFLA (D) UNESCO

5. e-Granthalaya is developed by
(A) NIC (B) DELNET
(C) ILA (D) INFLIBNET

6. Which of the following services is not possible through library automation?
(A) Current Awareness Service (CAS)
(B) Selective Dissemination of Information (SDI)
(C) Reference service
(D) All of the above services are possible

7. In which year Internet Corporation for Assigned Names and Numbers (ICANN) was founded?
(A) 1994 (B) 1996
(C) 1998 (D) 2001

8. Which of the tagline is associated with ICANN?
(A) Entire World. Entire Internet
(B) Universally Internet
(C) One World. One Internet
(D) Internet for Universe

9. RDBMS stands for
(A) Relational Database Manipulation System
(B) Relational Database Management System
(C) Relationship Database Method System
(D) Relational Database Management Specification

10. ERM stands for
(A) Entity-Relationship Method
(B) Entity-Relationship Model
(C) Entity-Replacement Method
(D) Entity-Representation Method

11. Which of the following organizations maintained the Protocol Address Space and the Domain Names and Numbers in world-wide?
(A) ICANN (B) NTIA
(C) OPAD (D) IEEE

12. Which of the following is an education and research network in India?
(A) DELNET (B) ERNET
(C) ADINET (D) CALIBNET

13. URI stands for
(A) Universal Resource Information
(B) Universal Resource Index
(C) Uniform Resource Identifier
(D) Uniform Resource Index

14. Which of the following is associated with DBMS/RDBMS?
(A) Data Description Languages
(B) Data Manipulation Languages
(C) Query Languages
(D) All of the above

15. Which of the following is true for metadata?
(A) Data about data
(B) Structure about structure
(C) Information about other information
(D) All of the above

16. NICNET stands for
(A) National Informatics Centre Network
(B) National Information Centre Network
(C) National Informatics Control Network
(D) National Information Communication Network

17. C-DAC formerly known as
(A) National Centre for Software Technology (NCST)

(B) National Institute of Software Technology (NIST)
(C) National Centre of Computer Technology (NCCT)
(D) National Centre of Information Technology (NCIT)

18. In which year NCST was established?
(A) 1983 (B) 1985
(C) 1987 (D) 1989

19. Which of the following is the web development tool?
(A) PHP (B) Python
(C) CGI (D) All of the above

20. 'Google Calendar' is the example of
(A) Web application
(B) A type of search engine
(C) A type of web server
(D) A kind of anti-virus

21. Which of the following is Apple's OS X system desktop search engine?
(A) Spotlight (B) Opera
(C) Kindle (D) Safari

22. Which of the following is a search engine?
(A) PHP (B) Ruby
(C) Bing (D) Python

23. Which of the following is related to the web development tool?
(A) Servlet (B) CSS
(C) JavaScript (D) All of the above

24. Which of the following is a standard language for Database Management System?
(A) SQL (B) C++
(C) Java (D) PHP

25. Digital Object Identifier (DOI) system was introduced in
(A) 2000 (B) 2002
(C) 2004 (D) 2006

26. Universal Unique Identifier (UUID) is used in
(A) E-books
(B) E-journals
(C) Software construction
(D) All of the above

27. Which one is not associated with LAMP?
(A) PHP (B) LINUX
(C) MSSQL (D) MYSQL

28. Which of the following web development tools is used for quick update of web page without the reloading the entire web pages?
(A) AJAX (B) SJAX
(C) MJAX (D) TJAX

29. Which of the following notations is used for dividing DOI name in two parts?
(A) Comma (,) (B) Plus (+)
(C) Asterisk (*) (D) Slash (/)

30. Who coined the term 'AJAX'?
(A) Ethan Marcotte (B) Jeffrey Zeldman
(C) Cameron Moll (D) Jesse James Garret

31. The Relational model was first proposed in
(A) 1960 (B) 1965
(C) 1970 (D) 1975

32. Which of the following is the documents identifier system?
(A) DOI (B) PII
(C) FAT (D) Both (A) and (B)

33. The advantage of Database System
(A) Data Consistency
(B) Program data dependence
(C) Controlled Redundancy
(D) Both (A) and (C)

34. Which of the following languages is used for making metadata structure?
(A) JAVA (B) ASP.NET
(C) JSP.NET (D) XML

35. DHCP stands for
(A) Data Host Configuration Protocol
(B) Dynamic Host Configuration Protocol

(C) Digital Host Configuration Protocol
(D) Direct Host Configuration Protocol

36. Which of the following is a satellite-based communication network of NIC?
(A) NICNET (B) INFLIBNET
(C) DELNET (D) ERNET

37. Which of the following is the metadata format?
(A) ONIX (B) FGDC
(C) MARC (D) All of the above

38. GILS is related to
(A) Database Server
(B) 4th Generation Language
(C) Metadata format
(D) Web Hosting

39. PII stands for
(A) Publisher Item Identifier
(B) Permanent Item Identifier
(C) Periodical Item Identifier
(D) Prenatal Item Identifier

40. In PII, what is the keyword for serial publication?
(A) S (B) SR
(C) SRL (D) SS

41. How many characters string in PII?
(A) 12 (B) 14
(C) 17 (D) 19

42. At present, the DELNET is known as
(A) Delhi Libraries Network
(B) Developing Library Network
(C) Digital Library Network
(D) Dynamic Library Network

43. Which of the following is a global character encoding system?
(A) PHP (B) XML
(C) UNICODE (D) HTML

44. Who maintain the MARC 21 format of bibliographic data?
(A) CILIP (B) LOC
(C) ALA (D) UNESCO

45. Match the following:

LIST-I	LIST-II
(1) INFLIBNET	(i) 1977
(2) DELNET	(ii) 1986
(3) NICNET	(iii) 1991
(4) ERNET	(iv) 1988

Codes:

	(1)	(2)	(3)	(4)
(A)	(iii)	(iv)	(i)	(ii)
(B)	(iv)	(i)	(iii)	(ii)
(C)	(ii)	(i)	(iii)	(iv)
(D)	(i)	(iv)	(ii)	(iii)

46. Which of the following is the specialized network?
(A) DESINET (B) ERNET
(C) CSIRNET (D) All of the above

47. WorldShare Management Service (WMS) is an integrated suite of cloud-based library management application, developed by
(A) IFLA (B) ASLIB
(C) UNESCO (D) OCLC

48. Who organized the CALIBER?
(A) DELNET (B) RRRLF
(C) INFLIBNET (D) DRTC, Bengaluru

49. Which of the following is maintaining the MODS (Metadata Object Description Schema) standard?
(A) LOC (B) IFLA
(C) UNESCO (D) IEEE

50. The maintenance agency of Dublin Core Metadata is
(A) UNESCO (B) IEEE
(C) DCMI (D) LOC

51. SOUL stands for
(A) Software for University Libraries
(B) Software for Universal Libraries

(C) Systematic Online University Libraries
(D) Systematic Online Users Libraries

52. The maintenance agency of Text Encoding Initiative (TEI) metadata format is
(A) UNESO (B) IFLA
(C) LOC (D) TIE Consortium

53. Which of the following is the freeware library automation software?
(A) SOUL (B) e-Granthalaya
(C) Koha (D) Both (B) and (C)

54. The maintenance agency of Encoded Archival Description (EAD) metadata format is
(A) Library of Congress (LOC)
(B) Society of American Archivists (SAA)
(C) EAD Consortium
(D) Both (A) and (B)

55. Which of the following online union catalogue services is provided by INFLIBNET?
(A) UnivCat (B) ICatt
(C) IndCat (D) WorldCat

56. Which of the following library automation/ repository software is made in New Zealand?
(A) Koha (B) GreenStone
(C) Both (A) and (B) (D) Verso

57. The maintenance agency of Metadata Encoding and Transmission Standard (METS) metadata format is
(A) CILIP (B) IFLA
(C) LOC (D) UNESCO

58. GreenStone has been developed and distributed in cooperation with
(A) UNESCO (B) Human Info NGO
(C) IFLA (D) Both (A) and (B)

59. Openbiblio was created in 2002 by
(A) Dave Stevens
(B) John S. Mark
(C) William S. Stevens
(D) Both (A) and (B)

60. The maintenance agency of RDF standard elements is?
(A) W3C (B) LOC
(C) IFLA (D) UNESCO

61. Which of the following statements is true for 'GreenStone'?
(A) It is a multilingual software
(B) It developed under the GNU General Public License (GPL)
(C) It sponsored by CILIP
(D) Both (A) and (B)

62. Which of the following statements is true for 'koha'?
(A) It gives union catalogue facility
(B) Off-line circulation facility is available
(C) It written in Perl language
(D) All of the above

63. The term 'Web 2.0' was first used by
(A) Darcy DiNucii (B) Allen J. William
(C) Tom M. Steve (D) John K. Michel

64. Which of the following is the metadata standard?
(A) METS (B) MIX
(C) TEI (D) All of the above

65. The process of organizing database relations to minimize redundancy is called
(A) Sorting (B) Splitting
(C) Normalization (D) Cascading

66. The Z39.50 is a search and retrieval protocol at the
(A) Application level
(B) Presentation level
(C) Session level
(D) Data Link level

67. The feature of Z39.50 protocol is
(A) Initializing the session between client and server
(B) Searching the records through structural query language

(C) Sorting the records according to any given sorting criteria
(D) All of the above

68. With the help of............, we can quickly notified the web users related to the web content.
(A) RSS (B) Cookies
(C) Tag (D) Attributes

69. A.....is a website that allows collaborative modification of its content directly from the users.
(A) Wiki (B) Blogs
(C) Cookies (D) RSS

70. Ubuntu is a/an
(A) Operating System
(B) Integrated Library Software
(C) Office Management Application
(D) Web Designing Language

71. GILS stands for
(A) Global Information Location Service
(B) Global Information Locator Service
(C) Graphical Information Locator Service
(D) Geographical Information Locator Service

72. The Z39.50 protocol was originally proposed in
(A) 1982 (B) 1984
(C) 1989 (D) 1991

73. ARCNET was developed by
(A) South Central Bell
(B) Datapoint Corporation
(C) Teltone Corporation
(D) Apricot Computers

74. ARCNET was developed in
(A) 1976 (B) 1982
(C) 1984 (D) 1986

75. WIMAX stands for
(A) Worldwide Interrelation for Microwave Access
(B) Worldwide Interoperability for Microwave Access
(C) Worldwide Interoperability for Multimedia Access
(D) Worldwide Internet for Multimedia Access

76. SRW stands for
(A) Search/Retrieve Web Service
(B) Search/Retrieve WideArea Service
(C) Search/Relational Web Service
(D) Search/Report Web Service

77. The birthplace of WWW is
(A) CERN (B) IBM
(C) Apple (D) NASA

78. SOAP stands for
(A) Synchronous Object Access Protocol
(B) Simple Object Access Protocol
(C) Systematic Object Access Protocol
(D) Standard Object Access Protocol

79. FOSS stands for
(A) Free and Open Source Software
(B) Frequently Open Source Software
(C) Fundamental Open Source Software
(D) Firewall Open Source Software

80. European Organization for Nuclear Research (CERN) is located at
(A) Paris (B) Geneva
(C) Berlin (D) Madrid

81. CMS stands for
(A) Complex Management System
(B) Compiler Management System
(C) Content Management System
(D) Command Management System

82. ....is an XML-based messaging protocol for information exchange among computers?
(A) FTP (B) SOAP
(C) TCP/IP (D) CORBA

83. Which of the following is the web service-based protocol for querying Internet indexes and database and then return search results?
(A) FTP (B) SRW
(C) SRU (D) Both (B) and (C)

84. The FOSS movement began in 1993 by
(A) Richard Stallman
(B) Manuel Blum
(C) Stephen R. Bourne
(D) Robert S. Boyer

85. Larry Page is the founder of
(A) Google (B) Yahoo
(C) Amazon.com (D) Apple

86. Which of the following Operating Systems (OS) is support by NewGenLib?
(A) Linux (B) Windows
(C) Mac OS (D) Both (A) and (B)

87. Which of the following is the example of Content Management System (CMS) software?
(A) Drupal (B) Joomla
(C) Wordpress (D) All of the above

88. Which of the following Operating Systems (OS) is support by 'Evergreen'?
(A) Linux (B) Windows
(C) Mac OS (D) All of the above

89. The database part of any integrated library software is called
(A) Front-end (B) Back-end
(C) User-end (D) Customer-end

90. Which of the following database software/ packages is used by 'e-Granthalaya version 4.0' for back-end?
(A) MySql 5.0 (B) SQL Server 2005
(C) PostgreSQL (D) Oracle 11g

91. How many bits are used in UNICODE for information interchange?
(A) 7 (B) 9
(C) 16 (D) 18

92. Which of the following statements is true?
(A) ASCII uses 7-bit character encoding
(B) EBCDIC is a 12 bit character encoding
(C) UNICODE is capable to encoded all the world languages
(D) Both (A) and (C)

93. UTF stands for
(A) Unicode Transformation Format
(B) Universal Transformation Format
(C) United Transformation Format
(D) UNIX Transformation Format

94. Which one is odd?
(A) UTF-8 (B) UTF-16
(C) UTF-32 (D) UTF-38

95. ISCII stands for
(A) Indian Script Code for Information Interchange
(B) International Script for Information Interchange
(C) Internal Script for Computer Information Interchange
(D) Internet Script for Computer Information Integration

96. ISCII uses.......bit encoding system for information interchange.
(A) Six (B) Seven
(C) Eight (D) Ten

97. Which of the following is/are metadata harvesting protocol?
(A) OAI-PMH (B) HTTP
(C) FTP (D) All of the above

98. Which of the following library automation/ repository software is developed in India?
(A) Koha (B) GreenStone
(C) Openbiblio (D) NewGenLib

99. Android is a/an
(A) CMS (B) OS
(C) Protocol (D) Device

100. Which of the following is a Citation Management Software?
(A) Zotero (B) Openbiblio
(C) Koha (D) DSpace

101. Which of the following is a query language for information retrieval?
(A) MQL (B) CQL
(C) FQL (D) TQL

102. CQL stands for
(A) Complex Query Language
(B) Contextual Query Language
(C) Command Query Language
(D) Content Query Language

103. NFC stands for
(A) Non-Frequency Communication
(B) Near Field Communication
(C) Numerical Field Communication
(D) Native Field Communication

104. Which of the following is the major principle for operation of RFID systems?
(A) Reductive Coupling
(B) Conductive Coupling
(C) Inductive Coupling
(D) All of the above

105. FTP is a/an
(A) Network protocol
(B) Application protocol
(C) Telecommunication protocol
(D) None of the above

106. HTTP is a/an
(A) Application protocol
(B) Network protocol
(C) Both (A) and (B)
(D) Telecommunication protocol

107. Which of the following is the foundation of data communication for the World Wide Web (WWW)?
(A) FTP (B) HTTP
(C) UDP (D) POP

108. Which of the following protocol is used for Mail delivery?
(A) SMTP (B) POP3
(C) IMAP (D) All of the above

109. SMTP stands for
(A) Simple Mail Transfer Protocol
(B) Syntax Mail Transfer Protocol
(C) Synchronous Mail Transfer Protocol
(D) Standard Mail Transfer Protocol

110. Which of the following is the wireless data interface?
(A) Infrared (B) Bluetooth
(C) Wi-Fi (D) All of the above

111. SAW stands for
(A) Simple Acoustic Wave
(B) Serial Acoustic Wave
(C) Synchronous Acoustic Wave
(D) Surface Acoustic Wave

112. IMAP stands for
(A) Internet Message Access Protocol
(B) Internal Message Access Protocol
(C) International Message Access Protocol
(D) Information Message Access Protocol

113. PsyINFO is a/an
(A) Database of abstracts of literature in the field of philosophy
(B) Medical database, developed by the IFLA
(C) Library network in the field of Psychology, developed by UNESCO
(D) Database of abstracts of literature in the field of Psychology

114. Which of the following organizations jointly published 'Survey on Digitization and Preservation'
(A) IFLA and CILIP
(B) IFLA and ALA
(C) IFLA and UNESCO
(D) UNESCO and CILIP

115. CDS/ISIS was first released in
(A) 1975 (B) 1978
(C) 1985 (D) 1988

116. The feature of FOSS software is
(A) Free software
(B) Open-source software
(C) Free licensed
(D) All of the above

117. Which of the following is the UNICODE implementation of CDS/ISIS?
(A) D-ISIS (B) E-ISISI
(C) J-ISIS (D) L-ISIS

118. Which of the following software tools is used for direct data exchange between CDS/ISIS and IDAMS
(A) IDAS (B) IDIS
(C) IDJS (D) IDUS

119. 'Serial Control' means
(A) Monitoring multiple issue of a serial
(B) Overdue alert
(C) Provision of grace period for receiving the serial
(D) All of the above

120. Which of the following is maintain and disseminate the IDIS?
(A) CILIP (B) IFLA
(C) UNESCO (D) ALA

121. Which of the following is a wireless non-contact radio system to transfer data from a tag attached to an object for automatic identification?
(A) SRW (B) WorldCat
(C) RFID (D) Web-OPAC

122. What is the range of Low Frequency (LF)?
(A) 20–100 kHz (B) 30–300 kHz
(C) 30–300 MKz (D) 300 MHz–30 GHz

123. SRD stands for
(A) Serial Range Devices
(B) Short Range Devices
(C) Synchronous Range Devices
(D) Simple Range Devices

124. In CDS/ISIS, fields within a record are identified by a code number called
(A) Tag (B) Key field
(C) Attribute (D) Relation

125. Which of the following is related to the security requirement of RFID?
(A) Authentication
(B) Encryption
(C) Prevention of malicious attack
(D) All of the above

126. The 'Code 39' is related to
(A) A type of application used in Barcode
(B) A protocol used for message transmission
(C) An encryption algorithm for sensitive data transmission
(D) A bibliographic description code developed by IFLA

127. When we send a message from Outlook Express, which protocol will responsible for sending such message?
(A) FTP (B) HTTP
(C) SMTP (D) SOAP

128. Which of the following is the freeware library automation/repository software?
(A) e-Granthalaya
(B) GreenStone
(C) CDS/ISIS
(D) All of the above

129. Which of the following is the utility software for CDS/ISIS?
(A) ISISAscii (B) ISISMarc
(C) JAVAISIS (D) All of the above

130. Which of the statements is true about DSpace?
(A) The first public version was released in 2002
(B) The original authors are MIT and HP Labs
(C) It is the platform independent software
(D) All of the above

131. Which of the following is the free and open source institutional repository software?

(A) DSpace (B) GreenStone
(C) Invenio (D) All of the above

132. Invenio is developed by

(A) UNESCO (B) CERN
(C) IEEE (D) IFLA

133. EAS stands for

(A) Electronic Article Surveillance
(B) Electronic Article Supply
(C) Electronic Application Surveillance
(D) Electronic Applicable Surveillance

134. Assertion (A): Library network is basically a group of libraries coming together with some agreements that helps to each other for result-oriented services.

Reason (R): INFLIBNET is an Inter-University library network in India.

(A) Both (A) and (R) are true
(B) Both (A) and (R) are false
(C) (A) is true, but (R) is false
(D) (A) is false, but (R) is true

135. Assertion (A): In freeware software we can download, copied without restrictions and freely used without any payment.

Reason (R): Freeware software like open-source that means we can change original source codes.

(A) Both (A) and (R) are false
(B) Both (A) and (R) are true
(C) (A) is true, but (R) is false
(D) (A) is false, but (R) is true

136. Assertion (A): Invenio is an open source software specially used for digital assets management.

Reason (R): Institutional repository software typically used for scholarly and published digital content as a Digital Library.

(A) Both (A) and (R) are true
(B) Both (A) and (R) are false
(C) (A) is false, but (R) is true
(D) (A) is true, but (R) is false

137. Assertion (A): In Cloud Ready Application, the entire applications are working as an enterprise mode.

Reason (R): In Digital Libraries, the cloud-based applications are best deployed as a collection of cloud services.

(A) Both (A) and (R) are false
(B) Both (A) and (R) are true
(C) (A) is true, but (R) is false
(D) (A) is false, but (R) is true

Answers Keys

1. (D)	2. (B)	3. (A)	4. (A)	33. (D)	34. (D)	35. (B)	36. (A)
5. (A)	6. (D)	7. (C)	8. (C)	37. (D)	38. (C)	39. (A)	40. (A)
9. (B)	10. (B)	11. (A)	12. (B)	41. (C)	42. (B)	43. (C)	44. (B)
13. (C)	14. (D)	15. (D)	16. (A)	45. (A)	46. (D)	47. (D)	48. (C)
17. (A)	18. (B)	19. (D)	20. (A)	49. (A)	50. (C)	51. (A)	52. (D)
21. (A)	22. (C)	23. (D)	24. (A)	53. (D)	54. (D)	55. (C)	56. (C)
25. (A)	26. (C)	27. (C)	28. (A)	57. (C)	58. (D)	59. (A)	60. (A)
29. (D)	30. (D)	31. (C)	32. (D)	61. (D)	62. (D)	63. (A)	64. (D)

65. (C)	66. (A)	67. (D)	68. (A)	105. (A)	106. (A)	107. (B)	108. (D)
69. (A)	70. (A)	71. (B)	72. (B)	109. (A)	110. (D)	111. (D)	112. (A)
73. (B)	74. (A)	75. (B)	76. (A)	113. (D)	114. (C)	115. (C)	116. (D)
77. (A)	78. (B)	79. (A)	80. (B)	117. (C)	118. (B)	119. (D)	120. (C)
81. (C)	82. (B)	83. (D)	84. (A)	121. (C)	122. (B)	123. (B)	124. (A)
85. (A)	86. (D)	87. (D)	88. (D)	125. (D)	126. (A)	127. (C)	128. (D)
89. (B)	90. (C)	91. (C)	92. (D)	129. (D)	130. (D)	131. (D)	132. (B)
93. (A)	94. (D)	95. (A)	96. (C)	133. (A)	134. (A)	135. (C)	136. (A)
97. (A)	98. (D)	99. (B)	100. (A)	137. (B)			
101. (B)	102. (B)	103. (B)	104. (C)				

CHAPTER

9 Research Methodology

Introduction

The systematic investigation, study of materials and source in order to establish facts and reach new conclusion simply called research. Research is not just a collection of facts but it considered as the manipulation of things, concepts that generalizing the principle, verifying the knowledge and sometime after research, some predefined thoughts or principles have been changed.

In research methodology, researchers use tools and criteria for solving or searching the given research problems and different sources use different type of methods for solving the problems.

Research in Library & Information Science (LIS) is a core aspect of library education and LIS is a rapidly evolving field. Therefore, research is needed for entire field of studies in LIS.

Today, we have seen so many classification schemes and cataloguing principles, number of indexing methods and various information dissemination methods. These are possible due to the research in LIS field. Therefore, research in LIS will explore the hidden strength of Universe of Knowledge and at present a progressive research in LIS is now making an independent discipline in Universe of Knowledge.

Therefore, in this chapter, we will discuss important points and plenty of questions with their answer according to the present trends of said examinations.

Important Points

- Research is a creative work contributing to the growth of knowledge for the benefit of man and society.
- According to *Encyclopedia of Social Sciences*, "research is the manipulation of things, concepts or symbols for the purpose of generalizing to extend, correct or verified knowledge, whether that knowledge aids in construction of theory or in the practice of an art."
- According to Grinnell, "research is a careful, systematic, patient study and investigation in some field of knowledge, undertaken to establish facts or principles".
- According to Grinnell, "research is a structured inquiry that utilizes acceptable scientific methodology to solve problems and creates new knowledge that is generally applicable".

- Systematic observation, classification and data interpretation are consisted the Scientific Method.
- Research methodology is a way to systematically solve the research problem by logically adopting steps.
- Scholarly research is systematic, well planned and scientific thinking, whereas everyday research is quick thinking, very personal decisions and casual sense.
- Basically, there are three types of research, viz.: (a) application of research study, (b) objectives in undertaking the research, and (c) inquiry mode employed.
- Research methodology not only deals with the research method but also considers the logic behind the methods.
- The surveys and fact-finding enquiries of different kinds are included in descriptive research.
- In analytical research, researchers have to use data, facts or information, which is already available and analyze these to make a critical evaluation of the material.
- Applied research is a research methodology used to solve a specific, practical problem of an individual group and this methodology of research is used to find solutions to everyday problems.
- Quantitative research is based on the measurement of quantity or amount.
- Qualitative research is concerned with qualitative phenomena and in this methodology, gathers information is not in numerical form.
- Empirical research is based on observed and measured phenomena and derives knowledge from actual experience rather than from basic theory, facts or belief.
- The specific statement of prediction in research is called hypothesis and it describes in concrete rather than theoretical terms of what happen during research study.
- According to William Zikmund, "research design is defined as a master plan specifying the methods and procedures for collection and analyzing the needed information".
- According to K.N. Kerlinger, "research design is the plan, structure, and strategy of investigation conceived so as to obtain answers to research questions and to control variance".
- In research, solutions to problems should be based on knowledge, not on personal beliefs, theories, or guesses.
- A concept which can take on different quantitative values is called variables, e.g. the concept age, weight, temperature, and height are variables.
- If one variable depends upon or is a consequence of other variable is called depend variable whereas a variable that is antecedent to the dependent variable is called independent variable, e.g. the variable date_of_birth is an independent variable and variable age is dependent variable because it determine through variable date_of_birth.
- In same case current-date and date_of_birth are independent variable and variable age is dependent for the variables current_date and date_of_birth.

- According to Gorge J. Mouly, "hypothesis is an assumption whose testability is to be tested on the basis of the compatibility of its implications with empirical evidence and previous knowledge".
- Hypothesis should be clear and accurate, state relationship between variables, and amenable to testing within a time bound.
- On the basis of research method, we can classify it into five categories, viz.: (a) philosophical research, (b) historical research, (c) survey research, (d) experimental research, and (e) case-study research.
- In research, the primary data can be collected either through experiment or through survey.
- The survey data can be collected through personal interview, through mailing of questionnaires or through electronic communication.
- Data collection through questionnaires method is quite popular in case of big enquiries.
- A sample is a small proportion of a population selected for observation and analysis.
- According to David S. Fox, "in the social sciences, it is not possible to collect data from every respondent relevant to our study but only from some fractional part of the respondents. The process of selecting the fractional part is called sampling."
- Probability sampling is generally used in fundamental research in which the purpose is to generalize the results.
- In behavioural sciences, the observation method is the most commonly used method for data collection.
- The reasoning that uses general principle to predict specific result is called deductive.
- In inductive reasoning, makes broad generalizations or construct general principles from specific observations.
- Deductive reasoning is a basic form of valid reasoning and during the research, the deductive reasoning is used to reach a logical true conclusion.
- Probability sampling is also known as random sampling or chance sampling.
- Snowball sampling (or Chain-Referral sampling) is a non-probability sampling technique that is used by researchers to identify potential subjects in studies where subjects are hard to locate and it is consider as non-probability sampling.
- A research method in which present-day events are studied with reference to the events that took place in the past is known as historical research.
- Semantic Differential (S.D.) scale was developed by Charles E. Osgood, G.J. Suci, and P.H. Tannenbaum.
- In experimental research, we collect primary data during the course of doing experiments.
- In descriptive type, we can obtain primary data either through observation or through direct communication with respondents.

- In descriptive method of research, we can collect primary data through (a) questionnaires, (b) interview, (c) observation, and (d) schedules.
- The data collection through questionnaire is relatively economical.
- Aristotle was the proponent of deductive method.
- The data collected by a researcher from the UGC is under the category of secondary data.
- Observation is the starting point for a research.
- In research method, a conclusion is drawn from two statements is called syllogism.
- Independent variable is the variable where researchers changes or manipulates.
- Blocking is the arrangement of experimental groups into similar groups.
- Errors are classified in three categories, viz.: (a) systematic error, (b) random error, and (c) blunder.
- The identified causes, where error is not determined by chance, but it introduced by an inaccuracy is known as systematic errors.
- Due to statistical fluctuations in either direction in the measured data and precision limitations of the measurement device, the Random errors are occurred.
- The blunder errors is an outright mistake, when a person may record a wrong value, forget single digit or some digits, misreading the scale measurement or such blunder mistake and that type of error will change whole research output.
- Zero error is a Systematic error.
- In scientific paper, the detailed report of the research work is prepared with standard format.

QUESTIONS

1. ....is designed to solve practical problem of the modern world, rather than to acquire knowledge for knowledge enhancement.

(A) Applied Research

(B) Basic Research

(C) Fundamental Research

(D) None of the above

2. A research based on testing a theory, measured with numbers, and analyzed using statistical techniques is called

(A) Qualitative Research

(B) Quantitative Research

(C) Collaborative Research

(D) None of the above

3. Users survey in a library is a/an

(A) Quantitative Research

(B) Collaborative Research

(C) Qualitative Research

(D) All of the above

4. Which of the following statements is true for Mailed Questionnaire?

(A) Its costs less to compare to others types of Questionnaire

(B) It covers wider geographical area

(C) The biggest disadvantage of Mailed Questionnaire is low response rate

(D) All of the above

5. Which one is an odd as a kind of Research Methodology?
(A) Historical Method
(B) Descriptive Method
(C) Scientific Method
(D) Real Time Method

6. ....describes the frequency of publication by authors in any given field.
(A) Zipf's Law (B) Lotka's Law
(C) Bradoford's Law (D) Garfield's Law

7. *Human Behavior and the Principle of the Least Effort* was written by
(A) G.K. Zipf
(B) Alfred J. Lotka
(C) Samuel C. Bradford
(D) Eugene Garfield

8. ....refers to reference in one source of text to another source of text with information where such text can be found.
(A) Citation Analysis
(B) Statistical Analysis
(C) Entity-Relationship Analysis
(D) Directory Analysis

9. The law of scatter of the articles over journal in given subject is described through..........
(A) Lotka's Law (B) Bradford's Law
(C) Zipf's Law (D) None of the above

10. The term 'Librametry' was coined by
(A) Alfred J. Lotka
(B) Samuel C. Bradford
(C) S.R. Ranganathan
(D) G.K. Zipf

11. ....is about word distributions in a given text.
(A) Bradford's Law (B) Zipf's Law
(C) Lotka's Law (D) Garfield Law

12. Co-citation Coupling is a method used to establish a/an......similarity between two documents.
(A) Text (B) Paragraph
(C) Line (D) Word

13. If answer a question with only "YES" or "NO" or any such type decision is called
(A) Closed-End Questions
(B) Open-End Questions
(C) Mailed Questionnaire
(D) Both (B) and (C)

14. ....are ones that require more than one word answer.
(A) Closed-End Questions
(B) Open-End Questions
(C) Short Questions
(D) Both (A) and (C)

15. A measurement scale that reflects the average number of citations to articles published in Science and Social Science journals.
(A) Impact factor
(B) Data factor
(C) Information factor
(D) Historical factor

16. Who says "Research is the key to the future of the profession and is an important means by which institutional programme is enriched"?
(A) S.R. Ranganathan (B) J.H. Shera
(C) H.P. Luhn (D) J.D. Brown

17. Which of the following is the primary data for researchers?
(A) Interview (B) Observation
(C) Questionnaires (D) All of the above

18. Which of the following is the secondary data for researchers?
(A) Government reports
(B) Web information
(C) Historical data
(D) All of the above

19. SPSS stands for
(A) Statistical Package for Social Science
(B) Systematical Package for Social Science

(C) Subject Package for Social Science
(D) Simple Package for Social Science

20. Impact factor is devised by
(A) Alfred J. Lotka
(B) Samuel C. Bradford
(C) S.R. Ranganathan
(D) Eugene Garfield

21. The h-index was proposed by......in 2005.
(A) George E. Hirsch (B) Paul J. Compton
(C) John K. Culler (D) Peter W. Cook

22. Match the following:

LIST-I	LIST-II
(1) Bibliometrics	(i) Studies quantitative aspects of science
(2) Webometrics	(ii) Studies quantitative aspects of Internet resources (WWW)
(3) Cybermetrics	(iii) Studies quantitative aspects of recorded information
(4) Scientometrics	(iv) Studies quantitative aspects of WWW as well as electronic resources

Codes:

	(1)	(2)	(3)	(4)
(A)	(iv)	(ii)	(i)	(iii)
(B)	(iii)	(i)	(ii)	(iv)
(C)	(iii)	(ii)	(iv)	(i)
(D)	(iii)	(ii)	(i)	(iv)

23. Bradford's Law is concerned with........ distribution over a range of source.
(A) Subject (B) Word
(C) Sentence (D) Paragraph

24. Zipf's Law is concerned with....... distribution over a range of source.
(A) Word (B) Subject
(C) Sentence (D) Paragraph

25. Which of the following is the midpoint of the steps of scientific method?
(A) Analysis (B) Observation
(C) Conclusions (D) Experiment

26. A conference or meeting to discuss a particular subject and will present papers on a particular subject by a number of contributors.
(A) Workshop (B) Symposium
(C) Congress (D) All of the above

27. The Web Impact Factor (WIF) introduced by.....in 1998.
(A) Peter Ingwersen
(B) James H. Curry
(C) Peter Chen
(D) Danese C. Cray

28. The.......is found by adding up all of the given data and dividing by the number of data entries.
(A) Mode (B) Median
(C) Mean (D) Frequency

29. The observation which occurs most frequently in a sample is the
(A) Mode (B) Mean
(C) Median (D) Frequency

30. What measure of central tendency is most sensitive to skewness?
(A) Mean (B) Mode
(C) Median (D) Frequency

31. Which of the following is not a common measure of central tendency?
(A) Median (B) Mode
(C) Mean (D) Range

32. Finding information patterns by analyzing citation patterns, word frequency for statistical analysis is called
(A) Bibliometrics
(B) Data collection
(C) Data gathering
(D) Data decentralization

33. Median is a/an

(A) Middle point (B) Highest point

(C) Lowest point (D) Average point

34. .....is the study of measuring and analysis science, technology and innovation.

(A) Scientometrics (B) Parametrics

(C) Webometrics (D) None of the above

35. Bibliometrics, Informetrics, and Scientometrics applied to the web is called

(A) Cybermetrics (B) Compumetrics

(C) Datametrics (D) Neteometrics

36. The.......of a set of data values is the middle value of the data set when it has been arranged in ascending order.

(A) Mean (B) Mode

(C) Median (D) Range

37. Match the following:

LIST-I	LIST-II
(1) Lotks'a Law	(i) 1926
(2) Bradford's Law	(ii) 1934
(3) Zipf's Law	(iii) 1949
(4) Bibliometrics	(iv) 1969

Codes:

	(1)	(2)	(3)	(4)
(A)	(i)	(ii)	(iii)	(iv)
(B)	(ii)	(iii)	(iv)	(i)
(C)	(ii)	(i)	(iii)	(iv)
(D)	(iv)	(ii)	(iii)	(i)

38. The term 'Bibliometrics' is coined by

(A) Alan Pritchard

(B) Alfred J. Lotka

(C) George K. Zipf

(D) Samuel C. Bradford

39. Which of the following is true for Questionnaire Method?

(A) Data collections are easy and quickly

(B) Empirical data can be collected

(C) It is the fruitless method

(D) Both (A) and (B)

40. Which of the following is true for Historical Research?

(A) It is the application of the scientific method for enquiry to historical problems

(B) It is the critical investigations of events

(C) It deals with the past experience

(D) All of the above

41. For Historical Research, the documentary source is

(A) Personal letters (B) Newspaper

(C) Diaries (D) All of the above

42. Which of the following software/packages is used for statistical analysis?

(A) SPSS (B) PSPP

(C) JASP (D) All of the above

43. Which of the following is the free and open source statistical analysis software?

(A) JASP (B) PSPP

(C) SPSS (D) Both (A) and (B)

44. ....is a way to systematically resolve the research problem.

(A) Research Methodology

(B) Information Technology

(C) Ethics

(D) Data collection

45. Which of the following statements is true for Structured Interview?

(A) Questions can be changed

(B) There is no predefined sequences of questions

(C) During interview, new questions can be added

(D) Contains of questions may be an Open-Ended or a Closed-Ended

46. After testing we have got 'taste of water is either nice or so nice', this type of information is called

(A) Qualitative information
(B) Quantitative information
(C) Statistical information
(D) All of the above

47. The output of validation of data may be
(A) Lists (B) Details reports
(C) Summary reports (D) All of the above

48. The notation of Null Hypothesis is
(A) H_0 (B) H_1
(C) H_2 (D) H_z

49. Which of the following is the first part of any research proposal?
(A) Introduction (B) Title
(C) Hypothesis (D) Objective

50. ....is an assumption, presumption or some condition or situation related to the research.
(A) Scope (B) Observation
(C) Hypothesis (D) Introduction

51. The.........Hypothesis is a hypothesis which the researcher tries to disprove or reject.
(A) Alternative (B) Null
(C) Empirical (D) Logical

52. Alternative Hypothesis is denoted by
(A) H_0 (B) H_1
(C) H_a (D) H_m

53. Which of the following statements is false?
(A) Inductive methods are generally associated with qualitative research
(B) Deductive methods are commonly associated with quantitative research
(C) Inductive methods are concerned with the generation of new theory
(D) None of the above

54. Deductive reasoning works from the........ to the............
(A) less general, more specific
(B) more general, more specific
(C) more general, less specific
(D) less general, less specific

55. Inductive Reasoning flow
(A) Top-to-down (B) Bottom-to-up
(C) Straightforward (D) Both (B) and (C)

56. The sequence of Deductive Reasoning is
(A) Theory-> Hypothesis-> Observation-> Confirmation
(B) Hypothesis->Theory->Observation-> Confirmation
(C) Observation->Hypothesis->Theory-> Confirmation
(D) Observation->Theory->Hypothesis-> Confirmation

57. Reasoning that uses general principle to predict specific results is called
(A) Deductive Reasoning
(B) Inductive Reasoning
(C) Special Reasoning
(D) Both (A) and (C)

58. Which of the following is the first stage of any research process?
(A) Observation
(B) Hypothesis
(C) Data Collection
(D) Terms and Conditions definition

59. An advantage of computer-based telephonic interview is
(A) Quality of data will be increased
(B) Data analysis is easy
(C) Time consuming is reduced
(D) None of the above

60. Which of the following is the advantage of Scientific Method?
(A) Reliable (B) Accurate
(C) Systematic (D) All of the above

61. Preliminary data collection is a part of
(A) Exploratory Research
(B) Descriptive Research

(C) Explanatory Research
(D) Both (B) and (C)

62. For theoretical framework of any research, which of the following is a solid basic foundation?
(A) Questionnaires
(B) Literature Review
(C) Referencing
(D) Survey

63. Research that is done to understanding the past event is called
(A) Archival Research
(B) Historical Research
(C) Event Research
(D) Document Research

64. Which of the following is the newer method of survey?
(A) Social Networking Survey
(B) Field Survey
(C) E-mail Survey
(D) Both (A) and (C)

65. In which types of interview, the questions are already prepared?
(A) Telephonic Interview
(B) Personal Interview
(C) Structure Interview
(D) Unstructured Interview

66. Who was the advocator of Deductive Reasoning?
(A) Aristotle (B) Plato
(C) Socrates (D) Aristippus

67. Who was the advocator of Inductive Reasoning?
(A) Aristippus (B) Plato
(C) Socrates (D) Francis Bacon

68. H-D method stands for
(A) Hypothetico-Deductive
(B) Hypertext-Deductive
(C) Hypermedia-Deductive
(D) Hippo-Deductive

69. An effective way of quantifying data from a sample group
(A) Interviews (B) Questionnaires
(C) Field surveys (D) Observation

70. A/an.....is defined as anything that varies or change in value.
(A) Variable (B) Data
(C) Information (D) Attribute

71. The variable that is the effect or is the result or outcome of another variable is a/an
(A) Dependent variable
(B) Independent variable
(C) Expensive variable
(D) None of the above

72. Who was the proponent of Hypothetico-Deductive method?
(A) Aristotle
(B) Plato
(C) Christiaan Huygens
(D) Socrates

73. Hypothetico-Deductive is a/an
(A) Scientific Method
(B) Experimental Method
(C) Observational Method
(D) Statistical Method

74. During research, ethics applying in
(A) Planning
(B) Statistical analysis
(C) During data sampling
(D) All of the above

75. The characteristics of Scientific Method is
(A) Empirical (B) Verifiable
(C) Deterministic (D) All of the above

76. A variable that is presumed to cause a change in another variable is a/an

(A) Independent variable
(B) Dependent variable
(C) Expensive variable
(D) Statistical variable

77. Research process consists of a number of ....related activities.
(A) Open (B) Closed
(C) Mixed (D) Both (B) and (C)

78. Cluster Sampling is related to
(A) Population (B) Bibliographic
(C) Abstracting (D) Indexing

79. Which of the following is the data collection method?
(A) Observation
(B) Personal interview
(C) Questionnaire
(D) All of the above

80. For researchers, the characteristics of secondary data is
(A) Reliability (B) Suitability
(C) Adequacy (D) All of the above

81. Which of the following is the Hypothesis-Testing method?
(A) Chi-Square test (B) T-test
(C) F-test (D) All of the above

82. The characteristics of Hypothesis is
(A) It should state the relationship between variables
(B) It should be accurate
(C) It should be unlimited in scope
(D) Both (A) and (B)

83. ANOVA stands for
(A) Analysis of Variance
(B) Annotation of Variance
(C) Anticipation of Variance
(D) Analysis of Variable

84. ANOVA was developed by
(A) Ronald Fisher (B) Jacob Cohen
(C) E.L. Lehmann (D) David Moore

85. The Scientific Method is preferred over other methods because it is more
(A) Systematic (B) Accurate
(C) Reliable (D) All of the above

86. The book titled *Novum Organum* was written by
(A) Francis Bacon (B) Alfred Aho
(C) Andrew Appel (D) Hal Abelson

87. Which of the following is true of S.R. Ranganathan's Scientific Method?
(A) The spiral moves forward in anti-clock direction
(B) Lowest end of the vertical line is called Zenith
(C) Left end of the horizontal line is called Ascendency
(D) Upper end of the vertical line is called Nadir

88. The upper end of the vertical line of Scientific Method is called
(A) Nadir (B) Zenith
(C) Ascendant (D) Descendent

89. Lowest end of the vertical line of Scientific Method is called
(A) Zenith (B) Nadir
(C) Descendant (D) Ascendant

90. Which of the following cardinal point of Scientific Method will solved the research problem?
(A) Zenith (B) Nadir
(C) Ascendancy (D) Descendant

91. Match the following:

LIST-I	LIST-II
(1) Quadrant I	(i) Hypothesis
(2) Quadrant II	(ii) Verification
(3) Quadrant III	(iii) Empirical
(4) Quadrant IV	(iv) Deductive

Codes:

	(1)	(2)	(3)	(4)
(A)	(iv)	(ii)	(iii)	(i)
(B)	(ii)	(i)	(iv)	(iii)
(C)	(iii)	(i)	(iv)	(ii)
(D)	(i)	(iii)	(iv)	(ii)

92. Match the following:

LIST-I	LIST-II
(1) ibid.	(i) here and there
(2) op. cit.	(ii) namely
(3) viz.	(iii) in the work cited
(4) passim	(iv) in the same place

Codes:

	(1)	(2)	(3)	(4)
(A)	(i)	(iii)	(ii)	(iv)
(B)	(iv)	(iii)	(ii)	(i)
(C)	(iv)	(i)	(ii)	(iii)
(D)	(ii)	(i)	(iii)	(iv)

93. Which of the following data collection methods is good for big enquiries?

(A) Observation Method
(B) Interview Method
(C) Questionnaire Method
(D) Schedules Method

94. Match the following:

LIST-I	LIST-II
(1) Quadrant I	(i) Zenith to Descendant
(2) Quadrant II	(ii) Descendant to Nadir
(3) Quadrant III	(iii) Ascendant to Zenith
(4) Quadrant IV	(iv) Nadir to Ascendant

Codes:

	(1)	(2)	(3)	(4)
(A)	(iv)	(iii)	(i)	(ii)
(B)	(ii)	(i)	(iii)	(iv)
(C)	(iii)	(iv)	(i)	(ii)
(D)	(i)	(ii)	(iii)	(iv)

95. Which of the following variables is applicable in research?

(A) Independent variable
(B) Dependent variable
(C) Controlled variable
(D) All of the above

96. A survey tool that requests an assessment of some variable from among a range of potential responses.

(A) Ratio Scale (B) Likert Scale
(C) Ordinal Scale (D) Hume's Scale

97. Which of the following is true for Nominal variables?

(A) We cannot perform any mathematical operations
(B) We cannot compare as logical operations
(C) We can count the number of observations
(D) All of the above

98. A rectangular graphical diagram that display data through bars of different heights is called

(A) Pie Chart (B) Histogram
(C) Line Chart (D) Area Chart

99. Which of the following research methods is applying for Library and Information Science Research?

(A) Historical Method
(B) Descriptive Method
(C) Scientific Method
(D) Any of the above

100. We can collect secondary data through

(A) Newspaper (B) Reports
(C) Trade journal (D) All of the above

101. Histogram was first introduced by

(A) Karl Pearson (B) Rudolf Bayer
(C) Edwin Catmull (D) John Crowcroff

102. Which of the following is a bibliometric software?

(A) Loktastats (B) Koha
(C) Bibmet (D) DSpace

103. Assertion (A): Research is a scientific and systematic work for significant information on a specific topic.

Reason (R): Research is a non-academic activity but using technical sense.

(A) Both (A) and (R) are true
(B) Both (A) and (R) are false
(C) (A) is true, but (R) is false
(D) (A) is false, but (R) is true

104. Assertion (A): Research design is the conceptual structure within research is conducted and it's associated with collection and analysis of data.

Reason (R): Research design is needed because time and budget cost can be easily analyzed.

(A) Both (A) and (R) are false
(B) Both (A) and (R) are true
(C) (A) is true, but (R) is false
(D) (A) is false, but (R) is true

105. Assertion (A): Survey and Experiment both are same because they are conducted in case of Descriptive Research.

Reason (R): In Descriptive Research, the samples have very larger because the percentage of responses generally happens to be low.

(A) Both (A) and (R) are true
(B) Both (A) and (R) are false
(C) (A) is false, but (R) is true
(D) (A) is true, but (R) is false

106. Assertion (A): One of the oldest methods of data collection is Observation Method for both scientist and social scientists.

Reason (R): Observation has to be done very carefully and systematical manner and most important its need for Impartial Observation.

(A) Both (A) and (R) are true
(B) Both (A) and (R) are false
(C) (A) is true, but (R) is false
(D) (A) is false, but (R) is true

107. Assertion (A): Historical Method is also called 'Documentary Method' because its main reliance on documentary source.

Reason (R): Both primary and secondary sources of information simultaneously important for this type of research.

(A) Both (A) and (R) are false
(B) Both (A) and (R) are true
(C) (A) is false, but (R) is true
(D) (A) is true, but (R) is false

Answers Keys

1. (A)	2. (B)	3. (A)	4. (D)	41. (D)	42. (D)	43. (D)	44. (A)
5. (D)	6. (B)	7. (A)	8. (A)	45. (D)	46. (A)	47. (D)	48. (A)
9. (B)	10. (C)	11. (B)	12. (D)	49. (B)	50. (C)	51. (B)	52. (B)
13. (A)	14. (B)	15. (A)	16. (B)	53. (D)	54. (B)	55. (B)	56. (A)
17. (D)	18. (D)	19. (A)	20. (D)	57. (A)	58. (A)	59. (C)	60. (D)
21. (A)	22. (C)	23. (A)	24. (A)	61. (A)	62. (B)	63. (B)	64. (D)
25. (B)	26. (B)	27. (A)	28. (C)	65. (C)	66. (A)	67. (D)	68. (A)
29. (A)	30. (A)	31. (D)	32. (A)	69. (B)	70. (A)	71. (A)	72. (C)
33. (A)	34. (A)	35. (A)	36. (C)	73. (A)	74. (D)	75. (D)	76. (A)
37. (A)	38. (A)	39. (D)	40. (D)	77. (B)	78. (A)	79. (D)	80. (D)

81. (D)	82. (D)	83. (A)	84. (A)
85. (D)	86. (A)	87. (C)	88. (B)
89. (B)	90. (B)	91. (C)	92. (B)
93. (C)	94. (A)	95. (D)	96. (B)
97. (D)	98. (B)	99. (C)	100. (D)
101. (A)	102. (A)	103. (C)	104. (B)
105. (C)	106. (A)	107. (B)	

CHAPTER 10 Information Technology

Introduction

The application of Information Technology (IT) is very broad and term "information technology" is often used to refer to all of computer system. IT is not a single entity but it is the broad subject concerned with all aspects of data processing and information management including data storing and retrieval.

In Library and Information Science, IT refers to anything related to computing technology, such as database management of library consortia, library network in in-campus and out-campus, making e-resource in integrated library software, centralization of library data, ordering of data in any desired order and much more.

At present, IT is not only a computer-based services but also a set of tools, methods and procedure.

After emerging of IT in our library house-keeping, we have seen lots of changes such as card catalogue to e-catalogue, Web-OPAC, metadata harvesting, data warehouse and data mining, document to e-document and the form of library also changed from conventional to digital library and hybrid library and now cyber library.

Therefore, at present IT-based services in library is highly demandable in entire library house-keeping. In this situation, we will take plenty of questions with answer related to present trends in information technology in various competitive examinations in Library and Information Science subject.

Important Points

- AJAX stands for Asynchronous JavaScript and XML and with the help of this technique we can create better, faster and more interactive web applications.
- Cascading Style Sheets (CSS) is a type of web language or style sheet language used for describing the web presentation of a web page written in a markup language.
- With the help of CSS, we set the page layout, colour, and fonts separately as an object.
- The CSS specifications are maintained by the World Wide Web Consortium (W3C).
- The file extension of CSS file is .css.

- The CSS web application techniques are developed by Hakon Wium Lie and Bert Bos and initial released on 17 December 1996.
- The Web Hypertext Application Technology Working Group (WHATWG) is a community of people interested in evolving HTML and other web development-related technologies.
- Internet is the global system of interconnect computer networks that use the TCP/IP to link devices worldwide.
- The Domain Name System (DNS) is a hierarchical decentralized naming system for computers, services, or any resource connected to the Internet or a private network.
- IP address is a set of numerical value assigned to computers and their devices for participating in a computer network through Internet protocol.
- There are two versions of IP (Internet Protocol), viz.: (a) IP version 4, and (b) IP version 6.
- In IP version 4, an address consists of 32 bits which is canonically represented in dot-decimal notation and it consists of four decimal numbers, each ranging from 0 to 255, separated by dot, e.g. 172.16.254.1.
- A random-access memory device allows data items to read and write.
- Robert H. Dennard invented Dynamic Random-Access Memory (DRAM) in 1968.
- Static Random-Access Memory (SRAM) and Dynamic Random-Access Memory (DRAM) are two widely used forms of primary memory.
- Read-Only Memory (ROM) is a type of non-volatile memory that means stored information can be retrieved even after power off and other examples of non-volatile memory are hard disk, magnetic tape, optical disks, flash memory, etc.
- Random-Access Memory (RAM) is the example of volatile memory, which means stored information can't be retrieved after power off the computer.
- Blu-ray Disc is a digital optical disc data storage format and it was designed to supersede the DVD format.
- A single-layer Blu-ray Disc can store up to 25 GB data whereas BDXL format of Blu-ray Disc can store 100 GB and 128 GB write-once discs and 100 GB rewritable discs for commercial applications.
- MPEG-2 is a standard for the generic coding of moving pictures.
- The primary characteristics of an HDD (Hard Disk) are its capacity and performance.
- PATA (Parallel Advanced Technology Attachment or Parallel ATA) and SATA (Serial Advanced Technology Attachment or Serial ATA) are computer bus interface that connects host bus adapters to mass storage devices such as hard disk drives, optical drives, optical disc drives.
- Serial ATA succeeded the older Parallel ATA standard.

- Forward Error Correction (FEC) or Channel Coding is a technique used for controlling errors in data transmission over communication channels.
- Hamming code (developed by R.W. Hamming at Bell Labs) is a set of error-correction codes that can be used to detect and correct bits errors in data communication, moved from one location to another.
- NAND Gate (Negative-AND) is a logic gate, produces an output which is false only if all its inputs are true.
- A modem (modulator-demodulator) is a type of network hardware device that modulates one or more carrier ware signals to encode digital information for transmission and demodulates signals to decode the transmitted information.
- In computer network, the RS-232 is a standard for serial communication transmission of data.
- The first packet switching network for computer network was ARPANET (Advanced Research Projects Agency Network).
- A set of communication standards for simultaneous digital transmission of voice, video, data, and network services over public-switched telephone network is known as Integrated Service Digital Network (ISDN).
- In computer networking, multiplexing is a method by which multiple analog or digital signals are combined into one signal over a shared medium and device that performs the multiplexing is called a multiplexer (MUX).
- In Linux, the wc command is used to count the total number of lines, words, and characters contained in a file.
- The kernel is the core application in Linux Operating System (OS).
- GNU stands for GNU's not Unix.
- The GNU Operating System (OS) is a complete free software and upward-compatible with Unix.
- Richard Stallman is the founder of GNU Project and project was conceived in 1983.
- In Linux, the sudo command allows a permitted user to execute a command as the super-user with full administrative work.
- In Operating System (OS), the filesystem is the data structures that used to keep tracks of files on a disk or partition and it is the way that files are organized on the disk.
- In Linux, everything is configured as a file and technically directory (folder) is also a file.
- In Linux, the mount command mounts a storage device or filesystem which make it accessible and attaching to an existing directory structure.
- Linux starts filesystem with root directory (/).
- List of filesystem of Linux under root directory are as follows:

Directory	Description
/	Root directory as well as first directory in Linux filesystem and all files and directories are created and managed under this root directory.
/home	This is default directory for user data and automatically creates a home directory matching with username in this home directory.
/root	This is administrative user's home directory and root user is the super user in Linux.
/bin	This is shareable by all the users and usually do not require any permission to run.
/usr	This directory contains user application software files, libraries, documentations, etc. for all user-related programs.
/var	This directory store all variable files and temporary files created by users such as log files, mail queue, download from the Internet, etc.
/etc	This directory contains system configuration files.
/boot	This directory contains Linux boot loader file.
/dev	This directory contains device files.
/tmp	This is the temporary location for applications during system execution.
/mnt	This directory uses for standard mount point for external filesystem, e.g. DVD-ROM, CD-ROM, pen drive or any USB enable external storage devices.
/sbin	This directory contains system administration command files and available only for root user.

- In Linux, the mkdir command creates a new directory.
- In Database Management System (DBMS), the data dictionary is a data structure (file or set of files) that contains a database's metadata.
- In SQL, the DROP INDEX statement to remove an index or domain index from the database.
- Oracle RDBMS, IBM DB2, Microsoft SQL Server, MySQL, Informix, PostgresSQL, Ingres are most popular Relational Database Management System (RDBMS) software.
- In SQL, the Grant statement is use to grant privileges on table, view, and procedure to other users or roles, whereas the Revoke statement use to take back privileges granted to other users and roles.

QUESTIONS

1. Tim Berners-Lee invented the World Wide Web (WWW) in......

(A) 1987 (B) 1989
(C) 1991 (D) 1995

2. The World Wide Web Consortium (W3C) was founded by

(A) Tim Berners-Lee (B) Ken Thompson
(C) Grace Hopper (D) James Gosling

3. In DBMS, the database schema is constructing through.......

(A) DCL (B) DML
(C) DDL (D) XML

4. Which of the following statements is true?

(A) The major contribution of ISO is to development of OSI model
(B) An analog signal is a continuously varying signal
(C) A digital signal has something or nothing in the form of binary
(D) All of the above

5. MIPS stands for

(A) Millions of Instructions Per Second
(B) Methods of Instructions Per Second
(C) Millions of Information Per Second
(D) Methods of Information Per Second

6. Which of the following components is the part of CPU?

(A) ALU (B) Microprocessor
(C) Cache (D) All of the above

7. A set of rules that govern data communication between sender and receiver is known as

(A) Law (B) Principle
(C) Protocol (D) Rule

8. Z39.50 is a/an

(A) Open Source Database Management System
(B) Compiler used in Linux Kernel
(C) International standard communication protocol for data searching and retrieving
(D) Fourth generation web designing language

9. How many codes are proposed by Edgar F. Codd for relational model for database?

(A) Nine (B) Ten
(C) Thirteen (D) Fifteen

10. Which of the query language is used in Z39.50 for data searching and retrieving?

(A) Command Query Language
(B) Complex Query Language
(C) Contextual Query Language
(D) All of the above

11. The purpose of Copy Tracker software is

(A) Easy copied the files from one location to another
(B) Encoding the lost files
(C) Retrieved the lost files
(D) To detect plagiarism in a document or research paper

12. Which of the following is the Copy Tracker software?

(A) Viper (B) EVE2
(C) Urkund (D) All of the above

13. The fundamental language for making metadata structure is

(A) PHP (B) JAVA
(C) XML (D) JSP

14. APDU stands for

(A) Application Protocol Data Unit
(B) Active Protocol Data Unit
(C) Associative Protocol Data Unit
(D) Asynchronous Protocol Data Unit

15. Measurement of audio signal in fixed intervals of time is called

(A) Audio data (B) Sampling
(C) Quantizing (D) Counting

16. In DBMS, which of the following views describes what data are actually stored in the database?
(A) External view (B) Conceptual view
(C) Internal view (D) All of the above

17. SDLC stands for
(A) System Development Life Cycle
(B) System Designing Life Cycle
(C) Structure Designing Life Cycle
(D) System Distributed Life Cycle

18. The first step of SDLC is
(A) System Analysis
(B) System Design
(C) Feasibility Study
(D) Preliminary Investigation

19. Which of the following is the Modulation Technique for signal coding?
(A) Amplitude Shift Keying (ASK)
(B) Frequency Shift Keying (FSK)
(C) Phase Shift Keying (PSK)
(D) All of the above

20. The whole block of data bits is transferred at once called
(A) Asynchronous Communication
(B) Synchronous Communication
(C) Isochronous Communication
(D) Full-duplex Communication

21. Which Multiplexing technique is used only for digital transmission?
(A) Frequency Division Multiplexing
(B) Time Division Multiplexing
(C) Statistical Time Division Multiplexing
(D) None of the above

22. Which topology is known as complete topology?
(A) Star topology (B) Ring topology
(C) Mesh topology (D) Bus topology

23. In which topology, each node is connected to every other node by direct link?
(A) Star topology (B) Bus topology
(C) Mesh topology (D) Ring topology

24. The topmost layer of OSI model is
(A) Physical Layer
(B) Data Link Layer
(C) Transport Layer
(D) Application Layer

25. Which of the following types of data can be transferred in Integrated Service Digital Network (ISDN)?
(A) Audio (B) Video
(C) Text (D) All of the above

26. NIC stands for
(A) Network Interface Card
(B) Network Interrelated Card
(C) Network Information Card
(D) Network Interface Circuit

27. Which of the following networks is used by X.25 protocol?
(A) LAN (B) WAN
(C) MAN (D) Both (A) and (C)

28. Which of the following statements is true for TCP/IP?
(A) It was developed before OSI
(B) It consists of five layers
(C) The highest layer is Application layer
(D) All of the above

29. In URL address .edu, .com, .ac are the example of
(A) IP address (B) Domain Name
(C) Client Name (D) Server Name

30. Domain Name System is a/an.......structure
(A) Binary (B) Decimal
(C) Tree (D) Circle

31. Which of the following is the Country Domain Name for India?

(A) .in (B) .ind
(C) .india (D) .indo

32. Match the following:

LIST-I	LIST-II
(1) ATM	(i) Planning tool
(2) PERT	(ii) Generic solution to problem
(3) Algorithm	(iii) System project management
(4) Gantt Chart	(iv) Real time system

Codes:

	(1)	(2)	(3)	(4)
(A)	(ii)	(iii)	(iv)	(i)
(B)	(iv)	(iii)	(ii)	(i)
(C)	(i)	(iii)	(ii)	(iv)
(D)	(iv)	(i)	(ii)	(iii)

33. Which of the following Protocols is used in Email?
(A) POP (B) SMTP
(C) JAR (D) Both (A) and (B)

34. Which of the following queries can be deleted a relation (Table) from the database?
(A) DELETE (B) DEL TABLE
(C) DROP TABLE (D) REMOVE TABLE

35. Which of the following is the disadvantage of Flat File Systems?
(A) Data isolation
(B) Unanticipated Queries
(C) Integrity problem
(D) All of the above

36. POP stands for
(A) Post Office Protocol
(B) Primary Office Protocol
(C) Permanent Office Protocol
(D) Proxy Office Protocol

37. SMTP stands for
(A) Simple Mail Transmission Protocol
(B) Simple Mail Transfer Protocol
(C) Synchronous Mail Transfer Protocol
(D) Synchronous Mail Transmission Protocol

38. For Wi-Fi communication, which of OSI model has been used?
(A) Physical Layer (B) Data Link Layer
(C) Transport Layer (D) Both (A) and (B)

39. Wi-Fi is the example of
(A) LAN (B) MAN
(C) WAN (D) WLAN

40. ODBC stands for
(A) Oracle Database Connectivity
(B) Object Database Connectivity
(C) Open Database Connectivity
(D) Online Database Connectivity

41. WLAN stands for
(A) Wide Local Area Network
(B) World Local Area Network
(C) Wireless Local Area Network
(D) Windows Local Area Network

42. In Hierarchical model, records are organized as
(A) List (B) Circle
(C) Tree (D) All of the above

43. Which of the following is primary memory?
(A) RAM (B) ROM
(C) CD-ROM (D) Both (A) and (B)

44. Example of Dynamic Web page is/are
(A) Facebook web page
(B) INFLIBNET web page
(C) UGC web page
(D) Both (B) and (C)

45. The first public version of DSpace was released in
(A) 1998 (B) 2000
(C) 2002 (D) 2005

46. DSpace is written in

(A) C++ (B) Java
(C) ASP.NET (D) Python

47. Which of the following Operating Systems is supported by DSpace?
(A) Microsoft Windows
(B) Linux
(C) Mac OS X
(D) All of the above

48. Which of the following is the example of open source software?
(A) DSpace (B) Koha
(C) GreenStone (D) All of the above

49. Which of the following Operating Systems is supported by Koha?
(A) Microsoft Windows
(B) Mac OS
(C) Linux
(D) All of the above

50. Koha is written in
(A) Java (B) C
(C) C++ (D) Perl

51. Which of the following is a content-management framework platform?
(A) DSpace (B) Drupal
(C) Koha (D) GreenStone

52. Drupal is written in
(A) Java (B) C
(C) C++ (D) PHP

53. Which of the following is the Linux distributor?
(A) Ubuntu (B) Fedora
(C) OpenSUSE (D) All of the above

54. Which of the following is a desktop environment for free and open source software?
(A) GNOME (B) MYNOME
(C) KNOME (D) DNOME

55. Which of the following statements is true?
(A) RAM is dynamic and volatile
(B) ROM memory cannot be erased and rewritten
(C) ROM is non-volatile
(D) All of the above

56. In database transaction, ACID properties are
(A) Atomicity, Consistency, Isolation, Durability
(B) Attributes, Currency, Isolation, Directory
(C) Application, Consistency, Isolation, Durability
(D) Applicable, Currency, Isolation, Distillation

57. A kind of memory that comes with computer as pre-written for computer booting.
(A) RAM (B) ROM
(C) Virtual (D) Cache

58. Which of the following statements is false for Primary Key field?
(A) It may be NULL
(B) Fully functional dependency not required
(C) Duplicate value may be stored
(D) All of the above

59. Which of the following is a comparison operator in SQL?
(A) SELECT (B) LIKE
(C) INSERT (D) UPDATE

60. In computer hardware, IAR stands for
(A) Instruction Address Register
(B) Information Address Register
(C) Interrelated Address Register
(D) Instruction Applicable Register

61. Which of the following is Input Device?
(A) Keyboard (B) Scanner
(C) Mouse (D) All of the above

62. OCR stands for
(A) Optical Character Reader
(B) Optical Currency Reader
(C) Optical Control Reader
(D) Optical Contact Reader

63. OMR stands for
(A) Optical Markup Reader
(B) Optical Method Reader
(C) Optical Mark Reader
(D) Optical Multimedia Reader

64. Which of the following is used by banks for cheque identification?
(A) OMR (B) OCR
(C) MICR (D) POS

65. Which of the following statements is true?
(A) Magnetic tape is a serial access storage device
(B) Optical disk is a direct access storage device
(C) Secondary storage devices may be serial access or direct access
(D) All of the above

66. Which of the following is the optical storage device?
(A) CD-ROM (B) DVD-ROM
(C) Pen Drive (D) Both (A) and (B)

67. A kind of special software/package that stores users information during web surfing.
(A) Cookies (B) Blue tooth
(C) Red software (D) Green software

68. Which of the following is Primary Memory?
(A) RAM (B) ROM
(C) Cache (D) All of the above

69. Which of the following types of RAM does not need frequent power refreshing?
(A) Dynamic RAM (B) Static RAM
(C) Flash RAM (D) Both (A) and (B)

70. From which generation of computer, Microprocessors has been used as switching device?
(A) Second Generation
(B) Third Generation
(C) Fourth Generation
(D) Fifth Generation

71. EBCDIC stands for
(A) Extended Binary Coded Decimal Interchange Code
(B) Executable Binary Coded Decimal Interchange Code
(C) Expanded Binary Coded Decimal Interchange Code
(D) Extendable Binary Coded Decimal Interchange Code

72. EBCDIC is a/an
(A) Eight-bit character encoding
(B) Seven-bit character encoding
(C) Nine-bit character encoding
(D) Eleven-bit character encoding

73. A single-layer DVD-ROM can hold.......... data.
(A) 4.7 MB (B) 4.7 GB
(C) 3.8 GB (D) 737 MB

74. In data storage devices, WORM stands for
(A) Write Once Read Many
(B) Write Once Recoded Many
(C) Write Once Recordable Media
(D) Both (A) and (C)

75. Which of the following is WORM device?
(A) CD-R (B) DVD-R
(C) DVD-RW (D) Both (A) and (B)

76. Magnetic tape was invented by?
(A) Fritz Pfleumer (B) Alan Tuning
(C) John Backus (D) John Mauchly

77. ....memory is a high speed memory device which stores high speed data from the processor before sending it to RAM.
(A) ROM (B) Virtual
(C) Cache (D) Both (A) and (B)

78. A kind of memory which is the part of the hard disk drive that can be used as 'RAM' to get extra memory for data processing.

(A) Virtual Memory
(B) Cache Memory
(C) Parallel Memory
(D) Users Memory

79. In.......Charles Babbage invented Difference Engine to compile mathematical tables.
(A) 1810 (B) 1815
(C) 1821 (D) 1829

80. Transistors was invented in 1948 at
(A) AT&T Bell Labs
(B) IBM Labs
(C) Apple Technology Labs
(D) University of Pennsylvania, USA

81. In which generation of computer technology, Integrated Circuit (IC) was used as a switching device?
(A) Second (B) Third
(C) Fourth (D) Fifth

82. The study of Artificial Intelligence (AI) of computer technology is known as
(A) Second Generation
(B) Third Generation
(C) Fourth Generation
(D) Fifth Generation

83. Which of the following is extremely fast printer?
(A) Line Printer (B) Ink Jet Printer
(C) Laser Printer (D) Dot Matrix Printer

84. Which of the following statements is true for dumb terminal?
(A) Very huge Primary Memory
(B) Monitor, keyboard and sometimes barcode scanner are attached
(C) It cannot do any processing or storage of data.
(D) Both (B) and (C)

85. A........is a communication pathway connecting two or more devices.
(A) Router (B) Bus
(C) Path (D) LAN

86. In computer system, the CPU, memory, and connectors for all inputs and outputs devices in a single board is called
(A) Memoryboard (B) Motherboard
(C) Connectorboard (D) Commonboard

87. Devices inside the computer is connected using
(A) Buses (B) Lines
(C) Interfaces (D) All of the above

88. Which of the following is the highest level memory in hierarchy in term of speed?
(A) Register (B) Cache
(C) Main Memory (D) DVD-ROM

89. Which of the following is the example of Database Management Systems (DBMS) software/package?
(A) DB2
(B) Oracle 11g
(C) MySQL Server 5.5
(D) All of the above

90. The loading of the Object Code into the memory of a computer is done by a/an
(A) Assembler (B) Compiler
(C) Loader (D) Interpreter

91. UNIX was developed at AT&T's Bell Labs in
(A) 1965 (B) 1969
(C) 1972 (D) 1976

92. In which year vacuum tube was invented?
(A) 1899 (B) 1900
(C) 1906 (D) 1912

93. BCD stands for
(A) Bits Coded Decimal
(B) Binary Coded Decimal
(C) Basic Coded Data
(D) Basic Coded Decimal

94. Which of the following components is optional for a computer system?
(A) CPU
(B) MU
(C) ALU
(D) Above all are mandatory

95. LINUX is a/an
(A) Multi-Tasking Operating System
(B) Multi-User Operating System
(C) Single-User Operating System
(D) Both (A) and (B)

96. ....is a combination of software and hardware that prevents unwanted programs from outside networks.
(A) Firewall (B) Firmware
(C) Antivirus (D) Compiler

97. Which of the following was the first electronic computer?
(A) ABC (B) ENIAC
(C) MARK I (D) Pascaline

98. 1 Petabyte is equal to
(A) 1024 KB (B) 1024 MB
(C) 1024 GB (D) 1024 TB

99. John Napier is best known as the inventor of
(A) Laptop (B) Java compiler
(C) Logarithms (D) Linux Kernel

100. ....was the world's first stored-program computer.
(A) EDSAC (B) ENIAV
(C) UNIVAC (D) ABC

101. Which of the following statements is false for Java language?
(A) Platform dependent
(B) Object-Oriented
(C) Multithreaded
(D) Robust

102. Among these, which one is smallest in term of data storage?
(A) Petabyte (B) Gigabytes
(C) Terabytes (D) Megabyte

103. FAT stands for
(A) File Allocation Table
(B) Field Allocation Table
(C) File Application Table
(D) File Applicable Table

104. FTP stands for
(A) File Transfer Protocol
(B) File Transmission Protocol
(C) Field Transfer Protocol
(D) Field Transmission Protocol

105. Which one is an output device?
(A) Mouse (B) Plotter
(C) Scanner (D) Light Pen

106. BIOS stands for
(A) Bytes Input Output System
(B) Binary Input Output System
(C) Basic Input Output System
(D) Bits Input Output System

107. Abacus was the first
(A) Mechanical calculator
(B) Electronic calculator
(C) Electronic computer
(D) Mechanical computer

108. DFD stands for
(A) Data Flow Diagram
(B) Data File Diagram
(C) Digital Flow Data
(D) Data Flow Device

109. Removing errors from a program is called
(A) Compiling (B) Assembling
(C) Debugging (D) Translating

110. In computer programming, logical errors can be detected through
(A) Compiler
(B) Assembler

(C) Programmer/user intelligence
(D) Interpreter

111. Who design a model for stored-program in computer memory for data processing unit?
(A) John Von Neumann
(B) Dennis Ritchie
(C) Ken Thompson
(D) Alan Turing

112. In Windows environment CTRL+ P is used.........
(A) For printing
(B) For print view
(C) For entire document selection
(D) For print pausing

113. What is the right combinations of keys for CUT and PASTE in MS Office?
(A) CTRL+X then CTRL+P
(B) CTRL+ X then CTRL+V
(C) CTRL+C then CTRL+X
(D) CTRL+ALT+X then CTRL+V

114. Which of the following is the hardware interface of a computer system?
(A) Register (B) Adder
(C) Transistor (D) All of the above

115. Which of the following software is used for translation of programs from Assembly Language to Machine Language?
(A) Assembler (B) Compiler
(C) Interpreter (D) All of the above

116. Microsoft Excel is a/an.........software.
(A) Database (B) Spreadsheet
(C) Presentation (D) Graphical

117. In Microsoft Excel, we can edit particular cell value through
(A) F2 (B) F3
(C) F4 (D) F5

118. Which of the following is the tool for Structured System Analysis and Design?
(A) DFD (B) CASE
(C) HIPO (D) All of the above

119. In Microsoft Excel, the formula begins from
(A) # (B) =
(C) & (D) $

120. In computing, Bug is a/an
(A) Hardware (B) LAN topology
(C) Error (D) Setup file

121. Microsoft Power Point is a/an........... software.
(A) Presentation (B) Spreadsheet
(C) Database (D) Statistical

122. In Microsoft Word, the short-cut key of 'Save As' is
(A) F3 (B) F8
(C) F12 (D) F4

123. MIS stands for
(A) Management Information Serial
(B) Management Information Sequential
(C) Management Information System
(D) Management Integration System

124. Which of the following is Object Oriented Programming (OOP) language?
(A) Java (B) C++
(C) C (D) Both (A) and (B)

125. In computing, a nibble is the aggregation of
(A) Four-bit (B) Half an octal
(C) 16 bits (D) Either (A) or (B)

126. Which one is the example of System Software?
(A) LINUX (B) MS Office
(C) Koha (D) Java

127. API stands for
(A) Application Programming Interface
(B) Application Programmer Interface

(C) Active Programming Interface
(D) Allocating Programming Interface

128. What is the key for 'Bootstrapping'?
(A) CTRL+ALT+DEL
(B) ALT+DEL+ SHIFT
(C) SHIFT+DEL+F9
(D) ALT+DEL+F10

129. Which of the following is not related to the generation of computer language?
(A) Machine Level Language
(B) Object-Oriented Language
(C) Mother Level Language
(D) High Level Language

130. Which of the following is not character-encoding scheme in computer system?
(A) ASCII (B) EBCDIC
(C) Baudot Code (D) System Code

131. The Binary equivalent of 45 is
(A) 00101101 (B) 00110011
(C) 00101111 (D) 00100011

132. In which year ARPA renamed the Defense Advanced Research Project Agency (DARPA)?
(A) 1965 (B) 1972
(C) 1976 (D) 1978

133. Which of the following is executable file?
(A) .exe (B) .apk
(C) .com (D) All of the above

134. Which of the following is an external memory in a computer system?
(A) RAM (B) ROM
(C) Cache (D) Hard Disk

135. In computing, the error detection scheme is
(A) Parity bits
(B) Checksums
(C) Cyclic Redundancy Checks (CRCs)
(D) All of the above

136. Which of the following is true for Intranet?
(A) It is a local area network uses within an organization
(B) Internet Protocol such as TCP/IP is used for communications within organization
(C) It is not accessible for outsiders
(D) All of the above

137. The first web browser 'Mosaic' was released in
(A) 1992 (B) 1994
(C) 1996 (D) 1998

138. Match the following:

LIST-I	LIST-II
(1) John Ambrose Fleming	(i) Standardization of ASCII
(2) Bob Bemer	(ii) Relational Model for Database
(3) Cleve Moler	(iii) Vacuum Tube
(4) Edgar F. Codd	(iv) MATLAB

Codes:

	(1)	(2)	(3)	(4)
(A)	(ii)	(iii)	(i)	(iv)
(B)	(iii)	(i)	(iv)	(ii)
(C)	(i)	(iii)	(iv)	(ii)
(D)	(iii)	(iv)	(i)	(ii)

139. How many bits are in an IP address?
(A) 16 (B) 32
(C) 38 (D) 64

140. ....is a networking device that forward data packets from one network to another.
(A) Router (B) Gateway
(C) Protocol (D) Bandwidth

141. ....is the data rate when communicating over certain media or devices.
(A) Router (B) Interpreter
(C) Bandwidth (D) Protocol

142. How many classes in IP address?

(A) Four (B) Five
(C) Six (D) Seven

143. Which of the following is first Octet Decimal Range of IP address for Class C category Domain Name?
(A) 192-223 (B) 184-237
(C) 189-256 (D) 123-267

144. The maximum host addresses for Class C IP address is
(A) 223 (B) 254
(C) 267 (D) 298

145. In which year Magnetic tape was invented in Germany?
(A) 1926 (B) 1928
(C) 1930 (D) 1935

146. For the first time who gave the idea 'information stored in digital form' known as Optical Digital Recording (ODR)?
(A) James T. Russell (B) Sophie Wilson
(C) John Backus (D) E. Allen Emerson

147. For the first time, the concept of Compact Disc (CD) was introduced by
(A) Leslie Lamport
(B) Claude Shannon
(C) Edsger W. Dijkstra
(D) James T. Russell

148. What is the Base of Hexadecimal number system?
(A) Base 2 (B) Hexa 10
(C) Base 16 (D) Base 12

149. A storage media that contains a small image or micro-production of a document is called
(A) Microform (B) Database
(C) Floppy disk (D) CD-R

150. Koha is a/an.....
(A) Application software
(B) System software
(C) Utilities software
(D) All of the above

151. A half-duplex circuits actually means
(A) The signal strength is weak
(B) The signal strength is strong
(C) Both sides talk at a time
(D) Only one side can talk at a time

152. Bandwidth is described in
(A) Gigabytes per minute
(B) Bits per second
(C) Kilobytes per hour
(D) Terabytes per half-hour

153. A kind of computer language that understood directly by the computer
(A) Machine Language
(B) Assembly Language
(C) High Level Language
(D) Both (B) and (C)

154. Which of the following can read High Level Language syntax and then translate it into equivalent Machine Language?
(A) Compiler (B) Interpreter
(C) Assembler (D) Both (A) and (B)

155. Which of the following OSI layers handles error detection?
(A) Physical Layer
(B) Transport Layer
(C) Data Link Layer
(D) Application Layer

156. How many layers in TCP/IP Protocol Architecture?
(A) Three (B) Four
(C) Five (D) Seven

157. Which of the following layers is not belonged to TCP/IP layer?
(A) Presentation Layer
(B) Transport Layer

(C) Internet Layer
(D) Network Interface Layer

158. Which of the following is an Internet-standard protocol for collecting and organizing information from network and configure network devices such as server, printer, router, etc.?
(A) TELNET (B) SMTP
(C) FTP (D) SNMP

159. Which of the following protocols is used for accessing remote computers over TCP/IP networks like the Internet?
(A) TELNET (B) FTP
(C) SMTP (D) All of the above

160. UDP stands for
(A) User Datagram Protocol
(B) Unix Datagram Protocol
(C) Universal Datagram Protocol
(D) Unified Datagram Protocol

161. In.........transmission, signals are transmit in only one direction where one station is transmitter and the other is receiver.
(A) Simplex (B) Half-duplex
(C) Full-duplex (D) Multiplex

162. In.........operation, both stations may transmit, but only one direction at a time.
(A) Full-duplex (B) Half-duplex
(C) Multiplex (D) Simplex

163. In.......operation, both stations may transmit simultaneously.
(A) Full-duplex (B) Half-duplex
(C) Multiplex (D) Simplex

164. Which of the following is unguided media?
(A) Mobile Communication
(B) Satellite Communication
(C) Microwave
(D) All of the above

165. Which of the following is guided media?
(A) Twisted pair wire (B) Coaxial cable
(C) Fiber optic cable (D) All of the above

166. Telephone is a/an......media.
(A) Half-duplex (B) Full-duplex
(C) Simplex (D) Both (A) and (C)

167. Walkie-Talkie is a/an.......media.
(A) Simplex (B) Full-duplex
(C) Half-duplex (D) Both (A) and (B)

168. Which of the following statements is true related to the TCP/IP model?
(A) It is a Client/Server architecture
(B) Transport Layer of TCP/IP is not guarantee delivery of packets
(C) It operated independently
(D) All of the above

169. Which of the following is a web page location?
(A) URL (B) HTML
(C) XML (D) Both (B) and (C)

170. A search engine is a/an
(A) Information
(B) Web pages
(C) Indexes of web pages
(D) Web pages for information according to the search term

171. Which of the following is the transmission impairments?
(A) Noise (B) Delay distortion
(C) Attenuation (D) All of the above

172. An antenna is a transmission and reception media for........
(A) Guided media
(B) Unguided media
(C) Short distance media
(D) Both (A) and (C)

173. PCM stands for
(A) Pulse Code Modulation
(B) Parallel Code Modulation

(C) Paired Code Modulation
(D) Proxy Code Modulation

174. Unit for Data Rate is
(A) Bits Per Second (B) Data Per Second
(C) Giga Per Hour (D) Mega Per Hour

175. A combinational circuit that forms the arithmetic sum of the three inputs bits is
(A) Half-Adder (B) Full-Adder
(C) Multiplex (D) Duplexer

176. A/an...........is a combinational circuit that converts binary information from input lines to an associated pattern of outputs bits.
(A) Binary decoder (B) Audio decoder
(C) Decompress (D) Video decoder

177. A/an..........is a combinational circuit that selects binary information from one of many input lines and directs it to a single output line.
(A) Encoder (B) Decoder
(C) Multiplexer (D) Full-duplex

178. Flip-Flop is a/an
(A) Parallel circuit
(B) Sequential circuit
(C) Analog signal
(D) None of the above

179. Which of the following is not the type of Flip-Flop?
(A) T Flip-Flop (B) JK Flip-Flop
(C) D Flip-Flop (D) Z Flip-Flop

180. BCD stands for
(A) Binary Coded Decimals
(B) Bits Codes Decimals
(C) Bytes Coded Decimal
(D) Basic Coded Decimal

181. In BCD, the system of writing numerals are assigns a........binary.
(A) 3-bit (B) 4-bit
(C) 6-bit (D) 7-bit

182. In..........Topology, each Network Host is connected to a central hub with a point-to-point connection.
(A) Star (B) Ring
(C) Bus (D) Tree

183. Which of the following is not the example to Network Topology?
(A) Bus Topology (B) Tree Topology
(C) Mesh Topology (D) Directory Topology

184. Routers operate which of the following layers of OSI model?
(A) Network Layer (B) Application Layer
(C) Session Layer (D) Physical Layer

185. Hubs operate which of the following layers of OSI model?
(A) Physical Layer
(B) Application Layer
(C) Transport Layer
(D) Data Link Layer

186. Which of the following tags is used for text Bold in HTML?
(A) <B> (B) <BD>
(C) <BLD> (D) <BLDT>

187. Which of the following HTML attributes provides the hyperlink of pages?
(A) href (B) ref
(C) uref (D) dref

188. A/an......is a text or an image we can click on, and jump to another document.
(A) Datalink (B) Megalink
(C) Hyperlink (D) Referencelink

189. Which of the following tags is using for Hyperlink in HTML?
(A) <F> (B) <L>
(C) <UL> (D) <A>

190. Which of the following tags defines the document's body in HTML?

(A)
 (B) <BODY>
(C) <!DOCTYPE> (D) <TITLE>

191. Which of the following is the High Level Web Programming Language?
(A) ASP.NET (B) PHP
(C) JSP (D) All of the above

192. Which of the following is metadata?
(A) Subject (B) Date
(C) Language (D) All of the above

193. The original Dublin Core Metadata Element Set consists of.........metadata.
(A) 12 (B) 13
(C) 14 (D) 15

194. DCMI stands for
(A) Dublin Core Metadata Initiative
(B) Dublin Core Metadata Interchanged
(C) Dublin Core Metadata Information
(D) Dublin Core Metadata Integration

195. The Dublin Core Metadata Element Set (DCMES) was published in
(A) 1996 (B) 1998
(C) 2000 (D) 2002

196. The metadata elements of Dublin Core are stored in the head of........documents.
(A) C++ (B) C
(C) HTML (D) COBOL

197. Which of the following metadata standards is written in XML?
(A) DDI (B) MODS
(C) METS (D) All of the above

198. Digital Object Identifier (DOI) is managed by
(A) IFLA
(B) International DOI Foundation
(C) LOC
(D) UNESCO

199. Which of the following is the metadata standard for digital preservation?
(A) PREMIS (B) EDOC
(C) METAE (D) FMETA

200. The address of web page is called
(A) URL (B) Internet
(C) Web Browser (D) Web Surfing

201. The relational model for database designing in RDBMS is introduced by
(A) E.F. Codd (B) L.B. Codd
(C) Chris W. Ware (D) S.J. Sansom

202. In database architecture, which of the following is not a schema?
(A) Physical Schema (B) Logical Schema
(C) Database Scheme (D) Control Scheme

203. DNS stands for
(A) Domain Name Server
(B) Domain Name System
(C) Digital Name System
(D) Directory Name System

204. SGML stands for
(A) Standard Generalized Markup Language
(B) Systematic Generalized Markup Language
(C) Standard Graphics Markup Language
(D) Standard General Multimedia Language

205. Which of the following is not true for Linux Operating System?
(A) Multiuser Capability
(B) Communication
(C) Not Secure
(D) Multitasking

206. The web browser 'Internet Explorer' is developed by
(A) Microsoft
(B) Tim Berners-Lee
(C) Apple technology
(D) ARPANET

207. In Linux, devices related files are stored in........directory.

(A) dev (B) device
(C) bin (D) tmp

208. ISP stands for
(A) Internet Service Provider
(B) International Service Provider
(C) Internet System Programming
(D) Internet Server Programming

209. Linux Kernel is written which of the following computer languages?
(A) Java (B) PHP
(C) C (D) VB.Net

210. Which of the following commands is used for listing of files and directories in Linux/Unix?
(A) ls (B) lst
(C) disp (D) display

211. In Linux/Unix, the notation......indicates that file is an ordinary file.
(A) d (B) f
(C) % (D) –

212. Which of the following commands is used for change the access permissions of files and directories in Linux/Unix?
(A) chmod (B) changemod
(C) revmod (D) delmod

213. Which of the following symbols is indicated that file is executable in Linux/Unix?
(A) e (B) x
(C) r (D) w

214. Web pages, FTP files and Databases are collectively called
(A) Internet Resource (B) Internet Service
(C) Web sites (D) Protocol

215. Which of the following is not a web browser?
(A) Firefox (B) Opera
(C) Kernel (D) Both (A) and (B)

216. Which of the following is like a read only memory in computer system?
(A) Freeware (B) OpenSource
(C) Firmware (D) Hardware

217. A computer system where computer connects two or more networks and enables users to access one network from another is called
(A) Gateway (B) Routeway
(C) Firmware (D) None of the above

218. ....is a webpage which gives the introductory information about to its owner and provides links to its other relevant pages.
(A) Home page (B) Header page
(C) Footnote page (D) HTML page

219. A network system which operates within an organization is called
(A) Internet (B) Intranet
(C) MAN (D) WAN

220. At present how many sets are present in IP address?
(A) Two (B) Three
(C) Four (D) More than five

221. The term.........is used to define an area where Wi-Fi access is available.
(A) Server (B) Client
(C) Hotspot (D) Circle

222. Which of the following is Web Server software?
(A) Apache
(B) Internet Information Server (IIS)
(C) XAMPP
(D) All of the above

223. Which of the following is web programming language?
(A) PHP (B) JSP
(C) ASP.NET (D) All of the above

224. The attribute of quality of information is
(A) Timeliness (B) Accuracy
(C) Relevancy (D) All of the above

225. Who creates PHP web programming language?

(A) Rasmus Lerdorf (B) Denis Richie
(C) James S. Lee (D) John K. Lee

226. SQL is a/an..........generation query language.

(A) First (B) Second
(C) Third (D) Fourth

227. Which of the following field names could be Primary Key in DBMS?

(A) ROLL_NO
(B) TOTAL_AMOUNT
(C) STUDENT_NAME
(D) CITY_NAME

228. Secondary storage devices are used for

(A) Data transfer from one computer to another
(B) Permanent data storage
(C) Data back up
(D) All of the above

229. A.........Key is a column (field) in a table that uniquely identify all the table records.

(A) Primary (B) Boolean
(C) Cluster (D) Transaction

230. Match the following:

LIST-I	LIST-II
(1) Relation	(i) Unique Identifier
(2) Attributes	(ii) Table
(3) Tuple	(iii) Column (field)
(4) Primary Key	(iv) Row(record)

Codes:

	(1)	(2)	(3)	(4)
(A)	(ii)	(iii)	(iv)	(i)
(B)	(iii)	(ii)	(iv)	(i)
(C)	(iv)	(ii)	(iii)	(i)
(D)	(iii)	(ii)	(i)	(iv)

231. A process where restoring the database from database crash or failure point is called

(A) Database recovery
(B) Database maintenance
(C) Database redistribution
(D) Database transaction

232. WAP stands for

(A) World Application Protocol
(B) Wireless Application Protocol
(C) Web Application Protocol
(D) Web Access Protocol

233. Which of the following data files is permanent in nature?

(A) Transaction File (B) Report File
(C) View File (D) Master File

234. KDD stands for

(A) Knowledge Discovery in Database
(B) Knowledge Dataware in Database
(C) KWIC Discovery in Database
(D) Knowledge Decision in Database

235. What is the decimal value for Hexadecimal 'F'?

(A) 10 (B) 11
(C) 13 (D) 15

236. Which of the following is not an image file format?

(A) BMP (B) TIFF
(C) GIF (D) PPT

237. ISAM is the example of File Management System, developed by

(A) Oracle (B) Microsoft
(C) IBM (D) Apple

238. Which of the following statements is false for Data Warehouse?

(A) It content large amount of data
(B) It available ready-only mode
(C) Data from different operational systems are integrated
(D) All of the above are true

239. GPS stands for

(A) Global Positioning System
(B) General Positioning System
(C) Geographical Positioning System
(D) Graphical Positioning System

240. The process of Normalization was first developed by
(A) David P. Anderson
(B) Tim Finin
(C) Edgar F. Codd
(D) Joseph Goguen

241. What is the possible query for 'GET THE TITLES OF ALL THE BOOKS WHOSE PUBLISHING YEAR IS 2012'?
(A) Select TITLE from CATALOGUE where PUB_YEAR=2012
(B) Select CATALOGUE where PUB_YEAR=2012 from CATALOGUE
(C) List TITLE from CATALOGUE where PUB_YEAR=2012
(D) Display TITLE from CATALOGUE where PUB_YEAR=2012

242. OLAP stands for
(A) Off Line Analytical Processing
(B) On Line Analytical Processing
(C) On Line Application Processing
(D) On Line Active Processing

243. Which of the following is the example of 'Schema' in DBMS?
(A) Defines the tables
(B) Defines the fields in each table
(C) Defines the relationships between fields and tables
(D) All of the above

244. GPRS stands for
(A) Global Packet Radio Service
(B) General Packet Radio Service
(C) Geographical Package Radio Service
(D) General Protocol Radio Service

245. Which of the following is the example of RDBMS/DBMS Software?
(A) Oracle 11g
(B) MySQL Server 5.5
(C) DB2
(D) All of the above

246. OLTP stands for
(A) On Line Transaction Processing
(B) On Line Transmission Processing
(C) On Location Transaction Processing
(D) On Line Tables Processing

247. The term OLAP was coined by
(A) Edgar F. Codd (B) John W. William
(C) Stephan S. (D) Joseph Goguen

248. In SQL, we can changed the structure of a table through
(A) ALTER TABLE
(B) CHANGE TABLE
(C) TABLE ALTER
(D) STRUCT TABLE

249. Database search from unknown patterns and information is called
(A) Data warehousing
(B) Data mining
(C) Data clustering
(D) Data summarizing

250. Which of the following is a standard language for Database Management System?
(A) Structured Query Language
(B) Structured Access Language
(C) Structured Updating Language
(D) Structured Storage Language

251. Which of the following is not an example of Database Model?
(A) Relational Model
(B) Hierarchical Model
(C) Network Model
(D) Physical Model

252. Which of the following is a Data Manipulation Language (DML) statement?

(A) CREATE (B) ALTER
(C) UPDATE (D) DROP

253. In Entity-Relationship (E-R) diagram, which of the following statements is false?

(A) Entity is represented by rectangular box
(B) Attribute is represented by eclipse
(C) Primary Key is identified by diamond box
(D) Entity name is written in uppercase

254. GIF stands for

(A) Graphics Interchange Format
(B) Graphics Internal Format
(C) Gigabytes Interchange Format
(D) Graphics Interchange File

255. Which of the following commands instructs the Linux that a file system is ready to use?

(A) cp (B) ls
(C) mount (D) grep

256. Which of the following is a universal gate?

(A) NAND (B) OR
(C) AND (D) XOR

257. In DBMS, DDL stands for

(A) Data Definition Language
(B) Data Direction Language
(C) Data Dimension Language
(D) Data Division Language

258. A/an........is an elementary building block of a digital circuit.

(A) Modem (B) Compiler
(C) Logic Gate (D) Multiplexer

259. If A = 0 and B = 1, what is output of XOR gate?

(A) 1 (B) 0
(C) NULL (D) Any of the above

260. Which of the following is/are example of an 'Entity'?

(A) Object (B) Person
(C) Place (D) All of the above

261. Cache memory is built-in between

(A) CPU and CD-ROM
(B) CPU and Hard Disk
(C) CPU and Main Memory
(D) CPU and Magnetic tape

262. RISC stands for

(A) Recall Instruction Set Computer
(B) Reduced Instruction Set Computer
(C) Replace Instruction Set Computer
(D) Removed Instruction Set Computer

263. Which of the following parts of computer performs the data processing functions?

(A) Control Unit (CU)
(B) Arithmetic and Logic Unit (ALU)
(C) Memory Unit (MU)
(D) Compiler

264. A/an.........requires the supporting refresh circuitry.

(A) Static RAM (B) Dynamic RAM
(C) EPROM (D) EEPROM

265. ....provide internal storage within the CPU.

(A) Cache (B) Registers
(C) Interpreter (D) Assembler

266. A hyperlink to a saved websites address is called.

(A) Bookmark (B) Tag
(C) Blog (D) Digital Footprint

267. RAID stands for

(A) Redundant Array of Independent Disks
(B) Replaced Array of Independent Disks
(C) Rebuilt Array of Interdependent Disks
(D) Random Array of Independent Disks

268. Which of the following was first 32-bit machine of Intel?

(A) 8080 (B) 8086
(C) 80386 (D) 80486

269. The digital assets in cyberspace is called
(A) Cloud Computing
(B) Digital Footprint
(C) Digital Property
(D) Virtual Property

270. Which of the following is the lowest layer of OSI model?
(A) Application Layer
(B) Session Layer
(C) Physical Layer
(D) Data Link Layer

271. The disconnection of online presence and activities in cyberspace in a long time is called
(A) OFF Line (B) Digital Death
(C) Digital Archive (D) Digital Afterlife

272. Match the following:

	LIST-I		LIST-II
(1)	First Normal Form (1NF)	(i)	Isolation of independent multiple relationships
(2)	Second Normal Form (2NF)	(ii)	Eliminate Columns (fields) not dependent on the key field
(3)	Third Normal Form (3NF)	(iii)	Elimination of redundant data
(4)	Fourth Normal Form (4NF)	(iv)	Elimination of repeating groups

Codes:

	(1)	(2)	(3)	(4)
(A)	(iv)	(iii)	(ii)	(i)
(B)	(i)	(ii)	(iii)	(iv)
(C)	(ii)	(i)	(iv)	(iii)
(D)	(iii)	(ii)	(i)	(iv)

273. In open source world, LAMP is a/an
(A) A kind of Operating System (OS)
(B) Hyperlink's tags
(C) Linux, Apache, Mysql and PHP/Perl
(D) Set of communication protocols

274. Storing and accessing the data and programs over the Internet instead of computer storage device is called
(A) Cloud Computing
(B) Digital Computing
(C) Online Computing
(D) Universal Computing

275. Assertion (A): Data Dictionary is a system database that contains database descriptions such as name of the tables, fields name and their data type within the database.

Reason (R): One of the most important parts of any DBMS/RDBMS is the data dictionary.
(A) Both (A) and (R) are true
(B) Both (A) and (R) are false
(C) (A) is true, but (R) is false
(D) (A) is false, but (R) is true

276. Assertion (A): In Database Management System, normalization is analysis, not database designing.

Reason (R): In normalization, data model is optimized for applications, not for ad hoc querying.
(A) Both (A) and (R) are false
(B) Both (A) and (R) are true
(C) (A) is false, but (R) is true
(D) (A) is true, but (R) is false

277. Assertion (A): In Database Management System, NULL is not an absolute value, but it uses absent of absolute value.

Reason (R): In Numerical field (Column), we can insert zero (0) in place of NULL for absent of any value.
(A) Both (A) and (R) are true
(B) Both (A) and (R) are false
(C) (A) is true, but (R) is false
(D) (A) is false, but (R) is true

278. Assertion (A): Linux systems have a single directory structure like tree.

Reason (R): All accessible storage must have an associated location in this single directory tree.

(A) Both (A) and (R) are true
(B) Both (A) and (R) are false
(C) (A) is false, but (R) is true
(D) (A) is true, but (R) is false

279. Assertion (A): Computer memory is organized into a hierarchy and Register is the highest level among these.

Reason (R): In memory hierarchy, the cost/bit is decreased but increased the data capacity.

(A) Both (A) and (R) are true
(B) Both (A) and (R) are false
(C) (A) is true, but (R) is false
(D) (A) is false, but (R) is true

Answers Keys

1. (B)	2. (A)	3. (C)	4. (D)	97. (B)	98. (D)	99. (C)	100. (A)
5. (A)	6. (D)	7. (C)	8. (C)	101. (A)	102. (D)	103. (A)	104. (A)
9. (C)	10. (C)	11. (D)	12. (D)	105. (B)	106. (C)	107. (A)	108. (A)
13. (C)	14. (A)	15. (B)	16. (B)	109. (C)	110. (C)	111. (A)	112. (A)
17. (A)	18. (D)	19. (D)	20. (B)	113. (B)	114. (D)	115. (A)	116. (B)
21. (B)	22. (C)	23. (C)	24. (D)	117. (A)	118. (D)	119. (B)	120. (C)
25. (D)	26. (A)	27. (B)	28. (D)	121. (A)	122. (C)	123. (C)	124. (D)
29. (B)	30. (C)	31. (A)	32. (B)	125. (D)	126. (A)	127. (A)	128. (A)
33. (D)	34. (C)	35. (D)	36. (A)	129. (C)	130. (D)	131. (A)	132. (B)
37. (B)	38. (D)	39. (D)	40. (C)	133. (D)	134. (D)	135. (D)	136. (D)
41. (C)	42. (C)	43. (D)	44. (A)	137. (B)	138. (B)	139. (B)	140. (A)
45. (C)	46. (B)	47. (D)	48. (D)	141. (C)	142. (B)	143. (A)	144. (B)
49. (C)	50. (D)	51. (B)	52. (D)	145. (B)	146. (A)	147. (D)	148. (C)
53. (D)	54. (A)	55. (D)	56. (A)	149. (A)	150. (A)	151. (D)	152. (B)
57. (B)	58. (D)	59. (B)	60. (A)	153. (A)	154. (D)	155. (C)	156. (C)
61. (D)	62. (A)	63. (C)	64. (C)	157. (A)	158. (D)	159. (A)	160. (A)
65. (D)	66. (D)	67. (A)	68. (D)	161. (A)	162. (B)	163. (A)	164. (D)
69. (B)	70. (C)	71. (A)	72. (A)	165. (D)	166. (B)	167. (C)	168. (D)
73. (B)	74. (D)	75. (D)	76. (A)	169. (A)	170. (D)	171. (D)	172. (B)
77. (C)	78. (A)	79. (C)	80. (A)	173. (A)	174. (A)	175. (B)	176. (A)
81. (B)	82. (D)	83. (C)	84. (D)	177. (C)	178. (B)	179. (D)	180. (A)
85. (B)	86. (B)	87. (D)	88. (A)	181. (B)	182. (A)	183. (D)	184. (A)
89. (D)	90. (C)	91. (B)	92. (C)	185. (A)	186. (A)	187. (A)	188. (C)
93. (B)	94. (D)	95. (D)	96. (A)	189. (D)	190. (B)	191. (D)	192. (D)

193. (D)	194. (A)	195. (B)	196. (C)	237. (C)	238. (D)	239. (A)	240. (C)
197. (D)	198. (B)	199. (A)	200. (A)	241. (A)	242. (B)	243. (D)	244. (B)
201. (A)	202. (D)	203. (B)	204. (A)	245. (D)	246. (A)	247. (A)	248. (A)
205. (C)	206. (A)	207. (A)	208. (A)	249. (B)	250. (A)	251. (D)	252. (C)
209. (C)	210. (A)	211. (D)	212. (A)	253. (C)	254. (A)	255. (C)	256. (A)
213. (B)	214. (A)	215. (C)	216. (C)	257. (A)	258. (C)	259. (A)	260. (D)
217. (A)	218. (A)	219. (B)	220. (C)	261. (C)	262. (B)	263. (B)	264. (B)
221. (C)	222. (D)	223. (D)	224. (D)	265. (B)	266. (A)	267. (A)	268. (C)
225. (A)	226. (D)	227. (A)	228. (D)	269. (C)	270. (C)	271. (B)	272. (A)
229. (A)	230. (A)	231. (A)	232. (B)	273. (C)	274. (A)	275. (A)	276. (B)
233. (D)	234. (A)	235. (D)	236. (D)	277. (C)	278. (A)	279. (A)	

CHAPTER

11 Miscellaneous Questions

QUESTIONS

1. Library of Congress was founded in
(A) 1800 (B) 1821
(C) 1825 (D) 1827

2. Library Research Round Table (LRRT) was founded in
(A) 1965 (B) 1968
(C) 1975 (D) 1980

3. The father of Information Science
(A) Paul Otlet (B) J.H. Shera
(C) S.C. Bradford (D) H.P. Luhn

4. DCMI stands for
(A) Dublin Core Metadata Initiative
(B) Dublin Core Metadata International
(C) Dublin Code Metadata Interchanged
(D) Dublin Core Metadata Information

5. In CCC, the Subject Analytical Entry is/are known as
(A) Cross Reference Entry
(B) Book Index Entry
(C) Cross Reference Index Entry
(D) All of the above

6. The Sears List of Subject Headings (SLSH) was first designed in 1923 by
(A) Minnie E. Sears (B) Aaren S. Sears
(C) Alena T. Sears (D) Elvina E. Sears

7. Who says "Search strategy is the mirror in the dark"
(A) S.R. Ranganathan (B) J.H. Shera
(C) William A. Katz (D) J.D. Brown

8. ZBB stands for
(A) Zero Based Budgeting
(B) Zero Balance Budgeting
(C) Zero Buying Budgeting
(D) Zero Budget Balancing

9. George Boole was a/an
(A) Mathematician (B) Logician
(C) Physicist (D) Statistician

10. How many tables in *DDC* 23rd edition?
(A) 4 (B) 5
(C) 6 (D) 7

11. Who invented Zato Coding?
(A) Calvin N. Mooers
(B) John W. Backus
(C) Wim Ebbinkhuijsen
(D) David Epstein

12. Which of the following statements is true for Cutter's Expansive Classification Numbers?
(A) The first part of the Call Number is the Class Mark
(B) The second part of the Call Number is known as the Author Mark/Book Mark
(C) The Book Mark may start with a number
(D) All of the above

13. Match the following:

	LIST-I	LIST-II
(1)	Philosophy of Library Classification	(i) 1963
(2)	Documentation and its Facets	(ii) 1931
(3)	Library Book Selection	(iii) 1973
(4)	Five Laws of Library Science	(iv) 1966

Codes:

	(1)	(2)	(3)	(4)
(A)	(iii)	(i)	(iv)	(ii)
(B)	(i)	(iii)	(iv)	(ii)
(C)	(iv)	(i)	(ii)	(iii)
(D)	(iv)	(ii)	(i)	(iii)

14. The book titled *Documentation and its Facets* was written by
(A) H.P. Luhn (B) J.D. Brown
(C) J.H. Shera (D) S.R. Ranganathan

15. The term 'Biomedical Sciences' was coined in 1955 for study of
(A) Medicine (B) Physical Sciences
(C) Biology (D) All of the above

16. A regularly updated website or web pages, generally run by an individual or similar group for expressing the thoughts in Internet world is called
(A) Chatting (B) Blogging
(C) Expressing (D) Communicating

17. The term 'Web 2.0' was popularized by
(A) Tim O'Reilly (B) Dale Dougherty
(C) John William (D) Both (A) and (B)

18. The term 'Web 2.0' was officially coined in 2004 by
(A) Dale Dougherty
(B) Leonard Kleinrock
(C) J.C.R. Licklider
(D) Robert Taylor

19. The term 'Fair Used' is most relevant to
(A) Systematic arrangement of books
(B) Books keep on the same location
(C) Related to the Copyright
(D) Not any underline or sketching

20. Which of the following books written by W.C.B. Sayers?
(A) *Canons of Classification*
(B) *Introduction to Library Classification*
(C) *Manual of Library Classification*
(D) All of the above

21. The book titled *Thesaurus of English Words and Phrases* was written by
(A) Peter Mark Roget
(B) Aldous Roget
(C) Alexander M. Smith
(D) D.H. Lawrence

22. Which of the following was the first book written by W.C.B. Sayers?
(A) *Manual of Library Classification*
(B) *Introduction to Library Classification*
(C) *Canons of Classification*
(D) *Grammar of Classification*

23. Who defined "documentation is the complex of process, involved in pin-pointed, exhaustive and expeditious service of nascent micro thought to the specialist"?
(A) S.R. Ranganathan
(B) J.H. Shera
(C) Paul Outlet
(D) H.P. Luhn

24. Which of the following was the ancient Indian writing material?
(A) Clay Tablet (B) Papyrus
(C) Palm leaf (D) Parchment

25. Which of the following layers does not exist among seven layers of OSI Model?

(A) Logical Layer (B) Data Link Layer
(C) Session Layer (D) Network Layer

26. ....is small extension but great intention.
(A) Macro Subject
(B) Micro Subject
(C) Classical Subject
(D) Synthesized Subject

27. Which of the following is the example of Thesaurus?
(A) MESH (B) TEST
(C) INSPEC (D) All of the above

28. The current edition of CCC is.......
(A) 3rd (B) 4th
(C) 5th (D) 6th

29. There are.......volumes in 20th edition of *DDC*?
(A) 3 (B) 4
(C) 5 (D) 6

30. Who invented the 'Retroactive Ordinal Notation'?
(A) E.J. Coats (B) J.S. Mills
(C) H.E. Bliss (D) S.R. Ranganathan

31. Who described "documentation as memory of mankind"?
(A) Rende Mahen (B) S.R. Ranganathan
(C) K.O. Murra (D) R.R. Shaw

32. The time period of patent in India is ....years from the date of filing of patent application.
(A) 15 (B) 18
(C) 20 (D) 23

33. A/an...........is a term describing a publishing house in which authors pay to have their book published.
(A) Unit press
(B) Vanity press
(C) Commercial press
(D) Payee press

34. What is the time period of protection of copyright granted in India?
(A) 45 years (B) 55 years
(C) 60 years (D) 65 years

35. Who gave the 'Verbal Communication Model'?
(A) Shannon and Weaver
(B) Harold Lasswell
(C) Richard Braddock
(D) David Berlo

36. CALIBNET was established in 1986 by
(A) NISSAT (B) NICNET
(C) NIC (D) ERNET

37. Which of the following is the synonym term for Thesaurus?
(A) Vocabulary Control
(B) Grammar Control
(C) Author List Control
(D) Document Control

38. The term 'Portico' is related to
(A) Communication protocol
(B) Preservation of digital publications
(C) An open source initiative
(D) Antivirus software

39. An unusually small size of book is technically called
(A) Bibelot (B) Monograph
(C) Pamphlet (D) Monogram

40. 'Influence of Religion on Education' is the example of
(A) Loose Assemblage Kind 1
(B) Loose Assemblage Kind 2
(C) Fusion
(D) Denudation

41. Who is the founded of Free Software Foundation (FSF)?

(A) Richard M. Stallman
(B) Bill Gates
(C) Paul Allen
(D) Warren Buffett

42. Delhi Public Library was established in
(A) 1948 (B) 1951
(C) 1953 (D) 1956

43. ANOVA (Analysis of Variance) was developed by
(A) R.A. Fisher (B) G.W. Snedecor
(C) W.H. Kruskal (D) Arthur Cayley

44. In which year Verbal Communication Model (Lasswell's Communication Model) was developed?
(A) 1946 (B) 1948
(C) 1951 (D) 1954

45. The article titled "The Structure and Function of Communication in Society" was written by
(A) Harold Lasswell
(B) George Gerbner
(C) Shannon and Weaver
(D) Denis McQuail

46. Match the following:

LIST-I	LIST-II
(1) NewGenLib	(i) 2002
(2) Koha	(ii) 2009
(3) DSpace	(iii) 2005
(4) SOUL 2.0	(iv) 2000

Codes:

	(1)	(2)	(3)	(4)
(A)	(iii)	(iv)	(i)	(ii)
(B)	(ii)	(i)	(iv)	(iii)
(C)	(iv)	(ii)	(i)	(iii)
(D)	(iii)	(ii)	(iv)	(i)

47. In which year AICTE was set-up?
(A) 1945 (B) 1948
(C) 1952 (D) 1956

48. Which of the following was the founder of Cultivation Theory?
(A) George Gerbner
(B) Claude Elwood Shannon
(C) Warren Weaver
(D) Harold Lasswell

49. The term 'Semantics' is coined by
(A) Michel Breal (B) C.E. Shannon
(C) D.K. Berlo (D) V. Schramm

50. The term Intellectual Capital (IC) is introduced by
(A) Tom Stewart Fortune
(B) Patrick H. Sullivan
(C) John Kenneth Galbraith
(D) C.T. Taylor

51. After which of the following recommendations, Central Medical Library in India was founded?
(A) Bhore Committee
(B) G.V. K. Rao Committee
(C) Kelkar Committee
(D) Yashpal Committee

52. Asiatic Society Library is suited at
(A) Mumbai (B) Chennai
(C) Kolkata (D) Ahmedabad

53. Which of the following is the Content Management System (CMS) tool?
(A) Joomla (B) WordPress
(C) Drupal (D) All of the above

54. The essay "As We May Think" was written by......in 1945.
(A) Vannevar Bush (B) Philip Kitcher
(C) L. Barsalou (D) James M. Nyce

55. The 'Jubilee Project' is associated with
(A) Evaluation of Electronic Information Services
(B) Standardization of Catalogue Code

(C) MARC Standardization
(D) Library Consortia

56. Which of the following is a classification scheme for medicine?
(A) NLM Classification System
(B) CLC Classification System
(C) KDC Classification System
(D) NDC Classification System

57. In Spiral of Scientific Method, the starting point is
(A) Zenith (B) Ascendant
(C) Nadir (D) Descendant

58. "The foundation of a library is a book, the foundation of librarianship is classification"—who says this?
(A) S.R. Ranganathan
(B) W.C.B. Sayers
(C) H.E. Bliss
(D) E.C. Richardson

59. Which of the following is a 'Noble Prize' winner and also great contributor in the field of Documentation?
(A) Henri La Fontaine
(B) Paul Otlet
(C) Luther H. Evans
(D) John Cotton Dana

60. In database, the unique value stored field is called
(A) Super Key (B) Compound Key
(C) Alternate Key (D) Primary Key

61. Match the following:

LIST-I	LIST-II
(1) British Museum Code	(i) 1952
(2) Prussion Instruction	(ii) 1841
(3) Vatican Code	(iii) 1899
(4) Nippon Cataloguing Rules	(iv) 1931

Codes:

	(1)	(2)	(3)	(4)
(A)	(ii)	(iii)	(iv)	(i)
(B)	(i)	(iii)	(iv)	(ii)
(C)	(iii)	(ii)	(iv)	(i)
(D)	(iv)	(i)	(ii)	(iii)

62. The modern term for the 'Book Selection' is
(A) Collection Management
(B) Library Collection
(C) Library Acquisition
(D) All of the above

63. 'Bibliotheque Nationale' is the National Library of
(A) Germany (B) Italy
(C) France (D) Netherlands

64. In book publishing, the term 'Exhausted edition' means
(A) Out of print
(B) Under process of printing
(C) Under process of compiling
(D) Just published

65. A field of study related to the area of 'Human-Computer Interaction' is called
(A) Natural Language Processing (NLP)
(B) Computer Language Processing (CLP)
(C) Compiler Language Developing (CLD)
(D) Natural Computer Processing (NCP)

66. C.A. Cutter graduated from Harvard College in
(A) 1853 (B) 1855
(C) 1857 (D) 1860

67. Which of the following is associated with the term 'Thesaurus' in the information retrieval context?
(A) Helen Brownson (B) S.R. Ranganathan
(C) H.P. Luhn (D) J.H. Shera

68. Who coined the term 'The Internet of Things'?

(A) Kevin Ashton (B) Vinton Cerf
(C) James Gleick (D) Richard Leghorn

69. Who developed the Automatic Indexing System?
(A) Herbert Ohlman
(B) J.H. Shera
(C) S.R. Ranganathan
(D) H.P. Luhn

70. Which of the following is associated with Semantic Web Collaboration Spaces?
(A) Wikis
(B) Social networks
(C) Social forums
(D) All of the above

71. The first edition of the book *Library Administration* was published in
(A) 1931 (B) 1933
(C) 1935 (D) 1945

72. Who coined the term 'Internet'?
(A) Vinton Gray Cerf
(B) Tim Berners-Lee
(C) Mark Prensky
(D) Richard Leghorn

73. In Intellectual Property Rights, the term 'Intellectual Property' means
(A) Sales is not possible
(B) Sales is possible
(C) Copy is not possible
(D) Both (A) and (C)

74. In book printing, a page without a folio number but including in pagination technically is called
(A) Unused page (B) Blank page
(C) Missing page (D) Uncounted page

75. Universal Bibliographical Control (UBC) is associated with
(A) CILIP (B) ALA
(C) IFLA (D) UNESCO

76. Which of the following year UNESCO was celebrated as International Book Year?
(A) 1965 (B) 1968
(C) 1972 (D) 1975

77. In 1886, the Bern Convention is related to
(A) Cataloguing (B) Classification
(C) Patent (D) Copyright

78. The term 'Invisible Web' is refers to
(A) Web content that we have not understand the language
(B) Web pages not open
(C) Web pages that blocked by government
(D) Web pages that hidden from the search engines

79. In India, which organization has been applied Library and Information Policy at national level?
(A) NISCAIR, New Delhi
(B) ILA, New Delhi
(C) RRRLF, Kolkata
(D) National Library, Kolkata

80. Which of the following is true?
(A) Data->Knowledge->Information->Wisdom
(B) Information->Data->Knowledge->Wisdom
(C) Data->Information->Knowledge->Wisdom
(D) Data->Wisdom->Information->Knowledge

81. Among five laws, which law is related to the extension service of library?
(A) Books are for use
(B) Every reader his/her book
(C) Every book its reader
(D) Save the time of reader

82. Library cess is specially for
(A) Public library
(B) Academic library
(C) Research library
(D) All type of libraries

83. IFLA founded in 1927 at

(A) Edinburgh (B) New York
(C) Manchester (D) Bristol

84. If search engine not able to locate the web pages or hidden from the search is called
(A) Blocked web (B) Blacked web
(C) Invisible web (D) Redirect the web

85. Who says "Librarianship is not a profession"?
(A) J.D. Brown
(B) Melvil Dewey
(C) Judith McPheron
(D) C.A. Cutter

86. The frequency of publication of J.D. Brown's journal *The Library World* was
(A) Quarterly (B) Monthly
(C) Bi-monthly (D) Bi-yearly

87. *Guinness Book of World Record* is published from
(A) Chicago (B) Washington
(C) London (D) Paris

88. In which year 'Browne Charging System' was started?
(A) 1892 (B) 1895
(C) 1899 (D) 1901

89. The term 'PPBS' is related to
(A) Indexing (B) Abstracting
(C) Budgeting (D) Reprography

90. The concept "the best reading for the largest number, at the least cost" is given by
(A) Melvil Dewey (B) S.R. Ranganathan
(C) C.A. Cutter (D) J.D. Brown

91. The concept "Right book to the right reader at the right time" is given by
(A) S.R. Ranganathan
(B) C.A. Cutter
(C) Mevil Dewey
(D) F.K.W. Drury

92. Which of the following works is related to the Acquisition Section?
(A) Accessioning
(B) Duplicate Checking
(C) Receiving request for new books
(D) All of the above

93. The first edition of book titled *Library Book Selection* of S.R. Ranganathan was published in
(A) 1949 (B) 1951
(C) 1955 (D) 1964

94. In research, the term 'hypothesis' is related to
(A) Reality (B) Fact
(C) Speculation (D) Truth

95. *Cutter's Rules for a Dictionary Catalogue* was published in
(A) 1873 (B) 1876
(C) 1880 (D) 1891

96. In which year IFLA was launched 'Advancement of Librarianship Programme (ALP)'?
(A) 1982 (B) 1984
(C) 1987 (D) 2000

97. In which year International Council for Science (ICSU) was started?
(A) 1931 (B) 1934
(C) 1938 (D) 1940

98. In which year ICSU Abstracting Board (ICSU-AB) was established?
(A) 1950 (B) 1952
(C) 1954 (D) 1958

99. Which of the following is not a Boolean search operator?
(A) AND (B) OR
(C) NOT (D) FOR

100. S.R. Ranganathan mainly derived the principles of Book Selection from the
(A) Canons of Classification
(B) Canons of Cataloguing

(C) Principle of Helpful sequence
(D) Five Laws of Library Science

101. Which of the following is the Business Information Database?
(A) ABI/INFORM (B) ASTINFO
(C) INIS (D) BIOSIS

102. The 'Inkblot' test is developed by
(A) Hermann Rorschach
(B) Richard J. Herrnstein
(C) Arthur R. Jensen
(D) Alexander R. Luria

103. Which of the following was the first chairman of IASLIC?
(A) J. Saha (B) A.K. Mukherjee
(C) S.L. Hora (D) S.R. Ranganathan

104. In Spiral Method, the highest level is
(A) Nadir (B) Zenith
(C) Ascendant (D) Descendant

105. Which of the following is famous in Citation Indexing?
(A) Eugene Garfield
(B) Julian J. Baggini
(C) James M. Baldwin
(D) William A. Katz

106. Which of the following is a CSIR-NISCAIR Online Periodicals Repository?
(A) NOPR
(B) DOPR
(C) TOPR
(D) NISCAIRONLINE

107. Lotka's Law especially related to
(A) Publisher's productivity
(B) Author's productivity
(C) Reader's productivity
(D) All of the above

108. The soul of a document is the........of document.
(A) Subject content (B) Title
(C) Physical format (D) Publishers

109. The term 'Kinesics' is related to
(A) Body motion communication
(B) Indexing system
(C) RDA
(D) Abstracting system

110. ....coined the term 'Statistical Bibliography'.
(A) E. Wyndham Hulme
(B) S.R. Ranganathan
(C) C.A. Cutter
(D) C.F. Gosnell

111. BOAI is related to
(A) Open access to the research literature
(B) Communication protocol
(C) Metadata standards
(D) Computer hardware

112. The term 'Kinesics' was first used in 1952 by
(A) Ray Birdwhistell (B) George Bateson
(C) James Hunt (D) Paul Broca

113. Person who classify the books according to the library classification scheme is called
(A) Classifier (B) Cataloguer
(C) Classificationist (D) Indexer

114. The term 'Bibliometrics' was first coined by
(A) Alan Pritchard
(B) C.A. Cutter
(C) S.R. Ranganathan
(D) Benoit Mandelbrot

115. In which type of library, the informal self-education is possible?
(A) Public library
(B) Academic library
(C) Special library
(D) All of the above

116. Who coined the term 'Ready Reference Service'?
(A) S.R. Ranganathan
(B) T.J. Allen
(C) Alan Pritchard
(D) Benoit Mandelbrot

117. Person who build the classification schemes according to the principles and canons is called
(A) Classifier (B) Indexer
(C) Classificationist (D) Librarian

118. 'Advises librarians to know the habits, education and occupations of their people' is given by
(A) W.C.B. Sayers
(B) S.R. Ranganathan
(C) J.D. Brown
(D) C.A. Cutter

119. Library Legislation is related to which type of library?
(A) Academic library
(B) Research library
(C) Public library
(D) All types of library

120. Who coined the term 'Technological Gatekeeper'?
(A) S.R. Ranganathan
(B) T.J. Allen
(C) Alan Prichard
(D) Margaret Hutchins

121. Which of the following is freeware DBMS?
(A) PostgreSQL (B) MySQL
(C) Firebird (D) All of the above

122. Who coined the term 'Reference Interview'?
(A) Margaret Hutchins
(B) T.J. Allen
(C) Alan Prichard
(D) W.C.B. Sayers

123. Who gave technical assistance for the foundation of INSDOC?
(A) UGC (B) IASLIC
(C) UNESCO (D) ISI, Kolkata

124. "Some books are to be tasted, others to be swallowed, and some few to be chewed and digest"—who says this?
(A) Francis Bacon
(B) C.A. Cutter
(C) Will Durant
(D) Benjamin Franklin

125. Match the following:

	LIST-I	LIST-II
(1)	Classification and International Documentation	(i) 1933
(2)	Classification and Communication	(ii) 1931
(3)	Five Laws of Library Science	(iii) 1951
(4)	Colon Classification	(iv) 1948

Codes:

	(1)	(2)	(3)	(4)
(A)	(iv)	(i)	(ii)	(iii)
(B)	(iv)	(iii)	(ii)	(i)
(C)	(iii)	(iv)	(ii)	(i)
(D)	(iii)	(ii)	(iv)	(i)

126. RFID stands for
(A) Radio Frequency Identification Device
(B) Radar Frequency Identification Device
(C) Radio Frequency Information Device
(D) Radio Frequency Interval Device

127. The RFID technique can be used....the data for physical object.
(A) to identifying (B) to tracking
(C) to processing (D) All of the above

128. The term 'Librametry' is coined by
(A) S.R. Ranganathan
(B) W.C.B. Sayers
(C) C.A. Cutter
(D) Alan Pritchard

129. Which of the following is not the valid keyword for citation references?
(A) Loc. cit (B) Op. cit.
(C) Ibid. (D) Ref.

130. A wireless technology standard for data exchange over short distance is
(A) Bluetooth (B) Wi-fi
(C) Hypermedia (D) Multimedia

131. Which of the following is the elemental kernel in library science?
(A) Title of the document
(B) Author of the document
(C) Subject of the document
(D) Book Number of the document

132. DOAB stands for
(A) Directory of Open Access Books
(B) Digitalized of Open Access Books
(C) Delivery of Open Access Books
(D) Documentation of Open Access Books

133. Disadvantage of Bluetooth is/are
(A) Low speed
(B) Limited range
(C) Cable replacement
(D) Both (A) and (B)

134. *Journal of Intellectual Property Rights* (*JIPR*) is published by
(A) CSIR-NISCAIR, India
(B) ALA, USA
(C) CILIP, UK
(D) ALIA, Australia

135. In 1998, the final report of FRBR was compiled by
(A) K.G. Saur (B) R.L. Jones
(C) L.C. Nelson (D) S.G. Harper

136. The frequency of publication of *JIPR* is
(A) Annual (B) Bi-monthly
(C) Half-yearly (D) Monthly

137. WIF stands for
(A) Web Impact Factor
(B) World Impact Factor
(C) WWW Impact Factor
(D) Windows Impact Factor

138. WIF is developed by
(A) Ingwersen Peter (B) John Peter
(C) C.S. William (D) P.S. Alan

139. Which of the following is the metadata standard?
(A) EXIF (B) DACS
(C) CDWA (D) All of the above

140. Which of the following methods is used for syntax errors checking in computer programs?
(A) Compiler (B) Interpreter
(C) Flowchart (D) Both (A) and (B)

141. Errors in computer programs/software is called
(A) Bug (B) Virus
(C) Tag (D) Attributes

142. Which of the following is the character encoding method?
(A) ASCII (B) UTF-8
(C) GB2312 (D) All of the above

143. Which of the following is the form of extension service?
(A) Book fair (B) Library orientation
(C) e-catalogue (D) All of the above

144. Which of the following is MOOC (Massive Open Online Course): a web-based platform for education?
(A) WizIQ (B) NPTEL
(C) Coursera (D) All of the above

145. Who founded the Indian Statistical Institute (ISI)?
(A) P.C. Mahalanobis
(B) C.V. Raman
(C) G.N. Ramachandran
(D) J.C. Bose

146. The term 'librametry' is coined by
(A) S.R. Ranganathan
(B) H.E. Bliss
(C) Melvi Dewey
(D) L.H. Evans

147. Which of the following is associated with a systematic use of users' education in library ?
(A) S.R. Ranganathan
(B) Melvil Dewey
(C) Patricia B. Knapp
(D) Peter F. Drucker

148. In which year S.R. Ranganathan coined the term 'librametry'?
(A) 1948 (B) 1951
(C) 1955 (D) 1958

149. An expert on bibliometrics is called
(A) Indexer
(B) Bibliometrician
(C) Librametrician
(D) Thesaurus Designer

150. Who coined the term 'Informetrics' for the first time?
(A) E.F. Codd (B) H.P. Luhn
(C) Otto Nacke (D) William A. Katz

151. Which of the following was the student of Melvil Dewey?
(A) W.A. Borden
(B) Ellen M. Richard
(C) Rubin J. Richard
(D) All of the above

152. A person who prepares the gist of the intellectual content of a book, article, etc. is called
(A) Bibliographer (B) Indexer
(C) Abstractor (D) Cataloguer

153. Which of the following is the academic search engine?
(A) Google Scholar
(B) Microsoft Office
(C) Open Office Org
(D) All of the above

154. What is rule for heading of three or more personal authors in CCC?
(A) Title of the document
(B) First author with 'and others' keyword
(C) All authors with 'and'
(D) First and second author and then 'and others' keyword

155. In which year Royal Asiatic Society of Bengal was established?
(A) 1784 (B) 1786
(C) 1788 (D) 1889

156. In first time in India which university started the Bachelor Course in Library Science?
(A) Banaras Hindu University
(B) Aligarh Muslim University
(C) Mumbai University
(D) Calcutta University

157. Match the following:

	LIST-I	LIST-II
(1)	Geological Survey of India	(i) 1916
(2)	Botanical Survey of India	(ii) 1857
(3)	Zoological Survey of India	(iii) 1851
(4)	Indian Metrological Department	(iv) 1889

Codes:

	(1)	(2)	(3)	(4)
(A)	(ii)	(iii)	(iv)	(i)
(B)	(iii)	(iv)	(i)	(ii)
(C)	(iv)	(iii)	(ii)	(i)
(D)	(i)	(iv)	(iii)	(ii)

158. Match the following:

LIST-I	LIST-II
(1) Indian Mathematical Society	(i) 1921
(2) Indian Botanical Society	(ii) 1931
(3) Indian Chemical Society	(iii) 1924
(4) Indian Statistical Institute, Kolkata	(iv) 1907

Codes:

	(1)	(2)	(3)	(4)
(A)	(iv)	(i)	(iii)	(ii)
(B)	(i)	(iv)	(ii)	(iii)
(C)	(ii)	(iv)	(iii)	(i)
(D)	(iii)	(i)	(iv)	(ii)

159. Saha Institute of Nuclear Physics is located at

(A) Kolkata (B) Chennai
(C) Bengaluru (D) Mumbai

160. In which year Society for Information Science (SIS), New Delhi was formed?

(A) 1975 (B) 1978
(C) 1981 (D) 1982

161. A common range of working area of Bluetooth is

(A) Up to 100 m (B) Up to 250 m
(C) Up to 300 m (D) Up to 400 m

162. Which of the following is the Operating System for Smart Phones?

(A) Android (B) BlackBerry
(C) iOS (D) All of the above

163. In which year Imperial Council of Agriculture Research was established?

(A) 1929 (B) 1931
(C) 1934 (D) 1944

164. In which year Indian Council of Medical Research was established?

(A) 1909 (B) 1911
(C) 1915 (D) 1920

165. In which year Indian Industrial Research Bureau was established?

(A) 1932 (B) 1934
(C) 1936 (D) 1939

166. CDMA stands for

(A) Code Division Multiple Access
(B) Code Division Multimedia Access
(C) Complex Data Multimedia Access
(D) Common Division Multiple Access

167. In which year H.W. Wilson Company was established?

(A) 1920 (B) 1925
(C) 1928 (D) 1935

168. Match the following:

LIST-I	LIST-II
(1) Classified Catalogue Code	(i) 1938
(2) Prolegomena to Library Classification	(ii) 1945
(3) Theory of Library Catalogue	(iii) 1937
(4) Elements of Library Classification	(iv) 1934

Codes:

	(1)	(2)	(3)	(4)
(A)	(iv)	(iii)	(i)	(ii)
(B)	(i)	(iv)	(iii)	(ii)
(C)	(iv)	(i)	(iii)	(ii)
(D)	(ii)	(iii)	(iv)	(i)

169. The unique number given to an item when recording its addition to the library is called

(A) Accession Number
(B) Class Number
(C) Book Number
(D) Collection Number

170. The field of library classification that explores computer involvement in classification requiring intelligence, and the use of natural language is called

(A) Artificial Intelligence
(B) Natural Intelligence
(C) Knowledge Intelligence
(D) Language Intelligence

171. A mathematical/logical procedure for solving a problem especially in a computer program is called
(A) Algorithm (B) Programming
(C) Procedure (D) Function

172. The first test of newly developed software or hardware in a computer lab is called
(A) Alpha test (B) Beta test
(C) Gama test (D) X-test

173. Amazon.com is a/an
(A) Search engine (B) Consortia
(C) E-commerce (D) Subject Gateway

174. In which year American Indian Library Association was founded
(A) 1973 (B) 1975
(C) 1977 (D) 1979

175. The formal record of the proceedings of an academy or organization is generally process in
(A) Bibliography (B) Index
(C) Annals (D) Directory

176. In Western world, which of the following methods is broadly used for assigning Book Number in the documents?
(A) Publication Number
(B) Author Number
(C) Year Number
(D) Accession Number

177. The capacity of a communication channel to transmit a signal in terms of data amount is called
(A) Bandwidth (B) Datawidth
(C) Channel strength (D) Half Duplex

178. Bibliographic Classification also known as
(A) Bliss Classification
(B) Dewey Classification
(C) Mathematics Subject Classification
(D) Expansive Classification

179. The representation of data by 1 or 0 is called
(A) Octal (B) Decimal
(C) Hexadecimal (D) Binary

180. Which of the following is/are Cataloguing tool?
(A) AACR (B) LCSH
(C) CCC (D) All of the above

181. Chinese American Librarians Association was formed in
(A) 1976 (B) 1983
(C) 1987 (D) 1989

182. The term 'crawler' is associated with
(A) Web Technology
(B) Abstracting
(C) Book Classification
(D) Indexing

183. In which year Digital Millennium Copyright Act Legislation was passed?
(A) 1996 (B) 1998
(C) 2000 (D) 2002

184. DOI stands for
(A) Digital Object Identifier
(B) Digital Optical Identifier
(C) Digital Oriented Identifier
(D) Digital Object Integration

185. DNS stands for
(A) Domain Name System
(B) Dynamic Name System
(C) Develop Name System
(D) Database Name System

186. In Dublin Core Metadata, total numbers of metadata elements are?

(A) 12 (B) 14
(C) 15 (D) 16

187. Which of the following is not belonged to Dublin Core metadata element?
(A) Title (B) Publisher
(C) Identifier (D) Data size

188. HTTP stands for
(A) Hypertext Transfer Protocol
(B) Hyperlink Text Transfer Protocol
(C) Hypertext Transmission Protocol
(D) Hypertext Translation Protocol

189. The 6th International Congress on Medical Librarianship (1990) was held at
(A) New York (B) Tokyo
(C) Belgrade (D) New Delhi

190. International Congress on Medical Librarianship was established in
(A) 1953 (B) 1955
(C) 1959 (D) 1964

191. ISBN system was adopted internationally since
(A) 1969 (B) 1971
(C) 1975 (D) 1978

192. An annual award 'Kate Greenaway Medal' is given by
(A) IFLA (B) CILIP
(C) ALA (D) SLA

193. In reference work, the Latin abbreviation 'loc. cit' means
(A) In the place cited
(B) Year of publication
(C) Place of publication
(D) Lack of appropriate reference

194. Lycos is associated with
(A) Web portal
(B) Indexing system
(C) Abstracting system
(D) Language translator

195. Which of the following is related to 'Data about data'?
(A) Transdata (B) Machinedata
(C) Metadata (D) Compiledata

196. Which of the following is the citation reference manual?
(A) MLA style (B) APA style
(C) Chicago style (D) All of the above

197. In IT, Safari is a/an
(A) Web browser
(B) Protocol
(C) Programming language
(D) Operating System (OS)

198. The term 'spider' is associated with
(A) Web technology
(B) Indexing system
(C) Book compilation
(D) Cataloguing

199. Which type of information source will patent?
(A) Primary (B) Secondary
(C) Tertiary (D) All of the above

200. Who says "Reference service is the establishing of contact between reader and book by personal service?"
(A) S.R. Ranganathan
(B) C.A. Cutter
(C) J.D. Brown
(D) William A. Katz

201. Which of the following is the publishing place of *Encyclopedia Americana*?
(A) Chicago (B) New York
(C) Washington (D) Los Angeles

202. In MARC21, the tag number for Language is
(A) 520 (B) 546
(C) 556 (D) 561

203. The ISSN International Centre (ISSN IC) is located at

(A) Netherlands (B) Washington
(C) Paris (D) Athens

204. Translated documents fall under which category of information sources?
(A) Primary (B) Secondary
(C) Tertiary (D) All of the above

205. Unpublished books/documents called
(A) Grey literature (B) Green literature
(C) Yellow literature (D) Imprint literature

206. The first English scientific journal was
(A) *Philosophical Transactions*
(B) *Philosophical Theory*
(C) *Journal of Philosophy*
(D) *Human Anatomy*

207. In which year the British Museum (now British Library) was opened for public?
(A) 1755 (B) 1759
(C) 1765 (D) 1771

208. National Botanical Research Institute is located at
(A) New Delhi (B) Lucknow
(C) Kolkata (D) Hyderabad

209. GPS stands for
(A) Global Positioning System
(B) Global Parallel System
(C) General Positioning System
(D) Global Posting System

210. INB has been published by
(A) Central Reference Library, Kolkata
(B) IASLIC, Kolkata
(C) ILA, New Delhi
(D) AIU, New Delhi

211. Stock verification is the part of
(A) Library Administration
(B) Library Classification
(C) Library Cataloguing
(D) Bibliography Service

212. What is 'URKUND'?
(A) Medical database
(B) Indexing system
(C) Anti-plagiarism software
(D) Biotechnology database

213. Who says 'Librarian is a salesmanship'?
(A) J.H. Shera (B) H.P. Luhn
(C) J.D. Brown (D) S.R. Ranganathan

214. In which year S.R. Ranganathan formulated the Five Laws of Library Science?
(A) 1925 (B) 1928
(C) 1931 (D) 1933

215. In which year Research Libraries Group (RLG) merged with OCLC?
(A) 2002 (B) 2004
(C) 2006 (D) 2009

216. The headquarters of American Library Association (ALA) is suited at
(A) Chicago
(B) New York
(C) Washington, D.C.
(D) San Francisco

217. Which of the following was the first secretary of American Library Association (ALA)?
(A) Justin Winsor
(B) Melvil Dewey
(C) Charles Ammi Cutter
(D) John Cotton Dana

218. Which of the following was the first president of American Library Association (ALA)?
(A) Justin Winsor
(B) Melvil Dewey
(C) Henry Munson Utley
(D) William Isaac Fletcher

219. Which of the following is the oldest library association of the world?

(A) CILIP (B) ALA
(C) IFLA (D) SLA

220. According to the Indian School of Cataloguing (S.R. Ranganathan's thought), the cataloguing rules called
(A) Prolegomena (B) Canons
(C) Dictionary (D) All of the above

221. Indian Library Science Abstracts is published by
(A) NISCAIR, New Delhi
(B) IASLIC, Kolkata
(C) ILA, New Delhi
(D) ISI, Kolkata

222. 'National Manuscript Library of India' is suited at
(A) Kolkata (B) Bengaluru
(C) Mumbai (D) Tanjore

223. The IASLIC Bulletin was first published in
(A) 1954 (B) 1956
(C) 1959 (D) 1962

224. The book titled *Planning Academic and Research Library Building* was written by
(A) K.D. Metcalf (B) Alan Moore
(C) A.P. Herbert (D) C.H. Lewis

225. Research Library Group (RLG) was founded in
(A) 1972 (B) 1974
(C) 1976 (D) 1977

226. British Museum was founded in
(A) 1749 (B) 1951
(C) 1753 (D) 1755

227. Which of the following is the encrypted virtual currency?
(A) Bitcon (B) Mycon
(C) ComCoin (D) VirtCoin

228. Which of the following is the Oriental Library of India?
(A) Rampur Raza Library, Rampur
(B) Asiatic Society Libraries, Kolkata
(C) Salar Jung Museum and Library, Hyderabad
(D) All of the above

229. Match the following:

LIST-I	LIST-II
(1) Andhra Desa Library Association	(i) 1921
(2) Maharashtra Library Association	(ii) 1914
(3) Bengal Library Association	(iii) 1925
(4) Punjab Library Association	(iv) 1916

Codes:

	(1)	(2)	(3)	(4)
(A)	(iv)	(i)	(ii)	(iii)
(B)	(ii)	(i)	(iii)	(iv)
(C)	(iv)	(ii)	(iii)	(i)
(D)	(i)	(iii)	(ii)	(iv)

230. Which of the following was started the first training programme in Library Science in India?
(A) William Alanson Borden
(B) Asa Don Dickinson
(C) Lala Labhu Ram
(D) Khan Bahadur Asadullah

231. The Kothari Committee recommended .....of the total college budget for library development.
(A) 5% (B) 10%
(C) 20% (D) 35%

232. Who was the founder of DRTC?
(A) S.R. Ranganathan
(B) P.C. Mahalanobis
(C) J.B.S. Haldane
(D) S.L. Hora

233. In which year Canadian Library Association was formed?
(A) 1921 (B) 1946
(C) 1950 (D) 1955

234. The Consortium of University Research Libraries (CURL) is now as
(A) Research Libraries UK (RLUK)
(B) United Kingdom Research Libraries (UKRL)
(C) Research Libraries Consortium UK (RLCUK)
(D) United Kingdom Research Libraries Consortium (UKRLC)

235. In which year China Academic Library and Information System was started?
(A) 1995 (B) 1998
(C) 1999 (D) 2002

236. Which of the following terms is used for Smart Phone software?
(A) Tag (B) Blogs
(C) Apps (D) Share

237. In India, which of the following is the second Ph.D. in Library and Information Science?
(A) S.K. Sharma Pandey
(B) M.P. Satija
(C) Krishn Kumar
(D) K.B. Asadullah

238. In which year first Card Catalogue was appeared?
(A) 1743 (B) 1768
(C) 1775 (D) 1784

239. According to C.A. Cutter, which of the following is true?
(A) Catalogue is a list of books which is arranged on some definite plan
(B) Catalogue is distinguish from a bibliography
(C) Bibliography is only a list of books in a library
(D) All of the above

240. MPEG-4: a standard for............
(A) Multimedia
(B) Transmission protocol
(C) Communication protocol
(D) OS standard

241. When input message is equal to the output message (i.e. input = output), called
(A) Communication standard
(B) Lossless
(C) Diffusion
(D) Lamination

242. According to AACR-II(R), which of the following is/are rendering under the Uniform Title
(A) Sacred texts (B) Folk tales
(C) Pseudonyms (D) Both (A) and (B)

243. In computer technology, P2P stands for
(A) Point-to-Point
(B) Peer-to-Peer
(C) Programs-to-Programs
(D) Position-to-Position

244. The Universal Bibliographical Control is associated with
(A) FID (B) ALA
(C) IFLA (D) CILIP

245. JPEG is an image compression standard which was accepted as an international standard in
(A) 1990 (B) 1992
(C) 1995 (D) 1996

246. In cataloguing, entries arrangement according to the code rules is called
(A) Entries code (B) Filing code
(C) Catalogue code (D) Book entries code

247. The RDA standard is related to
(A) Classification
(B) Cataloguing
(C) Communication protocol
(D) Database architecture

248. Which of the following is the official journal of ISKO?

(A) *Knowledge Organization*
(B) *Herald of Library Science*
(C) *SRELS Journal of Information Management*
(D) *Library Philosophy and Practice*

249. Source Code Theorem is represented by
(A) Shannon's 1st Theorem
(B) Shannon's 2nd Theorem
(C) Huffman's 1st Theorem
(D) None of the above

250. Channel Coding Theorem is represented by
(A) Shannon's 1st Theorem
(B) Shannon's 2nd Theorem
(C) Huffman's 1st Theorem
(D) None of the above

251. Information Capacity Theorem is represented by
(A) Shannon-Hartley Law
(B) Shannon-Mackay Law
(C) Shannon-Weaver Law
(D) Weaver-Hartley Law

252. MPEG stands for
(A) Motion Picture Expert Group
(B) Motion Pixel Expert Group
(C) Movie Picture Expert Group
(D) Motion Picture Experiment Group

253. In which year MPEG was formed?
(A) 1986 (B) 1988
(C) 1990 (D) 1992

254. Who says "Catalogue is as explanatory, logically arranged inventory and key to the books and their contents and it is confined to the books in a particular library"?
(A) C.A. Cutter
(B) J.D. Brown
(C) S.R. Ranganathan
(D) W.C.B. Sayers

255. In which year *MLA Manual and Guide to Scholarly Publishing* (3rd Edition) was published?
(A) 2002 (B) 2004
(C) 2008 (D) 2010

256. Which of the following tags is used for paragraph breaking in HTML?
(A) <PG> (B) <PB>
(C) <P> (D) <PL>

257. Which of the following is/are access point?
(A) Main entry (B) Added entries
(C) Call Number (D) All of the above

258. Which of the following is the 'Form' facet of Main Class 'Literature' in CC6?
(A) [P1] (B) [P2]
(C) [P3] (D) [P4]

259. In MARC, which of the following is Subject Headings field?
(A) 4XX (B) 6XX
(C) 7XX (D) 8XX

260. The paper titled "The Construction of a Faceted Classification for a Special Subject" was written by
(A) D.J. Foskett (B) S.R. Ranganathan
(C) D. Austin (D) J. Mills

261. "A Classification and Subject Index for Cataloguing and Arranging Books and Pamphlets of a Library" was written by
(A) Melvil Dewey
(B) Henry E. Bliss
(C) Margaret A. Edwards
(D) W.C.B. Sayers

262. Which of the following is true for 'Library of Congress Classification'?
(A) Classification was invented by J.D. Brown
(B) There are 21 Major Classes in this scheme
(C) The letter H is used for Education
(D) All of the above

263. In which year Digital Millennium Copyright Act (DMCA) was passed?

(A) 1990 (B) 1993
(C) 1996 (D) 1998

264. The paper titled "Classification, Coding, and Machinery for Search" was written by
(A) S.R. Ranganathan
(B) Henry E. Bliss
(C) Luther H. Evans
(D) W.C.B. Sayers

265. Which of the following is the ASLIB's publication?
(A) *Journal of Documentation*
(B) *Performance Measurements and Metrics*
(C) *Program: Electronic Library and Information Systems*
(D) All of the above

266. In CC6, the notation for Super Imposition Device (SID) is
(A) : (B) &
(C) – (D) ;

267. The structure of CCF is commonly an implementation of
(A) ISO-2709 (B) ISO-3098
(C) ISO-4165 (D) ISO-4628

268. Who says "The foundation of a library is a book, the foundation of librarianship is classification"?
(A) S.R. Ranganathan
(B) W.C.B. Sayers
(C) J.D. Brown
(D) H.E. Bliss

269. Which of the following programs was implemented after 'International Meeting of Cataloguing Experts' in Copenhagen (1969)?
(A) RDF (B) MARC
(C) AACR-II (D) ISBD

270. MARC XML was developed by
(A) LOC (B) IFLA
(C) UNESCO (D) CILIP

271. What is the frequency of publication of 'Management Information' (an ASLIB publication)
(A) Bi-monthly (B) 10 issues per year
(C) 8 issues per year (D) Annually

272. In library classification, who proposed the 'One Place Theory'?
(A) H.E. Bliss (B) S.R. Ranganathan
(C) C.A. Cutter (D) J.D. Brown

273. In which year 'the first International Cataloguing Code (Catalogue Rules, Author and Title Entries)' was published in both American and British editions?
(A) 1908 (B) 1910
(C) 1911 (D) 1923

274. Which of the following is the founder of VINITI?
(A) A.I. Mikhailov (B) M. Lomonosov
(C) E. Dynkin (D) M. Kravchuk

275. Who is authorized agency of Abridged and Medium Edition of Universal Decimal Classification (UDC) in English language?
(A) IFLA (B) UNESCO
(C) BSI (D) LOC

276. In which year 'Panizzi's 91 Rules for Standardizing the Cataloguing of Books' was approved by British Museum?
(A) 1836 (B) 1839
(C) 1842 (D) 1845

277. In which year 'American Library Association (ALA)' cataloguing rules—'Condensed Rules for an Author and Title Catalogue' was first published in 'Library journal'?
(A) 1881 (B) 1883
(C) 1888 (D) 1902

278. The UGC-INFONET Digital Library Consortium has been merged into
(A) e-Shodh Sindhu Consortium
(B) UGC-DAE Consortium for Scientific Research

(C) MCIT Library Consortium
(D) INDEST-AICTE Consortium

279. In which year, the draft of Functional Requirements for Authority Data (FRAD) was presented?
(A) 1998 (B) 2000
(C) 2002 (D) 2004

280. FRAD is based on
(A) Hierarchical Data Model
(B) Network Data Model
(C) Relational Data Model
(D) Flat File Data Model

281. In which year Library of Congress tested the MARC program in first time?
(A) 1965 (B) 1967
(C) 1970 (D) 1973

282. In 1954 *Cataloguing Principles and Practice: An Inquiry* was published by
(A) Library of Congress, USA
(B) Library Association, UK
(C) UNESCO
(D) FID

283. The first consolidate edition of ISBD was published in
(A) 1971 (B) 1985
(C) 1989 (D) 2007

284. In which year ILA became the member of IFLA?
(A) 1954 (B) 1957
(C) 1959 (D) 1962

285. The first edition of *Encyclopedia Britannica* was published and printed in
(A) London (B) Birmingham
(C) Edinburgh (D) Glasgow

286. Which of the following is not a Network Protocol?
(A) E6 (B) PPP
(C) Z39.50 (D) IMAP

287. Who quoted "Where is the Wisdom we have lost in knowledge? Where is the knowledge we have lost in information"?
(A) T.S. Eliot
(B) Richard Matthew Stallman
(C) Paul Outlet
(D) H. La Fontaine

288. Which of the following is/are composite media?
(A) Bar Code (B) Web page
(C) Book (D) All of the above

289. *Encyclopedia Americana* was first published in........volumes.
(A) 10 (B) 13
(C) 15 (D) 18

290. Grey Literature Network Service is founded in
(A) 1989 (B) 1992
(C) 1994 (D) 1996

291. Which of the following cities is associated with the foundation of IFLA?
(A) Edinburgh (B) Manchester
(C) Bristol (D) Belfast

292. The periodical *Index and Catalogue* is published under which parent body?
(A) IFLA (B) LOC
(C) CILIP (D) UNESCO

293. The first International Conference Series on Grey Literatures was held in
(A) 1993, Amsterdam
(B) 1995, Washington
(C) 1997, Luxembourg
(D) 2003, Amsterdam

294. Which of the following organizations is responsible for webpage standards worldwide?
(A) ANSI (B) NISO
(C) W3C (D) NASIG

295. Library and Information Science Abstracts (LISA) has been published since

(A) 1956 (B) 1962
(C) 1969 (D) 1971

296. *Indian Journal of Radio and Space Physics* is published by
(A) BARC, Mumbai
(B) NISCAIR, New Delhi
(C) ISRO, Bengaluru
(D) DRDO, New Delhi

297. Which of the following is an online digital library of education research and information?
(A) CILIP (B) ERIC
(C) Inspec (D) All of the above

298. Which of the following was founded by Melvil Dewey?
(A) Library Journal (B) Library Herald
(C) Library Trends (D) Library Review

299. In which year National Library of India adopted AACR-II?
(A) 1982 (B) 1985
(C) 1987 (D) 1989

300. POPLINE is a
(A) Health-related database
(B) A kind of communication protocol
(C) An indexing system developed by IFLA
(D) CILIP online repository

301. *Teacher Librarian: The Journal for School Library Professionals* has been published since
(A) 1988 (B) 2000
(C) 2005 (D) 2014

302. *School Libraries Worldwide* is published by
(A) IASL (B) UNESCO
(C) IFLA (D) CILIP

303. Which of the following was the founder president of Commonwealth Library Association (COMLA)?
(A) K.C. Harrison (B) H.D. Barry
(C) George Chandler (D) William S. George

304. COMLA Newsletter has been published since
(A) 1973 (B) 1975
(C) 1977 (D) 1979

305. The term 'Bandwidth' is associated with
(A) Telecommunication
(B) Classification
(C) Cataloguing
(D) Reprography

306. In which year Tim Berners-Lee proposed the Hypertext data system?
(A) 1985 (B) 1987
(C) 1989 (D) 2000

307. The term '3-tier application' is associated with
(A) Classification
(B) Indexing
(C) Abstracting
(D) Software development

308. CLI stands for
(A) Communication Line Interface
(B) Command Line Interface
(C) Compile Line Interface
(D) Complex Linux Interface

309. 'Bodleian Library' is located in
(A) University of Oxford, England
(B) University of California, Los Angeles
(C) Victoria University, Melbourne
(D) Deakin University, Melbourne

310. 'Centre for Information Quality Management (CIQM)' is founded by
(A) CILIP
(B) UK online User Group
(C) IFLA
(D) Both (A) and (B)

311. Which of the following is/are true for 'cheap edition' of a book?
(A) Reprint of an earlier edition
(B) Poorer paper
(C) Bound in a cheaper cover
(D) All of the above

312. The magazine *American Libraries* is published by
(A) Washington Library Association (WLA)
(B) American Library Association (ALA)
(C) Public Library Association (PLA)
(D) Pacific Northwest Library Association (PNLA)

313. International Association of Scientific and Technological University Libraries (IATUL) is located in
(A) USA (B) Germany
(C) United Kingdom (D) Italy

314. Which of the following is the European Bureau of Library, Information and Documentation Associations?
(A) CILIP (B) ALA
(C) EBLIDA (D) IFLA

315. The online version of *ALA Online Handbook of Organization* has been published since
(A) 2007 (B) 2009
(C) 2010 (D) 2011

316. Which of the following is published 'Cucolis'?
(A) Developing Library Network (DELNET)
(B) Calcutta Library Network (CALIBNET)
(C) Ahmedabad Library Network (ADINET)
(D) Mysore Library Network (MYLIBNET)

317. In which year h-index was proposed?
(A) 2001 (B) 2003
(C) 2005 (D) 2008

318. In which year g-index was proposed?
(A) 2002 (B) 2004
(C) 2006 (D) 2012

319. In which year Scientific Information Bureau (SIB) rename as Defence Scientific Information and Documentation Centre (DESIDOC)?
(A) 1963 (B) 1965
(C) 1967 (D) 1971

320. The h-index was proposed by
(A) Leo Eagghe
(B) J.E. Hirsch
(C) H.P. Luhn
(D) Claire K. Schultz

321. The g-index was proposed by
(A) J.E. Hirsch
(B) Leo Egghe
(C) S.R. Ranganathan
(D) F.W. Lancaster

322. In which year 'Herald of Library Science' was ceased?
(A) 2002 (B) 2003
(C) 2006 (D) 2008

323. The i10 index was introduced by
(A) F.W. Lancaster (B) Google
(C) IFLA (D) H.W. Wilson

324. In which year S.R. Ranganathan was honoured with the title 'National Research Professor'?
(A) 1961 (B) 1963
(C) 1965 (D) 1968

325. In which year 'ALA's Condensed Rules for an Author and Title Catalogue' was published in *Library Journal*?
(A) 1878 (B) 1882
(C) 1886 (D) 1893

326. In which year Congress of Southeast Asian Librarians (CONSAL) was formed?
(A) 1965 (B) 1970
(C) 1972 (D) 1976

327. In which year S.R. Ranganathan was awarded 'Padma Shri'?
(A) 1952 (B) 1954
(C) 1957 (D) 1961

328. In which year Melvil Dewey was opened the first formal library school?
(A) 1882 (B) 1887
(C) 1889 (D) 1901

329. 'International Literacy Day' (by UNESCO) is celebrate each year on
(A) 4 August (B) 8 September
(C) 12 August (D) 25 October

330. Buenos Aires Public Library (later the National Library of Argentina) was established in
(A) 1805 (B) 1810
(C) 1812 (D) 1834

331. Who was the first President of IFLA?
(A) Isaac Collijin
(B) Jorge Luis Borges
(C) Mao Zedong
(D) Christopher Okigbo

332. Universal Product Code (UPC) is a...... digit bar code.
(A) 9 (B) 12
(C) 14 (D) 16

333. In which year Libraries Act was passed in United Kingdom?
(A) 1847 (B) 1850
(C) 1855 (D) 1858

334. The default file name extension of MARC file is/are
(A) .mrc (B) .marc
(C) .mrrc (D) Both (A) and (B)

335. Who devised the Adjustable Classification?
(A) J.D. Brown (B) H.E. Bliss
(C) C.A. Cutter (D) Charles Goss

336. Which of the following is the principal association of major research libraries in Europe?
(A) IFLA (B) LIBER
(C) CILIP (D) All of the above

337. eGyankosh is associated with
(A) IIT, Kanpur
(B) IIT, New Delhi
(C) ISI, Kolkata
(D) IGNOU, New Delhi

338. Which of the following is/are scripting language?
(A) Perl (B) JavaScript
(C) Java (D) Both (A) and (B)

339. PRECIS Indexing System was developed under the direction of Derek Austin for
(A) BNB
(B) IFLA
(C) UNESCO
(D) MLA International Bibliography

340. International Federation of Classification Societies (IFCS) was founded in
(A) 1982 (B) 1985
(C) 1988 (D) 1991

341. A kind of software version where user will try before buy is called
(A) Freeware (B) Shareware
(C) OpenSource (D) All the above

342. *Te Puna National Bibliography* is published from
(A) USA (B) New Zealand
(C) Japan (D) France

343. *MLA International Bibliography* (formerly known as *MLA Annual Bibliography*) has been published since
(A) 1918 (B) 1922
(C) 1927 (D) 1937

344. The book titled *A Librarian Looks Back* is an autobiography of
(A) J.D. Brown (B) S.R. Ranganathan
(C) Melvil Dewey (D) H.E. Bliss

345. For research journal what term is used for ready to print?
(A) Camera Ready Copy
(B) Composing
(C) Compiling
(D) Drafting

346. The first edition of *Encyclopedia Americana* was published by
(A) K. Thomas (B) J.M. Stoddart
(C) S. William (D) Tony S.

347. SDK stands for
(A) Software Design Kit
(B) Software Development Kit
(C) Software Development Knowledge
(D) Software Designing Knowledge

348. The..........is the signaling rate of a line for number of transitions on the basis of voltage or frequency changes that made per second.
(A) Byte (B) Bit
(C) Baud (D) Decoder

349. An error in a computer program is called
(A) Byte (B) Boolean
(C) Bug (D) POST error

350. In which year Dewey's *Classification and Subject Index for Cataloguing and Arranging the Books and Pamphlets of a Library* was published
(A) 1845 (B) 1856
(C) 1876 (D) 1890

351. The Library Code of Ethics (created by American Library Association) was formed in
(A) 1931 (B) 1935
(C) 1939 (D) 1945

352. Who was the founder of Library Bureau in Boston?
(A) C.A. Cutter (B) Melvil Dewey
(C) Herbert Putnam (D) H.E. Bliss

353. The first conference of librarians was held in
(A) New York, 1853 (B) New York, 1867
(C) London, 1867 (D) Paris, 1882

354. Which of the following is the founder member of Association of Medical Libraries?
(A) George Gould
(B) Charles R. Drew
(C) Elizabeth Blackwell
(D) Harvey Cushing

355. Which of the following year 'Science Abstract Service' was started by 'Inspec'?
(A) 1917 (B) 1925
(C) 1945 (D) 1967

356. The book titled *An Investigation of the Laws of Thought* was written by
(A) Augustus De Morgan
(B) George Boole
(C) J.D. Brown
(D) H.E. Bliss

357. In which year, the National Innovation Council (India) was constituted?
(A) 2001 (B) 2005
(C) 2007 (D) 2010

358. Which of the following was the chief developer of the Library of Congress Classification Scheme?
(A) Charles Martel (B) H.E. Bliss
(C) Melvil Dewey (D) C.A. Cutter

ANSWERS KEYS

1. (A)	2. (B)	3. (A)	4. (A)	133. (D)	134. (A)	135. (A)	136. (B)
5. (A)	6. (A)	7. (C)	8. (A)	137. (A)	138. (A)	139. (D)	140. (D)
9. (A)	10. (C)	11. (A)	12. (D)	141. (A)	142. (D)	143. (D)	144. (D)
13. (A)	14. (D)	15. (D)	16. (B)	145. (A)	146. (A)	147. (C)	148. (A)
17. (D)	18. (A)	19. (C)	20. (D)	149. (B)	150. (C)	151. (A)	152. (C)
21. (A)	22. (C)	23. (A)	24. (C)	153. (A)	154. (B)	155. (A)	156. (B)
25. (A)	26. (B)	27. (D)	28. (C)	157. (B)	158. (A)	159. (A)	160. (A)
29. (B)	30. (A)	31. (A)	32. (C)	161. (A)	162. (D)	163. (A)	164. (B)
33. (B)	34. (C)	35. (B)	36. (A)	165. (B)	166. (A)	167. (A)	168. (A)
37. (A)	38. (B)	39. (A)	40. (A)	169. (A)	170. (A)	171. (A)	172. (A)
41. (A)	42. (B)	43. (A)	44. (B)	173. (C)	174. (D)	175. (C)	176. (B)
45. (A)	46. (A)	47. (A)	48. (A)	177. (A)	178. (A)	179. (D)	180. (D)
49. (A)	50. (A)	51. (A)	52. (A)	181. (B)	182. (A)	183. (B)	184. (A)
53. (D)	54. (A)	55. (A)	56. (A)	185. (A)	186. (C)	187. (D)	188. (A)
57. (C)	58. (B)	59. (A)	60. (D)	189. (D)	190. (A)	191. (A)	192. (B)
61. (A)	62. (D)	63. (C)	64. (A)	193. (A)	194. (A)	195. (C)	196. (D)
65. (A)	66. (B)	67. (A)	68. (A)	197. (A)	198. (A)	199. (A)	200. (A)
69. (A)	70. (D)	71. (C)	72. (A)	201. (B)	202. (B)	203. (C)	204. (C)
73. (B)	74. (B)	75. (C)	76. (C)	205. (A)	206. (A)	207. (B)	208. (B)
77. (D)	78. (D)	79. (C)	80. (C)	209. (A)	210. (A)	211. (A)	212. (C)
81. (C)	82. (A)	83. (A)	84. (C)	213. (D)	214. (B)	215. (C)	216. (A)
85. (C)	86. (B)	87. (C)	88. (B)	217. (B)	218. (A)	219. (B)	220. (B)
89. (C)	90. (A)	91. (D)	92. (D)	221. (B)	222. (D)	223. (B)	224. (A)
93. (B)	94. (C)	95. (B)	96. (B)	225. (B)	226. (C)	227. (A)	228. (D)
97. (A)	98. (B)	99. (D)	100. (D)	229. (B)	230. (A)	231. (B)	232. (A)
101. (A)	102. (A)	103. (C)	104. (B)	233. (B)	234. (A)	235. (B)	236. (C)
105. (A)	106. (A)	107. (B)	108. (A)	237. (A)	238. (A)	239. (D)	240. (A)
109. (A)	110. (A)	111. (A)	112. (A)	241. (B)	242. (D)	243. (B)	244. (C)
113. (A)	114. (A)	115. (A)	116. (A)	245. (B)	246. (B)	247. (B)	248. (A)
117. (C)	118. (A)	119. (C)	120. (B)	249. (A)	250. (B)	251. (A)	252. (A)
121. (D)	122. (A)	123. (C)	124. (A)	253. (B)	254. (B)	255. (C)	256. (C)
125. (B)	126. (A)	127. (D)	128. (A)	257. (D)	258. (B)	259. (B)	260. (A)
129. (D)	130. (A)	131. (C)	132. (A)	261. (A)	262. (B)	263. (D)	264. (A)

265. (D) 266. (C) 267. (A) 268. (B)
269. (D) 270. (A) 271. (B) 272. (D)
273. (A) 274. (A) 275. (C) 276. (A)
277. (B) 278. (A) 279. (D) 280. (C)
281. (B) 282. (B) 283. (D) 284. (B)
285. (C) 286. (C) 287. (A) 288. (B)
289. (B) 290. (B) 291. (A) 292. (C)
293. (A) 294. (C) 295. (C) 296. (B)
297. (B) 298. (A) 299. (C) 300. (A)
301. (D) 302. (A) 303. (A) 304. (A)
305. (A) 306. (C) 307. (D) 308. (B)
309. (A) 310. (D) 311. (D) 312. (B)

313. (B) 314. (C) 315. (B) 316. (C)
317. (C) 318. (C) 319. (C) 320. (B)
321. (B) 322. (C) 323. (B) 324. (C)
325. (D) 326. (B) 327. (C) 328. (B)
329. (B) 330. (B) 331. (A) 332. (B)
333. (B) 334. (D) 335. (A) 336. (B)
337. (D) 338. (D) 339. (A) 340. (B)
341. (B) 342. (B) 343. (B) 344. (B)
345. (A) 346. (B) 347. (B) 348. (C)
349. (C) 350. (C) 351. (C) 352. (B)
353. (A) 354. (A) 355. (D) 356. (B)
357. (D) 358. (A)

Appendices

Appendix A: Abbreviations

Entities	Description
AACR	Anglo-American Cataloguing Rules
AARL	Australian Academic and Research Libraries
ABLISS	Association of British Library and Information Schools
ACI	Anteriorising Common Isolates
ACMLA	Association of Canadian Map Libraries and Archives
ACRL	Association of College and Research Libraries
ADC	Abridge Decimal Classification
AGORA	Access to Global Online Research in Agriculture
AGRIS	International System for Agriculture Science and Technology
AI	Artificial Intelligence
AICTE	All India Council for Technical Education
AIU	Association of Indian Universities
ALA	American Library Association
ALIA	Australian Library and Information Association
ALIC	Archives Library Information Center
ALISE	Association for Library and Information Science Education
ALU	Arithmetic Logic Unit
ANSCR	Alpha-Numeric System for Classification of Recording
ANSI	American National Standard Institute
APA	American Psychological Association
API	Application Programming Interface

APIN	Asia and Pacific Information Network
ARP	Address Resolution Protocol
ARPANET	Advanced Research Projects Agency Network
ASCII	American Standard Code for Information Interchange
ASLIB	Association of Special Libraries and Information Bureaux
ASP	Active Server Pages
ATM	Asynchronous Transfer Mode
BBS	Bulletin Board System
BCD	Binary Coded Decimal
BGP	Border Gateway Protocol
BIOS	Basic Input Output System
BIOSIS	BioSciences Information Service of Biological Abstracts
BIP	Books In Print
BIS	Bureau of Indian Standards
BNB	British National Bibliography
BOF	Beginning of File
BRC	Bibliographic Retrieval Services
BUCOP	British Union Catalogue of Periodicals
CA	Chemical Abstracts
CAD	Computer Aided Design
CALIBNET	Calcutta Library Network
CAN	Campus Area Network
CARIS	Current Agriculture Research Information System
CAS	Current Awareness Services
CBD	Current Bibliographical Directory
CBI	Cumulative Book Index
CCF	Common Communication Format
CDC	Curriculum Development Committee
CDI	Comprehensive Dissertation Index
CDMA	Code Division Multiple Access

CDP	Collection Development Policy
CD-R	Compact Disc-Recordable
CD-RW	Compact Disc-ReWritable
CDS	Cataloguing Distribution Service
CDS/ISIS	Computerized Documentation System/Integrated Set of Information System
CERN	European Organization for Nuclear Research
CGI	Common Gateway Interface
CIEPS	International Centre for the Registration of Serials Publications
CIIL	Central Institute of Indian Languages
CILIP	Chartered Institute of Library and Information Professionals
CIP	Cataloguing-in-Publication Programme
CLA	Canadian Library Association
CLIEJ	Chinese Librarianship: an International Electronic Journal
CLIR	Council on Library and Information Resources
CMS	Content Management System
COBOL	Common Business-Oriented Language
CODATA	Committee on Data for Science and Technology
COMLA	Commonwealth Library Association
COPE	Committee on Publishing Ethics
CORC	Cooperative Online Resource Catalogue
CPU	Central Processing Unit
CRL	Central Reference Library
CSIR	Council of Scientific and Industrial Research
CSS	Cascading Style Sheets
CU	Control Unit
DAI	Distributed Artificial Intelligence
DAO	Data Access Object
DBLP	Database Systems and Logic Programming
DBMS	Database Management System
DDC	Dewey Decimal Classification
DDS	Document Delivery Service

DELNET	Developing Library Network
DESIDOC	Defence Scientific Information & Documentation Centre
DEVSIS	Development Science Information System
DHCP	Dynamic Host Configuration Protocol
DHTML	Dynamic Hypertext Markup Language
DMCA	Digital Millennium Copyright Act
DOAJ	Directory of Open Access Journals
DOI	Digital Object Identifier
DPI	Dot Per Inch
DRDO	Defence Research and Development Organization
DRM	Digital Rights Management
DRM	Data Resource Management
DRTC	Documentation Research and Training Centre
DSIR	Department of Scientific and Industrial Research (India)
DSSS	Direct Sequence Spread Spectrum
DVD	Digital Video/Versatile Disc
EBCDIC	Extended Binary Coded Decimal Interchange Code
EFF	Electronic Frontier Foundation
ENIAC	Electronic Numerical Integrator And Computer
EOF	End of File
ERIC	Educational Resources Information Centre
ERNET	Education and Research Network
ETDE	Electronic Technology Data Exchange
FAO	Food and Agriculture Organization, UN
FDDI	Fiber Distributed Data Interface
FDLP	Federal Depository Library Programme
FHSS	Frequency Hopping Spread Spectrum
FID	International Federation for Documentation
FID	International Federation for Information and Documentation
FRBR	Functional Requirements for Bibliographic Records
FTP	File Transfer Protocol
GAN	Global Area Network

GB	Gigabyte
GIF	Graphics Interchange Format
GIGO	Garbage In Garbage Out
GIS	Geographical Information System
GPRS	General Packet Radio Service
GUI	Graphical User Interface
HAN	Home Area Network
HD	High Density
HDD	Hard Disk Drive
HTML	HyperText Markup Language
HTTP	HyperText Transfer Protocol
I/O	Input/Output
IAALD	International Association of Agricultural Information Specialist
IAC	Information Analysis and Consolidation
IAEA	International Atomic Energy Agency
IALL	International Association of Law Libraries
IAN	Internet Area Network
IARI	Indian Agricultural Research Institute
IASL	International Association of School Librarianship
IASLIC	Indian Association of Special Libraries and Information Centers
IATLIS	Indian Association of Teachers of Library and Information Science
IBIS	Illinois Bibliographic Information Services
IBM	International Business Machine
ICAR	Indian Council of Agriculture Research
ICDD	International Centre for Diffraction Data
ICI	Indian Citation Index
ICLC	International Chinese Librarian Club
ICMP	Internet Control Message Protocol
ICMR	Indian Council of Medical Research
ICNBS	International Conference on National Bibliographic Services
ICSSR	Indian Council of Social Science Research
ICSU	International Council for Science

ICT	Information and Communication Technology
IDE	Integrated Development Environment
IDRC	International Development Research Centre
IE	Internet Explorer
IEC	International Electrotechnical Commission
IEEE	Institute of Electrical and Electronics Engineers
IFLA	International Federation of Library Associations and Institutions
IIS	Internet Information Service
IIT	Indian Institute of Technology
ILA	Indian Library Association
ILSA	Indian Library Science Abstract
IMAP	Internet Message Access Protocol
IMS	Information Management System
INB	Indian National Bibliography
INDEST	Indian National Digital Library in Engineering Sciences & Technology
INFA	India News and Features Alliance
INFLIBNET	Information and Library Network
INIS	International Nuclear Information System
INPADOC	International Patent Documentation
INSDOC	Indian National Scientific Documentation Centre
INSPEL	International Journal of Special Libraries
INSSPEL	Indian Social Science Periodicals Literature
IP	Internet Protocol
IPAIRS	Indian Patent Information Retrieval Systems
IPDC	Internet Protocol Device Control
IPR	Intellectual Property Rights
IRD	Imperial Records Department
IRRC	Illinois Research and Retrieval Centre
IRS	Information Retrieval System
ISA	Indian Science Abstract
ISA	International Sociological Association
ISBD	International Standard Bibliographic Description

ISBN	International Standard Book Number
ISCA	International Science Congress Association
ISDN	Integrated Services Digital Network
ISDS	International Serials Data System
ISI	Institute for Scientific Information
ISI	Indian Standards Institution
ISKO	International Society for Knowledge Organization
ISMN	International Standard Music Number
ISO	International Organization for Standardization
ISP	Internet Service Provider
ISRO	Indian Space Research Organization
ISSN	International Standard Serial Number
ITLA	Indian Theological Library Association
JCR	Journal Citation Report
JDK	Java Development Kit
JRE	Java Runtime Environment
JS	JavaScript
JSLIS	Japan Society of Library and Information Science
KBE	Knowledge-Based Economy
Kbps	Kilobyte Per Second
KQML	Knowledge Query and Management Language
KVM	Keyboard, Video, Mouse
KWIC	Key-Word In Context
KWOC	Key-Word Out of Context
LAN	Local Area Network
LASIE	Library Automated Systems Information Exchange
LCC	Library of Congress Classification
LCCN	Library of Congress Control Number
LCRI	Library of Congress Rule Interpretations
LCSH	Library of Congress Subject Headings
LDLSCP	Legal Deposit Libraries Shared Cataloguing Programme
LED	Light-Emitting Diode

LIS	Library and Information Science
LISA	Library and Information Science Abstracts
LISTA	Library Information Science & Technology Index
LLAMA	Library Leadership and Management Association
MAN	Metropolitan Area Network
MARC	Machine-Readable Cataloguing
MCI	Medical Council of India
MDPI	Multidisciplinary Digital Publishing Institute
MEDLARS	Medical Literature Analysis and Retrieval Systems
MESH	Medical Subject Headings
MGCP	Media Gateway Control Protocol
MIS	Management Information System
MLA	Modern Language Association of America
MPEG	Motion Pictures Experts Group
MS-DOS	Microsoft-Disk Operating System
MU	Memory Unit
NAAC	National Accreditation and Assessment Council
NARA	National Archives and Records Administration
NASA	National Aeronautics and Space Administration
NASSDOC	National Social Science Documentation Centre
NCERT	National Council of Educational Research and Training
NCES	National Centre for Education Statistics
NCSI	National Centre for Science Information
NCTE	National Council for Teachers Education
NIC	National Informatics Centre
NIC	Network Interface Controller
NISCAIR	National Institute of Science Communication and Information Resources
NISO	National Information Standard Organization
NISSAT	National Information System for Science and Technology
NIST	National Institute of Standards and Technology
NSA	Nuclear Science Abstracts
NTIS	National Technical Information Service

NTP	Network Time Protocol
NUEPA	National University of Educational Planning and Administration
OASPA	Open Access Scholarly Publishers Association
OCLC	Online Computer Library Center
OCS	Online Copy Catalogue System
OJAS	Open Journal Access System
OJS	Open Journal System
OODBMS	Object-Oriented Database Management System
OPAC	Online Public Access Catalogue
ORDBMS	Object-Relational Database Management System
OSI	Open System Interconnection
P2P	Peer-to-Peer
PAN	Personal Area Network
PCB	Printed Circuit Board
PCC	Programme for Cooperative Cataloguing
PCI	Peripheral Component Interconnect
PCI	Posteriorising Common Isolates
PHP	PHP: Hypertext Preprocessor
PLANNER	Promotion of Library Automation and Networking in North-Eastern Region
POST	Power-On Self Text
PPP	Point-to-Point Protocol
PSTN	Public Switched Telephone Network
RAID	Redundant Array of Independent/Inexpensive Disks
RAM	Read Only Memory
RDA	Resource Description and Access
RDBMS	Relational Database Management System
RFID	Radio Frequency Identification
RGB	Red, Green, Blue
RIP	Raster Image Processor
RIP	Routing Information Protocol
RLG	Research Library Group

RRRLF	Raja Rammohun Roy Library Foundation
RSC	Reader Service Card
RTP	Real-time Transport Protocol
SALIS	Society for the Advancement of Library and Information Science
SAN	Storage Area Network
SCI	Science Citation Index
SCTP	Stream Control Transmission Protocol
SDI	Selective Dissemination of Information
SDP	Session Description Protocol
SENDOC	Small Enterprises National Document Centre
SGCP	Simple Gateway Control Protocol
SIP	Session Initiation Protocol
SJR	SCImago Journal Rank
SMTP	Simple Mail Transfer Protocol
SNIP	Source Normalized Impact per Paper
SNMP	Simple Network Management Protocol
SOSIG	Social Science Information Gateway
SRELS	Sarada Ranganathan Endowment for Library Science
SSCI	Social Science Citation Index
SVGA	Super Video Graphics Array
TCP	Transmission Control Protocol
TDMA	Time Division Multiple Access
TERI	Tata Energy Research Institute
UBC	Universal Bibliographic Control
UCC	Uniform Code Council
UDP	User Datagram Protocol
UKOLN	United Kingdom Office for Library and Information Networking
UNDP	United Nations Development Programme
UNESCO	United Nations Educational, Scientific and Cultural Organization
UNISIST	United Nations Information System in Science and Technology
UPC	Universal Product Code
UPS	Uninterruptible Power Supply

URI	Uniform Resource Identifier
URL	Uniform Resource Locator
USB	Universal Serial Bus
UTF	Unicode Transformation Format
VAOLS	Value Added On-Line Systems
VGA	Video Graphics Array
VINITI	All-Russian Institute for Scientific and Technical Information
VPN	Virtual Private/Public/Protected Network
VRML	Virtual Reality Markup Language
VSAT	Very Small Aperture Terminal
W3C	World Wide Web Consortium
WAN	Wide Area Network
WAP	Wireless Application Protocol
WIF	Web Impact Factor
Wi-Fi	Wireless Fidelity
WIPO	World Intellectual Property Organization
WLAN	Wireless Local Area Network
WLIC	World Library and Information Congress
WMA	Windows Media Audio
WPAN	Wireless Personal Area Network
WSSN	World Standards Service Network
WWW	World Wide Web
WYSIWYG	What You See Is What You Get
XML	Extensible Markup Language

Appendix B: Abstracts, Index, Thesaurus, Bibliographies, Proceedings

Title	Year of Publication	Publisher/Sponsored
A Bibliography of Africana	1975	Greenwood Press
A World Bibliography of Bibliographies	1939	University Press, Oxford
Academic Index	1985	Information Access Company

American Bibliography	1903	Blakely Press
American Humanities Index	1975	Whitson Publication
American Reference Books Annual	1970	Libraries Unlimited
American Statistics Index	1974	Congressional Information Service
Annual Bibliography of English Language and Literature	1921	Chadwick-Healy (now ProQuest)
Applied Science & Technology Index	1914	H.W. Wilson
Applied Social Science Index and Abstracts	1987	The Library Association
Art Index	1929	H.W. Wilson
Art Index Retrospective	1929	H.W. Wilson
Arts and Humanities Citation Index	1975	Institute for Scientific Information
ASIS Thesaurus of Information Science and Librarianship	1994	American Society for Information Science
Bibliographic Index: A Cumulative Bibliography of Bibliographies	1938	H.W. Wilson
Bibliography of Asian Studies	1956	Association of Asian Studies
Bibliography of Comparative Literature	1960	Russell and Russell
Bibliography of Education	1897	D. Appleton
Bibliography of Indian Zoology	1960	Zoological Survey of India
Biography Index	1964	H.W. Wilson
Biological Abstracts	1926	Bioscience Information Service
Botanical Abstracts	1918	Baltimore, Williams and Wilkins Company
British Education Index	1954	University of Leeds
British Humanities Index	1962	The Library Association
British National Bibliography (BNB)	1950	British Library Bibliographic Services
Business Periodicals Index	1958	H.W. Wilson
Canadian Periodical Index	1948	Canadian Library Association
Chemical Abstracts	1907	American Chemical Society
Computer and Control Abstracts	1983	Inspec

Cumulative Book Index	1898	H.W. Wilson
Cumulative Index of Sociology Journal	1971	American Sociological Association
Cumulative Subject Index to the Reader's Digest	1935	Berrien Book Binder
Current Contents: Arts and Humanities	1972	Institute for Scientific Information
Current Contents: Social and Behavioral Sciences	1969	Institute for Scientific Information
Current Technology Index (formerly known as British Technology Index)	1962	The Library Association
Directory of Special Libraries and Information Centers	1963	Gale Research
Dissertation Abstracts International	1938	University Microfilms International
Doctoral Dissertation on Asia: A Semi-Annual Index	1975	Association for Asian Studies
Education Index	1929	H.W. Wilson
Energy Research Abstracts	1975	U.S. Department of Energy, Technical Information Center
Engineering Index	1883	Engineering Index, Inc.
General Science Index	1963	H.W. Wilson
Guide to Critical Review	1909	Scarecrow Press
Guide to Indian Periodical Literature	1964	Indian Documentation Centre
Historical Abstracts	1954	EBSCO
Human Resource Abstracts	1975	EBSCO
Humanities Index	1974	H.W. Wilson
Humanities International Index	1925	EBSCO
Hungarian Technical Abstracts	1948	Hungarian Central Technical Library
Index Medicus	1979	National Library of Medicine
Index to Conference Proceedings	1970	British Library Bibliographic Division
Index to Indian Medical Periodicals	1959	National Medical Library

Index to International Statistics	1980	Congressional Information Service
Index to Social Science and Humanities Proceedings	1979	Institute for Scientific Information
Index to Times of India	1973	Bennett & Coleman
Indian Books in Print	1955	Indian Bureau of Bibliographies
Indian Dissertation Abstracts	1973	Indian Council of Social Science Research
Indian Library Science Abstracts	1967	Indian Association of Special Libraries and Information Centers
Indian National Bibliography (INB)	1958	Central Reference Library, Kolkata
Indian Press Index	1968	Delhi Library Association
Indian Psychological Abstracts	1967	National Social Science Documentation Center
Indian Science Abstracts	1965	NISCAIR
Indian Science Congress Abstracts	1934	Asiatic Society
Industrial Arts Index	1913	H.W. Wilson
Information Science Thesaurus	1964	Drexel Institute of Technology
International Bibliography of the Social Science	1951	Routledge
International Index to Periodicals	1907	H.W. Wilson
International Political Science Abstracts	1951	University Press of France and Basil Blackwell
Library and Information Science Abstracts	1969	The Library Association
Library Science Abstracts	1950	The Library Association
Magazine Index	1959	Information Access Company
Masters Abstracts International	1962	University Microfilms International
Music Index	1949	Harmonies Park Press
National Index of Translations	1977	Indian National Scientific Documentation Centre
Nepalese National Bibliography	1983	Tribhuvan University Centre, Library and Nepal Research

New York Times Index	1913	New York Times
Nuclear Science Abstracts	1946	U.S. Atomic Energy Commission
Physics Abstracts	1903	Inspec
Political Science Abstracts	1980	Silver Platter Information
Population Index	1937	G.K. Hall
Psychological Abstracts	1921	American Psychological Association
Reader's Guide to Periodical Literature	1900	H.W. Wilson
Roget's International Thesaurus	1886	Thos Crowell
Roget's Thesaurus	1852	Longman
Science Abstracts	1898	Inspec
Science Abstracts of China	1958	Academia Sinica, Institute of Scientific Information
Science Citation Index	1963	Institute for Scientific Information
Social Science and Humanities Index (formerly known as International Index to Periodicals - 1913 and International Index - 1955)	1966	H.W. Wilson
Social Science Citation Index	1973	Institute for Scientific Information
Social Science Index	1974	H.W. Wilson
Social Sciences and Humanities Index	1907	H.W. Wilson
Sociological Abstracts	1953	American Sociological Association
Sri Lanka National Bibliography (SLNB)	1974	National Library and Documentation Centre
Statistical Abstracts of the Indian Union	1950	Central Statistical Organization, India
Statistical Reference Index	1980	Statistical Reference Index
Technical Book Review Index	1935	Special Library Association
The Bibliography of Asian Studies	1956	Association for Asian Studies
The Impex Reference Catalogue of Indian Books	1960	India Book Export and Import Company

The International Thesaurus of Quotations	1970	Crowell
The Librarian Thesaurus	1990	American Library Association
The National Bibliography of Nigeria	1975	National Library of Nigeria
The New York Index	1913	The New York Time
The Union Catalogue of Social Science Serials	1970	NASSDOC
Thesaurus of Information Science Terminology	1968	Communication Service Cooperation
UNESCO Thesaurus: A Structured List of Descriptors...	1977	UNESCO
Wall Street Journal Index	1958	Dow Jones & Company
Webster's New World Thesaurus	1985	Simon & Schuster
Women Studies Abstracts	1972	Women Studies Abstracts
World Directory of Social Science Institutions	1990	UNESCO
World Translation Index	1978	International Translations Centre

Appendix C: Catalogue Codes and their Inventors

Catalogue Codes	Inventor	Year
Panizzi's 91 Rules for Standardizing the Cataloguing of Books (Rules for Compiling the Catalogues of Printed Books, Maps and Music in the British Museum)	Antonio Panizzi	1841
Charles Coffin Jewett Code	Charles Coffin Jewett	1852
Rules for a Printed Dictionary Catalogue	Charles Ammi Cutter	1876
Rules to be Observed in Forming the Alphabetical Catalogue of Printed Book	Cambridge University	1878
Condensed Rules for an Author and Title Catalogue	American Library Association	1883
Compendious Cataloguing Rules for the Author Catalogue	Oxford, Bodleian Library	1883
San Francisco Cataloguing for Public Libraries	F.B. Perkins	1884

Condensed Rules for a Card Catalogue	American Library Association	1886
Library School Card Catalogue Rules: with 52 Facsimiles of Sample Cards for Author and Classes Catalogues	Melvil Dewey	1889
Prussian Instruction: Rules for the Alphabetical Catalognes of the Prussian Libraries	Fritz Milkau (Official Prussian Ministry of Culture)	1899
Vatican Library: Rules for the Catalogue of Printed Books	Vatican Library	1931
Rules for Compiling the Catalogues of Printed Books, Maps and Music in the British Museum (Revised edition)	Published by British Museum	1936
A.L.A. Cataloguing Rules for Author and Title (2nd edition)	American Library Association	1949
Rules for Descriptive Cataloguing in the Library of Congress	Library of Congress	1949
Nippon Cataloguing Rules	Japan Library Association	1965
Guide to the Cataloguing of the Serial Publications of Societies and Institutions	Library of Congress	1919
Anglo-American Cataloguing Rules (AACR I) 1st edition	American Library Association, Library of Congress, Library Association and Canadian Library Association	1967
Anglo-American Cataloging Rules (AACRII) 2nd edition	American Library Association, British Library, Canadian Committee on Cataloguing, Library Association and Library of Congress	1978
Anglo-American Cataloging Rules (AACRII) Rev. edition	American Library Association, Australian Committee on Cataloguing, British Library, Canadian Committee on Cataloguing, Library Association and Library of Congress	1988

Anglo-American Cataloging Rules (AACRIIR) Rev. edition	American Library Association, Australian Committee on Cataloguing, British Library, Canadian Committee on Cataloguing, Chartered Institute of Library and Information Professionals (CILIP) and Library of Congress	2002
Anglo-American Cataloging Rules (AACRIIR) Rev. edition	American Library Association, Australian Committee on Cataloguing, British Library, Canadian Committee on Cataloguing, Chartered Institute of Library and Information Professionals (CILIP) and Library of Congress	2005
Anglo-American Cataloging Rules (AACRIIR) Concise edition	American Library Association	2004
Classified Catalogue Code (CCS) 1st edition	S.R. Ranganathan	1934
Classified Catalogue Code (CCS) 2nd edition	S.R. Ranganathan	1945
Classified Catalogue Code (CCS) 3rd edition	S.R. Ranganathan	1951
Classified Catalogue Code (CCS) 4th edition	S.R. Ranganathan	1958
Classified Catalogue Code (CCS) 5th edition	S.R. Ranganathan	1964
Seymour Lubetzky's Code of Cataloguing Rules: Author and Title Entry	Seymour Lubetzky	1960
International Standard Bibliographic Description for Monographic Publications (ISBD(M))	IFLA	1971
Machine-Readable Cataloging (MARC I)	Library of Congress	1966
UNIMARC	IFLA	1977
UNIMARC (2nd version)	IFLA	1980
Machine-Readable Cataloging (MARC 21)	Library of Congress	1999
Common Communication Format (CCF) 1st edition	UNESCO/PGI	1984

Common Communication Format (CCF) 2nd edition	UNESCO/PGI	1988
Dublin Core Metadata Schema (DCMS)	OCLC/NCSA	1995
Functional Requirement for Bibliographic Records (FRBR) 1st final report	IFLA	1998
Resource Description and Access (RDA)	American Library Association, Canadian Library Association and CILIP	2010

Appendix D: Classification Schemes and their Inventors

Classification Schemes	Inventor	Year
Dewey Decimal Classification (1st edition)	Melvil Dewey	1876
Dewey Decimal Classification (2nd edition)	Melvil Dewey	1885
Dewey Decimal Classification (23rd edition)	Melvil Dewey Edited by John S. Mitchell	2011
Expansive Classification	C.A. Cutter	1891
Nippon Decimal Classification (NDC)	Japan Library Association	1929
Universal Decimal Classification (UDC)	Paul Otlet and Henri La Fontaine	1895
Universal Decimal Classification (UDC) 1st edition (French)	Paul Otlet and Henri La Fontaine	1905
Universal Decimal Classification (UDC) 3rd edition (Germany)	Paul Otlet and Henri La Fontaine	1934
Universal Decimal Classification (UDC) 4th edition (English)	Paul Otlet and Henri La Fontaine	1943
Universal Decimal Classification (UDC) 1st Abridged edition	Paul Otlet and Henri La Fontaine	1948
Library of Congress Classification (LCC)	Herbert Putnam	1897
Subject Classification	J.D. Brown	1906
Colon Classification (CC) 1st edition	S.R. Ranganathan	1933

Colon Classification (CC) 2nd edition	S.R. Ranganathan	1939
Colon Classification (CC) 3rd edition	S.R. Ranganathan	1950
Colon Classification (CC) 4th edition	S.R. Ranganathan	1952
Colon Classification (CC) 5th edition	S.R. Ranganathan	1957
Colon Classification (CC) 6th edition	S.R. Ranganathan	1960
Colon Classification (CC) 7th edition	S.R. Ranganathan Edited by M.A. Gopinath	1987
Bibliographic Classification	H.E. Bliss	1940
Korean Decimal Classification	Korean Library Association	1940
National Library of Medicine (NLM) Classification System	Mary Louise Marshall Revised by Frank B. Rogers	1951
Russian Library-Bibliographical Classification (BBK)	Russian State Library (Formerly known as Lenin State Library)	1959
British Catalogue of Music Classification (BCM Classification)	E.J. Coates expanded by Patrick Mills	1960
International Classification	F. Ridder	1961
Book Classification of Chinese Libraries (BCCL)	China's Administrative Bureau of Cultural Affairs	1975
BSO Broad System of Ordering: Schedule and Index	FID/UNESCO	1978

APPENDIX E: CITATION MANUALS

Name	Publisher	Year
The MLA Style Manual (1st edition)	Modern Language Association (MLA), USA	1985
MLA Style Manual and Guide to Scholarly Publishing (3rd edition)	Modern Language Association (MLA), USA	2008
MLA Handbook for Writers of Research Papers (8th edition)	Modern Language Association (MLA), USA	2016
The ACS Style Guide: A Manual for Authors and Editors	American Chemical Society (ACS)	1997
AMA Manual of Style: A Guide for Author and Editors	American Medical Association (AMA)	1962

The Business Style Handbook	McGraw-Hill	2012
The New York Times Manual of Style and Usage (1st edition)	Three Review Press	1950
The New York Times Manual of Style and Usage (5th edition)	Three Review Press	2015
APA Style (1st edition)	American Psychological Association (APA)	1974
Publication Manual of the American Psychological Association (Formerly APA Style) (6th edition)	American Psychological Association (APA)	2009
ASA Style (5th edition)	American Sociological Association (ASA)	2014
The Bluebook: A Uniform System of Citation	Harvard Law Review Association, The Columbia Law Review, The University of Pennsylvania Law Review, and The Yale Law Journal, USA	1926
The Chicago Manual Style (1st edition)	University of Chicago Press	1906
The Chicago Manual Style (16th edition)	University of Chicago Press	2010
Citing Medicine: The NLM Style Guide for Authors, Editors, and Publishers (2nd edition)	United States National Library of Medicine	2007
MHRA Style Guide: A Handbook for Authors, Editors and Writers of Theses (Formerly MHRA Style) (1st edition)	Modern Humanities Research Association, UK	2002
MHRA Style Guide: A Handbook for Authors, Editors and Writers of Theses (Formerly MHRA Style) (3rd edition)	Modern Humanities Research Association, UK	2013
Hart's Rules (Oxford Style Manual) 1st edition	Oxford University Press, UK	1893
Hart's Rules (New Oxford Style Manual) 3rd edition	Oxford University Press, UK	2016
Scientific Style and Format: The CSE Manual for Authors, Editors, and Publishers (1st edition)	Council of Science Editors, USA	1996

Scientific Style and Format: The CSE Manual for Authors, Editors, and Publishers (8th edition)	Council of Science Editors, USA	2014
Turabian's Manual for Writers of Research Papers, Theses, and Dissertations (1st edition)	University of Chicago Press, USA	1937
Turabian's Manual for Writers of Research Papers, Theses, and Dissertations (8th edition)	University of Chicago Press, USA	2013
Vancouver Reference Style	International Committee of Medical Journal Editors, Canada	1978
Australian Guide to Legal Citation (1st edition)	Melbourne University Law Review Association and Melbourne Journal of International Law	1998
Harvard referencing (AGPS 6th edition) based on Style Manual for Authors, Editors and Printers	Australian Government Publishing Service	2002

APPENDIX F: DATE OF CONFERENCE/ESTABLISHED/FOUNDATION

Entities	Year
Advanced Research Projects Agency Network (ARPANET)	1969
Ahmedabad Library Network (ADINET)	1994
All India Council for Technical Education (AICTE)	1987
Allahabad Public Library	1864
All-Russian Institute for Scientific and Technical Information (VINITI)	1952
American Chemical Society	1876
American Documentation Institute	1937
American Society for Information Science	1937
Australian Law Librarians' Group (ALLG)	1969
Australian Libraries Gateway (ALG)	1998
Austrian Library Network	2002
Bangladesh National Scientific and Technical Documentation Centre (BANSDOC)	1972

Berne Convention for the Protection of Literary and Artistic Works (Berne Convention)	1886
Boston Public Library	1848
British Copyright Act (Imperial Copyright Act)	1911
British Library	1973
British Library's Automated Information Service (BLAISE)	1977
Bureau of Canadian Archivists (BCA)	1976
Bureau of Indian Standards (BIS)	1986
Calcutta Public Library	1836
Canada Institute for Scientific and Technical Information (CISTI)	1924
Canadian Council of Archives	1985
Cataloguing-In-Publication (CIP)	1971
Central Institute of Indian Languages, Mysore, India	1970
Central Reference Library (CRL), India	1970
Centre for Information Quality Management (CIQM)	1993
Chartered Institute of Library and Information Professionals (CILIP)	2002
Committee on Publication Ethics (COPE)	1997
Committee on Data for Science and Technology (CODATA)	1966
Connemara Public Library, Chennai	1896
Consortium of European Research Libraries (CERL)	1992
Consortium of University Research Libraries (CURL)	1980
Council of Science Editors (CSE) (Formerly Council of Biology Editors), United Kingdom	1957
Council of Scientific and Industrial Research (CSIR)	1942
Council on Library and Information Resources (CLIR)	1995
Council on Library Resources (CLR)	1956
Defence Research and Development Organization (DRDO)	1958
Defence Scientific Information & Documentation Centre (DESIDOC)	1970
Delhi Public Library	1951
Department of Scientific and Industrial Research (DSIR)	1985
Developing Library Network (DELNET)	1988
Directory of Open Access Journals (DOAJ)	2003

Documentation Research and Training Centre (DRTC)	1962
Education and Research Network (ERNET)	1998
European Organization for Nuclear Research (CERN)	1954
French National Centre for Scientific Research	1939
Geographical Survey of India (GSI)	1851
Google Scholar	2004
Imperial Library Act (India)	1902
Imperial Library, Kolkata	1891
Imphal Public Library	1938
Indian Agricultural Research Institute (IARI) (Pusa Institute)	1905
Indian Copyright Act (amended in 2012)	1957
Indian Council for Cultural Relations (ICCR)	1950
Indian Council of Agriculture Research (ICAR)	1929
Indian Council of Medical Research (ICMR)	1949
Indian Council of Philosophical Research (ICPR)	1977
Indian Council of Social Science Research (ICSSR)	1969
Indian Institute of Science (IISc), Benguluru	1909
Indian National Digital Library in Engineering Science and Technology (INDEST) Consortium	2003
INDEST-AICTE (formerly known as INDEST)	2005
Indian National Scientific Documentation Centre (INSDOC)	1952
Indian Standards Institution (ISI)	1947
Indian Statistical Institute (ISI), Kolkata	1931
Indira Gandhi National Open University (IGNOU)	1985
INDONET Network (CMC Ltd.)	1986
Information and Library Network (INFLIBNET)	1991
Institute for Scientific Information (ISI), Philadelphia	1958
Institute of Information Scientist, London	1958
International Centre for Diffraction Data (ICDD)	1941
International Chinese Librarian Club (ICLC)	1995
International Council on Archives (ICA)	1948
International Council for Science (ICSU), France	1931

International Development Research Centre (IDRC), Canada	1970
International Electrotechnical Commission (IEC)	1906
International Federation for Information and Documentation (FID)	1895
International Federation of Library Associations and Institutions (IFLA)	1927
International Group of Publishing Libraries (IGPL)	1983
International Institute of Bibliography, Brussels	1895
International Network for the Availability of Scientific Publications (INASP)	1992
International Nuclear Information System (INIS)	1970
International Organization for Standardization (ISO)	1947
International Serial Data System (ISDS), Paris	1971
International Society for Knowledge Organization (ISKO)	1989
International Sociological Association (ISA)	1949
International Study Conferences on Classification Research (1st Dorking, England)	1957
International Study Conferences on Classification Research (2nd Elsinore, Denmark)	1964
International Study Conferences on Classification Research (3rd Mumbai, India)	1975
International Study Conferences on Classification Research (4th Augsburg, Germany)	1982
International Study Conferences on Classification Research (5th Toronto, Canada)	1991
International Study Conferences on Classification Research (6th London, UK)	1997
International System for Agriculture Science and Technology (AGRIS)	1975
International Working Group of Archival, Library and Graphic Restores	1957
Japan Society of Library and Information Science (JSLIS)	1953
Joint Academic Network (JANET), United Kingdom	1984
Keesing's Records of World Events	1931
Khuda Baksh Oriental Public Library, Patna	1876
Kolhapur Princely State Public Libraries Act	1945
Kolkata Library Network (CALIBNET)	1992
Library Associations, UK	1877
Library of Congress	1800

Madras Library Network (MALIBNET)	1993
Maharaja's Public Library, Jaipur	1866
Management Library Network (MANLIBNET)	1998
Mysore Library Network (MYLIBNET)	1995
National Information Standards Organization (NISO), Maryland, USA	1939
National Book Development Board (NBDB), India	1967
National Book Development Council (NBDC), India	2008
National Book Trust, India	1957
National Centre for Science Information (NCSI), India	1983
National Council of Educational Research and Training (NCERT)	1961
National Informatics Centre (NIC)	1976
National Informatics Centre Network (NICNET), India	1977
National Information Standards Organization (NISO)	1939
National Information System for Science and Technology (NISSAT)	1977
National Institute of Science Communication and Information Resources (NISCAIR), New Delhi	2002
National Knowledge Commission (NKC), India	2005
National Library and Information Services Infrastructure for Scholarly Content (NLIST) Consortium	2010
National Library of Australia	1960
National Library of India	1953
National Library of Russia	1795
National Medical Library (NML), India	1966
National Mission for Manuscripts (NAMAMI), India	2003
National Museum, New Delhi	1949
National Policy on Education (NPE), India	1986
National Sample Survey Office (NSSO), India	1950
National Science Library (NSL), India	1964
National Social Science Documentation Centre (NASSDOC)	1969
National University of Educational Planning and Administration (NUEPA), New Delhi	1962
Open Access Scholarly Publishers Association (OASPA)	2008

Online Computer Library Centre (OCLC) (formerly Ohio College Library Center)	1967
Paris Revision (Universal Copyright Convention Revision)	1971
Raja Rammohun Roy Library Foundation (RRRLF)	1972
Rashtriya Madhyamik Shiksha Abhiyan (RMSA)	2009
Rashtriya Uchchattar Shiksha Abhiyan (RUSA)	2013
Research Libraries Group (RLG)	1974
Rights to Education Act (India)	2010
Russian Academy of Sciences	1724
SAARC Documentation Centre, New Delhi	1994
Scientific and Industrial Research Network (SIRNET)	1989
Scopus	2004
SLA: Asian Chapter	1999
Small Enterprises National Documentation Centre (SENDOC)	1970
Society for Information Science (SIS), India	1976
Society for the Advancement of Library and Information Science (SALIS)	2002
Special Library Association	1909
Tata Energy Research Institute (TERI)	1998
UGC-INFONET Digital Library Consortium	2003
United Nations Educational, Scientific and Cultural Organization (UNESCO)	1946
United Nations Development Programme (UNDP)	1965
United Nations International Scientific Information System (UNISIST) Programme	1973
Universal Copyright Convention	1952
University Grants Commission (UGC), India	1956
University of Bombay	1857
University of Calcutta	1857
University of Madras	1857
World Congress of Universal Documentation (Paris, France)	1937
World Intellectual Property Organization (WIPO)	1967
World Wide Web Consortium (W3C)	1994

APPENDIX G: ENCYCLOPEDIA, YEAR BOOK, GLOSSARIES, DICTIONARIES, ETC.

Title	Authors/Editors	Year of Publication	Publisher/ Sponsored
A Dictionary of Acronyms and Abbreviations in Library and Information Science	R. Tayyeb and K. Chandna	1979	Canadian Library Association
A Dictionary of Physics (3rd edition)	Alan Isaacs	1996	Oxford University Press
A Dictionary of Social Sciences	J. Gould and William L. Kolb	1964	Free Press
A Glossary of Geographical Terms (3rd edition)	Dudley Stamp and Audrey N. Clark	1979	Longman
ALA World Encyclopedia of Library and Information Science (1 Volume)	Robert Wedgeworth	1986	American Library Association
An Atlas of World Affairs	Andrew Boyd	1998	Routledge
An Encyclopedia of Indian Archeology	Amalananda Ghosh	1990	BRILL (Compiled by Indian Council of Historical Research)
APA Concise Dictionary of Psychology (1st edition)	American Psychological Association	2009	American Psychological Association
Bharatiya Sanskritikosh (10 Volumes)	M. Joshi	1969	Bharatiya Sanskriti Kosh Mandal
Bhartiya Itihas Kosh	S. Bhattacharya	1989	Uttar Pradesh Hindi Sansthan
Black's Law Dictionary (9th edition)	Bryan A. Garner and Henry Campbell Black	2009	Henry Campbell Black
Britannica Book of the Year (Annual Publication)	Encyclopedia Britannica	1938	Encyclopedia Britannica
Chamber's Encyclopedia (15 Volumes)	Chambers Editors	2001	Chambers
Chamber's Encyclopedia Yearbook	Frank Preston	1968	International Learning Systems

Chemical Engineers' Handbook (5th edition)	Robert H. Perry and Cecil H. Chilton	1973	McGraw-Hill
Collier's Encyclopedia (24 Volumes)	Collier's Editors	1966	Collier and Macmillan
Columbia Encyclopedia (6th edition) (1 Volume)	Columbia University	2001	Columbia University Press
Commonwealth University Yearbook (75th edition) (2 Volumes)	Association of Commonwealth Universities	2000	Association of Commonwealth Universities
Compton's By Britannica (26 Volumes)	Encyclopedia Britannica	2008	Encyclopedia Britannica
Concise Encyclopedia of Special Education	Cecil R. Reynolds and E. Fletcher	1990	Willey
Dictionary for Library and Information Science	Joan M. Reitz	1994	Libraries Unlimited
Dictionary of Art (34 Volumes)	June Turner	1996	Grove
Dictionary of Bibliometrics	V.P. Diodato	1994	Haworth Press
Dictionary of Documentation Terms	Frank S. Wagner	1970	University Microfilms
Dictionary of Education (2nd edition)	Charter V. Good	1959	McGraw-Hill
Dictionary of Education Acronyms, Abbreviations, and Initialisms (2nd edition)	James C. Palmer and Anita Y. Colby	1985	Oryx Press
Dictionary of Information and Library Management (2nd edition)	Janet Stevenson	2006	A & C Black
Dictionary of Information Science	Eric Burger	1989	Elsevier
Dictionary of Information Science and Technology	Carolyn Watters	1992	Academic Press
Dictionary of Information Technology (2nd edition)	Dennis Longley	1986	Oxford University Press
Dictionary of International Agricultural Trade	Harry W. Henderson	1971	U.S. Foreign Agriculture Service

Dictionary of Library and Information Science	Pandey S.K. Sharma and O.P. Gupta	1986	Ess Ess Publication
Digest of Education Statistics	National Center for Education Statistics	1966	National Center for Education Statistics
Editor and Publisher International Yearbook	Editor and Publisher	1959	Editor and Publisher
Encyclopedia Americana (30 Volumes)	Joseph M. Castagno	2006	Scholastic Library Publication
Encyclopedia Britannica (32 Volumes)	Philip W. Goetz, Robert McHenry and Dale Hoiberg	2010	Encyclopedia Britannica
Encyclopedia of Indian Culture	R. Narayan Saletore	1981	Sterling Publishers
Encyclopedia of Associations (1st edition)	Frederick Gale Ruffner	1954	Farmington Hills
Encyclopedia of Astronomy and Astrophysics (4 Volumes)	Paul Murdin	2006	Taylor and Francis
Encyclopedia of Cryptography and Security (2nd edition) (2 Volumes)	Van Tilborg et al.	2011	Springer-Verlag
Encyclopedia of Education Research (6th edition) (4 Volumes)	Marvin C. Alkin	1992	American Education Research Association
Encyclopedia of Ethics (2nd edition) (3 Volumes)	Lawrence C. Becker and Charlotte B. Becker	2001 (1st edition-1992)	Routledge
Encyclopedia of Indian Literature	Amaresh Datta	1987	Sahitya Academy
Encyclopedia of Library and Information Science (1st edition) (73 Volumes)	Allen Kent et al.	1968	Marcel Dekker
Encyclopedia of Library and Information Science (2nd edition) (4 Volumes)	Miriam A. Drake	2003	Marcel Dekker
Encyclopedia of Library and Information Science (3rd edition) (7 Volumes)	Marcia J. Bates and Mary Niles Maack	2009	CRC Press

Encyclopedia of Management (6th edition) (1 Volume)	Jenai Mynatt	2009	Gale
Encyclopedia of Professional Management (2nd edition) (2 Volumes)	Laster R. Bittel et al.	1985	Grolier International
Encyclopedia of Religion and Ethics (1st edition) (13 Volumes)	James Hastings	1908	T & T Clark (in Scotland) Charles Scribner's Sons (in USA)
Encyclopedia of Social Education (2nd edition) (3 Volumes)	Cecil R. Reynolds	2000	John Wiley
Encyclopedia of World Art (17 Volumes)	Bernard S. Myers	1959	McGraw-Hill
Europa World of Learning	Europa	1949	Routledge
Forthcoming Books	R.R. Bowker	1966	R.R. Bowker Company
Funk and Wagnall's New Encyclopedia of Science (21 Volumes)	George C. Kohn	1986	Raintree Publication
Guide to Reference Books (11th edition)	Robert Balay	1996	American Library Association
Handbook of Research on Teaching (3rd edition)	Merlin C. Wittrock	1986	Macmillan Publishing Company
Hindustan Yearbook and Who's Who	M.C. Sarkar	1933	M.C. Sarkar & Sons
India Who's Who	India News and Feature Alliance	1969	INFA Publication
India: A Reference Annual	Research and Reference Division, Ministry of Information & Broadcasting, Govt. of India	1953	Research and Reference Division, Ministry of Information and Broadcasting, Govt. of India
Indian Antiquary (24 Volumes)	Royal Anthropological Institute of Great	2012	Ulan Press

	Britain and Ireland and Archaeological Survey of India		
International Encyclopedia of Linguistic (2nd edition) (4 Volumes)	William J. Frawley	2003	Oxford University Press
International Encyclopedia of Ethics (9 Volumes)	Hugh LaFollette	2013	Willey-Blackwell
International Encyclopedia of Library and Information Science (2nd edition) (1 Volume)	John Feather and Paul Sturges	2013	Routledge
International Encyclopedia of the Social & Behavioral Sciences (2nd edition) (20 Volumes)	J. Wright	2015	Elsevier
International Handbook of Universities (15th edition)	International Association of Universities	1998	International Association of Universities
International Wildlife Encyclopedia (22 Volumes)	Maurice Burton and Robert Burton	2002	Marshall Cavendish
Keesing's Records of World Events	Keesing's World wide	1931	Keesing's World wide
Larousse Dictionary of Science and Technology	P.M.B. Walker	1995	Larousse
Library of Congress Subject Headings: Principles and Application	Lois Mai Chan	1986	Libraries Unlimited
McGraw Hill Encyclopedia of Science and Technology (20 Volumes)	McGraw-Hill	2012	McGraw-Hill Education
New International Encyclopedia (21 Volumes)	Herbert Treadwell Wade	2010	Nabu Press
Oxford Classical Dictionary	Max Cary	1949	Oxford University Press
Random House Webster's Dictionary of Scientist (1st edition)	Tony Geiss	1997	Random House

Ranganathan Dictionary: Indian Terminology on Library and Information Science	V. Venkatappaiah and P.S.G. Kumar	1993	B.R. Publishing
Rourke's World of Science Encyclopedia (10 Volumes)	Jason George	1998	Rourke Education Media
Test Critique (10 Volumes)	Daniel J. Keyser and Richard C. Sweetland	1994	PRO-ED
The American Library Association Yearbook	American Library Association	1976	American Library Association
The Asia Who's Who	Pan-Asia Newspaper Alliance	1957	Pan-Asia Newspaper Alliance
The Blackwell Encyclopedia of Management (2nd edition) (12 Volumes)	Chris Argyris, William Starbuck and Cary L. Cooper	2005	Wiley-Blackwell
The Canada Yearbook	Census and Statistics Office, Canada	1906	Census and Statistics Office, Canada
The Complete Encyclopedia of Crafts (24 Volumes)	Marshall Cevendish	1975	Columbia House
The Concise Dictionary of Education	Gene R. Hawes and Lynne S. Hawes	1982	Van Nostrand Reinhold Company
The Encarta World English Dictionary	K. Rooney	1999	Bloomsbury
The Encyclopedia of Philosophy (2nd edition) (10 Volumes)	Paul Edwards and Borchert	2006	Thomson Gale
The Encyclopedia of Philosophy (1st edition) (8 Volumes)	Paul Edwards	1967	Macmillan
The Encyclopedia of Visual Arts (10 Volumes)	Lawrence Gowing	1985	Grolier Educational Corporation
The English Dialect Dictionary (6 Volumes)	J. Wright	1898	Frowde

The Europa World Yearbook	Europa	1989	Europa Publication
The Europa Yearbook	Europa	1959	Europa Publication
The Indian Labour Yearbook	Labour Bureau, India	1946	Manager of Publications
The Indian Yearbook	Bennett, Coleman	1947	Bennett, Coleman & Company
The International Encyclopedia of Higher Education (10 Volumes)	A.S. Knowles	1977	Jossey-Bass
The International Who's Who	Europa Publication	1935	Europa Publications
The Library Association Yearbook	Library Association	1976	Library Association (now CILIP)
The Longman Dictionary of Scientific Usage	A. Godman and E.M.F. Payne	1988	Longman
The New Encyclopedia of Science (9 Volumes)	Michael Allaby et al.	2003	Oxford University Press
The New International Yearbook	International Year Book	1908	Dodd, Mead and Company
The Oxford Dictionary of Quotations (1st edition)	Alice Mary Smyth	1941	Oxford University Press
The Statesman Yearbook (152nd edition)	Nick Heath-Brown	2015	Palgrave MacMillan
The Statesman Yearbook (1st edition)	Frederick Martin	1864	Macmillan
The Times Atlas of the World	Times Books et al.	1992	Times Books
The Times of India Directory and Yearbook Including Who's Who	Girilal Jain (for year 1983)	1914	Bennett, Coleman & Company
The World Almanac and Book of Facts	World Almanac	1868	World Almanac Education Group
The World Book Atlas	World Book, Inc	1986	World Book
The World of Learning	Allen & Unwin	1947	Allen & Unwin
The Yearbook of Education	University of London	1932	Evans Brother

The Yearbook of the Indian National Science Academy	Indian National Science Academy	1970	Indian National Science Academy
Times of India Directory and Yearbook	Times of India	1947	Times of India
U.N. Statistical Yearbook	United Nations	1949	United Nations
Ulrich's International Periodicals Directory (1st edition)	Carolyn Farquhar Ulrich	1932	R.R. Bowker Company
UNESCO Statistical Yearbook	UNESCO	1949	UNESCO Statistical Office
Universities Handbook: India	Association of Indian Universities	1975	Association of Indian Universities
Web Site Source Book (6th edition)	Pam Gaulin	2001	Omnigraphics
Who's Who in Indian Science (1st edition)	H. Kothari	1964	Kothari Publications
Who's Who of World Religions (1st edition)	John R. Hinnells	1992	Simon & Schuster
Who's Who of Indian Writers	S. Balurav	1983	Sahitya Academy
Wiley Encyclopedia of Management (3rd edition) (14 Volumes)	Cary L. Cooper	2014	Wiley Publication
World Antiques (10 Volumes)	Harriet Bridgeman	1970	Caxton Publishing
World Book Encyclopedia (22 Volumes)	World Book Authors	2016	Scott Fetzer Company
World Encyclopedia of Library and Information Services (3rd edition) (1 Volume)	Robert Wedgeworth	1993	American Library Association
World History Encyclopedia (21 Volumes)	Alfred J. Andrea et al.	2011	ABC-CLIO
World Patent Information	World Intellectual Property Organization (WIPO)	1979	World Intellectual Property Organization (WIPO)

World Yearbook of Education	Robert Evans	1932	Evans Brothers
World's Wild Places (13 Volumes)	Time-Life	1975	Time-Life International
Worldmark Encyclopedia of the Nations (7th edition) (5 Volumes)	Moshe Y. Sachs	1988	Willey
Writers and Artist Yearbook	Adam and Charles Black	1906	Random Adam and Charles
Year's Work in Indian Librarianship	T.S. Rajagopalan	1988	Indian Library Association
Yearbook Australia	Australian Bureau of Statistics	1978	Australian Bureau of Statistics

APPENDIX H: FAMOUS PERSONS IN LIBRARY & INFORMATION SCIENCE AND THEIR WORKS

Persons	Contributions
A.C. Foskett	Author of book *The Subject Approach to Information.*
Abraham Harold Maslow	An American Psychologist and best known for creating 'Maslow's hierarchy of needs'.
Ada Sara Adler	Danish classical scholar and librarian.
Alan Pritchard	Coined the term 'Bibliometrics' in 1969.
Alireza Noruzi	Applies S.R. Ranganathan Five Laws of Library & Information Science to the web.
Andrea Crestador	The first person to process that books could be catalogued by using keyword instead of the title of the book.
Antonio Genesio Maria Panizzi (Anthony Panizzi)	Creator of 'Ninety-One Cataloguing Rules'.
B.S. Kesavan	First librarian of the India's National Library.
Beesman	Propounder of the term 'Information Transfer'.
Brian Campbell Vickery	A British information scientist, classification researcher and from 1966 to 1973 he was the Research Director at Aslib.
C.W. Hanson	Classifies the documentary sources into two categories: Primary and Secondary.

Canon Cody	Quoted that 'Library is a great popular university/people university'.
Carl Savage	He used the concept 'Invisible College' for the first time.
Charles Ammi Cutter	He developed the Expansive Classification Scheme and also invented Dictionary Catalogue.
Charles Belden	Quoted that 'Library is Everyman's university'.
Claude Elwood Shannon and Warrren Weaver	They proposed Linear Model of Communication in Knowledge Based (called Shannon-Weaver Model of Communication) in 1948.
Conrad Gesner	He regarded as Father of Bibliography.
D.J. Foskett	Author of book *Classification and Indexing in the Social Science*.
Daniel J. Boorstin	Twelfth Librarian of the United States Congress.
Denis Grogan	Classifies the documentary sources into three categories: Primary, Secondary and Tertiary.
Derek Austin	Creator of the PRECIS Indexing Language and also Subject Editor at the British National Bibliography between 1963 to 1967.
Donna Scheeder	Present president of IFLA.
Douglas Murray McGregor	Developed Theory X and Theory Y.
Douglas Waples	Well known in the study of research methodology in Library & Information Science and social epistemology (social enterprise of libraries).
Edward Wyndham Hulme	Coined the term 'Literary Warrant and Information Indication'.
Elton Mayo	Father of Human Relation Theory.
Ernest Cushing Richardson	He defined that "Classification according to the order of likeness from the simplest to the most complex" and also defined notation as shorthand sign.
Eugene Garfield	Founder of Bibliometrics, Scientometrics, Institute for Scientific Information (ISI) and he created many bibliographic products, e.g. Current Contents, Science Citation Index and he is also the founding editor and publisher of *The Scientist* (a news magazine for Life Scientist).

Eva Verona	She was the first European librarian to receive the American Library Association's Margaret Mann Citation in 1976.
Florence Milnes	First Reference Librarian at the British Broadcasting Corporation (BBC).
Frederick Fred Gridley Kilgour (Fred Kilgour)	Founding director of OCLC.
Frederick Richmond Goff	Famous in incunabula.
Gottfried van Swieten	Introduced the world's first card catalogue in 1780.
Halsey William (H.W.) Wilson	He was the creator of the Reader's Guide, the Cumulative Book Index, and the Book Review Digest and also the founder of the H.W. Wilson Company.
Hari Nath De	First Indian librarian (from 1907 to 1911) of the Imperial Library, India.
Henriette Davidson Avram	A computer programmer who developed the MARC format at the Library of Congress.
Henry Evelyn Bliss	He developed the Bibliographic Classification Scheme.
Henry La Fontaine	He is the co-founder of International Federation for Information and Documentation (FID) along with Paul Outlet and he received the Nobel Prize for Peace in 1913.
Herbert Putnam	He developed the Putnam Classification System which would influence his later design of the Library of Congress Classification System.
James Christian M. Hanson	He devised the Library of Congress Classification System.
James Duff Brown	He devised three classification systems: Quinn/Brown in 1898, Adjustable Classification in 1898 and Subject Classification in 1906 and he produced a standard textbook on librarianship titled *The Manual of Library Economy* and also pioneer of open access system in British Libraries.
James Ingersoll Wyer	Propounded 'Conservative, Moderate, and Liberal Theories of Reference Service.
James R. Rettig	In 1992, he posited a Sixth Law (an extension of S.R. Ranganathan's Laws) and he conceived the Sixth Law as 'Every reader his/her freedom'.
Jesse Hauk Shera	Information Scientist who pioneered the use of Information Technology in libraries.

James Mackintosh	Founder of the Asiatic Society of Mumbai.
John Cotton Dana	Founded the Newark Museum in 1909 and also served as president of the American Library Association in 1895.
John J. Beckley	First librarian of the United States Congress (Library of Congress).
John Macfarlane	First librarian of the Imperial Library, India.
John S. Mitchell	Ninth Editor-in-Chief of DDC and also editor of 22nd and 23rd editions.
Justin Winsor	First president of the American Library Association and founder member along with C.A. Cutter, Samuel S. Green and Melvil Dewey.
K.C. Harrison	First president of the Commonwealth Library Association.
L.R. McColvin	He had known the demand and supply theory of book selection in 1925.
Lee Pierce Butler	Along with S.R. Ranganathan, he was one of the first to use the term 'Library Science' as the scientific study of books and users.
Lorcan Dempsey	Chief Strategist of Online Computer Library Center (OCLC).
Louis Timothee	He was the first American Librarian.
Luther H. Evans	Tenth Librarian of Congress and the third Director-General of the UNESCO and he was chairman of the United Nations delegation to the UNESCO Inter-Government Copyright conference in Geneva in 1952.
M.A. Gopinathan	Editor of seventh edition of Colon Classification System.
M.M. Kessler	He introduced the concept 'Bibliographic Coupling' for first time.
Makoto Nagao	First scientist who developed practical Machine Translation (MT) and also the first president of the Asia-Pacific Association for Machine Translation (AAMT).
Marjorie Cotton Isherwood	The first professionally qualified children's librarian in New South Wales, Australia.
Mary Eileen Ahern	Public Library movement in U.S.A.
Melvil Dewey	Inventor of the Dewey Decimal Classification System, founder of the Lake Placid Club, one of the founders of

	the American Library Association and also founder of *The Library Journal*.
Michael Gorman	First editor of the *Anglo-American Cataloguing Rules* (2nd edition in 1978).
Michael Panzer	Tenth Editor-in-Chief of DDC.
Muhammad Siddiq Khan	Founder of the University Department of Library Science, University of Dhaka.
P.N. Kaula	First emeritus fellow professor of Library & Information Science in India appointed by U.G.C.
Patrick Magruder	Second Librarian of the United States Congress.
Paul Marie Ghislain Otlet (Paul Otlet)	Inventor of the Universal Decimal Classification (UDC) and also was a lawyer, peace activist and also founder of International Federation for Information and Documentation (FID).
Peter A. Phyor	Introduced Zero Based Budget.
Peter Mark Roget	The term 'Thesaurus' was coined.
S.R. Ranganathan	Father of Library Science, Documentation, and Information Science in India, inventor of Five Laws of Library Science, developer of Analytico-Synthetic Classification System, originator of Colon Classification System, Chain Indexing and Classified Catalogue Code and author of several books in Library and Information Science discipline.
Samuel C. Bradford	He was a British Mathematician and developed the Bradford's Law (Law of Scattering) for bibliometrics and citation analysis of scientific publication and he also founded British Society for International Bibliography (BSIB) in 1927.
Sarah Byrd Askew	An American Public Librarian who was associated with development of public libraries in U.S.A.
Sayajirao Gaekwad	Father of the Library Movement in India.
Shen Zhurong	Father of the Library Science in China.
Suzanne Briet	Known as 'Madame Documentation'.
Theresa Elmendorf	First female president of the American Library Association.
Thomas Bodley	Founder of the Bodleian Library of University of Oxford.
Virginia Lacy Jones	First African-American President of the Association of American Library Schools in 1967.

William Alanson Bordern	Started first school of Library Science in India.
William Jones	Founder of the Asiatic Society (Kolkata).
Zenodotus	First librarian of the Library of Alexandria.

APPENDIX I: FREQUENCY OF PUBLICATIONS

Entities	Frequency
African Journal of Library, Archives and Information Science	Biannually
American Libraries	Monthly
Annals of Library and Information Studies	Quarterly
Aslib proceedings	Monthly
Australian Academic and Research Libraries	Quarterly
Australian Library Journal	Quarterly
Biological Abstracts	Monthly
British National Bibliography (BNB)	Weekly
Canadian Journal of Information and Library Science	Quarterly
Cataloging and Classification Quarterly	8 issues/years
Chemical Abstracts	Weekly
Cumulative Book Index (CBI)	Monthly
Current Biography	Monthly
DESIDOC Journal of Library & Information Technology	Bimonthly
First Monday	Monthly
Granthana: Indian Journal of Library Studies	Biannual
Harvard Library Bulletin	Tri-annual
Herald of Library Science	Quarterly
IASLIC Bulletin	Quarterly
IASLIC newsletter	Monthly
IFLA Journal	Quarterly
ILA Bulletin	Quarterly
Index and Catalogue	Quarterly

Index Indiana	Quarterly
Indian Agricultural Sciences Abstracts	Biannual
Indian Journal of Information, Library and Society	Quarterly
Indian Journal of Traditional Knowledge	Quarterly
Indian Library Science Abstract	Quarterly
Indian National Bibliography (INB)	Monthly
Indian Science Abstracts	Semi-monthly
Information Studies	Quarterly
Information Technology and People	Quarterly
Information, Communication and Society	Monthly
Insights	Tri-annual
International Information Communication and Education	Quarterly
International Information and Library Review	Quarterly
International Journal of Digital Curation	Biannual
International Journal of Metadata, Semantics and Ontologies	Quarterly
International Journal of Special Libraries	Quarterly
International Journal of the Book	Annually
Journal of Academic Librarianship	Bimonthly
Journal of Classification	Tri-annual
Journal of Digital Information Management	Quarterly
Journal of Documentation	Bimonthly
Journal of Electronic Resources in Medical Libraries	Quarterly
Journal of Information and Knowledge Management	Quarterly
Journal of Information and Organization Science (JIOS)	Biannually
Journal of Information Ethics	Biannually
Journal of Information Science	Bimonthly
Journal of Information, Information Technology, and Organizations (JIITO)	Annually
Journal of Intellectual Property Rights	Bimonthly

Journal of Librarianship and Information Science	Quarterly
Journal of Library Administration	8 issues/year
Journal of Library and Information Services in Distance Learning	Quarterly
Journal of Library Metadata	Quarterly
Journal of Scientific and Industrial Research	Monthly
Journal of the Canadian Health Libraries Association	Tri-annual
Keesing's Records of World Events	Monthly
Knowledge Organization	Bimonthly
Kriti Rakshana	Bimonthly
Law Library Journal	Quarterly
Library and Information Science Research	Quarterly
Library and Information Science Abstracts (LISA)	Biweekly
Library Herald	Quarterly
Library Quarterly	Quarterly
Library Trends	Quarterly
LIBRES	Biannual
Libri	Quarterly
MEDOC	Quarterly
POPLINE	Monthly
Progress in Informatics	Annually
Publishers' weekly	Weekly
Quaerendo	Quarterly
School Libraries Worldwide	Biannual
Scriptorium	Biannual
Serials Librarian	Quarterly
SRELS Journal of Information Management	Bimonthly
Sri Lanka National Bibliography (SLNB)	Monthly
Statistical Abstracts of India	Annually
The Electronic Library	Bimonthly

The Grey Journal	Tri-annual
Transinformacao	Tri-annual
Urban Library Journal	Biannual
VINE Journal of Information and Knowledge Management Systems	Quarterly
World Patent Information Journal	Quarterly

APPENDIX J: HEADQUARTERS

Institutes/Organization	Headquarter
Albania Library Association	Tirana, Albania
All-Russian Institute for Scientific and Technical Information (VINITI)	Moscow
American Chemical Society	Washington, D.C.
American Library Association	Chicago
Amnesty International	London
Art Libraries Society of Nordic Countries (ARLIS/NORDEN)	Helsinki, Finland
Art Libraries Society of Australia and New Zealand (ARLIS/ANZ)	Canberra
Art Libraries Society of North America (ARLIS/NA)	Ontario, Canada
Association for Health Information and Libraries in Africa (AHILA)	Bamako, Mali
Association of Special Libraries & Information Bureau (ASLIB)	Bingley, UK
Association of Commonwealth Archivists and Records Managers (ACARM)	London
Association of International Librarians and Information Specialists (AILIS)	Geneva
Association of South East Nations (ASEAN)	Jakarta
Australian Library and Information Association (ALIA)	Kingston, Australia
Canadian Library Association	Ottawa, Ontario
Charter Institute of Library and Information Professionals (CILIP)	London
Chemical Abstracts Service	Columbus, Ohio

Committee on Data for Science and Technology (CODATA)	Paris
Commonwealth Library Association (COMLA)	Kingston, Jamaica
Commonwealth of Nations	London
Consortium of European Research Libraries (CERL)	London
Controller General of Patents, Designs and Trade Marks (CGPDTM)	Mumbai
Council of Scientific and Industrial Research (CSIR)	New Delhi
Council on Library and Information Resources (CLIR)	Washington, D.C.
Defence Scientific Information and Documentation Centre (DESIDOC)	New Delhi
Development Library Network (DELNET)	New Delhi
Documentation Research and Training Centre (DRTC)	Bengaluru
EBSCO Information Service	Ipswich, Massachusetts
Education and Research Network (ERNET)	New Delhi
European Association for Health Information and Libraries (EAHIL)	Maarssen, Netherlands
European Association of Information Services	Amsterdam
European Bureau of Library, Information and Documentation Associations (EBLIDA)	The Hague
European Information Association (EIA)	Manchester
European Organization for Nuclear Research (CERN)	Geneva
Food and Agriculture Organization (FAO)	Rome
Indian Association of Special Libraries and Information Centers (IASLIC)	Kolkata
Indian Council for Cultural Relations (ICCR)	Kolkata
Indian Council of Agriculture Research (ICAR)	New Delhi
Indian Council of Medical Research (ICMR)	New Delhi
Indian Institute of Science (IISc)	Bengaluru
Indian Library Association	New Delhi
Indian Patent Office	Kolkata
Information and Library Network (INFLIBNET)	Gandhinagar, Gujarat

International Association of Bibliophiles	Paris
International Association of Orientalist Librarians (IAOL)	Moscow
International Association of Research, Scientific and Technical Libraries	Moscow
International Association of School Librarianship	Chicago
International Association of Technological University Libraries (IATUL)	Oxford, UK
International Atomic Energy Agency (IAEA)	Vienna
International Electrotechnical Commission (IEC)	Geneva
International Federation for Information Processing (IFIP)	Luxembourg, Austria
International Federation of Library Associations and Institutions (IFLA)	Netherlands
International Nuclear Information System (INIS)	Vienna
International Organization for Standardization (ISO)	Geneva
International Patent Documentation Centre (INPADOC)	Vienna
International Sociological Association	Madrid
International System for Agriculture Science and Technology (AGRIS)	Rome
International Telecommunication Union	Geneva
Latin American Association of Archives	Columbia
League of European Research Libraries (LIBER)	Cambridge, UK
Library of Congress	Washington, D.C.
Madras Library Association	Chennai
Medical Library Association of India (MLAI)	New Delhi
National Centre for Science Information	Bengaluru
National Informatics Centre (NIC)	New Delhi
National Institute of Science Communication and Information Resources (NISCAIR)	New Delhi
National Library of Russia	St. Petersburg
National Medical Library	New Delhi
National Mission for Manuscripts (NAMAMI)	New Delhi

National University of Educational Planning and Administration (NUEPA)	New Delhi
Online Computer Library Centre (OCLC)	Dublin, Ohio
Raja Rammohun Roy Library Foundation (RRRLF)	Kolkata
Rajiv Gandhi National Institute for Intellectual Property Management	Nagpur
Russian Academy of Sciences	Moscow
SAARC Documentation Centre	New Delhi
SLA: Asian Chapter	New Delhi
Small Enterprises National Documentation Centre (SENDOC)	Hyderabad
Society for Information Science (SIS), India	New Delhi
Society for the Advancement of Library and Information Science (SALIS)	Chennai
South Asian Association for Regional Cooperation (SAARC)	Kathmandu
Special Library Association	Alexandria, Virginia
Tata Energy Research Institute (TERI)	New Delhi
United Nations (UN)	New York
United Nations Development Programme (UNDP)	New York
United Nations Educational, Scientific and Cultural Organization (UNESCO)	Paris
United Nations Industrial Development Organization (UNIDO)	Vienna
Universal Postal Union	Berne
World Intellectual Property Organization (WIPO)	Geneva

Appendix K: ICT Tools, Terminologies, Computer Languages and their Developers, Creators, etc.

Entities	Descriptions
C (Computer programming language)	Created by Dennis Ritchie in 1967
C++ (Computer programming language)	Created by Bjarne Stroustrup in 1979

Fujio Masuoka	Inventor of Flash memory
HTML (Markup language)	In 1990s, Tim Berners-Lee was introduced for first time.
Java (Computer programming language)	Created by James Gosling in 1995.
Android (Operating System)	A mobile operating system developed by Google in 2008 especially for Smart Phone.
JavaScript (Script language)	Created by Brendan Eich in 1995.
Linux (Linux Kernel)	First released in 1991 under the direction of Linus Torvalds.
J. Presper Eckert	Invented the ENIAC.
Charles Bachman	A computer scientist known for Integrated Data Storage.
George Boole	A logician, philosopher and author of *The Laws of Thought* (1854) which contains Boolean Algebra.
Peter Wegner	One of the co-contributors for development of the theory of Object-Oriented Programming (OOP) concept.
Paul Baran	Invented Packet Switched Computer Networking.
Douglas Engelbart	Best known for working in 'Human-Computer Interaction'.
Grace Hopper	She was one of the first programmers of the IBM's Mark I Computer in 1944.
Yukihiro Matsumoto	Chief designer of the 'Ruby' Programming language.
Charles Babbage	Invented first Mechanical Computer and known as father of Computer.
Ramanathan V. Guha	He is main technical precursor of W3C's Resource Description Framework (RDF) Standard and Really Simple Syndication (RSS).
Wim Ebbinkhuijsen	Known as father of COBOL language.
John Warner Backus	Known as inventor of FORTRAN computer programming language.
Ada Lovelace	She is known as the first computer programmer.

Sergey Brin	Co-founder of Google Corporation.
Bill Joy	Co-founder of Sun Microsystems in 1982 and developer of BDS Unix.
James Handler	One of the originators of the 'Semantic Web'.
Manuel Blur	Founder of Computational Complexity Theory and its application to Cryptography.
Brian Kernighan	Co-developer of Unix operating system along with Ken Thompson and Dennis Ritchie.
Leonard Kleinrock	Played key role for the development of ARPANET.
John G. Kemeny	Co-developer of the BASIC programming language in 1964 with Thomas E. Kurtz.
Marvin Minsky	Famous for development of Artificial Intelligence (AI) and co-founder of the Massachusetts Institute of Technology (MIT)'s AI laboratory.
David Korn	Author of the Korn Shell (a command line interface for Unix).
Jean Bartik	One of the original programmers for the ENIAC.
Jean Ichbiah	Chief designer of Ada Computer language.
Steve Jobs	Founder of Apple Inc and creator of Apple 2 computer.
Philip Don Estridge	Known as 'father of IBM PC' for the development of IBM Personal Computer (PC).
Perl (Script language)	Created by Larry Wall in 1980s.
Peter Merholz	The term 'Blog' was coined.
Tracy Camp	She is famous for inventing the wireless networking.
Christopher J. Date	Famous for Relational Database Theory and also writer of a famous book *An Introduction to Database System*.
Vinod Dham	Known as father of the Pentium chip.
Michael Kolling	Known as developer of BlueJ (an integrated Development Environment (IDE) for Java Programming Language).
PHP (Script language)	Created by Rasmus Lerdorf in 1995.
Python (Computer programming language)	Created by Guido van Rossum in 1991.

Robert Elliot "Bob" Kahn (Robert E. Kahn)	Along with Vinton Gray Cerf, invented the Transmission Control Protocol (TCP) and Internet Protocol (IP).
Ted Nelson	He coined the terms Hypertext and Hypermedia in 1963.
Claude Elwood Shannon	Father of Information Theory.
Tim O'Reilly	The term 'Web 2.0' was popularized.
Unix (Unix Compiler)	Developed in the 1970s at the Bell Labs under the directions of Ken Thompson and Dennis Ritchie.
Vinton Gray Cerf	Father of the Internet.
William Gibson	Used the term 'Cyberspace' for the first time.
Edgar Frank "Ted" Codd (E.F. Codd)	Defined the thirteen rules ((numbered zero to twelve) for Relational Database Management System.
Jorn Barger	The term 'Weblog' was coined.
Norman Abramson	Inventor of Wireless LAN technology.
WWW	Invented by Tim Berners-Lee in 1989.
Robert Cailliau	Organized the first International World Wide Web Conference at CERN in 1994.
Louis Pouzin	Invented the datagram (a kind of basic transfer unit associated with a packet-switched network).
Twitter	A microblogging social network platform, created by Jack Dorsey, Evan Williams, Biz Stone, and Noah Glass and launched in 2006.
Facebook	A social networking service launched in 2004 by Mark Zuckerber.
LinkedIn	A business-oriented social networking service founded by Reid Hoffman.
Tumblr	A microblogging and social networking platform founded by David Karp in 2007.
reddit	An entertainment, social news networking services and news website founded by Steve Huffman and Alexis Ohanian in 2005.
Yahoo	An American multinational technology company founded by Jerry Yang and David Filo in 1994.

Opera	A web browser began in 1994 as a research project at Telenor.
Internet Explorer (IE)	A web browser developed by Microsoft corporation in 1995.
Netscape Navigator	A web browser developed by Netscape Communication Corporation and released in 1994 under the name Mosaic Netscape 0.9.
Firefox	A web browser developed by the Mozilla Foundation and launched in 2002.
Google Chrome	A web browser developed by Google and released in 2008.
Safari	A web browser developed by Apple and released in 2003.
Konqueror	A free open-source web browser and released on 2000.
Google	An American multinational Internet-based technology company founded by Larry Page and Sergey Brin in 1998.
Maxthon	A freeware web browser developed by Chinese company Maxthon Limited and released in 2005.
YouTube	A global video-sharing platform founded by Chad Hurley, Steve Chen and Jawed Karim in 2005.
Linus Torvalds	Principal author of the Linux Kernel in 1991.
MINIX	A Unix-like Computer Operating System based on a microkernel architecture created by Andrew S. Tanenbaum in 1987.
Ubuntu	A Debian-based Linux Operating System distributor and released in 2004.
Linux Mint	A Debian-based Linux Operating System distributor and released in 2006.
Fedora	An Operating System based on the Linux Kernel and released in 2003.
Debian	A Unix-like Computer Operating System which composed entirely of free software and released in 1993.

Ian Ashley Murdock	An American Software engineer and the founder of Debian project.
openSUSE	A Linux-based operating system distributor released in 2005.
Red Hat Linux	A Linux-based Operating System distributor released in 1995 and discontinued in 2004.
Bharat Operating System Solution (BOSS)	A free and open source Linux distributor based on Debian, developed by the National Resource Centre for Free/Open Source Software (NRCFOSS) of India and supported by CDAC and initial released in 2007.
deepin	A free Linux distributor based on Debian and launched in 2004.
Knoppix	An open source Operating System based on Debian designed to be run directly from a CD/DVD or Live USB and released on in 2000.
GNOME	A desktop environment which is composed entirely of free and open source software.
GNU	GNU stands for 'GNU's Not Unix', complete free software, mass collaboration project, announced in 1983 by Richard Stallman.
Instagram	An online photo-sharing, video-sharing social networking platform created by Kevin Systrom and Mike Krieger in 2010.
Flickr	An image hosting and video-sharing platform crated by Ludicopr in 2004 and acquired by Yahoo in 2005.
imgur	An online image sharing platform founded by Alan Schaaf in 2009.
Picasa	An image organizer, image viewer for editing and organizing digital photo and also integrated photo-sharing on website, created in 2002 and in 2004 Google acquired Picasa and offers it as freeware.
Freeware	The term 'freeware' coined by Andrew Fluegelman in 1982.

Skype	An application that provide video chat and voice call services created by Niklas Zennstrom and Janus Friis in 2003.
MySQL	An open-source Relational Database Management System) software released in 1995 and currently develops under the Oracle Corporation.
PostgreSQL	An Object-Relational Database Management System (ORDBMS) released in 1996.
Microsoft SQL Server	A Relational Database Management System (RDBMS) developed by Microsoft Corporation in 1989.
Oracle (Oracle RDBMS)	An Object-Relational Database Management System (ORDBMS) developed by Oracle Corporation in 1977.
Sybase	A Relational Database Management System (RDBMS) developed by Sybase Corporation (now subsidiary of SAP) in 1984.
IBM DB2	A Relational Database Management System (RDBMS) developed by IBM in 1983.
Intel	Founded by Gordon Moore and Robert Noyce in 1968.
John von Neumann	Father of the Modern Computer called von Neumann Architecture. He gave a theory that program and any data are both stored together and modern computer architecture is based on that principle.

Appendix L: Indexing Systems, Subject Headings, Thesaurus

Indexing	Inventor/Editor/Sponsor	Year
Arts and Humanities Citation Index	E. Garfield	1978
ASIS Thesaurus of Information Science and Librarianship (2nd edition)	Jessica L. Milstead	1998
Automated Indexing	H.M. Ohlman	1958
Chain Indexing	S.R. Ranganathan	1938
Citation Indexing	E. Garfield	1963

Coates' Subject Indexing	E.J. Coates	1963
COMPASS Indexing	BNB	1991
Contextual Indexing and Faceted Taxonomic Access System (CIFT)	James D. Anderson	1979
H-Index	Jorge Eduardo Hirsch	2005
Key Word Indexing	H.P. Luhn	1959
Library of Congress Subject Headings	Library of Congress	1898
MeSh: Medical Subject Heading	US National Library of Medicine	2001
NEPHIS	T.C. Craven	1986
POPSI	G. Bhattacharya	1984
PRECIS	D. Austin	1974
Relational Indexing	J.E.L. Farradane	1950
Science Citation Index	E. Garfield	1964
Sears List of Subject Headings	M.E. Sears	1923
SLIC Indexing	J.R. Sharp	1966
Social Science Citation Index	E. Garfield	1973
Subject Indexing	M.E. Sears	1923
Systematic Indexing	J.O. Kaiser	1911
UNITERM Indexing	M. Taube	1953
Zator System	C.N. Mooers	1947

APPENDIX M: LIBRARY ASSOCIATIONS

Entities	Foundation year
African American Library and Information Science Association	1993
African Medical Library Association (AMLA)	1984
Albania Library Association	1993
All Bengal School Librarian Association (ABSLA)	1990
American Association of Law Libraries	1906

American Indian Library Association	1979
American Library Association	1876
American Theological Library Association	1947
Andaman and Nicobar Library Association	1977
Andhra Library Association	1914
Art Libraries Society	1969
Art Libraries Society of Nordic Countries (ARLIS/NORDEN)	1986
Art Libraries Society of Australia and New Zealand (ARLIS/ANZ)	1975
Art Libraries Society of North America (ARLIS/NA)	1972
Art Libraries Society of United Kingdom (ALIS/UK)	1969
Asian/Pacific American Librarians Association	1980
Association for Health Information and Libraries in Africa (AHILA)	1988
Association for Information Science and Technology (ASIT & T)	1937
Association for Information Systems (AIS)	1994
Association for Library and Information Science Education (ALISE)	1915
Association for Library Collections and Technical Services (ALCTS)	1957
Association of Architectural Librarians	1974
Association of Architecture School Librarians	1979
Association of Austrian Libraries	1896
Association of Christian Librarians	1957
Association of College and Research Libraries (ACRL)	1889
Association of Commonwealth Archivists and Records Managers (ACARM)	1984
Association of International Librarians and Information Specialists (AILIS)	1963
Association of Jewish Libraries (AJL)	1965
Association of Parliamentary Librarians in Canada	1975
Association of Research Libraries	1932
Association of Special Libraries and Information Bureaux/Association for Information Management (ASLIB)	1924
Association of Vision Science Librarians (AVSL)	1968

Australian Library and Information Association (ALIA)	1937
Australian School Library Association (ASLA)	1969
Baroda Library Association	1910
Bengal Library Association (BLA)	1925
Bihar Library Association	1936
Bombay Science Librarians' Association (BOSLA)	1970
Botswana Library Association (BLA)	1978
British Library Association	1877
Canadian Association for Information Science (CAIS)	1970
Canadian Association of Children's Librarians (CACL)	1939
Canadian Association of College and University Libraries (CACUL)	1963
Canadian Association of Public Libraries (CAPL)	1972
Canadian Health Libraries Association (CHLA)	1976
Canadian Library Association (CLA)	1946
Canadian School Library Association (CSLA)	1961
Chinese American Librarians Association	1973
Commonwealth Library Association (COMLA), Jamaica	1972
Congress of South-East Asian Librarians (CONSAL)	1970
Council of National and Information Association	1942
Delhi Library Association (DLA)	1939
European Association for Health Information and Libraries (EAHIL)	1987
European Association of Information Services	1970
European Bureau of Library, Information and Documentation Associations (EBLIDA)	1992
European Information Association (EIA)	1991
European Theological Libraries	1961
Ghana Library Association (GLA)	1962
Gujarat Library Association (Geetha Govinda Samskrita Sangha (GGSS))	1976
Independent Research Libraries Association	1972
Indian Association of Special Libraries and Information Centers (IASLIC)	1955

Indian Library Association (ILA)	1933
International Association of Agricultural Information Specialists (IAALD)	1955
International Association of Aquatic and Marine Science Libraries and Information Centers (IAMSLIC)	1975
International Association of Bibliophiles	1963
International Association of Law Libraries (IALL)	1959
International Association of Music Libraries, Archives and Documentation Centers	1951
International Association of Orientalist Librarians (IAOL)	1967
International Association of Research, Scientific and Technical Libraries	1989
International Association of School Librarianship (IASL)	1971
International Association of Schools of Information Science	1997
International Association of Scientific and Technological University Libraries (IATUL)	1955
International Committee of Agricultural Librarians	1935
International Council of Library Association Executives (ICLAE)	1975
International Federation for Information Processing (IFIP)	1960
Jammu & Kashmir Library Association	1966
Japan Library Association	1892
Karnataka State Library Association (KALA)	1964
Kerala Library Association (KLA)	1972
Latin American Association of Archives	1973
League of European Research Libraries (LIBER)	1971
Libraries Association of New Zealand	1910
Library Association of Ireland (LAI)	1928
Library Association of the United Kingdom	1877
Library Leadership and Management Association (LLAMA), Chicago	1957
Library Public Relations Council	1939
Madras Library Association	1928
Maharashtra Library Association	1921

Manipur Library Association	1987
Masonic Library and Museum Association (MLMA)	1995
Medical Library Association (MLA)/Association of Medical Libraries	1898
Medical Library Association of India (MLAI)	1981
Mexican Association of Librarians	1924
Middle East Librarians Association	1972
Modern Language Association (MLA)	1883
Music Library Association	1931
Mysore Librarians and Information Scientist Association (MyLISA)	2001
Pacific Northwest Library Association (PNLA)	1909
Patent and Trademark Depository Library Association	1983
Punjab Library Association	1916
Rajasthan Library Association	1962
Society for the Advancement of Library and Information Science (SALIS)	2002
Society of School Librarians International	1985
Special Library Association	1909
Theatre Library Association	1937
Utkal Library Association	1944
Uttar Pradesh Library Association (UPLA)	1949
Washington Library Association (WLA)	1905
West Bengal College Librarian's Association (WBCLA)	1962
Young Adult Library Services Association (YALSA)	1957

APPENDIX N: COMMITTEES/COMMISSIONS

Committee/Commission	Year	Chairman
Library Development Committee	1939	A.A.A. Fayzee
University Education Commission	1948	S. Radhakrishnan
Secondary Education Commission	1953	A.L. Muduliar
Library Committee	1957	Dr. S.R. Ranganathan

Advisory Committee for Libraries	1957	K.P. Sinha
Review Committee on Library Science	1961	Dr. S.R. Ranganathan
Education Commission	1964	Prof. D.S. Kothari
Review Committee for the National Library	1968	V.S. Jha
Committee on Reorganization and Development of Polytechnic Education in India	1971	G.R. Damodaran
Mehrotra Committee	1983	R.C. Mehrotra
National Policy on Library and Information System (NAPLIS)	1985	Prof. D.P. Chattopadhyaya
Committee on National Network System for Universities Libraries	1988	Prof. Yash Pal
Curriculum Development Committee on Library and Information Science	1990	Prof. P.N. Kaula
Review Committee on National Policy Education, 1986	1990	Acharya Ramamurti
Consider on the Revision of Pay Scales and Career Advancement of the Academic Staff of the Universities and Colleges	1997/1988	Prof. R.P. Rastogi
UGC Model Curriculum: Library and Information Science	2001	Dr. C.R. Karisiddappa

Appendix O: List of Important Books, Publishing Year and their Publishers

Title	Author/Editor	Year of Publication/ Latest Edition	Publisher/ Sponsored
A Descriptive Account of the Colon Classification	S.R. Ranganathan	1965	Asia Publishing House
Administration of the College Library	R. Lyle Guy	1974	Wilson

A Manual of Library Classification (3rd edition)	W.C.B. Sayers	1964	Andre Deutsch
A Topography of Cataloguing	Mary Piggott	1988	Library Association Publishing
ALA Filing Rules	American Library Association Filing Committee	1980	American Library Association
ALA Glossary of Library and Information Science (1st edition)	Heartsill Young	1983	American Library Association
ALA Glossary of Library and Information Science (4th edition)	Michael Levine-Clark and Toni M. Carter	2013	American Library Association
ALA Rules for Filing Catalog Cards	Pauline A. Seely	1968	American Library Association
An Introduction to Library Cataloguing and Classification	Harry Dewey	1957	Capital Press
An Introduction to Library Classification (9th edition)	W.C.B. Sayers	1958	Grafton & Company
Anglo-American Cataloguing Rules (2nd revised edition)	Michael Gorman and Paul Winkler	1988	American Library Association
Aspect of Theory of Syntax	Noam Chomsky	1965	M.I.T. Press
Authority Control: Principles, Applications and Instructions	Doris H. Clack	1990	American Library Association
Authors and Titles	James A. Tait	1969	Clive Bingley
Basic Budget Practices for Librarians	Margo C. Trumpeter and Richard S. Rounds	1985	American Library Association
Building Library Collections	M.C. Carter	1969	Scarecrow

Cataloguing (2nd edition)	E.J. Hunter and K.C.B. Bakewell	1983	Clive Bingley
Cataloguing and Classification: An Introduction (2nd edition)	Lois Mai Chain	1994	McGraw-Hill
Cataloguing: Theory and Practice	C.G. Viswanathan	1965	Asia Publishing House
Classification and Communication	S.R. Ranganathan	1951	University of Delhi
Classification and Indexing in Science	B.C. Vickery	1959	Butterworths Scientific Publication
Classification: Theoretical and Practical	E.C. Richardson	1901	Scribner
Classified Catalogue Code: With Additional Rules for Dictionary Catalogue (5th edition)	S.R. Ranganathan	1964	Asia Publishing House
Collection Development: The Selection of Materials for Libraries	William A. Katz	1980	Holt
Colon Classification (1st edition)	S.R. Ranganathan	1933	Madras Library Association
Colon Classification (6th edition)	S.R. Ranganathan	1960 (reprint in 1963 with some amendments)	Asia Publishing House and Ess Ess Publications for Sarada Ranganathan Endowment for Library Science, Bengaluru has been published since 2006
Dictionary for Library and Information Science	Joan M. Reitz	2004	Library Unlimited

Documentation: Genesis and Development	S.R. Ranganathan	1973	Vikas Publishing House
Documentation and Information	B. Guha	1983	World Press
Documentation and its Facets	S.R. Ranganathan	1963	Asia Publishing House
Documentation and the Organization of Knowledge	J.H. Shera	1966	Archon Books
Early Public Libraries	Thomas Kelley	1966	Library Association Publishing
Elements of Library Classification	S.R. Ranganathan	1945	Asia Publishing House
Faceted Classification	B.C. Vickery	1960	Aslib
Five Laws of Library Science	S.R. Ranganathan	1931	Madras Library Association
Fundamental of Library Organization and Administration: A Practical Guide	E.B. Gorbett	1978	Library Association Publishing
Fundamental of Reference Service	Frances Neel Cheney	1980	American Library Association
Fundamentals of Library Classification	B.I. Palmer and A.J. Wells	1951	Allen & Unwin
Global Information Society	William J. Martin	1995	Aslib Gower
Grammar of Classification (4th edition)	W.C.B. Sayers	1935	Grafton
Guide to Reference Books (9th edition)	E.R. Sheehy	1976	American Library Association
Guide to Reference Material (5th edition)	A.J. Walford	1990	Library Association Publishing
Guidelines for Establishment in	UNISIST	1981	UNESCO

Development of Monolingual Thesaurus (2nd edition)			
Handbook for Information Systems and Services	Pauline Atherton	1977	UNESCO
Handbook of Information Systems and Services	J.K. Khanna	1996	Beacon Books
Harrod's Librarian Glossary	Raymond John Prytherch	1995	Gower
Heading and Canons: Comparative Study of Five Catalogue Codes	S.R. Ranganathan	1955	S. Viswanathan
Indexing and Abstracting in Theory and Practice	F.W. Lancaster	1991	Library Association Publishing
Indexing Concept and Methods	Harold Borko and Charles L. Bernier	1978	Academic Press
Indexing Language and Thesauri: Construction and Maintenance	D. Soergel	1974	California Melville Publishing
Information Brokering: A New Career in Information Work	Marshall J. Crawford	1988	Library Association Publishing
Information Retrieval Systems: Characteristics, Testing, and Evaluation (2nd edition)	F.W. Lancaster	1979	John Willey
Information Science in Theory and Practice	B.C. Vickery and A. Vickery	1987	Butterworths
Information System	B.C. Vickery	1973	Butterworths
Information System: Theory and Practice	John G. Burch and Flexi R. Starter	1974	Hamilton
Information Systems, Services and Centers	H.M. Weisman	1972	Becker and Hayes

Introduction to Cataloguing and Classification of Books	Margaret Mann	1930	American Library Association
Introduction to Cataloguing and Classification	Bohdan S. Wynar	1976	Libraries Unlimited
Introduction to Informetrics	Leo Egghe and Ronald Rousseau	1990	Elsevier
Introduction to Librarianship	J.K. Gates	1968	McGraw-Hill
Introduction to Library Classification (1st edition)	W.C.B. Sayers	1918	Grafton
Introduction to Patents Information	Stephen Van Dulken	1990	British Library
Introduction to Reference Work (1st and 2nd Volumes) 8th edition	William A. Katz	2001	McGraw-Hill
Introduction to Subject Indexing	A.G. Brown et al.	1976	Clive Bingley
Itself an Education	B.I. Palmer	1962	Library Association Publishing
Knowledge Base Retrieval System	Alister Kemp	1988	Aslib
Libraries of the Future	J.C.R. Licklider	1965	M.I.T. Press
Library Administration (1st edition)	S.R. Ranganathan	1935	Asia Publishing House
Library Administration: Theory and Practice (1st edition)	R.L. Mittal	1964	Metropolitan Book Company
Library Book Selection (1st edition)	S.R. Ranganathan	1951	Indian Library Association
Library Book Selection (2nd edition)	S.R. Ranganathan and M.A. Gopinath	1966	Asia Publishing House

Library Building: Planning and Design	P.N. Kaula	1971	Vikas Publication
Library Catalogue: Fundamentals and Procedures	S.R. Ranganathan	1950	University Microfilms
Library Classification: Fundamentals and Procedure	S.R. Ranganathan	1944	Madras Library Association
Library Manual	S.R. Ranganathan and K.M. Sivaraman	1951	Indian Library Association
Library Manual for Library Authorities, Librarians, and Honorary Library Workers	S.R. Ranganathan	1962	Asia Publishing House
Library of Congress Subject Headings (7th edition)	Lois Mai Chan	1986	Libraries Unlimited
Management Techniques for Libraries	G. Edward Evans	1976	Academic Press
Manual of Classification for Librarians and Bibliographers	W.C.B. Sayers	1944	Grafton & Company
Manual of Library Classification and Shelf Arrangement	J.D. Brown	1898	Library Supply Company
Methods of Analysis and Evaluation of Information Needs: A Critical View	Werner Kunz et al.	1976	Verlag Dokumentation
Modern Outline of Library Classification	J. Mills	1960	Chapman & Hall
Non Book Materials: The Organic Section of Integrated Collection	Jean Weihs et al.	1979	Canadian Library Association
Organization of Knowledge in Libraries	H.E. Bliss	1939	H.W. Wilson

and the Subject Approach to Books			
Organization of Knowledge of the System of Subject	H.E. Bliss	1929	Holt
Organizing Knowledge	J.E. Rowley	1987	Gower
Organizing Knowledge in Libraries: An Introduction to Classification and Cataloging	C.D. Needham	1964	A. Deutsch
Philosophy of Library Classification	S.R. Ranganathan	1951	E. Munksgaard
Planning Academic and Research Library Buildings	Keyes D. Metcalf	1966	McGraw-Hill
Planning and Design the Library Building	Godfrey Thompson	1973	Architectural Press
Planning the Special Library	Ellis Mount	1972	Special Library Association
Practical Reference Work (2nd edition)	Denis J. Grogan	1992	Library Association Publishing
PRECIS: A Manual of Concept Analysis and Subject Indexing	Derek Austin	1974	The British Library
Prolegomena to Library Classification (1st edition)	S.R. Ranganathan	1937	Madras Library Association
Public Knowledge: The Social Dimension of Science	John Ziman	1974	Cambridge University Press
Public Libraries Manifesto	UNESCO	1994	UNESCO
Ramanujan: The Man and the Mathematician	S.R. Ranganathan	1967	Asia Publishing House

Reference Library Stock: An Informal Guide	Lionel R. McColvin	1952	Grafton
Reference Service and Bibliography	S.R. Ranganathan and C. Sundaram	1940	Madras Library Association
Reference Service (2nd edition)	S.R. Ranganathan	1961	Asia Publishing House
Rules for a Printed Dictionary Catalogue/ Rules for a Dictionary Catalogue	C.A. Cutter	1876	Government Printing Office (Washington, D.C.)
Sayers' Manual of Classification for Librarians	Arthur Maltby	1975	Andre Deutsch
Semantic Information Processing	Marvin Minsky	1968	M.I.T. Press
Statistical Methods for Librarianship	Manfred Kochen	1967	American Library Association
Study of General Categories Applicable to Classification and Coding in Documentation	Eric De Grolier	1962	UNESCO
Subject Catalogues: Heading and Structure	E.J. Coates	1988	Library Association Publishing
Subject Classification (1st edition)	J.D. Brown	1906	Library Supply Company
Subject Indexing Systems: Concepts, Methods and Techniques	S.B. Ghosh and J.N. Satparthi	1988	IASLIC
Suggestions for the Organization of Libraries in India	S.R. Ranganathan	1946	Indian Branch, Oxford University Press
System of Bibliographic Classification	H.E. Bliss	1935	H.W. Wilson
Systematic Bibliography (4th edition)	A.M. Lewin Robinson	1979	Clive Bingley

Technical Services in Libraries	M.F. Tauber	1954	Columbia Press
Techniques of Information Retrieval	B.C. Vickery	1970	Butterworth
The Electronic Library (4th edition)	J. Rowley	1999	Library Association Publishing
The Five Laws of Library Science (1st edition)	S.R. Ranganathan	1931	Madras Library Association
The Foundation of Education for Librarianship	J.H. Shera	1972	Becker & Hayes
The Information Society	William J. Martin	1998	Aslib
The Mathematical Theory of Communication	C.E. Shannon and W. Weaver	1949	University of Illinois Press
The Mathematical Theory of Communication	C.E. Shannon and W. Weaver	1949	University of Illinois Press
The Measurement and Evaluation of Library Services	F.W. Lancaster	1977	Information Resource Press
The Principles of Cataloguing	L. Jolley	1960	C. Lockwood
The Subject Approach to Information	A.C. Foskett	1969	Archon Books
The Third Wave	Alvin Toffler	1980	Pan Books
The University Library: The Organization, Administration and Functions of Academic Libraries	I.R. Wilson and M.F. Tauber	1958	Columbia University Press
Thesaurus Construction and Use: A Practical Manual	Jean Aitchison and Alan Gilchrist	1972	Aslib

Treasures of the Library Congress (1st edition)	Charles A. Goodrum	1980	Harry Abrams
University Libraries for Developing Countries	Morris A. Gelfand	1968	UNESCO

Appendix P: Public Library Act in Indian States

States	Year
Tamil Nadu (Madras) Public Libraries Act	1948
Andhra Pradesh (Hyderabad) Public Libraries Act	1960
Karnataka (Mysore) Public Libraries Act	1965
Maharashtra Public Libraries Act	1967
West Bengal Public Libraries Act	1979
Manipur Public Libraries Act	1988
Haryana Public Libraries Act	1989
Kerala Public Libraries Act	1989
Goa Public Libraries Act	1993
Mizoram Public Libraries Act	1993
Gujarat Public Libraries Act	2000
Odisha Public Libraries Act	2001
Uttarakhand Public Libraries Act	2005
Uttar Pradesh Public Libraries Act	2006
Rajasthan Public Libraries Act	2006
Lakshadweep Public Libraries Act	2007
Puducherry Public Libraries Act	2007
Bihar Public Libraries Act	2008
Chhattisgarh Public Libraries Act	2009
Arunachal Pradesh Public Libraries Act	2009

Appendix Q: Year of First Print/Launched

Entities	Country	Year
African Journal of Library, Archives and Information Science	Nigeria	1991
ALA Glossary of Library and Information Science	USA	1983
ALCTS Newsletter	USA	1976
American Library Directory	USA	1908
Annals of Library Science (now Annals of Library and Information Studies (ALIS) since 2001)	India	1954
Annals of Library Science and Documentation (now ALIS)	India	1964
Archival Issues	USA	1976
Archival Science	Netherlands	2000
Archivaria	Canada	1975
Archives and Manuscripts	Australia	1955
Archives and Records	UK	1947
Archives and Records: The Journal of the Archives and Records Association (formerly known as Journal of the Society of Archivists)	UK	2013
Archives and Records: The Journal of the Archives and Records Association (formerly known as Journal of the Society Archivists up to 2012)	UK	1955
Ariadne	UK	1996
ARLIS/NA Newsletter	USA	1972
Art Documentation	USA	1972
Aslib Journal of Information Management (formerly known Aslib Proceedings)	UK	2014
Aslib Proceedings (up to 2013)	UK	1949
Australian Academic and Research Libraries	Australia	1970
Australian Library Journal	Australia	1951
Biblion	USA	1897

Biblios	Brazil	1955
Biological Abstracts	USA	1926
British National Bibliography (BNB)	UK	1950
Bulletin of Bibliography	USA	1897
Bulletin of the American Library Association	USA	1970
Bulletin of the Medical Library Association	USA	1911
Canadian Journal of Information and Library Science	Canada	1976
Canadian Library Journal	Canada	1944
Cataloging and Classification Quarterly	USA	1980
Catalogue and Index	UK	1966
Chemical Abstracts	USA	1907
Children's Literature Association Quarterly	USA	1976
Chinese Librarianship	USA	1996
Choice: Current Review for Academic Libraries	USA	1963
CLIS Observer	India	1984
COLLNET Journal of Scientometrics and Information Management	UK	2007
Cumulative Book Index (CBI)	USA	1898
Current Awareness Abstracts	UK	1973
Current Biography	USA	1940
Current Research in Library and Information Science	UK	1974
Cybermetrics	Spain	1997
DESIDOC Bulletin	India	1981
DESIDOC Journal of Library & Information Technology (formerly known as DESIDOC Bulletin of Information Technology)	India	2008
DESIDOC Bulletin of Information Technology (formerly known as DESIDOC Bulletin)	India	1991
D-Lib Magazine	USA	1995

EContent Quarterly	USA	2013
Education for Information	Netherlands	1983
Encyclopedia Americana	USA	1829
Encyclopedia Britannica	UK (1968-1901) USA (1901-present)	1768
European Journal of Information System	UK	1991
European Research Libraries Cooperation: ERLC	Netherlands	1991
FID New Bulletin	Hague	1951
FID: Federation International Information and Documentation Bulletin	Hague	1951
First Monday	USA	1996
General Information Program: UNISIST Newsletter	Paris, France	1973
Granthagar	India	1937
Granthalaya Vijnana	India	1970
Granthana: Indian Journal of Library Studies	India	1990
Harvard Library Bulletin	USA	1947
Herald of Library Science	India	1962
IASLIC Bulletin	India	1956
IASLIC newsletter	India	1966
IATUL Proceedings	Sweden	1963
Ibersid	Spain	2007
IFLA Journal	UK	1975
Index Indiana	India	1977
Indian Agricultural Sciences Abstracts	India	2001
Indian Archives	India	1947
Indian Citation Index	India	2009
Indian Journal of Information, Library and Society	India	2012
Indian Journal of Traditional Knowledge	India	2002
Indian Library Association Bulletin	India	1965
Indian Library Science Abstract	India	1969

Indian National Bibliography (INB)	India	1958
Indian Science Abstracts	India	1965
INFLIBNET Newsletter	India	1995
Information and Organization	UK	2001
Information Outlook	USA	1910
Information Processing and Management	UK	1963
Information Processing and Management (formerly known as Information Storage and Retrieval)	UK	1975
Information Retrieval and Library Automation	USA	1965
Information Services and Use	Netherlands	1981
Information Storage and Retrieval (now Information Processing and Management)	UK	1963
Information System Management (formerly known as Journal of Information System Management)	USA	1992
Information Technology and Libraries (formerly known as Journal of Library Automation)	USA	1988
Information, Communication and Society	UK	1998
Insights: The UKSG journal (formerly known as Serials: The Journal for the Serials Community)	UK	2012
INSPEL: International Journal of Special Libraries	Germany	1975
Interface	USA	1978
International Federation for Documentation: P-Notes	Hague	1931
International Forum on Information and Documentation	Russia	1975
International Information and Library Review (formerly known as International Library Review)	UK	1992
International Information, Communication and Education	India	1982
International Journal of Digital Curation	UK	2006
International Journal of Information Management	UK	1980

International Journal of Information Science and Management	Iran	2003
International Journal of Legal Information	USA	1968
International Journal of Metadata, Semantics and Ontologies	UK	2006
International Journal of Special Libraries (Inspel)	Germany	1966
International Journal of the Book	Australia	2003
International Journal on Digital Libraries	Germany	1997
International Journal on Semantic Web and Information Systems	USA	2005
International Library Review	UK	1969
International Library Review (now International Information and Library Review) up to 1991	UK	1969
Internet Reference Service Quarterly	USA	1996
JISS: The International Journal of Scientometrics and Informetrics	India	1995
Journal of Academic Librarianship	UK	1975
Journal of Chemical Documentation	USA	1961
Journal of Classification	USA	1984
Journal of Digital Information	UK	1997
Journal of Digital Information Management	India	2003
Journal of Documentation	UK	1945
Journal of Education for Library and Information Science	USA	1960
Journal of Electronic Resources in Medical Libraries	USA	2003
Journal of Electronic Resources Librarianship	USA	1989
Journal of Hospital Librarianship	USA	2001
Journal of Indian Library Association (formerly known as ILA Bulletin)	India	1965
Journal of Information and Organization Science (JIOS)	Croatia	1977
Journal of Information and Knowledge Management	USA	2002

Journal of Information Ethics	USA	1992
Journal of Information Science	UK	1979
Journal of Information System Management	USA	1984
Journal of Intellectual Property Rights (JIPR)	India	1996
Journal of Japan Society of Library and Information Science	Japan	1953
Journal of Librarianship and Information Science	UK	1969
Journal of Library Administration	USA	1980
Journal of Library and Information Science	India	1976
Journal of Library and Information Services in Distance Learning	USA	2004
Journal of Library Automation	USA	1968
Journal of Library History, Philosophy, and Comparative Librarianship	USA	1966
Journal of Library Metadata	USA	1997
Journal of Scientific and Industrial Research (JSIR)	India	1942
Journal of the American Society for Information Science	USA	1950
Journal of the Association for Information Science and Technology (JASIST)	USA	1950
Journal of the Canadian Health Libraries Association	Canada	1980
Journal of the Medical Library Association: JMLA (formerly known as Medical Library and Historical Journal)	USA	2002
Journal of the Society of Archivists	UK	1955
Journal of Web Librarianship	USA	2007
Knowledge Management Research and Practice	UK	2003
Knowledge Organization	USA	1974
Kriti Rakshana	India	2005
Law Library Journal	USA	1908
LIBER Quarterly (formerly known as European Research Libraries Cooperation: ERLC)	Netherlands	1999

Library Administration and Management	USA	1975
Library and Information Science Research: An International Journal	UK	1979
Library and Documentation Journals	Hague	1975
Library and Information Science	Japan	1963
Library and Information Science Annual	USA	1985
Library and Information Science Research	UK	1987
Library Herald	India	1958
Library Hi Tech	UK	1983
Library Journal	USA	1876
Library Philosophy and Practice	USA	1998
Library Quarterly	USA	1931
Library Resource and Technical Services	USA	1957
Library Review	UK	1927
Library Science with a Slant to Documentation (up to 1988) (now SRELS Journal of Information Management since 2000)	India	1964
Library Science with a Slant to Documentation and Information Studies (formerly known as Library Science with a Slant to Documentation)	India	1988
Library Trends	USA	1952
Libres	Singapore	1990
Libri	Germany	1950
Malaysian Journal of Library and Information Science	Malaysia	1996
Medical Library and Historical Journal	USA	1898
New Library World	UK	1898
OCLC Newsletter	USA	1967
OCLC Systems and Services (formerly known as OCLC Micro)	UK	1984
Pearl: A Journal of Library and Information Science	India	2007

Progress in Informatics	Japan	2005
Progressive Librarian	USA	1990
Public Library Quarterly	USA	1979
Publishers' Weekly	USA	1872
Quaerendo	Netherlands	1971
Reference Librarian	USA	1981
Reference Review	UK	1986
Reference Service Review	UK	1973
Research in Librarianship	Australia	1965
Research Journal of Library Sciences	India	2013
Resource Sharing and Information Networks	USA	1981
Rilisar Bulletin	India	1982
RQ: Reference and User Services Quarterly	USA	1960
School Library Research	USA	1998
Science Citation Index	USA	1964
Scientometrics	Netherlands	1978
Scire	Spain	1995
Scriptorium	Belgium	1946
Serials Librarian	USA	1977
Serials: The Journal for the Serials Community	UK	1988
Special Libraries	USA	1910
SRELS Journal of Information Management (formerly known as Library Science with a Slant to Documentation and Information Studies)	India	2000
Sri Lanka National Bibliography (SLNB)	Sri Lanka	1974
Statistical Abstracts of Indian Union	India	1950
The Electronic Library	UK	1983
The Grey Journal	Netherlands	2005
The International Library and Information Review	UK	1969
Transinformacao	Brazil	1989

The Library: The Transactions of the Bibliographical Society (formerly known as The Transactions of the Bibliographical Society)	UK	1893
UNESCO Journal of Information Science, Librarianship and Archives Administration	Paris, France	1979
Urban Library Journal	USA	1993
US Library of Congress: Information Bulletin	USA	1942
VINE Journal of Information and Knowledge Management Systems	UK	1971
VOEB-Mitteilungen	Austria	1948
Webology	Iran	2004
World Book Encyclopedia	USA	1917
World Patent Information	UK	1979

Bibliography and Web References

Bibliography

Batley, Susan (2005). *Classification in Theory and Practical*. Oxford: Chandos Publishing.

C.K. Sharma (2005). *A Practice—Handbook of Classified Catalogue*. New Delhi: Atlantic Publishers & Distributors.

Guha, B. (1983). *Documentation and Information: Services, Techniques and Systems*. 2nd ed. Kolkata: World Press.

Isaac, K.A. (2001). *Glimpses of Library and Information Science*. New Delhi: Ess Ess Publications.

IGNOU (2004). *Element of Library Classification*. BLIS-03, Block-01.

——— (2004). *Information Source System and Service*. MLIS, Unit 01.

——— (2004). *Academic Library System*. MLIS, Unit 01-08.

Katz, William A. (1992). *Introduction to Reference Work*. Vo. 1: *Basic Information Sources*. 6th ed. New York: McGraw-Hill.

Khan, M.T.M. (1997). *Information Organization and Communication*. New Delhi: Ess Ess Publications.

Khanna, J.K. (2000). *Documentation and Information Services, Systems and Techniques*. Agra: Y.K. Publishers.

——— (1994). *Analytico-Synthetic Classification*. New Delhi: Ess Ess Publications.

Krishan Kumar (1991). *Reference Service*. 4th ed. New Delhi: Vikas Publication House.

——— (2001). *An Introduction to AACR2*. New Delhi: Vikas Publishing House.

Mukherjee, A.K. (1975). *Reference Works and its Tools*. 3rd ed. Kolkata: World Press.

Ranganathan, S.R. (2006). *Classified Catalogue Code*. New Delhi: Ess Ess Publications for Sarada Ranganathan Endowment for Library Science, Bengaluru.

Ranganathan, S.R. (2006). *The Five Laws of Library Science*. New Delhi: Ess Ess Publications for Sarada Ranganathan Endowment for Library Science, Bengaluru.

——— (2006). *Library Adminisytration*. New Delhi: Ess Ess Publications for Sarada Ranganathan Endowment for Library Science, Bengaluru.

——— (2006). *Classification and Communication* . New Delhi: Ess Ess Publications for Sarada Ranganathan Endowment for Library Science, Bengaluru.

——— (2006). *Prolegomena to Library Classiifction.* 3rd ed. New Delhi: Ess Ess Publications for Sarada Ranganathan Endowment for Library Science, Bengaluru.

——— (2006). *Reference Service.* New Delhi: Ess Ess Publications for Sarada Ranganathan Endowment for Library Science, Bengaluru.

——— (2006). *Philosophy of Library Classification.* New Delhi: Ess Ess Publications for Sarada Ranganathan Endowment for Library Science, Bengaluru.

——— (2006). *Colon Classificatio.* 6th Ed. New Delhi: Ess Ess Publications for Sarada Ranganathan Endowment for Library Science, Bengaluru.

Riaz, Muhammad (1989). *Advanced Indexing and Abstracting Practice.* New Delhi: Atlantic Publishers & Distributors.

Sachdeva, M.S. (1980). *Colon Classification: Theory and Practice.* New Delhi: Sterling Publishing.

Satija, M.P. (1989). *Colon Classification. A Practical Introduction* (7th Edition). New Delhi: Ess Ess Publication.

Satija, M.P. and Comaromi, John (1992). *Beyond Classification: Book Numbers.* New Delhi: Ess Ess Publications.

Sharma, C.K. and Sharma, A.K. (2007). *Library Classification.* New Delhi: Atlantic Publishers & Distributors.

Sharma, Pandey S.K. (1990). *Universe of Knowledge and Research Methodology.* Delhi: Ken Publications.

Seetharama, S. (1997). *Information Consolidation and Repackaging.* New Delhi: Ess Ess Publications.

Singh, Kiran and Sharma, C.K. (2005). *Library Management.* New Delhi: Atlantic Publishers & Distributors.

Sunil Kumar (2009). *Elements of Library Classification.* New Delhi: Rajat Publication.

Web References

http://www.abc-clio.com/ODLIS/odlis_A.aspx

http://www.cobocards.com/

https://books.google.co.in/

https://www.britannica.com

https://www.britannica.com/topic/The-Encyclopedia-Americana

https://classify.oclc.org/classify2/

https://en.wikipedia.org/wiki/Main_Page

http://www.iva.dk

http://libraries.ucsd.edu/help/glossary.html

http://library-soup.blogspot.in/p/lis-tutorials.html

http://lib.colostate.edu/howto/gloss.html

http://karibouconnections.net/medlibafrica/training_module/pdf/module1.pdf

https://www.lib.ucdavis.edu/dept/instruc/research/guides/glossary.php

http://library.samford.edu/about/li/glossary.html

http://www.library.illinois.edu/learn/intro/glossary.html

http://libguides.usc.edu/libraryterms

http://nopr.niscair.res.in/

https://www.oclc.org/support/documentation/glossary/dewey.en.htm

http://publications.drdo.gov.in/ojs/index.php/djlit

https://www.reference.com

http://shodhganga.inflibnet.ac.in/

http://thebusinesscommunication.com

www.ukoln.ac.uk/dlis/models/models1/serials-mtg/serials-req-ill.doc

http://www.waikato.ac.nz/library/study/get-help/glossary-library-terms

https://www.worldcat.org

http://www.webopedia.com

ATLANTIC TITLES FOR UGC-NET/JRF

Commerce: For UGC-NET/SLET and Other Competitive Examinations (Objective Type Questions), *Atlantic Research Division*

Economics: For UGC-NET/SLET and Other Competitive Examinations (Objective Type Questions), Third Revised and Enlarged Edition, *K.R. Gupta*

Education: For UGC-NET/SLET (Objective Type Questions), 2nd ed., Revised, Updated and Enlarged, *Atlantic Research Division*

English: For UGC-NET/JRF/SLET (Paper II and III) and Other Competitive Examinations (Objective Type Questions), Third Edition Revised, Updated & Enlarged, *R.S. Malik*

History: For UGC-NET/SLET and Other Competitive Examinations (Objective Type Questions), 2nd ed., & Enlarged Edition, *Atlantic Research Division*

Library and Information Science: For UGC-NET/SLET and Other Competitive Examinations (Objective Type Questions), *D.K. Pandey*

Management: For UGC-NET/SLET and Other Competitive Examinations (Objective Type Questions), Second ed., Revised, Updated & Enlarged, *Atlantic Research Division*

Mass Communication and Journalism: For UGC-NET/SLET (Objective Type Questions), 2nd ed., Revised, Updated and Enlarged, *Atlantic Research Division*

Political Science: For UGC-NET/SLET (Objective Type Questions), *Atlantic Research Division*

Public Administration: For UGC-NET/SLET (Objective Type Questions), *Atlantic Research Division*

Sociology: For UGC-NET/SLET and Other Competitive Examinations (Objective Type Questions), *Atlantic Research Division*

PREVIOUS YEARS' SOLVED PAPERS

Commerce: For UGC-NET/SLET/JRF Paper I, II, and III, Previous Years' Solved Papers, *Atlantic Research Division*

English: For UGC-NET/SLET/JRF Paper I, II, and III, Previous Years' Solved Papers, *Atlantic Research Division*

Environmental Science: For UGC-NET/JRF Paper I, II, and III, Previous Years' Solved Papers, *Atlantic Research Division*

Geography: For UGC-NET/JRF Paper I, II, and III, Previous Years' Solved Papers, *Atlantic Research Division*

Graduate Aptitude Test in Engineering (GATE): Mathematics, Previous Years' Solved Papers, *K.R. Gupta*

Graduate Aptitude Test in Engineering (GATE): Physics, Previous Years' Solved Papers, *Atlantic Research Division*

History: For UGC-NET/SLET/JRF Paper I, II, and III, Previous Years' Solved Papers, *Atlantic Research Division*

Home Science: For UGC-NET/SLET/JRF Paper I, II, and III, Previous Years' Solved Papers, *Atlantic Research Division*

Library and Information Science: For UGC-NET/SLET/JRF Paper I, II, and III, Previous Years' Solved Papers, *Atlantic Research Division*

Management: For UGC-NET/JRF Paper I, II, and III, Previous Years' Solved Papers, *Atlantic Research Division*

Political Science: For UGC-NET/SLET/JRF Paper I, II, and III, Previous Years' Solved Papers, *Atlantic Research Division*

Public Administration: For UGC-NET/SLET/JRF Paper I, II, and III, Previous Years' Solved Papers, *Atlantic Research Division*

Sociology: For UGC-NET/SLET/JRF Paper I, II, and III, Previous Years' Solved Papers, *Atlantic Research Division*

हिन्दीः यू.जी.सी.-नेट/जे.आर.एफ. Paper I, II, and III, Previous Years' Solved Papers, *Atlantic Research Division*

Law: For UGC-NET/JRF Paper I, II, and III, Previous Years' Solved Papers, *Atlantic Research Division*

Education: For UGC-NET/JRF Paper I, II, and III, Previous Years' Solved Papers, *Atlantic Research Division*

Mass Communication and Journalism: For UGC-NET/JRF Paper I, II, and III, Previous Years' Solved Papers, *Atlantic Research Division*

Social Work: For UGC-NET/JRF (Previous Years' Solved Papers), *Atlantic Research Division*